Hrant Dink

Hrant Dink

An Armenian Voice of the Voiceless in Turkey

Tuba Çandar

With an introduction by **Gerard Libaridian**

Translated by **Maureen Freely**

Transaction Publishers
New Brunswick (U.S.A.) and London (U.K.)

English-language edition copyright © 2016 by Transaction Publishers, New Brunswick, New Jersey.

This book is printed on acid-free paper that meets the American National Standard for Permanence of Paper for Printed Library Materials.

Library of Congress Catalog Number: 2015018191
ISBN: 978-1-4128-6255-4 (hardcover); 978-1-4128-6268-4 (paper)
eBook: 978-1-4128-6209-7
Printed in the United States of America

This volume is based on the much longer work by the author Tuba Candar (Tüba Çandar) originally published in Turkish (Everest Yayinlari, 2010, Istanbul) as Hrant.

Library of Congress Cataloging-in-Publication Data

Gandar, Tuba Tarcan.
  Hrant Dink : an Armenian voice of the voiceless in Turkey / Tuba Candar; with an introduction by Gerard Libaridian; translated by Maureen Freely.
     pages cm. -- (Armenian studies)
  Includes bibliographical references and index.
  ISBN 978-1-4128-6255-4 (alk. paper) -- ISBN 978-1-4128-6209-7 (alk. paper) 1. Dink, Hrant, 1954-2007. 2. Armenians--Turkey--Biography. 3. Journalists--Turkey--Biography. 4. Political activists--Turkey--Biography. 5. Armenians--Turkey--Interviews. 6. Turkey--Ethnic relations. I. Freely, Maureen, 1952-, translator. II. Gandar, Tuba Tarcan. Hrant. III. Title. IV. Title: Armenian voice of the voiceless in Turkey.
  DR435.A7C362 2016
  305.891'9920092--dc23
  [B]
                                                                    2015018191

To Hrant Dink
in loving memory

The translation of this work was made possible by a grant from
Harry Parsekian, Boston

Contents

Preface to the
Transaction Edition

Tuba Çandar

This book is a first: the first biography of Hrant Dink. It is not a classic one. It was Hrant's death that convinced me I should seek another way. This was a conscious decision.

Hrant Dink was an Armenian intellectual of Turkey, a journalist and political activist who was targeted for his views and assassinated in front of his newspaper's offices in Istanbul on January 19, 2007. First, they tried to drive him from the country with the slogan "Love it or leave it." In response, he wrote of feeling as "frightened as a pigeon, though I know that in this country of ours, they never hurt pigeons." Before the ink of his pen was dry, they had shot him in the neck. I lived through this terror, pain, and shame, along with everyone else in this country with a conscience. I wrote this book so that Hrant Dink would not be forgotten. I also wrote it to heal my own soul.

And yet, when I first started writing Hrant's biography, the pain of losing my friend was still too fresh, too raw. To position myself as an omniscient narrator examining a life from a distance was, quite simply, inconceivable. Nor could I write as if I had witnessed his life firsthand. And so I decided that there would be no single narrator, no overarching "I" in the book. Instead, I would tell Hrant's life story by bringing together the accounts of the closest witnesses of each period of his life. Their voices would construct the book.

Hrant was the first Armenian of Turkey who spoke openly in defense of his people's minority rights and against the discriminatory policies of the Turkish state. He also spoke for the democratic rights of all citizens of Turkey. This included the right to speak freely of the genocide of Anatolia's Armenians in 1915. It was his advocacy of democracy that made him a threat to the Turkish state.

As the founder and editor in chief of the bilingual Turkish-Armenian newspaper *Agos*, Hrant became the first secular voice of the Christian Armenian minority. He also became one of the country's most prominent public intellectuals, calling for the democratization of the Turkish political system.

He dared to speak and write against all of the taboos of the regime, from the Kurdish question to the headscarf ban, always with the same commitment. In a country where non-Muslim minorities live in closed and anxiously silent communities, this risky undertaking was unprecedented. But until his last day, his courage never wavered.

Hrant was prosecuted three times for "insulting and denigrating Turkishness." Many prominent Turkish intellectuals were also brought to court under similar charges. They included Orhan Pamuk, Nobel Laureate in literature; Elif Shafak, another distinguished novelist; and several prominent journalists. While the charges against these others were dropped at the very first hearings, Hrant alone was convicted. This was an act of discrimination, leveled against him solely on account of his being Armenian. Hrant took his case to the Court of Appeals, where his sentence was confirmed six months later. Following this last verdict, the death threats he received became increasingly serious, but the government offered him no protection. Having exhausted internal appeal mechanisms, Dink finally appealed to the European Court of Human Rights to overturn the ruling. Two days later, he was murdered on the pavement in front of his newspaper's offices.

When I began work on my book, I did not yet know which voices to include from outside his family, but I had already decided which voices to exclude. I had no wish to make room for those who had taken aim at Hrant or hounded him to his death. I was not going to sully his story in the name of impartiality. Because I knew which side I was on . . .

My book was to begin with Hrant's birth and end on January 19, 2007. My task was to write an account of my friend's life. That's all I knew when I set out on my journey. I still did not know how I would reach my destination.

After his wife Rakel gave her blessing, I reached out to Hrant's family. First his son Ararat, and then his brother Hosrof, and then the others . . . I entered through the door they opened and started walking from one person to the next.

Over a period of three and a half years, I interviewed a total of 125 people. I taped each interview and filed them both chronologically and by subject. And when it came time to move on to the writing, I transcribed the recordings and classified them both chronologically and thematically. When committing their words to the page, I took special care to preserve the unique tone of each narration. Their voices came to be joined to each other within the natural flow of the text, as if each one paused only to pass the word to the one that followed.

But not a word was added to the testimony I'd collected. I edited out the stories people told about themselves, saving every story they told about Hrant. Wherever I quoted from their letters or writings, I made slight alterations to give their words the cadence of spoken language.

It was when his life story was beginning to take shape that Hrant in the heavens could no longer restrain himself. In that enthusiastic voice of his, he said, "You're not doing this without me!"

Hrant was not an archivist of private life. In a country where, until recent times, military coups occurred once a decade on average, and where, with each new coup, homes were routinely raided and searched, books banned, and private documents confiscated—with large numbers of people rounded up and sent to prison for their political views—people do not always feel inclined to keep records. It is only natural that Hrant, as an Armenian and a leftist, was one such person. In any event, the struggle to make a living gave him no time to do so. All that was left from his personal life were a few poems that he had written for his wife, and a number of letters that he had written his children.

Nevertheless, Hrant Dink was an avid archivist of oral culture. He spent years collecting stories that his people told him. As these stories combined with his innate knowledge, he became the living memory of a century of Armenians. During the last decade of his life, distilled versions of these stories made their way into his thinking and writing.

It was when the doors to his newspaper offices opened to me that I saw where the real treasure was. The many columns, studies, essays, travelogues, and works of reportage he had produced in the ten years of *Agos* were preserved in its archives.

This was not, of course, my first encounter with Hrant's writings. Even so, I struggled to hold my own against this abundance and intensity. I did not want my book to become a simple anthology of his work. With this in mind, I extracted his autobiographical writings, editing them to fit the chronological and thematic flow of the biography. And so it was that Hrant's unique voice joined the chorus.

Hrant's writings are tightly argued. Excerpting sentences or even paragraphs from writings that he constructed stone by stone was very difficult—and all the more so because his words come straight from the heart, astounding with their authenticity. I had a hard time, until at last I felt I had found his voice. But in the end, he was still Hrant, of course. He was never one to fade into the background. And that is why his words appear in bold type in the pages that follow.

With Hrant's voice added, the book assumed the quality of an epic. We can see Hrant's love for mystification not only in the style of his writings but also in the names he chose for the various stages of his life. For instance, he named the Armenian Children's Camp—built by the children at the orphanage where he spent his childhood—the "Lost Civilization of Atlantis." After it was seized by the military regime, he called it "Swallow's Nest." He also adopted an epic style when explaining the Armenian issue to the Turkish public, narrating the tragedy of 1915 and its aftermath through the simple everyday stories of the man on the street. I tried to capture this same spirit in my chapter titles and my book's overarching structure.

Hrant's brutal death was itself epic in nature. In Istanbul on January 19, 2007, Hrant himself was transformed into a myth. Thus, I began my book with the voices of his family on the pavement where he was shot. Then I returned to the Anatolian city of Malatya, where Hrant was born. Beginning with the story of his ancestors, I constructed a chronological account of his life, in which a moment arrived when it became necessary to divide the book in two. The first book became *Khent Hrant*, covering a forty-year period from his birth until the founding of his newspaper, *Agos*, in 1996. The second, *Baron Hrant*, related his struggle for identity first as a journalist and later as a man of thought and action. These two lives were utterly different in content.

The foundations of Hrant's personality were laid at the orphanage of the Gedikpaşa Protestant Church and shaped by the tough struggle to earn his daily bread. Added to this was his revolutionary leftism, fostered during the student movements of the late 1960s and early 1970s. The result was a daring young man known by his closest friends as *Khent*, an Armenian word that translates roughly as "crazy heart."

Baron Hrant is, by contrast, a contemporary tragedy, the ending of which we know from the very beginning. During the last decade of his life, those who worked with him at *Agos* called him *Baron*, the word that Armenian students traditionally use to address their teachers. In this, his "second life," Hrant Dink embarked on a struggle that was unprecedented in a country where the denial of the 1915 genocide was and continues to be official policy.

As different as the two books might seem, I used the same approach throughout: while both *Khent Hrant* and *Baron Hrant* follow a clear chronology, they are, at the same time, organized by theme. And so, in the end, I composed this biography of thirty-one chapters—like an oratorio in which Hrant and those who loved him come together to narrate the story of his life. I feel obliged to make this clear, lest the collage of voices in the pages that follow be misunderstood.

In his final days, clouded by anxiety, the Hrant Dink we knew as a leftist and an atheist sought refuge in the psalms of the Holy Book. That is why I chose to bid my friend farewell with the prayers of his Christian faith.

This book began as a journey and traveled a long way from Aleppo to Damascus and as far as Brussels, down the roads that so many Armenians took into exile. From Yerevan to Deir ez-Zor to their final resting places.

In the beginning, I asked myself, "Why me?" By the end, I knew the answer. I am indebted to this book for giving it to me.

İstanbul, February 2014

Acknowledgements

As for those to whom I am in debt . . . I would first like to thank the Dink family. They put their trust in me, and they broke their silence. They unlocked their hearts, and they shared with me even their deepest secrets. They did not try to influence the book's contents. If this book reflects the independence of thought in Hrant's spirit, it is thanks to their trust, their faith, and their poise.

When my work on the book was entering its second year, Karin Karakaşlı, who had served as Hrant's "right hand" during his years at *Agos*, came into my life. I am forever indebted to my friend for her faith in my project and for the love and respect she showed me.

From the day she wrote to congratulate me on the book, and through the time it took for us to reach this moment, writer and translator Maureen Freely was a constant friend; she reached out to Gerard Libaridian, the Armenian scholar who became my editor, and undertook the arrangements to publish the book in English. I am indebted to both of them for their determination to bring *Hrant* to an international audience.

After my publisher, Transaction Books, asked me to take my 700-page Turkish book and reduce it by half for its English version, it was necessary for me to go back to the original version four years after its publication in Turkey to revise and reshape it. I would like to take this opportunity to offer my publishers my deepest thanks for giving me this opportunity to spend more time with Hrant.

I thank each of those who found the time to speak to me and who granted me permission to quote their written words. There are hundreds of them, impossible to name them all. Some are old friends. Others came into my life through Hrant. Here I give them all my deepest thanks.

Introduction to the Transaction Edition

Gerard J. Libaridian

Hrant Dink was a friend to many, a gentle yet passionate soul, a man devoted to his family, a tolerant yet fierce interlocutor, and a man with cold logic and a warm heart. Hrant presented a seeming paradox of a man whose mild manners belied a firmness of character and determination to go where his values and judgments—indeed, his humanity—would lead him. He was also an intellectual who sought the roots of problems; he thought issues through and compelled others to think as well.

These qualities have not emerged because he is no longer with us. Those of us who knew him closely felt in the presence of an extraordinary person from the first moment we read his articles or met him; even those who disapproved of his views and politics and those who hounded him during his lifetime realized that Hrant Dink was a courageous, convincing, yet unconventional, thinker. He listened to his antagonists, including those who tried to demean him, and absorbed any hatred. He shunned no one and respected all; in doing so, he compelled others to face their own inconsistencies, their behavior, and, in many instances, their hatred-based discourse and irrationality. Maybe that is the reason he invited the wrath of those most steeped in conventions and myths, those who loved their problems more than solutions, those who were afraid to question their own comfortable beliefs and prejudices, extremists among both Armenians and Turks who could not tolerate challenges to their hardened yet simplistic positions.

Hrant was both simple and great; he elevated everyone he came into contact with, whether by his words, his deeds, or his touch, except those who had no capacity to be elevated. I have rarely met a person whose values, character, and politics were in such harmony yet at the same time was so troubled—troubled because, after much conflict and war, the world he inhabited was not in harmony with the basic values that humanity had created.

Hrant did not see the world merely as a product that he had to endure. He wanted to add something to it. He knew that his thought process, coupled with his inability to accept these dissonances, had placed him at the center of major battles far larger than any one person; for Armenia and Armenians and for Turkey and Turks, these were battles of competing identities and of policies—a dangerous configuration that pitted conflicting interpretations of the past and of the lessons of the past with opposing visions for the future.

Hrant knew, as others do, that identities are shaped and evolve. But, as opposed to others, he thought that these changes could have a conscious and rational dimension and be effectuated in a manner as to promote the resolution of conflicts. What is known euphemistically as the "Turkish/Armenian conflict" became, for him, the prism through which he would experience the world and its questionable practices.

The narratives that Turks and Armenians supported were not only separate but also conflicting. For most Armenians, Turks appeared in history as killers and Armenians as victims; for the Turks, the Turks were the victims—victims of Great Power imperialism whose help Armenians sought to pressure the Ottoman government and who the Great Powers used in order to extract concessions. The victims of imperialism were also, as Hrant strove to remind the Turkish state and his co-citizens, victimizers, responsible for the planned deportations and massacres of Armenians in that empire, which has since been aptly characterized as genocide.

Hrant Dink was one of the first to have empathized with both victims without losing sight of the perpetrators. He was the first journalist to articulate a narrative that attempted to integrate the two conflicting ones. That made many quite uncomfortable, especially the Turkish state, which continued to deny the genocide, and the "deep state" that considered itself the guardian of an orthodoxy—political and historical—whose integrity had to be maintained at any cost lest the structure of values and taboos crumble.

Stimulated by the rise of the national democratic movement, by the end of the 1980s, the Armenian world had plunged into a battle for what I have called elsewhere "the soul of the Republic" and, by extension, of Armenian identity. With some exceptions, the Armenian diaspora had come too close to equating being Armenian with being anti-Turkish. Anti-Turkism simplified policy making, left few choices, and freed the decision-makers from taking responsibility for their policies and actions.

Less vulnerable to the vagaries of a diasporan existence and to the meanderings of what passed for political thought in the diaspora, the people of Armenia were able to mount a frontal assault on identity politics and set out to forge a new path, one based more on statehood and independence. This meant independence not only from the Soviet Union but also from an identity based on victimization and a political discourse based on fear: fear of Turkey and, more dangerous, an attachment to that fear as a principle of public life. That battle, in which Hrant Dink engaged fully with his articles, talks, and discussions, is still being waged, although with far less success for opponents of conventional thinking than two decades ago.

The battle he fought in Turkey was merely the other side of that coin. Hrant's probing mind eventually linked the denial of the genocide and of violence in Ottoman and Turkish history to its nondemocratic nature. Was Turkey to continue as an authoritarian nationalistic state in which limitations on thought and freedom of action were justified with constant references to real and imagined security threats, or was it going to finally transform itself into a normal state, worthy of joining the new Europe? That battle is still raging in Turkey, although here, too, hopes are not as high as they were a decade ago. After all, while both Armenia and Turkey need normalcy, the extremists on both sides need each other to justify their extremism and, for some, their hold on levers of power that come in different forms.

Hrant's last two battles might have been the most surprising, yet the most natural. First was his fight for Turkey's membership in the European Union. Surprising, because most Armenians in the diaspora and some in Armenia opposed that membership; natural, because it followed his belief in fundamental and universal rights enshrined in European institutions—rights the respect of which he considered the precondition for the development of a democratic society.

Second, he argued against the pending French law on the criminalization of the denial of the genocide. Here, too, Hrant's stand was surprising because for most Armenians, sending to prison those who deny the genocide was a welcome relief from denialism and from the burden of unrecognized history. Yet here, too, this stand was natural: he knew that beyond other considerations, criminalization of denial, beyond its infringement on freedom of inquiry and speech, would be used in the same manner as other policies had been used in relations between Great Power and Turkey: using the plight of minorities as a cover for their own policies to pursue unrelated aims, often as irritants to Turkish policy-makers, to the detriment of those same minorities. The battle for Turkey's membership in the European Union is still formally being waged but with increasingly less enthusiasm on the part of European Turkey; Europe's enthusiasm regarding this issue was always suspect.

With all of these battles at hand, no doubt Hrant knew that he was fighting a war, maybe many wars, although he would have disapproved of the terminology. The Turkish/Armenian issue, in all of its dimensions and complexities, has been one of the most intractable in recent history; it is symptomatic of and integral to the wider battles being fought today in a world still seeking its moral compass. Hrant was one of the most determined and complex protagonists on this battlefield, a protagonist whose human-rights-centered moral compass dictated his assessment of what to do with historical events and political realities. He knew that judgment was as important as knowledge.

Hrant Dink fell in the middle of his battles, which now must be ours. He was bigger than life in life, and he is even greater in death. His absence simply highlights the vacuum that exists and that we will learn to live with. We will accept that he is no longer with us. But his values and principles are, and we must make sure that we continue to fight for them as a whole and not take on only that which is convenient from his life or from his death.

Hrant was, evidently, bigger than life: he was a foot soldier with an ever-expanding vision of the field of perception and action. Through his articles and speeches, and in his discussions with the widest variety of people, Hrant broke taboos and built bridges.[1]

Hrant bridged the closed world of Armenians in Turkey and the Turkish people. As a product of the post-genocide Armenian community of survivors—the last remnants of the Armenian people in Anatolia and historic Western Armenia and of their progeny—he tried to redefine the position of Armenians in Turkey. He wanted to be liberated and to transform a community that has been repressed and treated as a tolerated religious minority into full-fledged citizens with a right to their own memory and the right to participate in shaping the future of the new country of which they've found themselves citizens. He did not think that the memory of past victimization should have been turned into the means for a new mental servitude nor should it define his people as a minority with rights to its religious practices and limited cultural rights only.

He tried, in fact, to secularize the community, an essential component of his quest to free Armenians from being state-defined Armenians and of his quest to promote equality of all as citizens. In this respect, he was an emancipator who reflected and represented a new generation of Armenians and Turks. By casting this issue as one of democracy, within a historical perspective, he, along with his colleagues, constituted another attempt to make Armenians on that land be treated as citizens rather than as subjects. In the evolution of his political thinking, he came to see the treatment of minorities and of their history on Ottoman lands, including the Republic of Turkey, as symptomatic of the real character of imperial realms and political regimes.

Unlike others who have tried to change Turkey, Hrant Dink knew that unless change came from below and involved the common people, change would not be permanent—hence his readiness to allow himself to speak from the heart, as an Anatolian, to reach out to the most conservative elements in Turkey. His very genuine emotionalism was a weapon that he knew could be used for a good purpose, but when he needed to be, he was the most rational person in the room.

Hrant bridged the world of Armenians of Turkey and that of the traditionally defined Armenian diaspora in whose worldview Armenians in Turkey did not rank high. He engaged the rest of the diaspora and compelled its leaders and members to give him and his compatriots their rightful place and to listen to his message.

Hrant bridged the world of Armenians in Turkey and in independent Armenia. He was one of the first to support the new republic and its policy of seeking to normalize relations with Turkey without the precondition that

Turkey recognize the events of 1915 as genocide. In doing so, he also engaged Armenians in Armenia, overcoming age-old prejudices and antagonisms between the Eastern and Western segments of that people.

He bridged the gap between Turkey and Europe, along with so many other citizens of Turkey, by pushing the country toward reforms and higher standards in human rights and democracy.

Nonetheless, Turkish/Armenian relations remained at the center of his intellectual, emotional, and almost spiritual deliberations. The term Turkish/Armenian "relations" or "conflict" is too simple to describe the many levels at which those bearing either one of these labels functioned, especially in the 1990s. From the abstracted hatred articulated by an Armenian who first met a Turk to state-to-state relations between Armenia and Turkey, there is a whole world of academic, community, and lobbying politics in which the "conflict" is played out.

While building his position brick by brick and issue by issue, Hrant challenged assumptions and definitions taken for granted in Turkey and among both peoples. He challenged many prejudices, institutional obstacles, and closely held assumptions. It is difficult to determine whether it was his character that made him adopt the challenging views that he had developed or his views that built his character. There is no doubt that his personal moral values played a major role in his accepting and living by precepts that others ignored.

Hrant was neither a historian nor an academic, but he had the ability to internalize what he read and to perceive its logic. He was brutally honest with himself, even at the cost of contradicting himself. Yet these contradictions were always at the edges of his worldview; he had the strength to recognize even minor contradictions and to rethink. His greatest strength consisted in the fact that he knew he did not have all of the answers. Hrant Dink was always evolving and fighting within himself to find answers to ever-new questions. While eschewing essentialism in the understanding of the terms "Turk" and "Armenian," he found his mission in "saving both from the scourge of racism and nationalism." For many, ethnicity defined the outer boundaries of their identities. For Hrant Dink, the ethnic experience was the motivator to see the world and try to reform it.

Maybe all of that weight was too much for the fragile shoulders of one man. At least he tried.

Cambridge, MA
January 2015

Note

1. Hrant Dink, *Two Close Peoples, Two Distant Neighbours*, published by the Hrant Dink Foundation, Istanbul, in 2014, is the first of a series of volumes that will introduce the English-language reader to Hrant Dink's articles.

Guide to Turkish Pronunciation

a as in "father"
e as in "pet"
i as in "machine"
o as in "oh"
u like the *oo* in "boot"
ı like the *u* in "but"
ü like the *u* in "mute"
ö as in German: *schön*
c like the *j* in "jam"
ç like the *ch in "child"*
g as in "get" (never as in "gem")
ğ is almost silent, lengthening the preceding vowel
j as in French: *jamais*
ş like the *sh in "should"*

Rakel's Letter

Not long after my husband's assassination, Tuba came to see me. She had tears in her eyes, and she spoke with great hesitation, as if she feared she might break my heart.

"My dear Rakel," she said, "I would like to write Hrant's biography. If you consent, I promise to write from the heart, with the utmost sincerity. This is what I have come to ask. Would you accept me as his biographer?"

I was right to believe she was sincere. It was a mission given to her by God. This was what I believed, and this was why I gave her my support. I also prayed for her.

For more than three years now, she has been in our lives. It is almost as if she had been there with us all along, and with my Çutağ, throughout his fifty-three years of life. She shared our moments of happiness and exhaustion, sorrow, serenity, and hope. She entered our hearts. She went back in time with us to retrace a hundred years of memories, opening up her soul as if she herself had traveled along this path with us.

For three years, we cried together. For three years, we grieved with one heart. To this I can bear witness. Because I now regard her as a member of my family, I can also add, "Let us thank God that you came to us, that you took on this task. By embracing it as an honor, not a burden, you honored us, too."

Dearest Tuba, I thank you with all my heart for your love and dedication. And most of all, for your eternal friendship . .

İstanbul, September 2010, *Rakel Dink*

My Hrant

At first, my Hrant was a pair of eyes. A pair of sad eyes, watching me curiously. It was our friend Elâ's funeral. I was standing far from the crowd, head bowed, struggling not to cry, when I felt his eyes on me. I turned my head and saw those sad eyes so at odds with his big, lively body.

Then, suddenly, he became a hand on my shoulder. He remained there, perched. Then he flew away, as fast as he had come . . .

Hrant was a surprise at first, but soon he'd become a story. When the funeral was over, my husband Cengiz introduced us, saying, "This peasant you see before you is the Armenian community's secular leader. Standing next to him is the Armenian girl, Rakel, who for many years thought she was Kurdish. And this is my wife, Tuba."

Hrant burst out laughing and said, "You godless bastard! Why don't you introduce us properly?"

And then, God knows why, Hrant got into our car without Rakel. As he made himself comfortable in the front seat, I caught myself thinking, *He might be Armenian, sure, but to me he is definitely an Anatolian.*

We set out for the city, with my eyes on the back of his thick neck. They went off into a discussion of deep political matters, and I into my own daydreams . . .

When we reached Istinye, I was jolted by a voice shouting, "Are you hungry?" Seeing me nod, Hrant turned to Cengiz and said, "You park the car," and before I knew it, he had jumped out, opened my door, grabbed my hand, and taken me over to the fishermen. He was walking, probably, but I was running. And if I should so much as try to stop in front of one of the stalls, he paid no attention. He just kept going. I was struggling to catch my breath, and I couldn't understand the rush. But then, finally, he stopped in front of the little shack where the fishermen cooked their own food on a potbelly stove.

As he began bantering with the old man by the stove, he finally let go of my arm. In his most caring voice, he began with his questions: "Would you like mackerel or bluefish? Should they put lettuce and tomatoes on it? Do you like it with or without onions?" By the time Cengiz caught up with us, I was eating my fish and bread from Hrant's hands.

"Who is this man?" I remember asking in the car, after he had left us to go his own way. In the years that followed, I kept asking that question many times. Who was this man, really? Who was this man who'd fed me fish and bread, as my own father had done? With time, I came to know him. I came to understand who he was. He was just a single man, but he was too fiery to hold down. So they shot him down.

And then . . . Then he became my book.

Lying on the Pavement

HRANT DİNK

Dear God! I've been shot!

HOSROF (ORHAN) DİNK

On January 19, I went to our bookstore at around eleven in the morning. During my lunch hour, I read "Fluttering like a Pigeon," his last column. How hard his words hit me! My heart almost flew up through my throat. *I'm going to* Agos, I said to myself. Just when I was about to leave, someone came in to to to see me. *All right*, I said, *we can speak for ten minutes or so, and then I'm going out.*

The meeting lasted longer than I expected. At one or two minutes after three o'clock, a call came through. A voice was saying, "They've shot Baron Hrant!" I remember dropping the phone onto the floor at that moment. Nothing else . . . just darkness.

The screams brought me back to myself. I stood up. I didn't ask anyone anything. I ran all the way down from the fifth floor. One sentence kept ringing in my ears: "They've shot him." I was going straight to *Agos* to save him. I jumped into a taxi. I told the driver to take me to Osmanbey. He took the coastal road. On the way, I asked the driver to turn on the radio, and that was when . . . that was when I heard he was dead.

I must have punched the driver, punched the doors. The traffic was terrible. Nothing was moving on the roads. I must have gotten out at Kasımpaşa or somewhere near Bilgi University. From there, I ran all the way to *Agos*. All the way to that pavement . . .

YERVANT (LEVENT) DİNK

I was at the store, as always. I was in this room. On January 19, the tension in this room was unbearable. It was hard to breathe in here; it was as if the ceiling were pressing down on us. We were all feeling very bleak. I'd had this terrible headache, so we'd turned off the television. So anyway, one of the boys came in. He opened the door. I was on my feet at that moment; I was right next to the door.

Brother, have you heard the news?, he said.

Heard what? I asked.

What they just said on television, he said.

Man, what are you talking about? Go and get this damn thing turned on.

There was a newsfeed running along the bottom of the screen. Something about an assassination attempt. I remember thinking something like, *Damn it, someone's shot him in the leg. That won't be enough to bring him down, not a giant of a man like him.*

I ran downstairs and threw myself into a taxi. My head was spinning. I saw that the traffic wasn't moving, so I jumped out of the taxi. I began to run. It gradually dawned on me that getting shot in the leg wouldn't cause a traffic jam like this. When I got to the front of *Agos,* I saw him. There was this big man, lying on the ground . . .

HAYCAN DİNK

On January 19, I was on the base in Sarıkamış. We were doing training. At around five in the afternoon, our company commander summoned me to his office. I went there, thinking that our orders must have come through. "Have you spoken to your family lately?" the commander asked. I told him that I hadn't been in touch with them for a few days because the lines were cut off. And, anyway, my father and Uncle Orhan had just been here for my swearing-in ceremony. Uncle Hrant had really wanted to come, too, but they'd talked him out of it because they were worried for his safety. He'd rung me the day after the ceremony to say how sorry he was not to be there with me. Then, he'd said, "Your military service is almost over now. When you come back, you'll get married, and we can all love and cherish your children. What I want most of all, he said, is to see you all married before I die."

The commander was speaking. "You'll hear it on television soon enough, so it's best you hear it first from me." He uttered my uncle's name. For a moment, he paused. "There's been an armed attack. I offer my condolences." I just stood there. Couldn't take it in. I couldn't hold the words "uncle" and "death" together.

My uncle's laugh rang in my ears. Just before I went off to military service, we were at *Agos,* talking. My uncle had just won the Henri Nannen Prize in Germany, and he'd decided to distribute the prize money among us children. That day, he gave me my share, after which he told me about his plans for the next month. He was going to Norway to collect another prize, and, while he was there, he was going to give a few speeches. And I said, "Uncle, what if you stopped speaking for a while?"

First, he just froze. A number of his friends had already been trying to persuade him to take a few steps back on account of all of the threats. But I guess he'd never expected to hear this from me. He paused for a few seconds, and then he reminded me that I was soon going off to military service. He began to tease me, saying, "Watch your own back first, my boy! There, you'll see for yourself what the world is made of!" I at once offered to give him the

200 euros he'd just given me as hush money, but that didn't stop him. He threw his big arms around me as his big laugh filled the room . . .

The commander told me to call my family, but I went straight to the television and flipped to the news channel. At that moment, I saw the commotion in front of the newspaper office. The newsfeed was running along the bottom of the screen: "Journalist Hrant Dink assassinated." I waited for them to show my uncle, and finally I saw him. So, yes, it was in the military that I found out what the world was made of.

ZABEL DİNK

On Thursday, January 18, we were going to the parking lot for my daughter Zepür's driving lesson. To get there, we had to walk past Hrant Ahparig's house. As we were hurrying past his house, I heard the outside door closing. I turned back. And there was Hrant Ahparig. He couldn't see us. We were in a rush and walking pretty fast. But still, I found myself doing something I'd never done before. I kept turning back and watching him. Did I look at him because I missed him or because I wanted him to see us? I really don't know. I just knew it was very odd, because when Hrant Ahparig stepped outside, he looked left and right and then up at the apartments. Then he looked behind him. After that, he crossed the street. He took four or five steps, heading for the avenue, only to change his mind and turn onto the other street. The avenue would have taken him out to the main road, but, no, he just went onto the side street and lingered there for a while before turning back.

I watched him until we reached the main road, and Hrant Ahparig kept looking left and right and up and down; he kept coming and going. I just couldn't understand why. I didn't have any sense that something was going to happen to him, but I did feel strange. I put it into my mind that I should mention it to my husband—his brother—when he came home that evening. But I was asleep by then. Orhan came home late that night, and he'd already left again by the time I woke up. So I wasn't able to tell him.

I was at the house that morning. Suddenly, I heard screaming in the building. I can't figure out where it's coming from or what this sound is. I go out to the balcony to look. I can't see anything below. I go to the door. My sister-in-law Haygan lives in the apartment below me. I can't hear anything in there. Her door is closed. I can't hear any noise coming from upstairs, either. But the commotion continues. Then, my phone rings. A voice says, "Sister, how are you?" The moment I say that I'm fine, the phone goes dead. But the screaming still goes on.

Suddenly, it occurs to me that there might be a thief in Haygan's apartment. A thief must be inside there, suffocating Haygan. I have a spare key, so I thought that I'd better run down and rescue her. Then, suddenly, it's chaos. While I'm running around the house, looking for the key, my mobile starts ringing, and then the house phone. The phone that's connected to the Internet begins to ring, too, and also the doorbell. I feel like I'm losing my mind, with the screaming and all of these phones and bells ringing.

Now I'm picking up one phone, and now I'm picking up another. I hear a voice coming over the line. "They've killed my uncle!" I go into shock. "Who's your uncle?" I shout. I can hear Maral screaming, "'Maaaaamaaaa!'" But I just can't accept it, so I shout even louder. I answer another ringing phone. "Stop talking, stop calling me!" I shout.

Finally, I open the door. I'm off to see Haygan. I see Lusin on the stairs. "Auntie, please come quickly. Mama is in a very bad way." *Yes, I know. They're strangling her,* I tell myself. I run in, and there is Haygan weeping. *Well, at least they didn't strangle her,* I think. But why is she crying so hard? And at that moment, I turn to look at the screen. "Breaking news: Hrant Dink has been killed . . ."

DELAL (BAYDZAR) DİNK

On January 19, I was at my office in Brussels. I was at my computer, but I didn't feel well. Even one of my colleagues noticed. "You don't look well," he said. "Why don't you go home and get some rest?" I didn't even have the energy to do that. Then, Guillaume came over to me; his eyes were brimming with tears. He was shaking. "I need to talk to you about something," he said. I stood up, asking him what was wrong. He was heading down the corridor. He moved on ahead, and I was walking behind him. And at that moment, something happened. Time slowed down, and then it stopped altogether. As I walked down that corridor, I felt that my life was about to change. Something had happened, and nothing in my life would ever be the same. I could feel this in my bones.

Guillaume took me into one of the empty rooms along the corridor. He closed the door and said, "Your father . . ."

"No!" I cried. "Quiet! Don't say a word!"

"He's been shot," he said. And I kept shouting "no!" and trying to silence him. He stopped speaking.

"Have they taken my father to the hospital?" I asked. "They saved him, didn't they?"

"No," he said. "He's dead." I didn't believe him. I kept screaming "no!" When he realized that I didn't believe him, he pulled up the Internet edition of that notorious newspaper, *Hürriyet*, and showed it to me. That's where I read it. It was from this very newspaper that I found out my father had been killed—and this time, I believed it.

ARARAT DİNK

That day, I'd been at the bookstore since early morning. I was going to take my friend to the hospital in the afternoon. I left the store and got into a taxi. Brother Necdet was the first one to reach me. "Arat," he said, "they've shot your father." Then, he said something like, "I can't get through. Do you know what condition he's in?"

And I said, "What are you talking about?" My mind had gone numb. I immediately called my father. My father didn't answer. I dialed the *Agos* number. No one answered. I called one of my friends at *Agos* on his mobile. "Are you at Agos?" I asked.

"No, I'm not," he said.

"I can't get through," I said. "Give me the number of someone else at *Agos*." He gave me Lora's number. I called her. She told me that she was outside. But there was something in the tone of her voice, too. I could tell that they'd just heard the news. They could not tell me anything. I am talking about the first few minutes . . .

By now, I was kicking the doors of the taxi and punching the windows. I told the driver to take me to Osmanbey, to *Agos*. We were still stuck in Çapa. The traffic was like nothing you could believe. I was swearing like crazy now. The driver was frightened. I gave his car quite a beating. So, then, I called my mother. "Where are you?" I said. She told me where. "*OK*," I said to myself. It was clear that she didn't know.

Then, Sera called me. "Apar," she said, "something's going on. Something's happened to Father."

"No, girl," I said. "It's nothing. It can't be anything. I'm on my way to *Agos* right now. I'll call you as soon as I know."

"I'm on my way there, too," she said.

We keep going, the traffic looks like it's never going to clear up. We keep going on and on . . .

Sera must have gotten there first. She phoned, crying, saying, "They're saying Papa is dead."

"That can't be true," I said. "Don't talk nonsense. No, he's just wounded." I couldn't get her to talk. I couldn't believe it, not until I saw him. I didn't want to believe it. And I don't believe it. We were in Dolapdere by now. I gave up on the taxi and just jumped out. As I got out, I gave the driver a hundred liras.

I was on my way up the hill when I suddenly realized that I was acting as if I'd accepted that my father was dead. *No*, I told myself. *He can't be dead.* So I went back and asked the driver for the change. I ran and ran. Then, well . . .then I saw my father on the ground. No, no, I didn't see him right away. I couldn't see him through the crowd. When I first got there, there was a police cordon, as if there had been an incident. At that moment, my only wish was to see my father still alive. I tried immediately to get through, thinking that if they stopped me, they would keep me there for at least two hours, talking and asking questions. I ran fast, pushing my way through the police cordon. I was almost at the door, and that was when I saw my father. I saw him lying on the ground.

SERA DİNK

The last time I spoke to my father was the evening of January 18. That was the last time I saw him—that evening at the house. My mother and father were sleeping in the next room. I had read his column, "Why I Am a Target" which had come out the previous Friday. These were things that he had talked to us about in private, and when I saw that he had poured it all out into his writing, I was deeply upset and cried for a long time.

From that night on, before I went to bed to say my prayers, I'd stand at his door and watch my father. And on January 18, I at last found the courage to speak with him. I went over, gave him a kiss, and wrapped my arms around him. Then I told him that I'd read his article, and I asked him if he'd received any threats during the week since. Smiling, he said, "Of course not!" That took me by surprise. "How could that be?" I asked. "Think of how many cases they've opened against you and how many threats they've sent you when you hadn't done a thing. And now you're telling me that you received no threats after writing that column?"

My father smiled again and said, "No, my girl, all of those threats have stopped now."

"So, Father," I said, "does that mean that the threats have stopped for good?" He smiled as he nodded. Then I kissed him for the last time and went to my room. How could I have known that I would lose him the very next day?

On January 19, I was walking around Taksim with my friends. One girl's mobile rang. She answered, and, as she listened, her face went white. When I saw this, I automatically reached for my own phone. I called my father, because when anything goes wrong in my life, he's the one I call. The phone rang, but no one answered. *My father must be busy doing something,* I think, *and that's why he can't hear it ringing. He'll check his phone soon, and when he sees that I called, he'd call me back.*

Then my friends put me in a car. And for some reason, they took me to *Agos.* A crowd had gathered outside the newspaper. Someone was lying on the ground. You know, I never believe anything until I hear it from my father. Once again, my hand went to my phone. I called my father so that he could explain to me what was going on—so that he could tell me that he was all right, and then I could relax. But, again, he did not answer. It was after I'd hung up that I realized that the man on the ground was my father. After that, I remember nothing.

RAKEL

I remember him leaving home at half past ten that morning. He didn't eat much for breakfast, but, as always, he ate something. He seemed preoccupied when he got up to leave. Something was bothering him. I kissed him and wished him a good day. "Don't be sad. These things that are troubling you aren't important. They'll be gone by the time you get home tonight. The important thing is that we're here together," I said, without knowing that it was our last talk.

Then, he left for work. I had a prayer meeting, so I went out, too. When the meeting was over, a few of us stayed on to share our thoughts. One young friend said, "Rakel Kuyrig, how can anyone forgive the unforgiveable?"

"Even if someone is a murderer," I said, "we have to forgive him because that is what Jesus tells us we must do. If we live by his word, if we follow his teachings, we must find it in ourselves to forgive this person unconditionally, because that's what he has taught us." I shall never forget this conversation.

Then, my phone rang. It was my son. "Mama, where are you?" he asked. "Pray," he said. His voice was shaking.

"My son," I said, "where are you? Stay where you are, and I'll come find you." I thought something had happened to him.

"No, nothing's happened to me, Mama," he said. "You just pray."

He had just hung up when Sera called. "Mama," she said. "Papa . . .I'm going to *Agos*." Her voice was quivering. She hung up. It was one thing after another now—just then, the phone rang in the house where we were meeting. Our hostess answered. She turned pale.

Now, this is what happens to people at times like these. Certain possibilities flit through your mind, but you push them away. If you put any of these possibilities into words, it would mean you were taking them seriously, accepting them as true. And you don't want that. But those thoughts still keep coming back.

And perhaps the same thoughts are occurring to the friends around you, because one of them faints. I slap her on the face. "Get up now, fast," I say. "Today is the day you need to be strong." I'm weeping, of course. "Are we going to have to take care of you, too, while we're trying to be strong? We cannot let ourselves faint, because if we do, we'll lose our strength. Remember what Jesus says: 'When you are weak, you will feel my strength welling up inside you.' Now that day has come. Stand up and let's think what we must do."

But even as I am telling this friend to stand up, I feel my own knees giving way. If I let my guard down, I am going to collapse. But at just that moment, a verse from the Bible comes flashing into my mind like lightning: "When you are weak, when there is nothing more you can do, my strength will manifest itself in you."

"So, Jesus," I say, "if that's what you say, then that day has come. Could there be a day when we needed your strength more?" I put on my coat then and there, and I got ready to leave the house. A friend followed me out, insisting on coming with me.

"I want to go to Agos," I say.

"No," she says, "we need to go home."

We are still arguing when we get there. But I'm not really there. I'm in shock. We walk all the way home. When I glance over at the corner, I see my sister-in-law, looking disheveled, walking toward our house. Her aunt and a few other friends are all coming toward the house.

This is how you know that something bad has happened. Everyone leaves the place where they heard the bad news and comes to you. No one cares what state they're in or how they look. You can read the bad news on their faces.

We go into the house. I throw down my bag. I pick up the phone. The doorbell doesn't stop ringing. But no one says a thing; no one even turns on the television. No one says it, but everyone knows. I haven't put it into words, but I know what has happened. I dial the taxi number from memory, even though I've never memorized it. I am trying to talk to the taxi people when instead I find myself speaking to my brother in Brussels. "Mikhail," I say, "I was just calling a taxi. How did you get on the line?"

"Kuyrig," he says, "take good care of yourself. We're on our way."

"Oh, please, look after Baydzar," I say. "She's the one you should be looking after."

"We're together," he says. "We'll be flying out together, too."

I hang up. Out of shock, I dial his number again. Now, we are crying together. At last, I'm able to call a taxi. I'm also shouting at the people in the house: "I'm not letting any of you stop me! I'm going to *Agos*! If anyone wants to come with me, they can." I got into the taxi with two friends. It was the longest journey of my life.

When I got there, I saw Ararat with Sera. I embraced them. How strange we humans are! What I thought at that moment was that my children would never recover from this. Crushed, fatherless, their wings broken . . . These were the thoughts flying through my mind. These were the thoughts in my mind as I embraced them.

By the time I got there, they'd taken my husband away. I saw his blood on the pavement. Later, I was sorry. Why hadn't I lain down to sleep next to him? Later, I was so sorry . . .

As I was leaving *Agos*, I saw that they were washing down the pavement with soap and water. They were trying to clean it up. As if it were possible to clean it up. How can bloodshed be cleaned away like that, with soap and water? These are God's words: "When people are silent, blood demands justice." When justice is not done, it is blood that still insists. It never stops speaking. Not now, not in the future, and the same is true for the bloodshed of the past—it never stops speaking.

Raising Hrant from The Pavement

My friend's name was Hrant. If you asked me to describe him, I would say he was a man of great humanity. His soul was pure. He was the truest of friends. He had courage and a wild streak. He was one of life's caretakers. He watched over us all. He was our dearest treasure. There might be other ways to describe him. But, for me, he was simply a man like no other.

They took my friend's life away. They shot him in front of his newspaper. They shot him from behind . . .

That day, I was shot, too. Every person he touched while alive, everyone he ever took into his large arms and healed with his touch—they were all shot. We were all shot. But it was Hrant who died. The rest of us were left behind.

And we saw things. We saw Hrant lying on his face on the pavement. We saw the white paper they'd tried to cover him with and his shoes, with the holes in their soles. We saw it all.

And we knew. There was Hrant, offering his lifeless body as a bridge to the history of his ancestors, telling us the stories that he was never able to tell when he was alive. As always, with his body . . .

We did not see Hrant being lifted from the pavement, but as the ambulance siren mixed with our own screams, we saw the bloodstains on the pavement. And it didn't end there. In the years that followed, we would see him deprived of justice. Thus, we would learn that his blood was still flowing on that pavement. With that knowledge stripping our hearts bare, we would look back at that pavement and see Hrant still lying there.

Come and help us raise Hrant from that pavement. All of us who were shot on that day but left behind—let us lift him up together.

Let us tell his story to the world.

Who knows? Perhaps he will hear our voices. Perhaps he'll add his own words to our chorus. And then—maybe—we shall all begin to heal.

TUBA ÇANDAR

Book One

Khent Hrant

Part I

An Abandoned Child

1

The Hamam of the Infidels

YERVANT (LEVENT) DİNK

Manuel Aşotyan Efendi was an Armenian tradesman living in Gürün, between Malatya and Sivas, and the father of five children. He sent his eldest, Ardaşes, to study in America. One night, when the whole family still was eagerly awaiting a letter from Ardaşes, there was a knock on the door. They thought it was the postman, but was the gendarmes!

It's 1915! A cable sent from Istanbul decreed that the deportations should begin. They rounded up the Armenians. Little Lusiye—her father used to call her his one and only Ahçik—is waiting with her brothers, waiting to find out what will become of them. People hunters were coming from all over at that time, and if a girl or a teenage boy caught their eye, they would ask the families "nicely" if they could take them away with them. Mihri Bey picked three girls out of the convoy and took them off with him to work in his house. One of these girls is Ahçik. She said goodbye to the family she will never see again and goes off to the mansion.

Some time later, the Agha's wife—it's not clear if she suspected Agha's good will—secretly summoned the housekeeper, "Hagop the Infidel," and asked him to take the three girls by night to an orphanage that's opened up in Sivas. Hagop immediately did as she has asked.

The Sivas orphanage was a haven for all of its children, and it was their salvation. But it didn't last long, for soon the founder and director fell ill, and when she died, the orphanage closed, and the children were farmed out to the community.

Anto was an Armenian from Erzurum; at the onset of war, he had a wife and children. An order arrived, and he was taken off by force to work on a labor regiment, making roads. Time passed, but he had no news from his family. In the meantime, he heard all sorts of rumors. He couldn't bear it anymore, so he found a way to escape. He reached his village, and what a terrible sight to see. There was nothing left of his home and no sign of his children. He fled to the mountains.

Some time later, word went out, offering amnesty to all those who fled to the mountains. Anto of Erzurum descended to the plain and went to Sivas.

One day, he was wandering through the market when he ran into someone from his village, who told him what had happened. He was devastated.

Everyone in his family had perished. The flame of revenge fired up in Anto's heart. His fellow villager understood this and tried to talk him out of it. He told him of an Armenian girl from the orphanage who was working in the fields; all the young men had their eyes on this girl, but because her courage was legendary, none of yet had tried their luck. There was only one way out of this catastrophe: to take this girl as his wife and start a new family.

So Anto, who is older than thirty, married Lusiye Ahçik, who had only just turned sixteen, and they moved to the Kangal district. They had six children— three girls and three boys. They gave each one the name of a loved one they had lost. In spite of the studied carelessness of the census takers, the names they give their children were unmistakably Armenian.

For a long time, they waited for people to come back. Of Anto's seven lost siblings, only one returned alive.

A brief account of our ancestors' share: a population of forty-three, and only four survived. Ahçik, part of whose life I have described, is the mother of Hrant's mother, Nvart; in other words, Hrant's grandmother. Those who knew her said that Hrant had Ahçik's temperament. As Hrant had said on so many occasions, "Every Armenian is a document!"

ARMENAK ÇAKIR

My name is Armenak Çakır. I am Hrant's uncle. I was born in Sivas, in the Kangal district, in 1928. Lusiye Çakır was my mother. Her father used to call her "Ahçik." In Armenian, that means "my daughter." The name stuck. We are six siblings in all. My mother's people came to Sivas from Gürün. They'd been under the protection of someone called Mihri Bey. This was during the deportations, during the massacres. Women were carrying their children in saddlebags on donkeys; along the way, my mother lost her twin sister. Many elderly people and children perished during the forced marches. They were gathering up Armenian girls at that time, so my mother stayed for a time in the home of Mihri Bey. A few years later, Mihri Bey's wife took her to the American college and left her there. There was an American college in Sivas in those days. It had an orphanage connected to it. They were bringing together Armenian children, and my mother stayed there for a time.

My father, Anto, was from Erzurum. When they were deported, my father and his mother left in a carriage with two of his brothers. They marched for months, and, in the end, they reached Sivas. My father found work there, and he married my mother. They settled in Kangal. That's where we were all born. Kangal is a tiny little town; there was no work there. In 1945, when my oldest brother returned from his military service, we moved with him to Malatya. My mother came with us. My father, Antranik Çakır—people called him Anto—stayed in Sivas. My mother knew very little about 1915. She would only speak of her own life story, nothing more, and she had one older brother, who'd been sent to America earlier. We had no idea what had happened to her other two siblings. We tried hard to find them, but we never did.

SİRANUŞ YAŞGÜÇLÜKAL

My name is Siranuş Yaşgüçlükal; my maiden name was Çakır. I am Hrant's maternal aunt, so you think they'd call me "teyze," but actually the children call me "hala." That's the custom with us—we call maternal aunts "hala" and paternal aunts "bibi." I was born in the Kangal district in Sivas in 1938. I was the youngest of six. I was seven years old when we moved to Malatya. When my oldest brother, Haygaz, came home from his military service, everyone wanted to move because Kangal was such a small place. There wasn't much work there. I can't remember the exact year, but it was sometime during the war—that would be World War II—but the soldiers came and asked if they could have the bread in the oven, and my mother said, "Leave enough for the children and take the rest." That's how poor people were!

When my brother Haygaz returned from the army, from Diyarbakır, he said, "Let's just move to Istanbul." My father, Antranik Çakır—they called him Anto—was a butcher in Çetinkaya. This was a train station on the Sivas or the Erzincan line. "Istanbul is too far away," he said. "Better if you go to Malatya. That's closer." My father stayed in Çetinkaya. For many long years, he worked as a butcher; he would join us each winter and go back every summer.

Both my father and my mother would talk a great deal about 1915. My father is from Erzurum. He was already married with a child when the deportations happened. They took them off to be slaughtered. They were seven siblings, and only my grandmother and two of my father's brothers survived.

My mother, Ahçik, was from Gürün, and it was from there that she moved to Sivas Kangal. There was a haberdasher named Mihri Bey, and he was rich. He had a shop and a mansion. He had scooped up thirteen beautiful Armenian girls who had come to Kangal and taken them all to his mansion. Mihri Bey, the owner of the mansion, was a rake, but his wife was a very good woman. Of course, the man had his way with a number of the girls.

There was an Armenian cook at the mansion named Hagop. Taking pity on my mother and her friend Elmas, he helped them escape; he took them to Sivas and left them at the orphanage there. This was an orphanage set up for Armenian children who had lost their families in 1915. Later, when my mother went to stay in the country, she was working in the potato fields. And there was a strapping young man—a Turk and a Muslim. Handsome, too. And my mother was a beautiful young girl. This man asked for her hand in marriage. My mother said, "I refuse to marry a Turk." She married my father instead. He was much older, but because there were no other men to choose from, my mother married him. She became my father's second wife just because he was Armenian.

ZABEL ÇAKIR

My name is Zabel Çakır, and my maiden name is Yastangeçkol. I'm Armenak Bey's wife. So I am Hrant's aunt; also, Sarkis's father, Ohannes, is my father, Arsen's, brother. In other words, Hrant's grandfather is my uncle.

To put off going into military service, my uncle Ohannes chose a different surname, and I understand that it was Dink. I was born in Malatya in 1935, on September 15, like Hrant; we share a birthday. Actually, since Hrant's father, Sarkis, was my cousin, and we were brought up as sister and brother, you could say I was Hrant's cousin. But because I am married to Armenak, they call me his aunt.

My father was originally from Gürün. My father moved to Malatya from Gürün when he was nine years old—or, rather, they were sent into exile during the slaughter in 1915. The oldest—Hrant's grandfather, Ohannes—came first, and then my Aunt Flor and my father, Arsen. There was also my Uncle Mihran; he went on to Aleppo later on. My father, my uncle, my aunt, and I, we all lived in the same house. Sarkis, his older brother, Rupen; and my Uncle Mihran—we all grew up together like brothers and sisters.

In the beginning, they earned their keep by renting fields and growing potatoes. When we were children, my father and my Uncle Ohannes also worked as dyers; they dyed material. In the old days, whatever villagers wore was always cotton. So, you see, the merchants in the market would give our people rolls of material, and they'd dye them. They dyed this material at the house. They would boil up ten to fifteen oil tins every day. Each of those tins could hold 18 kilos—just think of it! We would all help them until evening fell, and then we'd hang up the material in the street to dry.

Our house was in Salköprü. People called the neighbourhood the "Hamam of the Infidels." Everyone there was Armenian. My father and my uncle were considered to be doctors of some sort—if someone had a headache, he came to us.

Our elderly spoke the best Armenian; everyone in the neighbourhood would point us out. If a letter came from abroad, they'd bring it to us to read and to write an answer because my father and my uncle had gone to the Armenian school in Malatya. There was a school there that the French had opened. My father and my uncle had been educated there in the Protestant faith. They knew French, Armenian, Turkish, and old Ottoman Turkish. After the slaughter, the school was turned into an orphanage for the children who had survived, but lost their families in the slaughter. After that, it became the Tobacco Monopoly Factory. When we were growing up, there was no school for us to go to. All the Armenian schools had been closed, so we weren't able to go to an Armenian school. We learned only Turkish.

In our house, we never worked after three in the afternoon on Saturdays. All work would stop. Until Monday morning, no one did a bit of work. I remember Sarkis's mother—in other words, Hrant's paternal grandmother—best; her name was Baydzar. She would bathe herself, take out her clothes and get dressed, and then brush her long, long hair. There were three women in the house. We called our uncle's wife "harsa." That's our word for an uncle's wife, and it also means daughter-in-law.

So my uncle's wife, Baydzar, would sit with my Aunt Flor and my mother, and they would sing hymns. We didn't have anything like a radio or electricity.

In other words, there was no other way to amuse ourselves. They'd light gas lamps. Sometimes, they would talk about 1915. Baydzar was the one who'd talk about it most. She'd sing hymns and she'd talk. The whole family would sit and listen.

VARTANUŞ ÇAKIR

My name is Vartunuş Çakır. I was born in Malatya in 1930. I'm married to Nvart's eldest brother, Haygaz, or, to put it differently, I'm the wife of Hrant's eldest uncle. We married in 1949 with the help of a matchmaker. Afterward, we went to live in Haygaz's family home. It was in a place they called the "Hamam of the Infidels," like the "Quarter of the Infidels" in Diyarbakır.

There were two big churches in Malatya. One was in the market, and the other was derelict and not in use anymore. Children would go in there to play. That church was just behind the hamam. That's why they called our neighborhood the Hamam of the Infidels. They also called it Salköprü. It got that name when they slaughtered the Armenians, and the name stuck. They'd swing people from the bridge, or so the story went. It was mostly Armenians living there, and a few Alevis. Our landlord was Naciye, an Armenian who'd converted to Islam. We lived there all together, my mother-in-law, Ahçik, and my sister-in-law's family. My husband Haygaz was doing his military service then. We were engaged after he returned.

It was around that time that Nvart and Sarkis married. Nvart was a clever girl. She was quiet and serious. In the beginning, her father was against the match because of Sarkis's gambling. Haygaz was against it, too. They hoped marriage would straighten him out, and so, in the end, they agreed.

UNCLE ARMENAK

They called Hrant's father something else, too, in Malatya—they called him "Haşim the Tailor." He was a good tailor. He was a good man, actually, apart from the gambling. He had a pure heart. But the moment he started gambling, he wouldn't have cared if the sky fell in. He'd get in so deep that he'd even gamble away the money for the children's food. When they asked for Nvart, my father was in Sivas. They came and asked my brother instead. Sarkis's mother, father, and uncle all came to ask Nvart to marry their son.

Sarkis's father, Ohannes, had gone to school in Malatya, and he was a respected member of the community. He was known to read religious books and other books, too. He had really beautiful handwriting. He was employed as a foreman in a cotton mill. He was a truly learned man. They also used to dye cloth in their house. They were well off. Then came the Wealth Tax, and that was the end of it. They started to take their cloth to the villages to be dyed.

Almost everyone else in Sivas Kangal was Kurdish. We'd do our bargaining in the markets in Kurdish, and at home, we'd speak Turkish. We didn't know Armenian. We could understand this and that, but we couldn't really speak it. But in Ohannes' house, they spoke Armenian. Even when he spoke Turkish, he'd throw in a word of Armenian now and again. So, anyway, we accepted Haşim's proposal. In time, the girl wanted to get married, too, I believe. And we didn't want go back on our word, so we gave our sister in marriage.

Haşim got very drunk at the wedding. I took him by the arm and got him out of there, to avoid any incidents. After they were married, they moved into his father's house. *Now he'll pull himself together*, we thought. Sarkis's father had even opened up a shop for him. But he went back to the gambling. In a month or two, he had to shut the shop down. His father would track him down and take him away from the gambling table; he would stand over him and make him sew clothes. But it was all for nothing.

AUNT ZABEL

They called Sarkis "Haşim the Tailor," but they also called him "Master Haşim." He worked in the market. He was tall and handsome. He didn't take much care with his appearance; he was a bit scruffy. Yervant is the son who most resembles him. Hrant looked like Nvart. We were in primary school at the time; we'd hear my uncle and my father talking to each other about an Armenian family that had just moved from Sivas Kangal with a daughter who was ill. They must have been talking about Satenik. We'd pass by the house they were living in on our way to school. When we walked to and from school, we'd try to peek through their windows, and if the door was open, we couldn't stop ourselves going inside. Then we'd run away, of course. It's the way children think, isn't it? After all, we'd heard about a child who was ill . . .

Time passed, and now I was a young girl. I heard that our elders had gone to them, proposing that Sarkis marry their daughter, Nvart. Before marrying, Sarkis had caused his family a lot of anguish with his gambling. After the marriage, he caused his wife anguish, too. I was caught between the two families because we'd all grown up in the same house like brothers and sisters. When Sarkis married Nvart, Nvart came to live in our house. The newlyweds started to live with my Uncle Ohannes. We were living in two rooms. They were living in two rooms. When Hrant was born, I was engaged to his Uncle Armenak. When Hrant was forty days old, we got married. I moved to the house where Nvart had lived until marrying. In a way, the two households exchanged families.

Hrant was born in Salköprü, in the house at 1 Boncuklu Street. Salköprü was right next to the Çavuşoğlu district. It was near the municipal headquarters, where they said that the old train tracks were. These were historic places in Ottoman times and all that . . .

There was a large courtyard. Inside the courtyard, there were between five and ten houses. Just about fifty people lived there, all in all. The houses were two stories high at most, each standing alone, made of mud-brick and composite stone. Families lived communally to keep the costs down. They baked their bread in the oven in the courtyard. It was mostly Armenians living here, but there were Muslims, too, in our neighborhood. When we were children, we were very close.

Hrant was born on September 15, 1954, in our house. It was Uncle Ohannes who gave him his name in a ceremony with hymns and prayers.

AUNT SİRANUŞ

It was Hrant's grandfather who gave him his name. Put together two Armenian words—*hur* and *yerant*—and you get "Hrant." *Hur* means "flame," and *yerant* means "vitality." So Hrant means something like "lively flame." It was almost as if they knew what he would become when they gave him that name. After all, his grandfather was an educated man, God rest his soul, because he'd studied at a college that, in those days, taught Armenian and foreign languages. He owned a great big Bible, which he read voraciously. And Hrant took after him.

Hrant came a bit earlier than expected. He was a strapping boy, weighing more than 4 kilos. He was blond. His head was big, but he was a beautiful baby. My older sister was beautiful, too, by God. Those eyes, those eyebrows, and those long eyelashes . . . Hrant looked like her. She was clever, too, my sister. She'd taught herself how to read and write. We confided in each other a lot. She was in her nineteenth year when Sarkis came into her life. My mother was against the match, and so was my father, but in the end they consented. My father came all the way from Sivas to be there to put on the ring. So then she was married. And the troubles began.

She was still a fresh young bride when the gambling trouble began. There were scenes. After Hrant was born, they left Ohannes Bey's house for good. Nvart was hoping that if Sarkis left his father's house, then maybe he'd start taking his responsibilities seriously and stop gambling. The place to which they moved was also in Salköprü.

One thing I'll never forget is when Hrant was around one year old. He was still a babe in Nvart's arms. The riots of September 6–7 had just happened in Istanbul. Some people had heard about it on the radio. In those days, we were renting a house from Yusuf Agha. My older brother, Haygaz, was in the market, in the coffeehouse, that day. Whoever heard about the riots on the radio had passed on the news, and then women, children, and young people began to flock to our house because our house was a very big one with a staircase and everything.

They poured into the house, searching for a safe haven. There was shouting in the street. They said that there was some sort of a "meeting." Now how were we to know the meaning of a foreign word like "meeting?" So there we waited, expecting the worst. We got ready to throw stones from the upstairs windows if they came to attack us. We hid all of our valuables. We were all in tears. Then my brother Haygaz turned up. When he saw the state we were in, he was shocked. Then he cried, "So they're having a demonstration—what's it to you?" Then he told us what the "meeting" was about, after which, he said, "So now, everyone go home." I remember how Nvart headed off to her new home with Hrant in her arms. You see, they moved many times in Malatya. They kept falling behind on the rent and having to move on.

AUNT VARTANUŞ

When Nvart and Sarkis left Ohannes Bey's home, they didn't have a thing to their name. A bed and a cradle—nothing else. Then, Haygaz, may his soul rest in peace, thought it only right to buy two Antep *kilim*s for them, and they spread them on the floor. But that was all we could afford. They stayed in that place for about a year, and then, when Ohannes Bey refused to pay their rent any longer, they moved to the Çavuşoğlu district. They had these row houses there. They'd rent these places by the room. Two or three families would share a house. So, anyway, Sarkis was under Haygaz's thumb in those days. Haygaz kept a close eye on Sarkis to keep him from gambling. It was around then that Hosrof was born. Then, they left that place.

They moved near the Çekem family, who was very rich and owned a pottery kiln. So they went to live in their outhouses, and that was where Yervant was born. And that was where the real trouble started. Sarkis stopped coming home. He owned a sewing machine, but it went to pay a gambling debt. Haygaz went and paid the debt, got back the sewing machine, and turned it over to Ohannes Bey. But it was all for nothing. If he wanted to, Sarkis could make a suit in an hour; he had such quick hands, but they went idle. And he was such a good man, but he gambled and told lies. He cared for no one. And it was his wife who suffered, with his children.

AUNT SİRANUŞ

Before they moved into the Çekem compound, they lived in another place in the Çavuşoğlu District. One day, Nvart couldn't take it anymore, so she swept up her children and went back to her mother's house. I was still unmarried at that time. We were all sitting at the table, eating. Sarkis arrived to take his wife and children home. My brother Haygaz invited him to sit down. "Sit down, and let's talk about this nicely," he said. "Don't act like this. Get back to work. I can help you."

And so they went on, talking nicely, when Sarkis flared up and said, "I'm never going to change." My brother Armenak picked up a knife off the table and went for him. God must have been watching over us, because no one was injured. The rest of us just sat there in shock. I began to cry; I ran and grabbed my brother's arms.

After Yervant was born, they came back again to Salköprü, our neighborhood, somewhere near the ruined church. Nvart would bring Hrant and Hosrof to us; it was where they got fed. I'd make riding horses for them from the branches of a poplar tree. They'd play at being horsemen.

There were about fifty households there. The houses looked out onto a shared courtyard. The women would gather together in this courtyard to wash wool and dry apricot pips. In the middle was a washhouse. We'd take water from the pool and boil it. They'd wash the children in that courtyard, girls and boys, kicking and screaming, in huge copper basins. No one paid attention to whose child was whose; they'd take all the children and scrub them clean. This was the way we led our lives.

After that, Sarkis went back to gambling in a big way, and he ran up big debts. Hrant must have been three or four years old. They'd moved to the Çekem compound. By now, I was married, too. My son had just been born. One day, Sarkis had been gambling again, and he couldn't pay his debt. The gamblers raided his house. Nvart seized her children and fled to our brother Haygaz's house. And wouldn't Sarkis come straight to our house that same day? My father-in-law had summoned him so they could talk this over. And then, what do you know? Three or four of the gamblers came to raid our house, too! They must have followed him.

All hell broke out at the house. My father-in-law and my mother-in-law beat them off with sticks. They forced them out of the house. But this incident proved to be the straw that broke the camel's back.

It was clear that they couldn't stay in Malatya, so they decided to move to Istanbul. Or else it was the elders who made the decision for them. That part, I don't know . . .

HOSROF DİNK

I don't have a single picture in my mind of Malatya. Hrant remembered it because he was older than me. Later on, when my uncle and his family were still living there, I went to Malatya to visit. That time, Grandmother Ahçik had me sleep in her room. She was always suffering from headaches. I remember her always being in bed. But when she was on her feet, she ruled the house.

My mother, Nvart, was the poorest of her children, so Grandmother Ahçik always tried to help us. She had a strong sense of fairness. She knew that no one would dare to stop her. It was always like this, both in Malatya and when she came to Istanbul to visit. She ruled the roost, our grandmother, but she loved us dearly—at least that was how I felt. But I never saw my Grandfather Anto; I never knew him.

Hrant was always fascinated by Grandmother Ahçik's story, and Grandfather Ohannes's story, too. In the old days, our people in Anatolia used to write down their family records on the backs of their Bibles. Hrant had memories of Grandfather Ohannes reading a lot and writing things down. That's why he spent such a long time looking for books in which he might have written down our family's records. He spent a long time looking, but he never found anything.

HRANT

Our elders used to tell stories. They said that my grandfather was a voracious reader. He gave everything deep thought. When he was able to escape the summer sun, he would pull his wicker stool into the shade made by the vine on the courtyard wall, and he'd begin to turn the pages. As he turned the pages, moistening his fingers with his lips to separate the ones that had stuck together in the humidity, he would sometimes grow tired of the noise that his grandchildren were making around him,

and he would vent his anger on the sand flies, hitting them one by one with the covers of his books. When he couldn't bear the crying babies any longer, he would call out to my grandmother and say, "They've done enough running around out here. Take them inside!" And we would know that something he'd read had upset him. He always had a roll-up in his mouth, and its last dregs stuck to his lips. He burned his lips quite a few times when he was reading.

My grandfather could read Armenian. He could read English, too. So could his father. And they say, as my grandfather sat on his stool in the shade by the wall, swatting flies, there were more than four thousand Armenian schools across all Anatolia.

Again, our elders would tell their stories . . .

On the day when they were told, "You've got to leave this place," and they bundled up as much as they could carry, they could have buried their gold, but they picked up all the books God gave them and carried them on their shoulders. And they carried them as far as they could. "My son," the elders would tell me, "our grandfathers left their gold behind, but they took their books with them."

I salute my ancestors who left their gold behind and took their books with them.

I salute those who kept those books on their backs so that we still have them today. And I salute those who will do so in the future.

2

The Fisherman's Basket

UNCLE ARMENAK

In the spring of 1958, I came to Istanbul. I opened a shop and started to work. A year later, Hrant's father, Sarkis, arrived. He tracked me down, and we met. "I've come for good," he said. "I'm looking for work."

We were living at opposite ends of the city. We didn't see much of each other. When we met one time, he said that he was apprenticed as a tailor. After a short while, his father, Ohannes Bey, brought my sister Nvart with her three children to Istanbul.

AUNT SİRANUŞ

In Kumkapı, there was a fisherman. When they first came to Istanbul, they lived in his house. They had good days in that house. For a year, Sarkis worked well. He brought his money home. Then he found friends and started going to the coffeehouse. When he started gambling again, they were forced to move.

HARUT ÖZER

Hrant's family came to Istanbul after us. We came around the time of the 1960 coup. I remember that we hadn't quite settled down yet when they arrived. Their house was very close to ours. They lived on the ground floor of a dark, unplastered house.

This particular street in Kumkapı was where Armenians coming in from Anatolia tended to gather. These were modest houses shared by four or five families—each family in one big room. The toilets and kitchens were shared. Brother Sarkis was always out at the coffeehouse. They had the same coffeehouse culture in Malatya. The men would play cards, and our mothers would send Hrant and me to the coffeehouse to call our fathers home. The men never paid us any attention.

After Sister Nvart asked for a divorce, Brother Sarkis came to the front door to speak to her. They were speaking through the window, and I could see them. At some point, they must have started arguing, because Sister Nvart took the clog off her foot and threw it at him. Swearing and pounding on his back, she pushed him down the hill. They were running between the cars. We never saw Brother Sarkis in those parts again.

AUNT ZABEL

It was the end of 1959. We all boarded the same train for Istanbul: my Uncle Ohannes, Nvart with her three children, and me with my daughter. Our journey took three days.

Sarkis had rented a house in Kumkapı. Our house was close to theirs. We had just one room, and so did they. After coming to Istanbul, they lived together as man and wife for only three or four years. Then, Nvart came to us. My mother-in-law Ahçik Hanım had come to Istanbul from Malatya. She was the one who brought Nvart to us. Nvart couldn't take it anymore, apparently. I remember this happening while she was a neighbor to Baydzar.

BAYDZAR BOZUK

We became neighbors when they moved to their second house in Kumkapı. To be more accurate, Sarkis built a room, a kitchen, and a toilet in the back garden of our house. It's all gone now. They tore it down ages ago. We had the same landlord.

We lived like two sisters there. There was no one we knew from before. We met there. Sarkis, for example—well, he was our brother, too, but to tell the truth, we felt closer to Nvart. In those days, none of us had anything, but poor Nvart had the least of all.

Sarkis was working as a tailor. Nvart and I were doing little jobs by hand; for instance, sewing trousers, shirt buttons, coat linings—whatever we could find. There was no sewing machine at the house, of course; we sewed by hand.

Nvart suffered a lot. Sarkis wouldn't let her take in work. We had this neighbor, for instance, and Nvart would do her laundry just to get her hands on a few *kuruş*. Sarkis didn't want her doing that; he railed against her.

But if Nvart didn't work, he wouldn't give her any money, either—or if he did give her money, he'd come and ask for her to give it back so that he could go gambling. That was why Nvart did her sewing secretly. Whatever she earned, she hid behind the sofa so that Sarkis wouldn't see it.

Sarkis was a good tailor; he knew how to hold a pair of scissors. When he wasn't gambling, he was a good man, Nvart would say. That's why I still had time for him. When it came to money, he'd go off to play with just two and a half lira. Not more. But really, he had nothing.

People in those days were very abstemious. Very stoic. They worried what people would say; there was shame. You were expected to get married and make do in your new home. If you quarreled, they'd say "so-and-so's daughter went off to her husband but didn't make do, and that was a great shame."

Everyone accepted their lot and suffered. But poor Nvart, she suffered more than any of us. I'd always say that if Nvart fell ill, it was because she suffered so much. She was mother and father to her children. She was the sort of person who made something out of nothing. There was always trouble in that house. For example, Nvart came to me one day and said that Sarkis had flown into a rage because she wouldn't give him money for gambling, and he had hurled a pair of scissors at her. We could see into her window from the garden. We saw how the children lived in there. They were very good children. If you told them, "You're not crossing this line over here," they'd listen.

Nvart couldn't pay for electricity or water in our house. When they couldn't pay the rent, either, the landlord would say, "I'm taking them to court, and you're going to appear as witnesses."

"I'm not doing that," I would say. But the landlord had a conscience. He was Armenian, too. He was very patient, out of respect for the Lord. In the end, they moved to another house. Later, I heard that they'd separated.

UNCLE ARMENAK

Zabel had gone to Malatya. I said to myself, *Why don't I pay my sister and her children a visit*? I took food packages with me. The children would play in the little *meydan* near the Patriarchate. Hosrof and Yervant came and wrapped their arms around my legs. "Uncle," they said, "did you bring us some food to eat?"

"Yes, I have," I said.

My sister was in the house, doing laundry. "Has Sarkis come home?" I asked.

"Not yet," she said.

I went to the bakery and bought four or five loaves of bread. Then, I went to the coffeehouse. I looked through the window. Three people were sitting at a table, gambling. Nvart had already told me the year before that she couldn't bear it and that she was going to leave him. I didn't accept that. But when I saw him there in the coffeehouse that day, I thought, *Fine, it's over!* A man who goes off to gamble, leaving his children hungry, well, he's no longer a man. I took Nvart back home with me.

One day, I was home fixing an electrical plug. Sarkis walked in. He was coming to the house a lot, planting himself outside it. He'd come to see Nvart. He'd call the children to his side. Hrant was beginning to figure things out, and he was ashamed. He'd run away and hide, but the others would always go run to their father. He intended to use the children to soften up Nvart, you see. The whole neighborhood would come to the window to watch them.

At the top of the hill, there was a grocery store. When the grocer couldn't bear it any more, he went outside and said, "Enough is enough. You're disgracing yourself, do you know that?" So Sarkis took the boys and left. Five minutes later, I looked out and saw that he'd come back. By now, I'd lost my patience, so I ran outside to chase him away. They came after me and held me back. They wouldn't let me go after him. After this incident, Nvart went to court to ask for an official divorce.

AUNT ZABEL

What a situation we were in now; we had no idea what to do. Sarkis was my uncle's son, and Nvart my husband's sister. I ended up caught in the middle a lot. It really wore me down. All that coming and going, and so many shouting matches. Sarkis was not a bad person. He knew what he'd done wrong. When Armenak got angry and shouted at him, Sarkis would say, "You're right, big brother." He respected those who were older than him—that was his way. He was a good person. He knew how to take one piece of bread and share it with ten people, but he couldn't stop gambling—that was the problem.

UNCLE ARMENAK

It must have been in 1963. At the second hearing, Nvart and Sarkis were granted a divorce. The court gave custody to the father. But how was this father going to care for his children? I felt so sorry for them. Hosrof and Yervant were still little, at least. They couldn't understand much. But Hrant! He was very sensitive. He was a quiet, thoughtful child. He had his own way of talking and his own way of walking. I even remarked on that one day. "Look at how this one walks," I said. "He walks like a full-grown man. He's going to do great things when he grows up." He was still little then, but he looked out for his brothers; he took responsibility for them. He was a very proud child.

AUNT ZABEL

When Nvart came to stay with us, we were living in one room. We didn't have much furniture—just one double bed. My husband and I took our daughter into bed with us. On the other side of the room was a divan big enough for one person. That's where Nvart slept. Nvart stayed with us for a year. From time to time, my mother-in-law Ahçik would come to visit from Malatya. When that happened, we would give her our bed. We'd spread out bed mats for the rest of us, and we'd sleep head to toe. When my mother-in-law came to Istanbul, she'd stay for six months. She was the one who saw the type of situation that Nvart was in and took her out of her husband's house and brought her to us. She's also the one who put the children into the orphanage, I recall. But I don't remember anything about a fisherman's basket.

UNCLE ARMENAK

I never heard anything about a fisherman's basket . . .

YERVANT

Hrant was the one most affected by the fisherman's-basket incident. That's because he was older and understood more of what was going on. Many years later, when we three brothers sat down to talk about it, Hrant told the story as if he were reliving it step by step, and his greatest fear was that something might happen to his little brothers. He did something big that day, without knowing it, and maybe this was his first act of rebellion, the first time he stood up against life. He never asked us to go with him. But we saw him as our only source of safety, and that's why we went with him. Hrant was only seven years old, but already, in his gut, he had that spirit of resistance. That's where it all began, and it continued all his life.

HOSROF

Even now, when I go to Kumkapı, it still gives me the shivers. My roots are there . . . I have almost no memories of it. but its smell is still inside me. I don't remember much about the time we ended up on the streets. But I remember how I felt. Was it one night, or more than that? I remember what it was like to be outside all night. It felt like hiding behind a door . . .

YERVANT

When my mother and father divorced, the court gave my father custody of us children. Then, my father tried to take us back to my mother, and my mother didn't know what to do. "You will look after them," she kept saying. She was so, so poor. She was staying in her brother's house when she divorced my father.

That day, my father marched us up to their house. He stood at the corner, egging us on, pointing at my uncle's house and saying, "Go on, off you go to your mother." My poor, helpless mother kept shooing us away. "Stay away," she said. "Stay with your father." And she was screaming bloody murder at my father. Suddenly, Hrant took off, running downhill toward Kumkapı. And we ran after him. I don't remember what happened next, but I remember this part. I remember it because of the expression on my mother's face. If you had given her kerosene right then, she would have set herself on fire and taken us with her. That's how she looked.

HRANT

My earliest memory is of three children who've run away from home and are wandering the streets, lost. Three brothers, running away from their mother and father. How they fought, those two. On that day, my mother was shouting at us from the window, "Go to your father!" And my father was saying, "Go to your mother!" We were caught in the middle. Then, suddenly, I found myself heading down the slope, with my brothers running alongside me. This way and that, through the streets of Kumkapı, we ran and ran and ran . . . I don't know how long this went on.

It was the police who finally found us. In a fishermen's shack in Kumkapı, inside a fishing basket. The three of us, fast asleep in each other's arms. Hungry, of course, and thirsty. They told us we'd been gone for three days. Apparently, they had notified the police when we disappeared. I was seven years old, Hosrof was five, and Yervant two. This is my earliest memory.

3

The Orphanage

HRANT

Growing up as I did, in the orphanage in the basement of the Gedikpaşa Armenian Protestant Church, I was, until the age of fifteen, steeped in Protestant culture. They called it the *Joğvaran*, but it would have been more accurate to call it the *Puyn*, the Armenian word for "nursery," because we weren't all orphans. A few of us were, certainly, but for most of us, it was a nursery for children who had been brought to Istanbul from Anatolia, where there were no Armenian schools. And there were quite a few children with families that had fallen apart in some way, or who had lost either their mother or their father. In short, this orphanage was a nursery where orphaned, half-orphaned, poor, and abandoned children could find both shelter and education. My brothers and I, for example . . . Our parents had divorced, and we were left homeless. If it had not been for that nursery, who knows what would have become of us?

YERVANT

Apparently, it was after we were found sleeping in the street that we were admitted to the orphanage. The director, Hrant Güzelyan, gave us the details much later. It happened like this: Grandmother Ahçik was in Istanbul at that point. When she saw what a terrible state her daughter and grandchildren were in, she went off to the Gedikpaşa Protestant Church. She asked Güzelyan, the orphanage director, to take us in. "We can't," he said. "We have no room."

"The eldest is school age. Take him, at least," she pleaded.

The director said, "We take in only children brought from Anatolia. We have limited means," and he sent my grandmother away.

Then Güzelyan's own mother told him about the fisherman's basket. She told her son that three Armenian children had been found sleeping in the streets of Kumkapı. Then, the director sent out word that they should bring the children to him. And that is how the three of us were accepted into the orphanage. This decision was the turning point in our lives.

HRANT

In the Gedikpaşa Protestant Nursery, where I spent much of my childhood, we'd draw pictures on paper twice a year, in our childish hands.

On one side, we'd write a greeting in Armenian—*Sireli Pareraris* ("To my dear benefactor")—and write a few lines of thanks to our benefactors. Every pupil had his or her own benefactor.

This dialogue continued throughout our education, and, from time to time, they'd send letters, presents, and family photographs, which we'd keep next to our beds to remind us of the people we thought of as our second families. One of my most vivid and important childhood memories was visiting the sights of Istanbul with the family that came all the way from America to get to know me better.

HOSROF

Güzelyan, who was the founder of the orphanage as well as its director, met our costs with donations from Armenian benefactors from abroad. He was the minister of the Gedikpaşa Armenian Protestant Church. He was also a carpenter. He originally founded this place for six Armenian children he'd brought back from Anatolia. In our time, he was sheltering more than a hundred children there. These were all children between the ages of seven and twelve except for us. When you left primary school, you left this place, too. From then on, you had to fend for yourself.

This place we called the "orphanage" was no more than a two-room dormitory. Children from different classes all slept side by side on cots. In the dining hall, we were responsible for setting the tables and clearing them. The little children were responsible for the cleaning—everything from washing the dishes to sweeping the floor. We were split up into groups and put on a rotation for the cleaning duties. Because the orphanage was part of the Gedikpaşa Protestant Church, we received a Protestant education. Our church services were very simple. There were no big rituals.

HRANT

Growing up in that orphanage meant several Bible readings each day. I knew by heart which verse was where. I memorized all of the psalms. I'll never forget the phosphorescent cross I won when I won first place in a psalm memorization competition. I hung it on the wall over my bed, and it would glow in the dark. I remember the psalm I won with; it was Psalm 91, which begins with: "He that dwelleth in the secret place of the Most High/shall abide under the shadow of the Almighty./I will say of the Lord/'He is my refuge and my fortress'" It was very long, but I used to read it in Armenian, never skipping a line.

When I was a child, I was so well grounded in the details of Protestant teachings that I could have been a preacher.

So why didn't I become one? There was the service on the day of the Lord. And every Wednesday, there was an evening service. In addition to these, there were always several other morning and evening services. "There's a new sermon for you to hear," they'd say. "Off to church. Today

Brother So-and-So is giving a talk, so off to church." Three times a day, we said our prayers before eating. And three times a day, we said them after eating. Then there were our bedtime prayers.

As for Sundays, the service would start at ten in the morning and finish at noon. Straight after lunch, there was Sunday school... This was a bit livelier than the usual routine of listening to stories. When we sang hymns, there was a certain tempo. They did things to keep us children interested. For example, they'd show us pictures illustrating Christ's saying for the day...

GARABET ORUNÖZ

On Sundays, we had margarine and jam with breakfast. We never threw the margarine wrappers away; we used them to shine our shoes. Then we would put on our best clothes and go upstairs to the church for Sunday service and our prayers of thanks. Then there was lunch in the garden. This was the only time during the week that we had meat. After lunch, we would stay and talk in the garden, and visitors would go off into the corner for their heart-to-hearts. In the garden, we played dodgeball, marbles, football, and volleyball. After that, we had an evening service. Later, we came to realize that Sunday ended when this service was over. The visitors would leave, and the big kids would console the little ones who cried. After supper, we'd wash our feet, and once we'd all said our prayers at the foot of our beds, we'd all go to sleep.

HRANT

During that same period, I went from time to time to the Armenian Orthodox Lusavorçagan Church, which seemed to me like a magnificent theater. Usually, my friends and I would sneak in there to steal candles. On the walls was an Armenian inscription that we couldn't understand ... And all sorts of paintings ... And that great gleaming display at the front ... How different it was from our own.

Our church was a simple room with a pulpit and benches and, at most, a wooden cross. For Sunday services, we would bring in a few flowerpots and put them in places where they could best be seen. That was all the decoration we had in our church.

For special services and holiday rituals, we added a bit of color to this Protestant church. Especially on *Dznunt* (Christmas) and *Zadik* (Easter), we couldn't get enough of our Armenian nativity or miracle plays. We dramatized scenes from *Surp Zadik*: the capture, incarceration, and persecution of Jesus; the stations of the cross; and his resurrection. We all wanted to play Jesus, but only the big boys and the privileged ones were chosen. And none of us wanted to play Judas, who turned Jesus in.

As for me, I usually had some small part in every play. Please don't laugh, but the part I loved most was the angel who brought the news of the resurrection. They put two wings on me, and my lines were: "Ye women, why are you looking for a living man amongst the dead? He's no longer here;

he's been resurrected." I could say that those days are long gone, that now we're grown men, as tall as posts, but I don't know how, every Christmas and Easter, we still return to those innocent joys of our childhood years, and we still enjoy them as much as ever. A strange little mystery, this is.

HOSROF

In the orphanage, they wanted us to speak Armenian. If we didn't, the director got very angry. We knew Turkish from our family already, so from an early age, we had two languages. In the orphanage, discipline was tight. There was a strict hierarchy. Güzelyan, the director, was at the top. He had all of the authority. Beneath him, there were supervisors, or the *hsgiç*. They were something like mentors or counselors, but they were a bit more than that for us. Some of them would stay with us in the orphanage at night. Wednesdays and Saturdays were bath nights. The *mayrig* (mother) who prepared our food also did our laundry.

YERVANT

My earliest memory of the orphanage was the peeing incident. When we got there, I was only three or four years old. There were bedwetters among the older children, too, and so they'd wrapped nylon around the mattresses so that the urine wouldn't soak into them, and we were regularly taken to the toilet at night. I was never punished because I was so small, but when the older children wet their beds, they were punished. To avoid punishment, they used to switch their sheets with mine. Once after this happened, Güzelyan, the director, got very angry with me. And I started to cry, saying that I didn't do it. The director said, "I'm not going to punish you, but you shouldn't lie," and I was so upset that I lowered my trousers to show him that my pants were completely dry. Later, they found out who had done it, and he was punished. They weren't strict with me until I reached the age of six. I don't know why, but if I started crying, they wouldn't stop me. But once I started primary school, I lived by the same rules as everyone else, of course.

HOSROF

Because Yervant and I were small, Hrant always looked out for us. He took responsibility for us. After starting primary school, we were no longer just three but many brothers. Because there was an age difference between us, we each made our own friends. And this is how we got used to living collectively.

While we were living in the Joğvaran, we attended the İncirdibi Armenian Protestant School in Gedikpaşa. Here, there were boarders as well as day pupils, but most of the pupils were children who lived at the orphanage. So, in a sense, the orphanage was the school's boarding department. In primary school, we followed the national curriculum, and we also studied Armenian. After the March 12 coup in 1971, they shut the school down. The Joğvaran was shut down during the same period.

In school, as in the orphanage, Hrant rose to the top. He was very smart and a good reader who could grasp ideas quickly, and it was clear even at that age that he had leadership qualities. He was more outgoing than Yervant and I were. He was not just older than us, he was also sociable, enterprising, and responsible, someone who could stand tall under pressure. He made friends with everyone. He had self-confidence. I can never remember him expressing shame or frustration. If he looked poor, it's because we were all poor.

Living in an orphanage and sharing the work there gave us a strong ethos about helping others. To share the load, to share the pain of those around us who were suffering injustice—even at that young age, we learned those values.

AUNT ZABEL

So, after all that, they put the children in the church orphanage, you see. They couldn't have stayed with us at night. We had no room for them to sleep. Sometimes, if they were very ill, Nvart would bring them to the house. She'd have them sleep with her on that narrow divan. And then, I beg your pardon, but I got pregnant again. So Nvart said to her brother, "You have so little room here. It's time for me to move somewhere else."

We found her a house near the school in Gedikpaşa. Grandmother Ahçik went to live with her there for a while. By now, Nvart was doing the finishing work on coats. She'd go to the tailor and bring back work to do at home—making buttonholes, sewing on buttons, things like that. But Sarkis would just never leave her alone. He was spying on her, no doubt. Nvart would be ready to take her work back to the tailor, and the moment she walked into the street, there would be Sarkis, right behind her. How he loved his wife! He couldn't stop watching her and following her. Nvart wasn't in love with her husband—not really. She longed to get rid of him, but what could she do? If a woman's husband leaves his children hungry, if he doesn't know her worth, if he won't do an honest day's work, how is she going to love him?

HOSROF

One day, my father came to our primary school for some reason, and there was a scene with my Uncle Armenak. He and his family were still in Istanbul at that time. They'd not yet gone back to Malatya. What I remember is that my Uncle Armenak chased my father around the school dining room, waving a huge knife.

UNCLE ARMENAK

No, we never had a fight like that at the school. The orphanage had a wonderful effect on those children. They truly benefited from the education and the discipline they got there. They've all grown up well. They brought each other up, I might say. Because we moved back to Malatya around then, we weren't there to watch them grow up.

YERVANT

Uncle Armenak chased my father off with a knife on two occasions. The first time was in Malatya, and I can't remember it. The second time was when we were in primary school. This one, I remember. I'd just started first grade. My father had come to see us, and he was probably also trying to find out about my mother—that was his nature, sadly.

We were with our father in front of the school kitchen. Just then, Uncle Armenak came in through the door. When he saw my father, he began to grumble. My father could see what was coming, so he went into the kitchen. My uncle went in after him. I was standing at the door, watching the events unfold. There was a big stove in the middle of the kitchen. My uncle grabbed a knife that was laying next to the stove and attacked my father. They started running around the stove, my father in front, and my uncle behind him. I started to cry. Just then, the school janitor came into the kitchen and took the knife from my uncle's hand. My father took this opportunity to run away.

UNCLE ARMENAK

After my sister put her children into the orphanage, she came back to stay with us in Malatya for a time. We were there all together withour mother, Ahçik, and our older brother Haygaz. But my sister just couldn't settle down. Her nerves were shot by then. She was anxious and sad. This was probably the beginning of her depression. She stayed with us for two or three months. Then she couldn't bear it anymore without the children, so returned to Istanbul. She had no family left there, but she couldn't bear to be away from the children. And that was when her illness began in earnest.

YERVANT

I must have been around five years old. One day, my father came to the orphanage. He must have not been able to bear it—my mother's leaving for Malatya to join her family—and he'd poisoned my mind. So, anyway, that day the orphanage sent me to the *hamam* for a bath. I was playing with the water, waiting to be scrubbed. And then, suddenly, who should open the door but my mother? I didn't know what to do. My father had put so many thoughts in my head that I didn't want her anywhere near me. "Stay away from me! You're not our mother anymore!" Even today, I can hear myself screaming those words.

My mother tried to take me in her arms, but I pulled myself away from her and jumped out of the bath and ran naked into the garden. My mother was running after me and crying. I remember that I locked myself in the outhouse. My mother didn't show her face for a long time after that. My father heard about it and told me I'd done well.

HOSROF

Every morning, we would leave the orphanage two by two, holding hands, and go up the slope in a long line for about a kilometer to get to our primary school. My mother rented a room for herself that looked out onto this slope so that she could peep out her window and watch us coming and going without anyone seeing. Of course, she didn't tell us, because she knew that if she did, we'd run away from the orphanage and come to her. To make sure we couldn't see her, she never opened her window or her curtains to look down into the street.

She was living right under the nose of the orphanage, but we had lost all hope in her by then. We had no idea where she was. One day, by chance, I saw her parting the curtains. "Mama!" I yelled. Of course, she pulled away at once, but I had seen her. There was nowhere for her to hide. And so she came back into our lives.

It was just one room that she lived in. She slept and worked in it. She made buttonholes and sewed on buttons and tried to make her living. On these slim earnings, she struggled to make do. I remember how my mother was always trying to get us to eat things. Meat, eggs, whatever she had found that day. Whatever her strength allowed. Then, to be closer to us, she volunteered to do the orphanage children's laundry. There was one washing day a week—for the children as well as for the laundry. So, after Mother volunteered, she would also wash a few children. After that, she never went away again. She was always near us.

BAYDZAR BOZUK

Then Nvart moved close to the orphanage. Sometimes, we would run into each other in the street. We were always glad to see each other, but we never really sought each other out.

When we were neighbors, she wasn't sick. She got sick later. I couldn't bear it when I saw her. Oh, how I'd cry. And apparently she would tell her sister-in-law Zabel that this Baydzar was in even worse shape than she was, so every time she saw me, she cried, too.

Nvart was both mother and father to her children, even when she was ill. None of us could have matched her as a mother. Not once did she say, "I handed them over to the orphanage, so they eat what they can find. It's no longer my responsibility." They said she got some help from her big *Ahparig*; I think his name was Haygaz. She also had a mother, they called her Ahçik. She took her under her wing, too.

YERVANT

In the beginning, our mother hid herself away so that we—especially me—didn't make a fuss, but as soon as she rented that room on the same hill as the orphanage, she kept a close watch over us. Around then, the thing that upset us the most was that on holidays, most of the children had visitors who took them out for the day. The three of us would be left behind. But later, when we had discovered my mother's house, that sorrow ended, because we would sneak over there to visit her whenever we wanted.

We didn't like any food with onions in it. Because my mother knew this, she'd call us to her house and feed us secretly, but this was against the rules. Then, my Aunt Siranuş moved into a house right next to the orphanage. She would let us know somehow when she was cooking meat, and then she would feed us.

HOSROF

Aunt Siranuş used to mother us, too. Whenever my mother was having difficulties, my aunt was the first person she'd go to. As for the three of us, we didn't want to be a burden on anyone. We weren't comfortable about staying over or eating at other people's houses. My aunt's house was the only place where we didn't feel like strangers because she really did treat us like her own. I know Hrant always felt that way. He was very close to our aunt.

AUNT SİRANUŞ

Then we moved to Istanbul as a family, too, and we became my big sister's neighbors. My sister was living alone at the time, but Sarkis just wouldn't leave her alone! My sister was so upset about this. Her whole mind was on her children. She was living in a single room, and from there she could look down on the children's road. Then my sister fell ill. "I can look after the children," I said. "Let them come to me." They were still spending their nights at the orphanage, but they'd come to me to eat. All three of them loved the food I cooked. The one who came to me the most was Hosrof. Hrant was a little older than the others, and he was a little shy; he didn't want to come too often. He was a very proud child.

HOSROF

Did my father come to see us once a month? Maybe less often than that. Actually, when my parents got divorced, the court gave my father custody of all three of us. But, like my mother, he wasn't in a position to care for us. During the years we were in the orphanage, my father would come and see us "when he had the time," as he put it.

He worked for a tailor in Beyazıt, and on some Saturdays, he'd take us there. Sometimes he came to see us. I remember one New Year's . . . at New Year's, children were sent to the families that invited them over. Somehow, my mother and father had each made arrangements to take us out. But this time, Güzelyan, the director, said, "I'm not giving them to either of you." Maybe he wanted to punish them both to get them to cooperate. Who knows? But in the end, we were the ones to suffer because all of the other children went off, and we were left by ourselves at the orphanage.

During those years, we started helping our mother out a bit by taking things back and forth for her. There were tailors all around Beyazıt. We found out where they were. We'd carry five or ten coats at a time, whatever they could load on our backs. We'd take them back to the house. My mother would do the buttonholes and finish them off, and then she'd load the same things onto our backs—the jackets and coats and what have you—and send us back. And when we got there, they'd give us a new load, and we'd rush back to the house. We'd race up and down that slope, three little men loaded down with all of those big coats.

There was one other moneymaking possibility in those days. Hrant was seven or eight, and I was five or six. We'd sell hard biscuits in the streets.

If my father didn't come to see us, once we were old enough, Hrant would take us to see him. My father was living in Kurtuluş in those days. Hrant must have been in the last years of primary school—eleven or twelve at the most. On Sundays, he'd get permission from the director. We'd get on a bus, get off somewhere, and walk for hours, us three. It never mattered how old Hrant was. He was always our big brother, always the one who looked out for us.

YERVANT

Even in primary school, Hrant was the one who protected me and cared for me. He'd never tell us much. He carried all the responsibility because he was the oldest. We'd tell him everything that was bothering us. He was tall. Well-built and athletic. The perfect big brother. He was quiet about looking out for us. For instance, regarding that peeing incident that I mentioned earlier, he put pressure on the boy who switched his sheets with mine and made him confess. Years later, I heard about this from the boy himself. But my brother never said a word to me about it. He'd watch over me by pretending not to watch. He was very subtle about it. It was the women in the kitchen and the laundry who looked after me in those years, mostly. But on bath days, it was Hrant who washed me because I wouldn't let anyone else. My big brother washed me many times, but I only washed him once: on January 23, 2007 . . .

4

The Lost Civilization of Atlantis: The Armenian Children's Camp

HRANT

One morning, they took twenty of us children, and we went by foot from Gedikpaşa to Sirkeci, and from there by boat to Haydarpaşa, and from Haydarpaşa by train to Tuzla Station. From the station, we walked for an hour until we reached a vast, flat field bordering the lake and the sea.

In those days, Tuzla was not covered with the villas of bureaucrats and rich people; it was an untouched stretch of fine sand, bordering on the lake and the sea. On this vast field, there were just one or two houses, a fig or an olive tree here and there, and blackberry bushes lining the ditches. And we were little puny primary-school children from second to fifth grade.

We started digging at once. We planted our tent pegs into the holes we had dug for them, we planted the saplings into the holes we had dug for them, and we dug a well. Under the supervision of a foreman, we dug the foundations and started building up. Next to the main building, we put up a chicken coop and a stable. Believe me when I say that we spent that whole summer digging.

For three full months we toiled away, and as that barren soil grew greener and more colorful and the buildings went up, we turned it into a place that made people sigh and say, "Ah! This land has been touched by human hands; this is a place where people can live." We went to live the camping life, and by the time we had finished setting up that camp, we went back to our boarding school. But the summers of being condemned to the concrete garden of Gedikpaşa Orphanage were over. And so this is how we built what we called our Atlantis Civilization.

HOSROF

Tuzla Camp was the orphanage's summer home, you could say. Those of us who lived in the orphanage during the winter would go to Tuzla Camp for the summer. The Gedikpaşa Protestant Church Foundation bought the land in 1962. It was Güzelyan again who drove the project, turning it slowly into a children's camp.

There were about twenty children between the ages of eight and ten in the first group of children to go out; Hrant was one of them. A builder called Hasan Usta was in charge; they worked all summer and built a chicken coop and a stable and dug a well. They got it all going, in other words. After that, we little ones went there every summer. We planted trees. We turned part of the field into a market garden. Every morning, we would do exercises outside. We made a field for playing ball. We were all responsible for keeping the whole place clean. It was a summer camp through and through. There was work and there was play.

AGOP KALDILI

I was Hosrof's classmate. Hrant was two years older than us, but he was very kind to us little ones. He'd always help us. When school finished in the summer, we'd be taken by train to Tuzla Camp. Even before we got there, we were elated, because we were escaping from the concrete playgrounds at school and at our orphanage. Here, we had nature. We had a safe space. We had devotion and brotherhood. If only the trees could speak, they could tell such stories . . .

We produced food at Tuzla Camp, too. We produced the meat and milk and yogurt and cheese and fruit and vegetables that we ate in the orphanage during the winter. We even had animals there. And a stable. This was where we came to know nature. We were very happy there.

HRANT

One summer followed another. Every one, we spent at Tuzla Camp. And every year, there were more children. We dug more wells and found more water, and the land grew steadily greener. After many years of pulling up water by hand and carting it back and forth in big vats, the system was motorized. As the years passed, the trees grew taller than us. They gave shade to the buildings. Soon the entire camp was shaded, and the fierce sun beat down on us no more.

And it was our childish voices that fertilized our childish toil, and perhaps nature, too. After waking up at dawn and working until the middle of the night for three long summers, we at last finished the main building. The shortest of us children, Kütük (our name for Zakar), carried a bag of cement right up to the roof. We'd be so tired at night that we'd wet ourselves in our sleep. We remembered our families only at night, as we watched the city lights sparkling in the distance. Whoever came, whoever saw what we had done, they were envious. "Bravo," they'd say. "'Bravo.'"

LEVON MİKAYELOĞLU

We all worked, but Hrant worked the hardest. He never seemed to get tired. But he was naughty, too . . . as naughty as the rest of us. He was the smartest of the bunch. He always had a runny nose. You know how they say that it's the smart ones who have runny noses?

We had a playing field. We'd divide into teams and play ball. We put up swings in the garden. And there was the sea, too. It's still there, but then it was sparkling clean.

HRANT

The sea always speaks to me of freedom . . .
Whenever the air grows warmer and the sea calls to me,
It takes me back to those heady childhood days . . .
The time of day we imps loved the most was sunset.
We'd run to the sandbar between the lake and the sea,
Plunging our little bodies into the silence of the hour.
As the red sun slipped behind the islands,
We swam swiftly towards it,
But it would always sink before we got there.
And when we were way, way out, we would shed our last rags
And dive deep
As if by stripping off, we could set ourselves free.
Naked, we'd revel in the freedom of the water
Until we tired,
And never once did a fish nibble on our bits.

SİLVA ÖZYERLİ

We built our own pond, too. We put ducks and frogs in it. We had fish. Later on, we even had two monkeys. Greenery everywhere, topped with flowers.

The last time I went to Tuzla Camp was in '75. I never heard another thing about it from my friends. Then, in the '90s, I happened to be looking at *National Geographic*. There was an Afghani girl on the cover. The girl looked wild. The moment I set eyes on her, I thought of Tuzla Camp. "That's Rakel!" I cried. Those fearful eyes, that wild beauty, that air of mystery—she looked just like Rakel. That was what she looked like when they brought her to Tuzla from Cudi Dağı.

Rakel was brought to the camp from southeastern Anatolia with several children who were younger than her. Some were her siblings; others were from the same tribe. They didn't know Turkish or Armenian. What they spoke among themselves was Kurdish. Güzelyan, the director, would always scold them. "Don't speak Kurdish," he would say. Rakel was a strikingly beautiful girl. She had very long, raven-black hair.

HERDEM ÖCAL

When Rakel arrived, she could speak only Kurdish, but she quickly picked up both Turkish and Armenian. We all looked up to her. She was poor, too, but there was something different about her. She was the daughter of the *Agha* of her tribe; maybe that was why. She was young and small, but there was something about her that set her apart.

ARMENUHİ DİKMEN

Rakel was my friend. The two of us shared a room with *Morakuyr*. This is Armenian for aunt, but this woman was more like a mother. She was the one who sewed our dresses, taught us how to keep clean, and combed our hair. She was our teacher. Our "mademoiselle." They called Rakel and me "Morakuyr's girls." We were expected to set an example for the others.

RAKEL YAĞBASAN

I was only nine years old when I left my family and my village to be taken to Istanbul. The children with me were from the same tribe; they were my relatives. My father, Siament Agha, wanted his children to be educated. I was almost past school age. They sent us to Istanbul to learn how to read and to learn our language and religion.

First, they took us to Tuzla Camp. It was autumn. The schools opened while we were still there. The first half of the year, they didn't enroll us in school so that we wouldn't be overwhelmed. For a while, we stayed at Tuzla Camp. They gave us a bit of schooling there. That's where I first began to learn Armenian. Then we were taken to the orphanage in Istanbul. And in the second half of the year, we started school.

Tuzla Camp was just one building then. For the rest of our time in primary school, they took us there every summer. Inside the camp was a road shaded by poplars, which led to the sea. I helped make that road. My labor went into that camp, too. We always did everything together. Isguhi Morakuyr looked after the girls, and she put me in her group. They called us "Morakuyr's girls." This meant that we took greater responsibility for making sure that the children were kept clean and well cared for. It meant setting an example.

HRANT

Isguhi Morakuyr was the mother of the orphanage and of Tuzla Camp. She had lived through the painful days of 1915, and she was one of the last remaining members of the generation who could remember those days in detail.

The number of Armenian Protestants had dwindled, and she was also one of their last. She never married. She dedicated her life to the girls in the orphanage. We could call her a Protestant minister. Her faith was very pure.

She imparted to the girls in her care a Christian ethos. Every morning as she braided their hair, she would whisper prayers into their ears. She was devoted to Christ and to the girls she raised. My wife, Rakel, is just one of hundreds of girls she raised.

GARABET ORUNÖZ

If İsguhi Morakuyr was the girls' mother, then Hrant Güzelyan was father to us all. He had devoted his heart to gathering up the grandchildren of the Anatolian Armenians who had been spared the sword. Both the the orphanage and Kamp Armen—that's what we called the Tuzla Children's Camp—were his work, and the girls and boys in the orphanage worked with him to make them realities. By the time I went for the first time in 1970, it was already a haven. It was no wonder that Hrant Ahparig called it the Atlantis civilization.

OHANNES TECER

When we were brought in from Anatolia, we were just little children, separated from our parents. They never let us miss them. If it hadn't been for Mr. Güzelyan, how many generations of Armenian children might have been left to the streets? It's thanks to him that we grew up to become able-bodied, hard-working, family-minded men. He was as beautiful as his name, Güzelyan. But he was very strict. We took many beatings from him. He even had a stick made from cherry wood.

ARUS TECER

Mr. Güzelyan was always at the helm, at both the orphanage and the camp. He was both a Protestant minister and a head teacher. He taught us everything from mathematics to geography, and then, on Sundays, he would teach Sunday school. He had this little stick made from cherry wood. The moment we saw it, we made ourselves scarce, especially the boys. I'm glad to say that I never got a beating from him.

HRANT

I mentioned that I went to Tuzla when I was eight years old. I gave it twenty years of my life. I met my wife, Rakel, there. We grew up there together, and it was there that we married and where our children were born. Then they arrested our director, charging him with "raising Armenian militants." The charge was entirely unjust. None of us had grown up to become militants, after all . . .

And now the camp, like its buildings, stands deserted. It's a toothless, sunken-cheeked, stumbling old man. One by one, our beautiful green trees were chopped down, and those still standing are dry and twisted.

The other day, I was thinking about Tuzla Camp. I thought about all of the ripped off, confiscated child labor.

What should I say? "Well done?"

Part II

Madcap

5

Heartbreaker

HOSROF

By now, we were growing up—or, rather, Hrant was growing up. We tried to catch lizards on the train tracks—or, rather, Hrant and his friends did. I was too small for him to take along. One day, when they were going on a lizard hunt, I made a scene. "I'm coming, too," I said. He said no. I insisted. In the end, he told me that I was not going, and he pushed me. I fell down. Nothing broken, but I split my lip. I'll never forget how fast I ran. When he caught up with me, he picked me up, and off we ran to the pharmacy. They sewed me up there, without anesthetic, and I have never forgotten how much it hurt. The scar on my lips is a memory of Hrant that will always be with me.

By now, Hrant had finished primary school and was attending Bezciyan, the middle school right next to the Armenian Patriarchate. Hagop Minasyan, who had been one of our mentors from the orphanage, was there. Minasyan was a Catholic Armenian, but he came to teach at the Protestant orphanage, and he put a lot of work into all of us. He was Hrant's guardian angel. Because there was no school for İncirdibi Primary School to feed into, most of the Armenian children brought in from Anatolia suffered a rupture after finishing primary school. When they moved out of the orphanage, most went off to look for work in the Covered Bazaar—whatever work they could find—and they'd start work there as apprentices. So when Hrant, after finishing school, started saying things like, "What was the point of studying?" Minasyan caught him, and he ended up in middle school.

HAGOP MİNASYAN

At that time, I did not have the status of an Armenian Catholic priest. I was an Armenian Catholic priest; I was still a postulant. I made no distinction between Catholics and Protestants; whatever child passed before me, I tried to help. At the school, I would teach mathematics and religious studies, and in the evenings, I would go to the orphanage as a mentor. Generally poor Armenian families from Anatolia were not disposed to education; they wanted to send their children into work to earn a living.

When I met Hrant in 1967, he was in the fifth grade at İncirdibi Primary School and living at the orphanage. Unlike the other children, who were alone because their families had stayed in Anatolia, he was at the orphanage because his parents had separated; the family had fallen apart. So, in a sense, he had no one, either.

First, I went to his mother, but she wouldn't listen. Then, I tracked down his father, and I paid him many visits. Each time, he chased me off. Finally, he gave in. "Fine," he said, "do as you like. But you're getting no pocket money from me." He took out Hrant's primary school reports and diploma and threw them at my feet. I picked up the diploma and embraced him in thanks. That's how I was able to get Hrant into middle school.

I was his guardian. The director, Mr Onnik Fıçıcıyan, accepted Hrant by waiving the registration fee. In those years, we would often go together to his mother's house. We'd sit and talk and drink tea. Sometimes, if she could afford it, Nvart Hanım would serve us bowls of soup. As for Hrant's father, he always treated me well. Whenever I dropped by to see him, saying that Hrant needs this or Hrant needs that, at first he'd resist, but eventually he'd say, "Come on, then, let's go and buy it for him." And after that, he'd always take me for a meal. As poor as he was, he was still a generous man. He'd always tell me his troubles . . .

AUNT SİRANUŞ

When Hrant was studying at Bezciyan, I dropped in on my big sister one day. I found her crying. Hrant had written a poem for her, for Mother's Day, and won a prize. He'd taken the poem and the prize money to give to his mother. The poem was in her hand. We read it together, and then we both cried. How proud she was of her son.

HAGOP MİNASYAN

Hrant was an interesting child. I never saw him studying, but he did well each year without any help. He also won various prizes at school—prizes for compositions, for poems. Once, they even awarded him a big, thick book. He brought it over to show me. I'd often find him deep in thought. He seemed to be living in his own world.

HARUT ÖZER

When Hrant was in middle school, I was one class ahead of him. I only discovered that I was Armenian when I got beaten up as a child. The neighborhood children came and beat me up, calling me an infidel. After that, I became a bit timid. Even at that age, though, Hrant was different. He stood up for his rights. He never shrank back. The rest of us might have been frightened sometimes, but he was fearless. And bold.

Hrant was a good student in middle school. And he knew how to win hearts. He protected all of the girls in the school. For instance, there was one girl who came to school in an old Mercedes. That Mercedes would pick him and me up, and off we'd go to the girl's house to give her lessons. Her family had asked us to help her with her homework. They would make us five o'clock tea with biscuits.

Another thing I remember is that he always used to wipe his nose on his sleeve. I even asked his classmates once, "Does he do that in class, too?" "Of course," they replied.

When Hrant was in the last year of middle school, our neighbor's son gave us his chess set. That year, we started sitting in front of the door and playing chess. He was very good at chess, too.

OHANNES TECER

When we were at middle school together, he'd take me to his mother's house. She was very poor, but whenever I visited, she would make me sit down so she could feed me. We went on lots of adventures, even at that age. The first time I ever played hooky and went to see a film, it was with Hrant. Girls were always falling for him. But he only had eyes for Rakel.

YERVANT

When I was at middle school with Hrant, he used to go of his own accord to the orphanage to mentor the little ones. And he stayed there at night. This was his quiet way of staying close to us, perhaps. Or maybe it was to stay close to Rakel—because my brother was in love with Rakel even then. On weekdays, he would stay at the orphanage, and on weekends, he would go to Mother to help her sew buttonholes.

Hrant was a forthright, straight-talking, open-hearted child. He never tried to hide what he did out of shame. They call some people "pacesetters," and this was his nature. Leadership came naturally to him. Wherever you saw Hrant, you saw him taking on that sort of role. Even then, when Mr Güzelyan couldn't be at the orphanage, he would chair meetings. In soccer matches, he was always the player with charisma.

HOSROF

In middle-school music class, they taught us the notes. Hrant improved his skills all by himself. When he came back to the orphanage to mentor, he would sing for the children and recite prayers. But he was best at playing the *saz*. When he fell in love with Rakel, he went and bought himself a saz and taught himself how to play it. After that, he used the saz to express his feelings, his love. But in primary school, when Mr. Güzelyan had set up a choir, he had not let Hrant in, saying that he didn't like Hrant's voice. Years later, when I listened to Hrant playing the saz, I noticed with some shock how different his voice was. He was a great admirer of Aşık Veysel. He did a wonderful rendition of his song "My Road is Long." His voice was so sad, so deep.

After finishing primary school, I began to work at the Kayzer Photographic Studio in Beyoğlu. One day, I looked up and saw Hrant there, with that big saz in his hands. He took out a picture of Rakel. It was a little picture, for a document. He had it enlarged. We put it on the back wall, and he went in front with his saz. He had his picture taken in that pose. Like the minstrels. Like Aşık Veysel . . .

HARUT ÖZER

When we were in middle school, the children who were able to bring food from home would have lunch on the top floor. But the poor children—thirty or thirty-five of us—ate together on the ground floor. I always sat at Hrant's table.

In those years, we'd have small scuffles. We'd compete for the most candy. Just outside the school, they sold something called Damascus semolina cake. Hrant loved it, but we never had enough money. You know how they pass out candy at weddings? Well, because my father worked as a cleaner at the Three *Horan* Church, they would give him some of this candy after every wedding. I'd bring it to school with me. Hrant and I would give it to the candy seller in exchange for Damascus semolina cake. Sometimes at school he'd wheedle with me, saying, "So, my son, where's the cake?"

HOSROF

In those days, children read comics, like *Tom Mix* and *Texas*. And we had no money, of course. Once in a while, we'd lift a few comics from the grocery store on the corner near our mother's house. My big brother played no part in these escapades. He just read them. He always kept his nose clean. I would make the plan and execute it. Yervant would be my partner in crime. The magazines were all hanging from strings at the grocery store. I would pull them from the peg and race off down the slope. All very childish . . .

One day, Yervant and I had taken a few comics from the grocery store without paying for them; rather, we'd lifted them. My mother saw them in our jacket pockets. "You don't have any money," she said, "so how did you get these?" She kept pressing us. And when we confessed, she took us by the ears and marched us off! She dragged us into the shop. "My children took these without paying," she said, "and I don't have the money to pay for them." And she gave them back. I shall never forget how ashamed I was. Or how honest my mother was. In spite of everything she'd been through, she always kept herself going with honesty.

YERVANT

Hrant was mad about comics, especially *Tom Mix* and *Texas*; in other words, Çelik Bilek ("Steel Wrist"). And the habit passed to us . . .

In middle school, everyone would smoke in the toilets. I started smoking very early. When I was thirteen or fourteen, I played tombala and won three packs of cigarettes. The tombala man didn't want to give me the cigarettes. I'm pretty puny, but I'm good at arguing. So this man and I argued about it, and somehow I won—and he handed over the three packs of cigarettes. I was just walking off when his associates pounced on me and beat me up badly.

Some others there pulled them off and took me to the pharmacy. I came back to the house looking a sight. And suddenly, Hrant was there. When he saw what shape I was in, he was furious. I told him what had happened. "Get up," he said. "We're going out."

There was this coffeehouse where the tombala men gathered. He asked around and found out where it was. We walked in, Hrant in front and me behind. The place was packed. And Hrant gave them a piece of his mind. Not a sound from any of them. I looked, and there was the tombala man I'd argued with, sitting at a table with the three packs of cigarettes in front of him. He was drinking tea. I went over and picked up the cigarettes. And still, not a sound. No one was prepared to stand up to this plucky youth.

I gave Hrant a once-over. *Well, who would have thought it?*, I said to myself. *My big brother is Steel Wrist, my favorite comic book hero.* In a flash, we were home again. I slept for two days. But I cannot say if it was because I was so tired or so happy.

HOSROF

My brother played soccer, too. From middle school on, he played soccer all the time. He had an amateur league license. He framed it and put it on his wall. Later on, when he was in high school, he played with Taksim Spor and, after that, on the Galatasary Youth Team. He was a left winger. But then, he decided that he couldn't study and also play soccer, so he gave it up. I never once heard him say that he wished he hadn't. But, of course, he never said he was sorry about anything he did in life.

HARUT ÖZER

In those years, Hrant started reading books. He would read the Nazim Hikmet poems he got on tape from Sarkis Çerkezyan, one of our leftist role models. Sarkis's son Ğazaros was a friend of ours. We'd go to his house after school. That's where we became more interested in reading. Along with Nazim, we read Sait Faik, Yaşar Kemal, and Orhan Kemal. Onnik Fıçıcıyan, the late director of Bezciyan, was also an important figure in Hrant's life. It was because Hrant was influenced by his ideas that he started reading the left-leaning *Cumhuriyet* newspaper at around that time.

Also at school was our French teacher, Ayda Hanım. We loved her dearly. But she loved Hrant the most, I think . . .

AYDA TANİKYAN

In those years, I was assistant director at Bezciyan, and later I became director. I met Hrant when he was in his second year of middle school, so I was his teacher for two years.

Hrant was a tall boy, even taller than me. He was handsome but not at all concerned with his looks. He was not one of those people who showed off to get noticed. He was a serious and respectful student. He was never naughty, not even within acceptable limits. He was the one who took everyone else under his wing, and this was evident from the very beginning. I remember him as shy, but not painfully so. Quite the contrary, he had the aura of a leader. He drew people to him. He bowed to no one, nor did he have expectations of others.

He was not one of those students who rubbed teachers the wrong way. He had a strong nature, even if it had been suppressed since his childhood.

Yes, he was a heartbreaker. He was not afraid to speak openly. That's how he kept himself free of worry. In those days, teachers didn't like pupils standing up to them. They knew nothing about giving them the right to speak.

Hrant needed warmth. He didn't share his pain. He didn't show his feelings. His pride was probably his greatest asset, and it helped him stand straight. He was always trying to help those around him get out of trouble.

He was a good student, but not because he worked hard so much as the fact that he was smart. There aren't many middle-school students who were interested in composition. But in the final exam, Hrant took great care with both his Armenian and his Turkish. The teachers remarked about this at staff meetings.

The first time we had harsh words in class was when I noticed that he wasn't listening. He was reading a comic in class without making any attempt to hide it. I took away the comic. I was his homeroom teacher as well, so we had a long talk. From then on, whatever little problems we had, we resolved through dialogue. Hrant was still more of an Anatolian than a city person. It was impossible not to like him.

YERVANT

In middle school, he got a reputation for never studying. He never took textbooks to school. He was a very good listener. He would take in what the teacher was saying and take good notes. During his years in middle school, Hrant started reading a lot of books, thanks to his French teacher, Ayda Hanım. She and her husband, the lawyer Diran Bakar, took Hrant under their wing. They didn't just open their house to him, but also their library. By the time he finished middle school, he'd read most of the books in it.

After that, Ayda Hanım moved to France and became the director of a school in Nice. Every time she came to Turkey, she always inquired about Hrant. Years later, when my brother went to France, they met . . .

AYDA TANİKYAN

When Hrant moved on to high school, he continued to visit us. If there were books he wanted to read, he'd take them, and some he never brought back. Years later, he boasted about some of the books he'd lifted. As he made his confession, he burst into great peals of happy laugher. And I said, "How happy the bookseller whose books are stolen."

I kept track of Hrant during the years that followed, through his brothers and teacher friends. Though he'd been brought up to be highly disciplined, he didn't like taking orders. He could never stop feeling rebellious. Over the years, his love of reading and history kept growing.

I knew how in love with Rakel he was, and how determined he was. He'd have kidnapped her, if he'd had to. In fact, I never knew people who called Hrant *Khent*. But when first I heard this, I wasn't at all surprised. In a world that revolves around lies, hypocrisy, and emotional abuse, to tell the truth and to stand up for your principles—today as yesterday—is left to the mad ones.

6

First Rebellion

HAGOP MİNASYAN

I was the one who made it possible for Hrant to go on to Tbrevank High School after finishing middle school. Tbrevank was a boarding school. Granted, Hrant's family was in Istanbul, but in difficult circumstances. He had nowhere to live when he was in middle school, so, like it or not, he'd stayed on at the orphanage as a mentor. But when he finished middle school, that ended, too. But he was getting good grades, and he got himself through middle school. When we explained his situation, it wasn't hard to get him a place at Tbrevank. I can't say I spent much time with Hrant while he was in high school. By now, he was deep into leftist politics. But in those days, so was the rest of the younger generation.

HRANT

Before they describe their time at Tbrevank, everyone begins by saying where they're from. It's always one of the towns or villages of *Kavar*, the Armenian word for Anatolia. By this, I mean that Tbrevank and Anatolia are one and the same—so much so that everyone had the idea that it was only for students from Anatolia, and it was a long time before students from Istanbul were accepted. Until the 1970s, you could still count the number of Istanbul pupils on two hands.

Tbrevank High School settled in its home in Üsküdar, on the Asian side of the Bosphorus, in the 1950s. These were the years during which people were just waking up to the plight of the Armenians left in Anatolia.

MIGIRDİÇ MARGOSYAN

Tbrevank High School was founded in 1953 in Üsküdar. I was one of the first children to be brought in from Anatolia. I was brought there from Diyarbakır's "Quarter of the Infidels." Tbrevank had been set up as a boarding school because all of the pupils were Armenian children who had been taken away from their families and brought to Istanbul. None of us had anywhere to stay. We were, as they say, children who had fallen on hard times. Or, rather, we were the children of an entire people who had fallen on hard times.

HRANT

To understand why Tbrevank was founded, you have to go back to 1915. As we now know, the events of 1915 did not just result in the expulsion and slaughter of Anatolian Armenians; at the same time, it forced a significant group to suffer an erosion of their identity. This mass erosion began with the multitudes that escaped "deportation" by converting to Islam, and thousands of children were left with trusted neighbors so that they wouldn't come to harm on the roads of deportation.

In the 1950s, not counting the Islamized Armenians lost from view, there were still 170,000 Armenians living in Turkey who had held on to their identity. Not one school was left in Anatolia, and not one church. With the arrival of the 1942 wealth tax, levied against the nation's Christian and Jewish minorities, Anatolia's Armenians also lost their economic security, and it became all the more difficult to preserve their identity. There was growing anxiety about the future of Anatolian Armenians who had not converted to Islam. It seemed increasingly impossible to carry from Istanbul into Anatolia everything they needed to practice their religion and educate their children. The only way forward was for Istanbul to open its doors to Armenian pupils from Anatolia.

At this point, that great man, Patriarch Karekin Khaçaduryan, became involved. The Armenians of Anatolia were accustomed to entrusting their children to each other, but now they were to entrust them to their people's true father. When it opened its doors in 1953, the Surp Haç Tbrevank High School became the new home for children left in trust. Although Patriarch Khaçaduryan's ostensible purpose at the outset was to set up a divinity school, his true aim was to "find lost sheep" and take them into his care.

MIGIRDİÇ MARGOSYAN

When we got there, they were still painting and whitewashing the school building. First, they opened the middle school, and then the high school.

Having become one of the school's first graduates, I returned to serve as headmaster of Tbrevank between 1966 and 1972. At that time, we gave precedence to students coming from Anatolia. We would also admit students from Istanbul whose economic circumstances were very difficult. That is why we took Hrant into the school.

Tbrevank was actually a very strict school. Not only did we follow the curriculum set by the National Education Ministry but we also gave lessons in Armenian. There was no repeating years. If you failed the year, you had to leave the school.

In the time of Patriarch Şnorhk in the late 1950s, they'd also opened a divinity college. It later closed, partly due to a shortage of teachers and partly due to a shortage of students. By the time of Patriarch Şnorhk Kalustyan, it had become a private high school overseen by the National Education Ministry.

HRANT

I was drawn into a life of reading and writing by my "father," Patriarch Şnorhk. That's why I tried so hard to depend only on myself.

I came to love my church and stay connected to it because when I was in my first year of Tbrevank High School, he invited me and my friends to sing in church.

And I've been close to him ever since.

ARTİN (KEMAL) YASULKAL

The Patriarchate elders gave the boys in the school the status of *tbir*, but that arrangement had ended by the time I got to the school. I think it was still in place when Hrant Ahparig was there in his first year. Any student had the right to take on religious duties if he so wished. After the March 12, 1971, coup, when the divinity school on Heybeliada was closed, Tbrevank ceased to be a divinity school and became a private high school. In other words, the military leadership wanted the training of clerics to come to an end. It had nothing to do with the number of students.

HRANT

All in all, I studied at Tbrevank for two years. Probably because he knew what an obstinate boy I was, Baron Vahan said this to me after I finished the second year of high school: "It would be better for you to move to another high school because these people are never going to let you graduate." With that warning, I left the school. But, by then, the Tbrevank spirit was well established within me.

How much we were like chicks just hatched from their eggs in those days. Just think how chicks new to daylight will snuggle into each other. This is instinctive, and we did the same: we took refuge in each other because we didn't know what else to do. This sort of camaraderie, born of necessity, is the Tbrevank spirit.

OŞİN ÇİLİNGİR

They said that Tbrevank was founded to train clerics, but Patriarch Khaçaduryan's true aim was to rescue Anatolian Armenians vulnerable to assimilation and bring them to Istanbul. And, in the end, he was successful. First, they brought the children. To stay connected to their children, their families joined the community. Thanks in part to the Patriarchate and also thanks to the Istanbul schools with links to minority foundations, they could still live as Armenians in Istanbul.

The children brought in from Anatolia could speak neither Turkish nor Armenian properly. Whatever they learned about their language, their religion, and their community, they learned here, and what they learned, they shared. This was the place where they found the family nests they'd lost. This was the essence of the Tbrevank spirit.

YETVART TOMASYAN (TOMO)

The Tbrevank spirit was about helping people; it was about working together. Because it was about Anatolia, it was about poverty and wretchedness. These were children of great misfortune. Their families were far away in their villages in Anatolia, and they were here, in a boarding school. If you're talking about Istanbul Armenians, they were only admitted if they were very poor. The school didn't look kindly on Istanbul Armenians like me. But throughout those six years, even if we came from different worlds, we all lived like brothers. All of that poverty brought us together.

If you're talking about what happened after we left school, we all helped each other keep afloat in the struggle to make a living. If one of us got married, the other would rush to be his best man. If he needed to rent a house, he would ask one of his Tbrevank brothers. If he wanted to set up a business, he would find a few Tbrevank brothers, and they would pull together a few *kuruş* here and a few kuruş there and come in as partners. This was the true Tbrevank spirit.

HRANT

Tbrevank never fit in with the prevailing order—indeed, it existed to challenge and subvert it—and once it began sending its young out into the world, it became famous. So much so that between 1970 and 1980 it was said, in the language of the Istanbul bourgeoisie, to have become a "nest of communists." From its very foundations, Tbrevank was designed for such a label.

Having been brought to a boarding school to live far from their Anatolian families, these children would inevitably come to feel solidarity in the face of the changing conditions in Turkey and the world. Their fine education had accustomed them to reading and asking questions, so it was inevitable that left-wing traditions would find a home on that hill in Üsküdar.

Add to this what is rarely found in other schools: the sense of community and the continuity of relations between Tbrevank graduates and its new students. Tbrevank graduates who had gone on to college made sure to send us all of their left-wing literature; this was nothing more than spreading propaganda and agitation to schools, and it was very effective.

If Tbrevank truly wishes to be proud of something today, it should be the children it sacrificed to the leftist cause. Tbrevank should be praised for harboring the genuine left.

ARTİN (KEMAL) YASULKAL

When Hrant Ahparig was still in middle school, he knew about the revolutionary youth movement, and he was an admirer of the young man considered to be its leader, Deniz Gezmiş. During his years at Tbrevank, this interest steadily increased. After the March 12, 1971, coup, when one of our Tbrevank brothers, Orhan (Armenak) Bakır, became the leader of this now-illegal left-wing movement, it grew all the more intense. Hrant and Armenak were inseparable at school. It was almost as if they did not sit side by side but inside each other. They both looked out for each other.

In 1970, Hrant Ahparig was in first year of high school. By his third year, he was gone. We spent two years in boarding school together. Even though he was one year older than me, he was my big brother at school. He paid extra attention to me on account of my being from Malatya.

Hrant Ahparig was most interested in literature and social issues, but because he was so fond of our science teacher, Baron Vahan, he did well in science, too. He stood out as a student. He was open about being a leftist. He was very bold, and sometimes we would have to warn him. And he would say, "Listen, boys, I'm afraid of no one." He wouldn't listen to anyone. The one exception was the bond he felt with Baron Vahan Ajemian. Baron Vahan certainly played a part in his embracing the left.

HRANT

Baron Vahan, who taught us science, was a very good teacher. His dynamic way of speaking made it easy for his students to absorb the mechanics of physics and chemistry, but what students remembered best about him was the way he was with his students. In everything he did, he imparted to his students the importance of acting honorably and honestly. There was no need for him to give lectures; the way he lived and acted was enough. All we had to do was to learn from his example. He was our teacher at the time when Turkish youth were wandering into politics.

We students came mostly from the parts of Anatolian society that had been economically depressed. It was unthinkable that we would remain separate from the political movements of the time, and inevitable that we would be drawn into the current.

ĞAZAROS (GAZİ) ÇERKEZYAN

Baron Vahan taught not just at Tbrevank but also at the Sahakyan and Esayan high schools. I feel proud to have had him as a teacher. Hrant has, as always, voiced the views that we all shared.

Because my family lived in Istanbul, I wasn't able to attend Tbrevank. My mother worked in the orphanage kitchen, feeding the children, and my father was the well-known leftist Sarkis Çerkezyan. He was the one who gave Hrant his first leftist books. As for Tbrevank, it was the leftists' castle in those days. All of my friends were there, and Hrant was out in front. I'd spend my week-ends there. Sometimes they even arranged for me to sleep in the dormitory. That's how it was in those days, so much so that there wasn't a single man there who didn't call himself a leftist.

HRANT

It was around the time of March 12. University students were out in the streets. There was no way that we weren't going to be affected by that.

And so our school was living through the darkest days of its history. Around that time, the final-year students came into the class where we second-year students were in the middle of English class, and because our teacher had been harsh with us, they beat him up,. The school was in chaos. While the school management tried to remove those responsible from the school, Baron Vahan was crying blood, trying to get them to understand what state the students were in, and never giving up.

What we felt was that his mind was scolding us but his heart understood us. Even though I'd tried to save the teacher who'd been beaten up, the biggest blame fell on me, and I had come to the point of being suspended. From that moment on, I took on all of the attributes of an anarchist student. I wouldn't go to class, or, if I did, I sabotaged it. I was so angry that I even pulled stunts such as going into a class taught by a teacher like Baron Vahan wearing no shoes or socks.

After a moment spent erasing the blackboard, and without turning around to look at me, Baron put me nicely in my place. "Hrant, my son, without any socks, you'll catch cold!"

And then, in the end, he took me into a corner to say those words I'll never forget. "Look, Hrant, my son, these people are going to throw you out. The best thing is not to give them that pleasure. You leave Tbrevank voluntarily and go finish high school somewhere else." And that is what I did. As for this man, whose classes I did everything to ruin, this man who stood up to our anarchism with quiet determination, and the common sense he showed to integrate us back into society, I shall never forget him.

ARTİN (KEMAL) YASULKAL

This is how Hrant Ahparig came to leave the school: We had an English teacher named Aykvarkt Demirci, may he rest in peace. Well, the entire student body turned on him. The assault occurred in Hrant Ahparig's class, but the ones who carried it out were from the class above. A group of students, including his two best friends, Armenak and Stepan, burst into the room where Hrant Ahparig was in class and assaulted the teacher. According to what we know, Hrant stepped in and, with great difficulty, pulled the teacher out into the corridor. But, in the end, he still got punished.

MIGIRDİÇ MARGOSYAN

In truth, as the headmaster of Tbrevank, I didn't like sending students to the disciplinary committee. But I think that's what happened to Hrant. I have no memory of Hrant from school; he must have been somewhat withdrawn as a child. But I remember Armenak Bakır. Here was the problem: Being a leftist was no reason to be sent to the disciplinary committee because everyone there was a leftist. It may be that Hrant and Armenak Bakır were a bit more open about it. And it's possible that as headmaster I took a dim view of this, but at the end of the day, my own thinking was not much different from theirs. But there may well have been some discipline problems of this kind with Hrant. My memories of all that are vague. But let me also say this: It was no great thing for a student to be thrown out of school for discipline problems. He could have fallen afoul of the school and wanted to leave. That's not such a serious matter.

ARTİN YASULKAL

The headmaster at that time was Mıgırdiç Margosyan. He sent them to the disciplinary committee, and the ringleaders were expelled. Hrant had become involved to stop the assault, but because he was so close to those responsible, it was as if he'd been involved. And I think pride and altruism played their part. He might not have wanted to abandon Armenak, who was such a close friend of his—I just don't know. What I do know is that Margosyan was a very harsh teacher and a very harsh headmaster. If that hadn't been the case, he could have resolved this thing easily. He may have found it more convenient to forget about both Hrant and this incident.

YETVART TOMASYAN

Somewhere around the time that Hrant left Tbrevank is when he and I met. When he was sent to the disciplinary committee, he was sure that they were going to kick him out. It was close to the end of the year, anyway. So he finished that year and withdrew.

He enrolled in the Şişli May 19 High School. The headmaster there said that to enrol, he had to have a guardian. So Hrant came to the Tbrevank Alumni Association. At the time, I was its director. When he told me what his problem was, I got up and went over to the Şişli May 19 High School and became his guardian. He was eighteen, and I was twenty-four or twenty-five. That's how we first met.

He was a brash kid, Hrant was. Courageous. Generous. He liked to do what he set his mind to; he didn't like being under someone's thumb. We called him *Khent.* That's Armenian for "crazy." But that doesn't really capture its meaning. It means something more like "crazykid" or "crazyheart" or "madcap."

MARİ TOMASYAN (MAYRİG)

When I first met Hrant, he had just left Tbrevank, and my son Tomo had helped him get into a Turkish high school. He used to come to our house a lot in those days. He was like another son. And at nineteen and twenty, Hrant was a strapping lad. Better than handsome. He had light brown hair. He couldn't keep still. They called him *Khent.* I'm not sure who gave him this nickname, but Tomo used it all the time.

Hrant was quick to get angry. If you ask me, that was his only flaw. But it would all be over quickly. He never stayed angry. He used to call me "mother dear" and *Mayrig.* He'd give me a good squeeze on his way out, too. He'd bite my cheek. We'd laugh a lot. "You're my mother!" he'd say. He didn't really see much of his own mother in those days.

He'd eat and drink as if it were his own house; he'd stretch out in the sitting room. We were all poor in those days, what can I say? But Hrant didn't even have five kuruş to his name. He was very poor—very. But he never wanted to talk about his troubles. He was a proud boy.

SARKİS SEROPYAN

At the time, I was the director of an Armenian school in Balat. We'd rented a house or two near the school to accommodate students coming in from Anatolia—one for girls, and the other for boys. And we needed a mentor, a *hsgiç*, to take these children to and from school and supervise their study halls. We put an advertisement in the paper, more or less saying that we were looking for a fool who would be willing to do a lot of work for very low pay. And we got not one, but two, young men applying. One was Hrant Dink, and the other was Armenak Bakır. "We're volunteering," they said. "If you give us both places to sleep, we'll share the salary." Both were in the leftist movement at the time. They'd been expelled from their boarding school. Armenak's family was in Diyarbakır. Hrant's family was in difficult circumstances. They were on the street, literally. So, of course, we said yes.

HRANT

Armenak and I first crossed paths at Tbrevank. He was from Diyarbakır and I from Malatya, but it was in Istanbul that we met. We carried all of the problems of the country on our backs. And we were making our way through leftist literature. Before long, we were comrades. In the end, we brought about the school's first and last student protest, and the school asked us both to leave.

We were penniless, with nowhere to live. For a while, we slept at the Tbrevank Alumni Association, but then we heard that they were looking for mentors at a school in Balat. We went over and offered to share the salary if they could find beds for both of us. Our offer was accepted . . .

7

A New Name and a New Life

HRANT

When Armenak and I first became leftists, we worked for the Armenian community. The new generations of Armenians still scattered all across Anatolia were forgetting Armenian, on account of there being no schools. Around that time, it emerged that there were, especially in the east and the southeast, Armenian villages in which they spoke only Kurdish. When we found out about this, we decided to go out and collect these young Armenians and bring them back to Tbrevank. With this in mind, we went to Mardin-Midyat. In Silopi, we found Siament Agha's Varto tribe. Here we stayed with the villagers who lived in tents. That's how we first made contact with my [future] wife Rakel's village and its inhabitants. After that, we went to find the Armenians in neighboring villages.

A cleric from Diyarbakır helped us with our travels—Der Giragos, who had traveled the length and breadth of eastern and southeastern Turkey on horseback to find the Armenians who had survived 1915. In the beginning, it was Patriarch Khaçaduryan who supported us in our search, and after him it was Patriarch Father Şnorhk Kalustyan who helped keep his mission going. So, when Armenak and I went to Der Giragos, we were playing our small part in this effort. We did everything in our power to resist the erasure of Anatolian identity in Anatolia.

SÜSLÜ BAKMAZ

I am Armenak's older sister. I don't know his date of birth, but I do know that he was older than twenty-five. He moved to Istanbul from Diyarbakır after finishing primary school. In those days, church leaders were coming out and gathering up the children and taking them to Istanbul to be educated. My brother studied at Tbrevank, too. He'd come back to us for New Year's, and that was all. Once, he came back with Hrant. They went out and found Der Giragos, and then they went out on the road with him.

While they were staying with us, I did their laundry. No matter how much I pleaded with him, Hrant wouldn't take off his socks because they smelled so bad. "Come on now, I'm a village woman, I can take anything," I told him. "And I'm telling you now, I'm washing those socks." Still he, wouldn't take them off. That day, I'd made them *baba ghanoush*. Hrant hardly ate a thing.

My mother and I had no idea that these two were leftists. The two of them even got kicked out of school for being leftists.

HRANT

Tercüman, the biggest right-wing newspaper of the time, kept putting out negative pieces about Armenians in left-wing organizations. They kept saying that left-wing Armenians were trying to drag Turkey into the morass of terrorism. And so Armenak was worried that the Armenian community would be made to pay the price for our own left-wing activities. Besides, it was a problem being Armenian inside left-wing organizations. For example, you're campaigning to become the director of a syndicate, and word gets out that you're Armenian—they were hitting below the belt. Armenak was aware of this, too. But his main concern was that our people would become targets on his account; he didn't want them being victims. So we went to court and acted as each other's witnesses, and we changed our names. And so Hrant became Fırat . . .

MASİS KÜRKÇÜGİL

Hrant had already changed his name when I met him, but of course I never called him Fırat. This Hrant was a wild one—did you know that? From the very beginning, I called him *Khent.* He was wild, this guy—in his passions, his pleasures, his projects, his attitude toward life. Always chomping at the bit. He had a very broad outlook; sometimes it bordered on the eccentric. He would accept the craziest things as normal and go to enormous lengths to bring others around to his ideas. *Khent* means "irrepressible." There is little affection in the term.

I can't remember why I started calling him Khent, but it was probably sometime between 1974 and 1980, and it must have come out after one of our intense political discussions. I think that's why it stuck. He was khent, but he was also the most respectful person you could ever meet in this life. And the most honest. There was no one like him.

This taking a Turkish name—it was another first. As you know, most of us Turkish Armenians also have Turkish names. Our parents knew that we were going to have a hard time in this country on account of being Armenian, so they added a Turkish name. At home, people used their Armenian names, and outside the house, their Turkish names. This is particularly helpful in the workplace, so as to avoid discrimination. But we keep just one name from birth. And then Hrant! What does he do? After all those years, he goes to court and asks for a Turkish name!

HRANT

We were three friends: Armenak, Stepan, and me. During the political turmoil of the March 12 military regime, all three of us were drawn to a left-wing faction called TİKKO (Turkish Workers' and Peasants' Salvation

56

Army) and we wanted to work with it. To keep our community from suffering if something happened to us, we went to court and had our names changed. Armenak became Orhan, I became Fırat, and Stepan became Murat. Armenak went up into the mountains, where he died. He's remembered as Orhan Bakır. But I was never more than a sympathizer. Because that was around the time I fell in love and got married . . .

After that, it did not cross my mind to change my name back to Hrant. It didn't matter to me what it said on my identity card. I used the name Hrant anyway. And I also loved the name Fırat; I had taken it from a Yılmaz Güney film. I moved in leftist circles, and we'd go to visit Yılmaz Güney in prison.

MASİS KÜRKÇÜGİL

This name-changing business never sat well with me. There's a military regime, and you want to take left-wing ideas to rural areas, so isn't it like waving a red flag? So what if Stepan becomes Murat, and Armenak Orhan, and Hrant Fırat? Even if all you did was to go into a coffeehouse and sit, those villagers would pack you up and deliver you to the gendarmes in no time at all. This was what happened, I mean. But never mind . . .

Hrant and I first met in 1974. He was very tight-lipped about it, but we all knew he was linked with a left-wing organization known as TİKKO. We didn't know if he was a member or just a sympathizer, of course, but we knew that he was very close to Armenak Bakır. It was at around that time that Armenak's other name, Orhan Bakır, began circulating among the leaders of TİKKO, but I never got to know him.

SÜSLÜ BAKMAZ

In 1975, when we moved to Istanbul, Armenak was nowhere to be seen. Hrant would come and go, but he never stayed long. Every time he came to visit, he brought news of my brother. I'll never forgetwhen Hrant and his brothers went into business together and opened that photography shop in Feriköy. I went to see it. Hrant was standing there. That was the first time he asked me, "What should I call you?" Then, he said, "The best thing is if you become our sister." He embraced me. That's how we became sister and brother. My mother's name was Meryem, but Hrant would never use her name; he would always call her "Mother."

After Armenak disappeared, Hrant would come and stay with us sometimes. He would wear his suit around the house. "Does this suit look good on me?" he'd ask. I'd say that it did. But he never wore it outside the house.

MARİ MAYRİG

If you want the truth, Hrant first came with Armenak to our garden house in Bakırköy; that's where I got to know him. My son Tomo wasn't with them. He must have given them our address, and so they came and went. He was a warmhearted boy, Hrant. He came into the house, saying, "I'm Tomo's friend." One time, he even said to me, "What sort of shape is this house in?" as if he were the landlord.

Hrant pulled me into a corner and pointed at Armenak. "This one's leaving, Mayrig. He's leaving Istanbul. Let him stay here tonight," he said. And I said it was fine. Armenak was very quiet and withdrawn. He must have come once more to stay with us, but that was a long time afterward. If you want the truth, they were hunting down everyone by then. Was there anyone they weren't after?

HRANT

I had crossed over from being just a sympathizer. I'd come to a crossroads. Either I was going up into the mountains, or I was going to stay in Istanbul. Armenak chose the first road. But I was in love. I wanted to marry the girl I loved. He knew that, so he said I should stay in Istanbul. They needed people here, too. And so I stayed ...

RAKEL

When we married, I knew he was a leftist, but we never talked about such things. I knew he was involved with an organization through his friend Armenak, of course. When we heard that Armenak had been captured, we went together to Izmir to see him in prison. After that, my husband went with Armenak's mother and sister on their prison visits. There were other young people he knew through Armenak around then. They were probably friends from the organization, both Turks and Armenians. They were always coming and going, and sometimes they stayed at the house. That's how he helped his friends.

At the time, we were living with his father in Feriköy. Sometimes his father said nothing, and sometimes he'd get angry and complain. In the end, my husband chose to remain a sympathizer. "If I hadn't chosen love, I would have gone up into the mountains. I would have ended up like Armenak," he said. In my opinion, Armenak had an influence on his decision, too. He respected the fact that Hrant was in love with me, and so he made sure not to draw him into action. At least that's what I think.

SÜSLÜ BAKMAZ

After Armenak was caught, Hrant, Rakel, and I went to see him in prison in Izmir. He had many friends, but Hrant was the closest. Whatever Armenak said, he honored it. When they moved him from the prison to the hospital, it wasn't because he was ill. It was when they were taking him to the hospital for a medical examination that his organization made off with him.

After he got away, my brother came to Istanbul. Hrant and Tomo were both here. I'm not sure if they were the ones who found hiding places for him. I think Mari Mayrig might have taken him in, but they hid all this from me.

I did ask Hrant once, but he said, "Such questions are best left unanswered, sister. Don't worry. He's in safe hands."

RAKEL

It was 1980. My husband sent someone with a car. He sent word for me to get the children ready and come to Tomo's. My daughter Baydzar was two years old, and Ararat was around one. Off we went to Tomo's. And there was Armenak. He'd wanted to see the children one more time before leaving Istanbul. Of course, I knew that they were looking for him. How could I not know that? But, no, it never crossed my mind to worry that we might be putting ourselves in danger. I, too, loved him like a brother. And if I was just mentioning the children, don't make too much of that. I was a child then myself. I wasn't even twenty years old yet.

SÜSLÜ BAKMAZ

Then we got news that Armenak had been shot. Hrant called me with the news. He was always the one who kept us informed. This time, it was dark news. He said that he had read it in the paper. He stayed in Istanbul to arrange the funeral. I went with a friend's relative to Elazığ, where he had been shot. They dug up the grave so that we could identify him, and they covered it right up afterward. They wouldn't give us his body for a funeral. Then Hrant came to us one day, and he took away Armenak's photos, saying that they needed them. After that, he, too, was arrested. After the September 12 coup, they were rounding up everyone. Hrant spent some time in prison, too. During those days, Hrant's father was worried that the soldiers would come and search the house, so he took away Armenak's photographs and buried them. Then it rained, and they were all ruined.

After Armenak died, Hrant never left my side. I carried on being his sister. Hrant had just four words for me: "How are you, sister?" He'd say it in Kurdish, too: *çavaye başe*.

In the beginning, Hrant shied away from writing Armenak's story in *Agos*. In the end, on a Mother's Day, he published an interview with our mother under the headline "May Armenak's Bones Be Brought in from the Cold."

MASİS KÜRKÇÜGİL

I never knew Orhan Bakır, but whenever I thought of Hrant, I thought of him. I believe Hrant always felt him at his side, as if he were living through him, with him. They were a couple, really . . . Blood brothers. They became friends by sharing their Armenian identities, their Anatolian pasts, and their poverty. They went together into revolutionary politics and became comrades. They even died in the same way. In this country of ours, they were threats just by being alive. They were both shot and killed, one in the countryside, and the other in the middle of the city.

HRANT

Armenak and I met at Tbrevank. I was in the first grade of high school, and he was in the second. He'd always sit in the back row. He was left-handed. He didn't do much out of class, but he was always reading. He was from Diyarbakır, and he'd lost his father. There were seven children in all, and he was the eldest of four brothers. It was the Aykvart Demirci incident that brought us together.

We were each suspended from school for a week. We had nowhere to sleep, so that week we went to the Tbrevank Alumni Association. There we lived happily on bread and cheese. We listened to Ruhi Su.

We went back to school and finished the year. He was a year older than me, so he was finishing that year. But I left the school. There was nowhere for us to stay. We became mentors together at a school in Balat. He had started university, and I was in the last year of high school. He was the first one to take me and show me around the university.

In Balat, I met up with Rakel. I fell in love with her. Armenak was the first one I told. And he told me that his first love was the girl to whom he was giving private lessons. Armenak, Stepan, and I celebrated New Year's together, and I shall never forget it. When the Balat school closed, Armenak left, and I was transferred to Kumkapı. That summer, he started moving closer to the countryside, and we saw him only rarely. One day, when we were fishing off Kınalıada, I told him that I wanted to marry Rakel. I also told him my mother's reaction.

We went together to Diyarbakır and Silopi and then to Diyarbakır a second time. After that, Armenak left Istanbul. Then, we heard that he had been caught. We went to see him in Izmir. Later, we attended his trial there. After his organization helped him escape from the hospital in Izmir, he came to us. He stayed for a week. He wanted to see Rakel and the children. The heist in the Covered Bazaar happened while he was with us. We read the story in *Hürriyet*. I found him some money, and he left. Months later, we heard of his death.

Part III

Eternal Love

8

Rakel, the Girl from the Mountains

RAKEL

I was born in 1959 in the town of Silopi outside Mardin. I don't know exactly where I was born. We were living as nomads. We would set up our tents for the night in one place, and in the morning we'd be off again. By the time we settled in a village, I was already four or five. That place I remember: a village made up mostly of horsehair tents, with a few stone houses. It was known as Varto village. The name comes from my grandfather Vartan.

After my grandfather settled in this mountain village, he went down to the city. In 1963, he registered the land as Varto. He got the deed. Now they've changed the name; it's now called Yolağzı. It's most probably in the jurisdiction of Şırnak.

My father, Siament Yağbasan, was the chieftain of the Armenian Varto tribe. Our tribe was made up of several families that had survived the slaughter in 1915. They'd all escaped with their wives and children to Mount Cudi back then, and, for years, they'd stayed there. That's why they spoke Kurdish. My grandmother told me that they'd been saved by a Kurdish family that took them in. She was even married. The Kurds protected her. Because her skin was very pale, they rubbed ash from the stove on her face so that no one could see she wasn't Kurdish. Years later, some people recognized her, and she was able to get back together with her husband.

In our tribe, everyone was related to everyone. There were about 300 people in the village. To be Siament Agha's daughter didn't make me feel different than the others, but I was always proud of my father. He was a brave man. He bore no grudges. He didn't throw his weight around, but he had a certain presence. He deserved his position. Physically, too, he was larger than life. He was tall—a great giant of a man with blue eyes and blond hair. There's a legend about someone named Siabento, and they adapted it for my father. That's how highly he was rated.

HRANT

Who first discovered this Armenian Varto tribe in Silopi has yet to be determined. I think Der Serope must have been the first person to track

them down. Der Serope would, from time to time, explore the most remote villages of the East and Southeast, locate all of the Armenian families, and perform all of the baptisms and marriages that were waiting to happen. In Diyarbakır or Mardin, he was given directions to Silopi and found Siament Agha's village. He looked and saw this tribe living in tents, and he stayed with them for a few weeks. Then, he went back and told our Patriarch, Father Şnorhk Kalustyan, the story of the Varto Tribe.

RAKEL

In those days, we had neither an Armenian church nor an Armenian school. We knew we were Armenians, but we couldn't speak Armenian. We spoke Kurdish, like everyone in the Kurdish villages around us. Priests, what we then called monks, would visit a village close to us. There were Catholic and Protestant Christians living there. And Chaldeans. The priests and ministers visiting that village discovered us, too, and then they started coming to our village. We knew that we were Christian, but we had no Armenian Church. If you ask about worship, we used a big tent as our church. My father would sing hymns in Kurdish. He recited the psalms in Kurdish. Some of the priests taught us prayers in Assyrian. Or Aramaic, the language that Jesus spoke. This is what they told us. When they found out that our village was Armenian, Armenian priests started visiting us, too. When they came, it was a great event. Everyone rejoiced.

HRANT

Then Der Giragos went to see the village. At the time, Der Giragos was the prelate of Diyarbakır, and now he started visiting. He also provided the tribe material support from Patriarch Şnorhk.

In the many scenes you see with nomads in films from the East, you'll see someone following the caravan, walking strangely, looking this way and that. He's the one who's gathering up those the caravan left behind. Der Giragos was doing the same thing: gathering up those left behind on Anatolia's roads of exile.

RAKEL

I was eight years old when my mother died in Silopi. I remember her, but I cannot picture her face. My mother's name was Delal. She was thirty-five years old when she died. She was a courageous woman. Here's one thing I remember: The Kurds in the Muslim villages around us wouldn't leave us in peace. They were always trying to claim our fields. When these land disputes wouldn't stop, my father went down to the city again. He wasn't in the village when we heard that the shepherds from the next village had sent their sheep into the fields where we were growing crops. No one in the village would lift a finger, so my mother ran out there alone. She went after the shepherds, brandishing a shovel, and later she scolded our own villagers, saying, "And you call yourselves men!"

They said I looked like my mother—physically and also in nature. My voice also sounded like hers. When people hear me singing folk songs, that's what they say. It's not clear why she died. In the village, they say it was the evil eye . . .

I remember her last day. My mother was lying on a mattress. My father had gone out to give his sheep to the shepherd. My mother raised her head, and then she surrendered her soul. The whole village was crying. They put the children to sleep, but me, no, I wasn't going to sleep. I was going to stay next to my mother, I told them. And I did as I said. That whole night, I waited at her side.

Then the next day, they asked for water outside the tent and they washed her, to bury her. It was Good Friday—that I'll never forget. They'd cooked cracked wheat pilav with meat. Our mother had died, and they were putting food in front of us. They also shut the door on us. They'd lit a fire, and they were washing her outside. I don't know how I managed to kick that pilav and open the door, but I do know that I walked out through the crowd and watched them wash my mother.

HRANT

But if the fate of the Varto tribe changed, it was thanks to Hrant Güzelyan. He was both a concerned man and the right man for the job. In his view, the Bible's most important teaching was to find and save lost people. And so he set out for Diyarbakır. From there, he embarked on a long and tedious journey, arriving at long last in Siament Agha's village of Silopi in Mardin.

RAKEL

It was 1968. One day, the priests sent from Istanbul by the Armenian Patriarchate came to the village. A few days later, they took a group of us, all children, back to Istanbul with them. My father, the chieftain of our tribe, escorted us all the way. My two brothers came with us as well as the children of several relatives. I was just nine years old, and I didn't yet know that after the events of 1915, in the last years of the Ottoman Empire, the schools and churches had slowly all closed. What use are schools and churches when there's no one left to attend them?

Conditions were already difficult for the Armenians who'd survived, and there was pressure from the state. That's why so many migrated to Istanbul during the Republican era. With that, Anatolia's Armenian population dwindled even more, and the remaining schools and churches closed their doors. Then, the population decreased again until the only Armenian community was in Istanbul. I knew none of this, of course. What I knew was that my father put importance on his daughters' education. I was almost past school age. If we were to learn our religion and our language properly, we were going to have to leave our families and our village.

When we got to Istanbul, it was autumn. The schools had already opened. For a time, they kept us at the Armenian children's camp in Tuzla to give us some lesson before we started school. That's where we began to learn Armenian for the first time. My husband says that he saw me first at the camp in Tuzla, but I remember seeing him for the first time at Joğvaran, the orphanage where we were taken next.

YERVANT

When Rakel came to the orphanage, she was a girl with hair down to her waist, and they never cut it. Rakel arrived at the school with a group of boys. They were all our age, but they put them into the lower classes because they didn't know Armenian. They could speak only Kurdish. With time they mastered Armenian and, after that, Turkish.

RAKEL

I remember going into Gedikpaşa Church for the first time. How big it looked to me. And how dark it was inside. There was a lot of big wooden furniture. We'd come from a village. And at Tuzla Camp, there were tents, and there was grass. Whatever we saw in that church, we were seeing for the first time in our lives.

During the first two years, when we were staying at the orphanage, they put us into a room at the foot of the stairs. After that, they took us to a house in the same neighborhood, next to İncirdibi Primary School, and Isguhi Morakuyr was our housemother. Later on, we were sent to live in Beşiktaş. The last house to which we were moved was in Balat. So, you see, until we finished primary school, we were carried from one place to the next, like kittens. Because whatever they opened, the state would eventually shut down. And then they would enroll us boarders somewhere else. Of course, we didn't understand any of this at that age, but this was after the 1971 coup, and the military was in charge. My father would come to Istanbul several times a year, and he'd come and see us wherever we were boarding at that time.

One summer, our director, Mr Küçükgüzelyan, took us back to our village. We stayed there until school started. My father had married again. I already had a new brother. His mother was Bedro, my mother's uncle's daughter. And when she went to work in the fields, I looked after the little baby. It was hard to call her "Mother." I hardly said it, actually. I was studying in Istanbul, and I soon went back. Then, I got married. I never really lived with my second mother. I was very angry with my father at the time, but she was a decent woman, and she deserved my father. With time, I came to love and respect her. There were six of us from the first marriage—two girls and four boys—and from Bedro, there were seven. So thirteen in all . . .

BEDRO ANA

My name is Bedro Yağbasan. I was born in 1946 in Silopi. I am Rakel's mother, Delal Kuyrig's, uncle's daughter. In 1969, three years after her death, I became Siament Agha's second wife. Rakel was studying in Istanbul at the time.

Hrant was very interested in the story of our tribe. Siament Agha did not like to talk about the slaughter or the expulsion. He preferred to talk about his land disputes with our neighbors in the surrounding Kurdish villages and his struggles over the deed to the land. But Hrant kept pressing. So then he described how our people had escaped to Mount Cudi and lived in the caves there and survived. I'd heard it from my grandmother: A shepherd fell asleep while his sheep were grazing. In his dream, he saw a white bird, and the bird said, "Go and tell the Armenians. My name is Cudi. Tell them to come here and I shall save them." So he ran down to the village and told them about the dream, and that's how they came to the mountain. They stayed there until the trouble was over, and then they came down to Silopi.

From then on, we lived as nomads. The Kurds protected us. Although there were some who stole our animals and looted our property, others were very good to us, of course. They thought of us as their brothers. There were good relations, and there was buying and selling. "Come to us and convert to Islam," the Kurds would say. Our people refused, but they left their language behind. So as not to stand out too much, they abandoned Armenian and spoke only Kurdish—that was out of fear, of course. We don't know Armenian or Turkish, either. The only one in our tribe who could speak Turkish was Siament Agha. He learned it while he was in the military.

By 1963, we were well and truly settled. The name of our village was Varto. After that, they found us. When the Armenian Patriarchate in Istanbul heard of our existence, they sent Der Giragos to us. It was the first time we had ever seen an Armenian priest. It was such a surprise. The whole village rose up. Some cried with joy; others were ululating. After that, Küçükgüzelyan came to the village. Once again, Siament Agha did the translating. Our village was not just afraid of sending children out of the village. we were all afraid of leaving the village. But our visitors were the leaders of our church. "You never got a chance to go to school," they said, "but let your children have that chance. Let them learn their religion." And that was how they managed to convince Siament Agha.

HRANT

The Silopi Armenian Varto tribe of 300 Armenians lived in the foothills of Mount Cudi. We became aware of them during the 1960s and established relations. After their children were brought to our school, the late Patriarch, Şnorhk Kalustyan, took a sustained interest in their welfare.

Every year, he would travel the world, gathering support, and he did whatever he was able to do to help with the development of the village. At the top of his list was a project to bring water to the village from a

considerable distance. I myself visited Varto village twice. I helped with the installation of the pipeline. We got it done in record time, too.

To get there, we went by train from Haydarpaşa to Diyarbakır, from Diyarbakır by bus to Mardin, from Mardin by minibus to Silopi, and from Silopi by foot and by horse to the village, but not before we'd spent two days and two nights on the road.

BEDRO ANA

When Hrant first came to the village, it was the summer of 1970, I think. As far back as then, he and Rakel had surrendered their hearts to each other. And he'd heard about our tribe, so he came and found us. It was clear that he had come so that Siament Agha could see him. He had a friend named Armenak with him. We were delighted, of course. These Armenian youths had come to see us. They stayed for two weeks, and then they left. Hrant loved children, and he loved the poor; he was a good-hearted young man. Later on, Siament Agha said to me that he had never regretted giving his daughter to him. Hrant was never anything but respectful to his father-in-law. He was a very handsome man, Hrant, but not as handsome as Siament Agha. I've never seen any man as handsome as my husband.

MİKHAİL YAĞBASAN

And then, in 1978, my father took the rest of the tribe and moved them all to Istanbul. We migrated to Istanbul because they were giving us such a hard time out there. The people in neighboring villages kept trying to take away our land.

I know how many times my father went to court and was beaten up, and how many times he came home wounded. In my grandfather's time, our tribe rented the land to these people, but then they tried to make it their own. In the meantime, there was one dispute after another. In the end, my father got tired of it and decided that we should move on.

The move to Istanbul happened in stages. First, the children. They went to school there and got jobs. Soon, the families followed. The first wave was in the 1970s, and our family was the last to arrive. My father wouldn't leave the village until everyone else had gone. For a time, we stayed at a church near the Patriarchate in Istanbul.

YETVART TOMASYAN (TOMO)

His Eminence Patriarch Şnorhk put his heart into his work with this Varto tribe—bringing them out from Silopi, keeping them fed, treating their illnesses, and finding them shelter. He let the other business of the Patriarchate slide and put everything he had into this project. When they first arrived, he put them in a church near the Patriarchate. They made plywood rooms in the church hall and moved the families in there.

These people from the southeast had the innocence of villagers as well as their cunning. I sometimes felt that they were taking advantage of our

Patriarch's weakness. They could speak neither Armenian nor Turkish. They spoke Kurdish, but they addressed the Patriarch with the Turkish word *baba*. That pleased him to no end. There was only one other person who called him "Father," and that was Hrant.

HRANT

"Domestic collaboration with enemies abroad," That is the subject that causes us minorities the greatest anxiety especially if it's to seek something other than material assistance or to send help to a foundation outside the country. Immediately the slap on the label "domestic collaboration with enemies abroad." By and large, our only relations were with the Armenian diaspora. To seek anything beyond that called for an impossible amount of courage.

The man who made the greatest effort in this regard was Patriarch Şnorhk Kalustyan, whom we remember, with the utmost gratitude, as our "father." We shall never forget how he traveled the world, seizing every opportunity to garner support for the children he had brought in from Anatolia and their families. With his black cloak and his sharp eyes, he was like the eagle in its nest at the top of the precipice, flying out to feed its young. He'd fly to the ends of the earth and return with his hands full, and whatever he had gathered, he distributed among his people. One by one, he nurtured his young.

MİKHAİL YAĞBASAN

Then the Patriarchate settled us in a house at the foot of Galata Tower. My father was old by then, and he didn't work. We children took on various jobs and kept the family going. My sister Rakel was living with Hrant Ahparig near Feriköy Cemetery. I'd go over there a lot. My father couldn't really find his way around the streets of Istanbul, so Hrant would come often to visit us with my sister Rakel. Later, when they moved to Bakırköy, we moved into their ground floor flat in Harbiye. We lived there for two years.

In the 1980s, a few of our tribespeople left us to move to Armenia, but they couldn't make a go of it there, so they came back. My father really agonized over the decision to emigrate to Brussels. He made this decision for the sake of the children's futures. He was still suffering the stigma of being Armenian; the problem persisted in Istanbul. The 1970s were difficult, on account of ASALA [the Armenian Secret Army for the Liberation of Armenia]. And things became even more difficult after the September 12, 1980, coup.

He was a proud man, my father. My mother was molested, for example. My father wanted to make a complaint, but because he was Armenian, they took no notice. This had an influence on his decision to leave Turkey. Most of the tribe had emigrated by then. So, at last, in 1988, my father decided to emigrate to Brussels. The whole family left, with the exception of my sister Rakel. My father left behind the child he loved most. He never asked her to come, either, because now her place was with Hrant Ahparig and with her own family.

Others from our tribe were already in Brussels, but still, the early days weren't easy. We didn't know the language. We didn't know our way around. We lived as best we could. With time, we even managed to find work for ourselves. We educated our children, thank goodness. If you added up everyone in Holland and Belgium, our tribe now numbered 2,000. My father always wanted us Armenians to multiply. His wish came true.

BEDRO ANA

I never wanted to come to Brussels, but here we are. Moving to a new country is hard. For a whole year after we arrived in Istanbul, the water stank, and the bread was inedible. I kept longing for our beautiful village water. Sometimes I didn't want to drink any water at all. Tea was all I could drink. So now think what it was like for me in Brussels.

The place I loved most in Istanbul was Tuzla. That looked a little like a village. But we didn't go there very often. One day, when we were there, Siament Agha asked me to make bread. Someone important was coming, he said. So I made bread from 15 kilos of flour. Flatbread. I kept working, and the work wouldn't end. Then Siament Agha came and said, "I'm telling you—hurry! The big man is already here." I looked out, and it was Patriarch Şnorhk. The children were already at the table. I went and threw myself at his feet. I started ululating. And you can't do that without shouting.

HRANT

"There are two things that will start us going '*tilililili*,'" Rakel explains. "The first thing is joy, and the second is grief." Sometimes we do it to give thanks, and sometimes to rebel. It's not shouting, and it's not crying. It's just an exclamation. Neither your tongue nor your mouth plays any part in creating this sound. The sound comes straight from the heart."

Every time I hear someone ululating, I think at once of Rakel's mother, Bedro. I think of the Armenian Varto tribe. They lived in an entirely Armenian village in Silopi, Mardin, and they spoke Kurdish. When their children were brought to Istanbul to be educated at Armenian schools, they must have been missed, because one by one the flock left behind those lands for which they held deeds and followed their leader, Siament Agha, to Istanbul. Time passed. Istanbul began to feel too small. So, once again, they went forth. This time, it was Europe, with Siament again leading the flock.

I was just saying that I think of Bedro every time I hear that "tililili." She was beside herself, you see, when the late Patriarch Şnorhk came to visit the Tuzla Children's Camp. We were sitting at the table with the children and our "Father," giving our prayer of thanks. We were still praying when Bedro flew out and planted herself in front of Şnorhk. Staring straight into his eyes, she began to ululate. While we sat there, mortified, not knowing what to do, our dear departed Father waited patiently. When it ended, all he said was, "Amen."

I think that the holy man understood. It was her way of expressing the helplessness lived for a century, on Mount Cudi, without a church, without a "shepherd."

Bedro is still the same person that she was that day—this I know. Even if she lives in Europe, even if she learns French, this woman will never forget where she's from. See for yourself, if you'd like. Pick up the phone and call her. Someone will say *"Oui*?" in elegant French. This is Bedro. So then say, "Bedro, we're celebrating the 535th anniversary of the Istanbul Patriarchate right now. And guess who's come down from Etchmiadzin to be with us? Our Father!" Believe me when I say that she'll throw that French veil right off as, with all the strength she can muster, she cries, "Tilililili!"

9

Love at First Sight

HRANT

I felt met Rakel when she was nine and we were both boarders at the Joğvaran. And even at that age, I warmed up to her that wherever she went, I found some way to follow. For a long time, Rakel had no idea how I felt about her. The love I felt for her was genuinely platonic. I kept my feelings to myself, thinking that no one knew, that the world was blind.

RAKEL

I remember first seeing my husband at the orphanage. But this is not like a girl remembering a boy. I knew him as Hrant Ahparig, and I loved him as that person. He was helping me learn both Armenian and Turkish. He was at middle school and working as a mentor at the school.

While we were at the orphanage, Patriarch Şnorhk Kalustyan paid us no attention. He certainly visited the Armenian Protestant Church around the time it was founded. In my childish way, I understood that there was a difference between Orthodox and Protestant. Then I discovered that Protestants had no ceremonies or rituals, but that was the only difference. They teach the psalms of the Holy Book, by which I mean the prayers written by King David, in the simplest way possible.

But that wasn't the problem. While we were studying at the school connected to the Gedikpaşa Protestant Church, they took us back to the village during the summer after we had finished third grade. There must have been rumors that the orphanage people were trying to turn us into Protestants. My father was furious. And at the end of that summer, he took us out of İncirdibi Primary School. He sent us to the Patriarchate and they enrolled us in the Armenian Horanyan Primary School. They took us out of the orphanage, of course, and moved us to a house in Beşiktaş. Later, they moved us to a house in Balat. But wherever I went, it wouldn't be long before Hrant Ahparig turned up.

HRANT

Our home was the half-ruined front section of Meryem Ana Church. The children brought in from Anatolia were boarded there, and I was working there as a *hsgiç* (mentor). I would take them to and from school,

shop for the food, and sometimes help the children with their home-work. In other words, I did everything I could to live close to Rakel.

RAKEL

That summer, we were sent from Balat to the Kınalıada Children's Camp. Hrant Ahparig came with us, again as a mentor, and he stayed with us all summer. And that was when the first whispers about us began. When winter came, we left the island, but the apartment where the girls had been boarded in Balat had been closed, so they moved us to a broken-down section of Meryem Ana Church. We were still going to Balat for school.

YETVART TOMASYAN

Our Father the Patriarch would spend his summers at the Patriarchate's prop-erty on Kınalıada. While he was there, he required the services of a special messenger to keep on top of his correspondence. This meant picking up a dossier of private documents every morning and returning in the evening with the responses. Our Father the Patriarch asked me to recommend someone I knew. I recommended Hrant.

HRANT

I had just finished high school. I was looking for a job that wouldn't get in the way of my attending college. I had made a bit of a name for myself by then in the Interscholastic Armenian Composition Contests, and I'd published a few pieces in the Armenian daily newspapers.

Someone, I can't remember who, told me to go to the Patriarchate, where they were looking for a young man to join the staff. My first job was as a messenger, I recall, and after that I remember doing some typing for them. I also remember that I'd been working there for days, and I still hadn't seen His Eminence . . .

Then, one day, he called me to his office. After I had kissed his hand, he asked me my name, and then he handed me a sealed envelope. "Take this, my son, and deliver it to the *Marmara* newspaper. But don't idle along the way—get there as soon as you can, because the paper is about to go to press." I quickly left the office, and I got into a taxi, clutching the envelope. Ho hum . . . but he'd given me an important job. And, at last, I had met him. At last, I was a big man.

The next day, I went to the shop to buy the *Marmara*. I opened it while I was still on the street. I saw his piece. How proud I was! It was no small thing, was it? I was the one who had taken that piece to the paper.

After that, I would type up the pieces passed to me by the general sec-retary of the Patriarchate. Go buy the newspaper. Type this up. If there's something to take somewhere, take it. These were all routine jobs. Every time my teacher from Bezciyan Middle School saw me, she said, "What are you doing in that moldy place? Go out and find yourself something more creative." I paid no attention. I had begun to see myself as the Patriarch's secretary.

YETVART TOMASYAN

Once Hrant began working in the Patriarchate's summer residence on my recommendation, his admiration for our Father only increased. Later on, he began to work at the Patriarchate full time. He served as their special messenger for two or three years. I'm not sure that they paid him anything. I think His Excellency gave him only travel expenses. But Hrant didn't care about money. He had just finished high school that year, and, as always, he was having trouble finding a place to live.

HRANT

My relations with "Father Patriarch" grew steadily warmer. I was going into his room a few times a day, at least. But each time I went in, I still felt compelled to kiss his hand.

He was always reading and writing. He gave particular attention to the religious columns he wrote for the *Marmara* several times a week. His daily program was always the same. He would arrive at the office at the same time and go back upstairs at the same time. He would take a short break around noon. I'd go upstairs, to his house, and even his bedroom. Once, when he was in the bath, he dropped the brush he used for his back, and he called for me. I didn't even look for the brush. Instead, I rubbed his back with the loofah.

There were some benefactors who criticized him for paying so much attention to the people coming in from Anatolia. He would only rarely give the benefactors interviews, but we could go in and see him whenever we wished and tell him of our troubles. Those others would get angry at him, but we felt only his radiance.

I spent an important part of my life, my adolescence, at his side. He was Father to us, and I was one of his sons. He might not have been a magnificent Patriarch, but he was a true spiritual leader.

YETVART TOMASYAN

Hrant put his heart and soul into that job. And he considered Patriarch Efendi his own father. And, of course, he had the same affection as his Father, the Patriarch, for the Varto tribe . . . or, rather, Hrant loved the legendary Rakel.

RAKEL

The first time we were together as girl and boy was when I was in my last year of primary school, I recall. One Sunday, we were in the church in Balat. Hrant Ahparig had come with several friends. For the first time ever, he reached out to shake hands. I remember blushing then. I was thirteen. He was eighteen. For him, it had begun much earlier, of course. I was actually aware of this because every once in a while, I'd say, "What are you doing here? Why are you always following us?" Actually, I think I was being a bit of a coquette, because I liked making him angry. But, by now, they were beginning to whisper. This made me feel very ashamed because everyone knew that he was in love with me, and they were talking about it. But it was in that church, when he shook my hand, that I first had feelings. How surprised I was! What was it, this warmth radiating from my heart and making my cheeks so hot? I still remember thinking that.

HRANT

I thought that no one knew, that it was just inside my head, but it wasn't like that. Even the director of the orphanage, Digin Makruhi, had noticed. To tell the truth, she was pleased about it. She'd discussed it with Oyrort Azniv, and the two had decided to "bring us together." After that, they took Rakel off to the side, and they tried hard to convince her. Rakel dug in her heels. She had become aware of my interest a short time earlier, and it wasn't as if she wasn't pleased, but the girl was right. She had started school late, and even if she looked older, she was still only in her last year of primary school. Most of all, she was embarrassed about her friends knowing. "How can anyone be in love at this age?" they would say, and that made her pull back.

RAKEL

At last, I finished primary school, and I had a tonsillectomy. I was worried that he might come and see me in the hospital, so I warned everyone, asking them to make sure I was never alone. I was afraid of gossip. People would ask, "Who's this boy?" But somehow he managed to get around everyone, and he came to see me—and by now, I had begun to feel like his sweetheart. But I still played hard to get, and that was another matter.

That year, when we were still in those rooms at Meryem Ana Church, I took on more responsibility and began to work as one of the children's helpers. I was in charge of the kitchen, and because he was working there as a mentor, we were together every day. We'd organized a music hour for the children. He would sit at the piano, and I would sing, and the children would dance.

And now it reached my father's ears about Hrant Ahparig pursuing me. There was even a day when the boys from our tribe came and threatened him. "Aren't you ashamed of yourself? You were her teacher, and now you have your eye on her," they said, and then one of them pulled out a knife. I was there. In other words, I was an eyewitness. I didn't see the knife, but I saw the scuffle, of course. The fight had started. I just sat there watching, perfectly still. Honestly, that's what I did. I probably was thinking that he deserved this after causing all of that gossip.

MİKHAİL YAĞBASAN

Among the children they'd brought in from Anatolia were some adolescent boys from our village. They were staying in the boarding school in Balat, and they noticed that Hrant Ahparig was trying to get close to my sister. And they probably began to threaten him. These rumors found their way back to the village.

RAKEL

And then, we became *Çutak* and *Taşnak*. The headmistress of our boarding section was a lady named Digin Makruhi, and she discussed the matter with another elderly teacher named Oryort Azniv. They called me in and said, "Look, Rakel, love is hard to find, and not everyone will know it, and this boy is truly fond of you." They did their best to try and persuade me.

I had feelings, too, of course. And I liked him—I liked his courage, and I liked the way he stood out. But once I'd called him Ahparig. How could I ever call him husband? I just couldn't get past that. I was still a child . . .

Then, the two Digins said something else. Because they'd been aware of our situation for a long time, they'd given us nicknames so that no one would know when they were discussing us. They'd called him Çutak, and me Taşnak. The violin and the piano. He was Çutak because he was like a violin, slender and long and handsome. And I was Taşnak, because pianos and violins go together. When I heard this, I was very pleased. I loved it that we had those nicknames, and I was also very glad because I could call him by this other name. This made me feel more relaxed. I had a hard time calling him Hrant because after the name Hrant came the word Ahparig. I'd come to think of him as an older brother, and that was how I still addressed him. But now he had a name that had nothing to do with that! He's been Çutak for me ever since. He was Çutak when he was my sweetheart and Çutak when we were married. Always Çutak!

HRANT

Yes, Rakel took a lot of persuading, but finally she accepted my proposal of marriage. But now she had an even bigger problem: what would her father say of all this? And Digin Makruhi! What would she do?

She went straight to our Father Şnorhk to tell him of this inescapable malady of mine. Our Father said nothing to me. He waited for the school holidays. That summer, Rakel's father, Siament Agha, came to take the Silopi children back to the village. We put him up in the dormitory for several days. I was trying to find a way to approach him, but he acted as if I wasn't there, and his expression was stormy. It was clear that he had heard things, and he was uneasy.

Those were the most difficult days I ever lived through. Here is Rakel, about to go back to her village. Something was afoot. We heard that

Rakel's father might never send her back. In the village, they were saying that they would be marrying Rakel off that summer. My emotions were all over the place; I was in agony.

RAKEL

Finally, I told our female directors that I'd been persuaded and agreed to the marriage. By now, Çutak had learned how to say "I love you" in Kurdish. He whispered these words in my ear. I said nothing. All I gave him was a glance. Then, we started holding hands. By now, we were being seen together; we were going out to places and sitting down and talking.

What I remember best is not how he asked me to marry him, but when he touched me for the first time. We had been taken out to Kınalıada on a picnic. It was springtime. We were climbing up to the top of the hill. There are those steep slopes there. We're all used to that—we're from the village, after all. So we're all climbing, the children up in front, and me behind them, and Çutak behind me. I was wearing white shorts that day and a waist-length spotted blouse. I know because I still have a picture that was taken that day.

So there we are, climbing up the hill and pulling back the bushes. And then, suddenly, I was clinging to this bush in the middle of the slope. I was about to fall over. And there was Çutak, right behind me. Afterward he told me that he had looked up and seen that I was falling. And that blouse of mine was short, so he was thinking, *How am I going to catch her if I have to touch her flesh?* But then he looked, and he saw that I was sliding right back. Either he was going to catch me, or I was going to fall. He grabbed me by the waist. Then he took me by the hand, and we climbed up to the top together. Whenever he told people this story, he'd say, "And from then on, she snuggled up to me like a kitten." And that is why I came to say yes. For me, this episode was much more important than the proposal itself. I even turned to him and said, "Please don't tell anyone." Over and over, I warned him, "Don't tell anyone that you saved my life." It was after that that I agreed to marry him.

10

Happily Ever After

HRANT

I found myself pressed against Father Patriarch's door, listening in silence while, through the keyhole, I watched him speaking with my prospective father-in-law. "No, Father, no," said Siament Agha. "We never give our daughters to anyone outside our village. Also, this boy's parents are divorced. Who is this boy, and who does he think he is? What if he up and divorced my daughter? In our village, that's unheard of."

In that quiet voice of his, Father Patriarch was trying to calm the Agha, and he praised me at length. "This is how good this boy is," he said, making it clear that he was on my side. The Agha was dead set against it, but our Father wouldn't back down, either. "I've made inquiries, and it seems that the girl loves the boy, too. Digin Makruhi had a talk with her. Come on, now, don't stand in the way. Say yes, too, so that we can bring this to a happy conclusion. Let us build a nest for our children."

The Agha remained stubborn. "What is love, Father? What does it mean? We have no such custom. And here I am, the Agha of a huge village. And in this village, the custom is to pay a bride price. So where are this boy's parents? If I give my daughter without receiving a bride price, how can I hold up my head as an Agha? Do you want me to be the laughingstock of my own village?"

"Listen, Siament Agha, I'd heard that you were talking about this. But what's this bride-price business, anyway? There's nothing like that in our religion. It's a sin. What if he were my son? Would you be asking me for a bride price?"

Siament was silent; Siament was shocked. What was the poor man to say? The two men looked grim, and there I was, peering through the keyhole, quaking.

And then, just when it all seemed to be over, that brilliant man, my Father the Patriarch, says, "But you are the Agha, and of course you cannot allow yourself to look foolish in front of your people, so listen. Consider this boy as my son. What do you want from me?" My father-in-law then set his price at 40,000 liras, a princely sum for the time. Whereupon our Father says, "Examine your conscience, Siament. I am a poor man." And so they bargained until Siament came down to 5,000 liras. Siament, who doesn't want to take the money, said, "If this is how it is, then so be it." But our Father pulled totaling 5,000 liras from his pocket and forced my future father-in-law to put it into his. Even today, I can replay that scene in all its detail.

RAKEL

My father didn't want me to marry Çutak. "My girl," he said, "this boy's parents are divorced. We have none of that in our tribe. Tomorrow or the next day, this boy will leave you because this is what he's seen in his own house." No matter how hard I tried to convince him that Çutak was different, I couldn't bring him around.

My father knew nothing about Çutak's father's gambling habit. All he cared about was the divorce. And there were also rumors that my father wanted to marry me to someone from our tribe. I'm not sure if this was true or not, but they never allowed girls to marry outside the village. I was the first one. In the end, Patriarch Şnorhk stepped in. "I want your daughter for my son," he said, and my father agreed at last because he loved Patriarch Şnorhk and had the highest respect for him.

HRANT

After meeting with our Father, Siament Agha spent two more days with us. He still wouldn't speak to me. He was a bit cross with Rakel, too. When he went to take the other children to the train, I accompanied him. When we were saying our farewells, he at last let me kiss his hand, and he embraced me.

On the way back, when I dug into my pocket to buy my ticket for the ferry, the train was well on its way. How I longed to kiss his hand and embrace him once more. Without my knowing, he had slipped the Patriarch's five thousand liras into my pocket.

Oh, Siament Agha, my dear father-in-law . . . In time, he came to love me very much.

As time went on, he came to Istanbul a great deal, sometimes for medical treatment and sometimes for business. Every visit, he went to knock on Father Patriarch's door. After all, they were in-laws . . .

RAKEL

But it wasn't just my father who opposed the marriage. Çutak's mother did, too. Her reasons were a little different, of course. She wanted her son to marry a rich girl, and she didn't think I was worthy of her son. She had a few prospects in mind, I think—wealthy families willing to take a son-in-law into their homes. Thankfully, though, Çutak was not the sort of person who would ever go along with that. And, anyway, he was in love with me, so how could he love someone else? I never spoke to him about this, but you know how first impressions can create a certain distance in someone's heart? Well, this was why I always felt a certain distance from his mother. His father loved me dearly, though. And his aunt, and his great uncle . . .they were very happy for us, I recall.

Çutak went to Malatya to seek the blessing of his family elders. This was on the occasion of his cousin's marriage. Uncle Haygaz and Uncle Armenak were both there then. And Çutak's grandmother, Ahçik Hanım, was still alive. She'd aged a great deal. We kissed her hand. "So," she asked her grandson, "this is the dark skinny thing you're marrying?" Which is to say that she didn't like me. But Uncle Haygaz accepted me at once. He loved me very much. Once they got to know me, the others did, too. And as I got to know them, I grew to love them back.

HOSROF

Hrant fell in love with Rakel, and he was blind. Rakel was just a tiny little girl then, and Hrant was a strapping young lad. In the summer, when his hair went blond, he was truly striking. My mother had big plans for Hrant. She wanted him to marry a very rich and very beautiful girl. Around the time he was working at the Patriarchate, she'd heard about a number of wealthy families that had their eye on him. And then, of course, her dreams grew more elaborate. It was a very Anatolian attitude: after all of this poverty, let him save himself by marrying someone rich. That's why she opposed Rakel.

HAGOP MİNASYAN

I am the one who arranged for Hrant and Rakel to be engaged. I gave them their engagement rings; we went to the jeweler together to choose them. We had the ceremony in Hrant's father's house, and I was the one who put the rings on their fingers. And this is interesting: after the ceremony, our Hrant went over to Patriarch Şnorhk as if he wasn't engaged yet because he wanted Father to put the rings on their fingers, too. In other words, these two got engaged twice.

At the ceremony at his father's house, the only other people from his family were Hrant's brothers along with a few of his Tbrevank brothers. What a neighborhood that house was in! As you come up to the last bus stop in Kurtuluş, there's a Christian cemetery on your right. You took the battered track down past the cemetery, and, along the way, you even had to step over tombstones with Armenian inscriptions on them. After you had hopped over all of these, you got to a garden gate. The house was two stories, but it was a wreck. There was a well in the garden, too. Hrant's father lived there with with his sister, who they called Mari Bibi. And this was the house where Hrant and Rakel lived in such primitive conditions for many years. We'd go visit them there for meals, sometimes in the house and sometimes in the garden.

RAKEL

It was February 1975. We had a little celebration one evening at his father's house. Later, there was another engagement ceremony in the side building of

Meryem Ana Church near the Patriarchate. Patriarch Şnorhk put the rings on our fingers. Some of the *Ahparigs* from Tbrevank were there, too. From his family, there were Uncle Haygaz, Aunt Siranuş, and Uncle Haygaz's daughter— I think that was all. And now we were engaged.

YETVART TOMASYAN (TOMO)

I went to the engagement ceremony, of course. You know that section of Meryem Ana Church that they gave to the Armenians who'd migrated from Anatolia? Well, that's where they held the ceremony. The Tbrevank brothers were all there. We lined the chairs up against the wall. We ate, we drank, and we put on some tapes. We did the *halay*, we danced . . . Rakel was a tiny girl then. Thin as a branch. She called him Çutak and nothing else. You could see from her eyes how much she was in love. And in Hrant's eyes, passion.

RAKEL

That summer, we went back to Kınalıada, to be counselors at the children's camp. From 1973 on, Çutak had been spending his summers there to work alongside Patriarch Şnorhk. And that summer, I was invited, too. I started staying in the summer residence. By now, I was almost his daughter.

There were no plans to get married right away, but when Patriarch Şnorhk went to America on a fundraising trip in the summer of 1976, certain difficulties emerged. As much as our Patriarch tried to reconcile with us upon his return, we were very offended, and so we left. If this hadn't happened, they would have married us, and our lives would have proceeded differently. But that was not how it worked out. We were forced to leave the Patriarchate's summer residence as well as the boarding department next to Meryem Ana Church.

About a year passed between the engagement and the marriage; our official wedding was on April 16, 1976. We were married in the Beyoğlu Marriage Bureau. It took another year—finding the money, making the decision, convincing this person and then that person—before we could be married in church. We were officially married, but I was still staying with my husband's Mari Bibi.

One day, we were sitting there, talking. Talking about what we wanted to do in life, our hopes, our future, and maybe even our children, and in the middle of all that, we dropped off to sleep, right where we were on the divan. When she woke us up, Mari Bibi gave us such a knowing look that I couldn't even look at her again, or my future father-in-law. And we said, well, if that's what they think we're up to, then we might as well sleep side by side. That's why we came to live in the same house as a family. But we still hadn't had our church marriage, and that's why Mari Bibi didn't breathe a word to anyone outside the house. It became our secret. I was sleeping at his side, openly.

Çutak and I began a custom there. It started there, and it went on until his last day. We always kept a light on the room where we were sleeping so that we could look into each other's eyes as we fell asleep and, when we opened our eyes again, to see each other before we saw anything else.

YETVART TOMASYAN

At the time, there was no house for Rakel to leave as a bride, but Toros Hapik, one of our Tbrevank brothers, took it upon himself to figure this out. He was a jeweler. He made all of the arrangements. And then there was another friend from school, Garabet Gündüz, also from Malatya; he was Hrant's best man. And this is how they were married.

When they married, Hrant may have just started shaving, but Rakel, she was still a child. If you told her a donkey could fly, she would have believed you—that's how pure and innocent she was. And she still is. Her passion for the Bible comes out of that same innocence. In our family, we consider Rakel a saint. But that, of course, is another matter.

RAKEL

Finally, on April 23, 1977, we married in church. We were both very young. That day, his friends even joked that they had married two children on April 23, the Turkish national holiday for children. Really, it was the Tbrevank *Ahparigs* who married us. The one who was the best off played the baptismal priest, holding the cross; they called him "Yellow Garabet." Another brother was the best man.

We had a henna night. We put on henna. I was taken to the hamam. One of our friends bought us nightgowns and pyjamas. They adjusted the bridal gown of a friend for me. They put him into a wedding suit. It was in a dark color, with pinstripes, and he looked very handsome in it.

It was Patriarch Şnorhk who arranged the church wedding. It took place in Narlıkapı Church. That day, an important meeting came up, and our Patriarch was unable to join us, but we went straight from the church to kiss his hand. After the wedding, we went to live in Çutak's father's house. They'd prepared some food. We ate and we drank. We played music. We danced.

I was the one who wanted the church wedding the most. For me, it was a must. For me, it meant blessing our union and undertaking to continue in that same sacred spirit, because the blessing that the priest gave in church had been given to him by Christ by the Messiah. So now we had gone from being two bodies to being just one, and our union had been blessed.

We really did become one. We lived and thought in the same body. However much the Lord loves his creatures, however much he wished for us to bind ourselves unto him, so the Lord wished us to bind ourselves unto each other forever. He wanted the love between a man and a wife to serve as an example of this love. The love between a man and a wife is a sacred love because as much as you give, you receive. As much as you open yourself up, you are filled. I cannot find the words to describe the love and goodness that a man and a wife can share, nor can I find a way to describe such harmony. There are no words for such things. What I know is that this is God's gift to us. And if the Lord's subjects open their hearts to him, then this can come to pass, because the Lord has spoken of this to his subjects.

There's also something I learned from Mademoiselle İsguhi Morakuyr in the girls' orphanage. Before the wedding, she took me aside and said, "Our elders told us that the marriage bed was sacred and heavenly. Protect that sacred purity, and savor the taste of heaven." Years later, when I recalled those words, I asked myself, *What exactly does it mean, to compare a bed to heaven?* To protect its sacred purity means that the man and wife should not soil it with infidelity. Fine, but where's the heaven? When I discovered the answer, I even shared it with Çutak: what makes it like heaven is not a husband and a wife surrendering to each other, and it's not that there is no bargaining, or hunger, or poverty, or loss at the moment of climax. It's simply the contentment that love brings. That's where the heaven is; that's why it's like heaven. All you have there is innocence and purity, and yourselves, and the love you've brought with you. This is what heaven is in the Holy Book, too. Hatred cannot enter it, materialism cannot enter it, nor can jealousy or lies. What the Lord said about man and wife—that's heaven on earth.

Part IV

The Struggle to Make a Living

11

The First Family Business

HOSROF

When Hrant and Rakel got married, we three brothers came to live in our father's house. This was the first time in our lives that this had happened.

My father and our aunt, Mari Bibi, were living in a little shack of a house, and we would stay out most of the day and go there to sleep. And there was the struggle to make a living . . .

Around that time, we opened the Brothers Photography Studio nearby. We literally had no money, and as hard as it may be to believe, we had become "self-employed entrepreneurs."

Actually, this is how we got into the photography business: After failing a class in middle school, I went out to work. I apprenticed myself to a good master, and, from him, I quickly learned the business. Three or four years later, I was a serious photographer, working at the famous Studio Spot. By now, Hrant was at college. He was studying and selling watches . . . and also some other job that I think Hagop Minasyan had found for him.

HAGOP MİNASYAN

I got Hrant a job in the offices of the Saint Antoine Foundation, so that he could earn a bit of money. He'd just finished high school, but this was Hrant! He could never stay in one place. He got bored and left, and for a while I didn't see him. Then, one day, he appeared. He'd joined some company, and he was wandering around, selling watches. He even sold me one on an installment plan.

HOSROF

So while I was working at this photographer's studio, I got Yervant a job there, too. We were both very hardworking, and the owner hardly ever came by. It was our second year there, I think, when wallpaper became fashionable. Yervant and I started making wallpaper with the old engravings of the city.

We would photograph the engravings and then enlarge them to the size of walls and turn them into wallpaper. They were beautiful, but how were we going to sell them? We looked around and saw that Hrant was already hawking watches. *Let him sell our wallpaper, too*, we said. We'd even prepared a catalog. Hrant went off, and, two or three days later, he'd come back with a good order. We printed them up, and he delivered them and then he came back with another order. We printed up that one, too, and he went off to deliver it. When he came back with another order, he said, "Listen, why don't we just print these ourselves? We don't need a studio. We can print these in our father's house. I can get the orders. We can do the work ourselves." We agreed. Hrant went and got a loan from a friend, and when went out and bought equipment to enlarge the photos. It's still in my brother's house as a reminder of our incredible will to prevail.

It was around then that my brother finally succeeded in his pursuit of Rakel: Rakel's father had been persuaded, and they were engaged. Hrant had decided that they would marry at the first opportunity if he could manage to find a way to live independently. So you could say that his entrepreneurial spirit came from his falling in love with Rakel.

We made a wooden bath to develop the images. Rakel helped us with this, too. Hrant was the salesman. He went and got us orders, and when he came home at night, the four of us would work out in the garden. We didn't have a darkroom, so we would wait until night fell before beginning work. To enlarge the photographs, we would shine a light on the wall and print on the paper. Then we washed them in the bath. Don't even ask what effort all of that took!

RAKEL

The three brothers went into these jobs together. So, for example, it was Hosrof who thought up the photography idea. He was the one who knew that work the best. But it was the three of them who made it happen. I helped, too, as a volunteer.

The entrance of the house was a square hallway. There was a tiny room leading off of it. We turned that into the darkroom. We put chemical water into a basin. That's where we washed the film. They also bought a machine called an enlarger. We used it to enlarge photographs of the old engravings and sold them as posters.

In the garden was a well. Its motor was broken. We would pull water up from that well and wash those enlarged, wall-sized photographs on the snow. Then we would hang them up to dry, on pegs, like laundry.

And so we began to earn a living. We were very happy. Çutak was the salesman. But we didn't have that much paper. We printed only on commission. Whenever we sold some, we'd get another commission. I'll never forget. Once we had eleven orders. This was a big deal for us. We didn't know what to do. That was when they rented a little shop in Feriköy, and that's where they began to do serious photography. They called it the Brothers Photography Studio. I worked there, too, of course. I even learned how to do retouching.

HOSROF

When we began to get serious orders, we went and rented a small shop. After every commission, we pushed ourselves a little harder. In five or six months, we were able to start our own studio. We called it the Brothers Photography Studio. We were as surprised as anyone, but we succeeded. With no money to speak of, we'd set ourselves up in business. While we were setting up the business, we used the little pot of money our mother had put aside from her buttonholing. And so, for years, my mother would say to us, "Everything you've earned is mine."

AUNT SİRANUŞ

They were about to open this photography studio. I looked up, and there was Hrant. My neighbor had a phone; we still didn't have one. We went downstairs to the neighbor. Our Patriarch in those days was Father Şnorhk. Hrant loved him dearly. The man was a father to him. He called the Patriarch. He spoke in Armenian so that the neighbor wouldn't understand. There was this studio that they were about to open, and they needed money. The Patriarch said, "No, I'm not giving you any money." Hrant looked so pale; I'll never forget how pale he looked.

We went back upstairs, and I said, "Hrant, dear, how much do you need?" He wouldn't say. I had a little money in the bank at the time. We went there together, and I took the money out. How overjoyed he was as he walked away! And, oh, how happy I felt that I'd had the money to give him.

RAKEL

The Brothers Photography Studio was the first shop they opened. Later, they opened up a nicer place inside the market. That one was called the Maral Photography Studio. Then, just before our daughter Baydzar was born, they opened up a little bookstore. They called that the Maral Stationers. That continued for a while. After the children were born, I spent more time at home. I'd cook food and take it to the shop. In the evening, if I had time, I would make cake and take it over to the shop. If there was work to do, I'd stay and help. I'd do the receipts. We were a family business.

YETVART TOMASYAN (TOMO)

After the Hrant brothers went into business together and opened up that photography studio, it became the Tbrevank brothers' meeting place—our home, almost. The teapot was always full and simmering. We could smoke our cigarettes and talk. What else could the Tbrevank brothers need? It was only a few streets away from the Tbrevank Alumni Association, after all, and that was our other home. I saw a lot of Hrant in those days, either in the studio or at the association.

The association was pretty much a haven for leftists. There wasn't anyone from Tbrevank who wasn't drawn to leftist thinking. Our Armenian community didn't like giving its daughters to boys from Tbrevank. They didn't like us because we were leftists. The whole country was rising up, but our Armenian community was still asleep. This is what our community was like. Also, the

Istanbul Armenians didn't accept the Armenians coming in from Anatolia. And if they were leftist on top of it, then forget it!

Hrant always opposed this mentality, even from a young age. And later, at *Agos*, he had a lot of trouble with those people. He wouldn't mince his words with any of them. He was proud to be an Anatolian, and he wore that identity with pride. We called him *Khent*. He was a wild one. Not just about politics. About everything. It was in his veins, I mean. He would hold his ground. Do whatever it was he'd put his mind to. Whatever he put his mind to, he always did.

ARTİN YASULKAL

We all spent a lot of time at the Tbrevank Alumni Association. They had a big ping-pong table there. We never played cards, but there was a chess set, and Hrant Ahparig played well. We had folklore projects. And talks. We talked a lot about politics, personal problems, money trouble—we shared everything. We were all leftists. We'd heard about Hrant Ahparig being called *Khent*. We all knew this nickname, but we never used it because he was our big brother. The only ones who could call him that were the Ahparigs who were older than him.

MASİS KÜRKÇÜGİL

Don't pay any attention to that nickname. In fact, he was a man with a huge number of responsibilities. He always had been, from his earliest years. They were three brothers, and he had to be the big brother. Because of his legendary love for Rakel, he married her at a very young age, and his responsibilities multiplied—because when they themselves were still children, they had two children of their own. And, yes, the whole time, this child named Hrant was caring for his own mother and father.

When I knew him, he had a little shop that was partly a toy store, partly a stationery store, and partly a bookstore, and it was on the corner of the street where I lived. A little further on, there was the Brothers Photography Studio. Hrant and Rakel worked there, too. Later, in 1979, they opened Beyaz Adam (White Man) Bookstore in Bakırköy. That very first day, I helped them at the counter.

RAKEL

The struggle to make a living continued. Çutak was an optimist. Never once did I see him worry about what might become of us. He changed jobs a lot, but he never let his spirits slide. We did all sorts of jobs in those days, but you couldn't really say that we made money.

It was when we were able to rent a house for the first time that we also opened up the first Beyaz Adam. It was not the shop you see now; it was a tiny place on the ground floor, and it opened just before our second child, Arat, was born in the summer of 1979. Whose loans made that possible? Only they know. Who had enough confidence in them to loan them money? I have no idea. All I know is that during those first years at the Beyaz Adam, they worked harder than they'd ever done before. Taking a loan from one friend to pay off another—that's how they kept themselves afloat. That's how the the bookstore started, but the story goes on for years. It came to be the family's main source of income.

YETVART TOMASYAN

When Hrant was setting up the Beyaz Adam, he came to me. "The owner doesn't trust me," he said. "He needs a guarantor." So I became a guarantor, of course. I had a little money saved up, and I put that in, too. I had a friend named Nişan Ekmekciyan, and he came in as a partner, too. Nişan's nickname was "Beyaz Adam" (white man), and that is how the shop got its name. He was from our school, too. When Hrant talked about the Tbrevank spirit, this is what he was talking about. Everyone ran to help a brother in need. If it was money they needed, you took it out and handed it over.

When Hrant started this business, he had no money to his name, but he was fearless. Maybe that's what earned him his nickname. There he was, penniless, and he opened up a bookstore. Then he took it from one place to the next, and slowly it grew. In the end, it became the huge multi-story stationer-bookstore we know today. He built it up so much over ten years that it soon had no equal in Istanbul. But when it first opened, it was a tiny, ramshackle little place.

MİKHAİL YAĞBASAN

It was in '78–'79. One day, Hrant Ahparig came to our house, and he said to my father, Siament Agha, "Would you please allow your son to come and work with me in this new store we're about to open?" And so our years at the Beyaz Adam began. The first store was nothing like the one you see today, of course. It was a little place on the ground floor. The stairs weren't even built yet. We built them ourselves, like workmen. During my years there, I became closer to my Hrant Ahparig, of course. I began to do 90 percent of the book carting. Only at the start of the season would they rent a car to buy wholesale. The rest of the time, we carried the books on our backs. His brothers were still running the photography studio at the time. So it was just him and me, and some of his friends. Sometimes my father would get fed up, and he wouldn't want me to go to work. "Why, father?" I'd ask.

"He's not paying you, why else?" he said.

When business was bad, Hrant Ahparig didn't give me my weekly paycheck, but I'd still go back. I loved working with him. It was a place where everyone worked together.

YETVART TOMASYAN

All of the friends from Tbrevank helped get the Beyaz Adam off the ground. The same spirit was at work there. But the most important help came from Brother Nişan. He put every penny of his small savings into the store. They called him "Beyaz Adam" (white man), because he had no eyebrows, eyelashes, or hair.

He was so sad the day he lost his father that they all fell out, and they never grew back. In the beginning, he'd come to the store, and we'd work together. Then, he couldn't bear Hrant's carelessness anymore, and he said, "If I have to go on working with this man, I'll eat his head [an Armenian expression that means "'I will destroy him']." And so he left. He was an accountant; he worked in a registry office, and Hrant knew nothing about such things.

OŞİN ÇİLİNGİR

One of the partners was Nişan Ekmekçiyan. He'd lost all of his hair; he ws totally bald. His way of greeting people was an echo of a Native American saying: "Hail! The white man will die!" When they were trying to think of a name for the store, they sat up all night, and then Hrant thought of this one.

Beyaz Adam first opened in 1979 and went through several incarnations. The first shop was on a side street in Bakırköy. It was a little place on the ground floor with a narrow entrance. Then the store moved to another street nearby, and finally to the place where it is now. It moved three times, and it grew every day until it became a seven-story store on the busiest avenue in Bakırköy. It's the biggest in all of Istanbul, and it has another branch in Pangaltı. His brother Yervant ran that one.

YERVANT DİNK

When my brother was opening the bookstore, he had no money, of course. He did everything on loans—paid one and took out another. We faced failure with each store, but we were accepted as honest men who would pay their debts. Thankfully, we never had to eat our words—we never came undone. If our situation was bad, we'd say so openly. In the end, we were able to pay off all of our debts.

When we first opened Beyaz Adam, it was a tiny shop. The first thing we did was to move into the photography studio. We called ourselves a bookstore, but we'd also go from school to school, doing photos for identity cards. It was always Hrant with the original ideas. He was always the one out in front. If you have nothing to start with, you can sometimes achieve the impossible because you're nothing, and you have nothing to lose. But when you start becoming someone, you begin to take more care, you're more cautious. So, anyway, that's what it takes to make something work.

RAKEL

They had just opened the bookstore, and they were struggling to get if off the ground. They had not been at it for a year yet when the news came that Armenak (Orhan Bakır) had been shot. It was May 1980. It was a huge shock for us all. We were mad with grief. He'd been like a brother to my husband, and I'd loved him very much, too. I'd known he was in danger, but of course we hadn't been expecting this. I didn't realize then that we were heading for the September 12 coup. I had no idea that we would soon be in danger, too.

12

A Student Like No Other

RAKEL

Çutak was struggling to make a living and at the same time trying to keep up with his university studies. It all got very complicated. Actually, it was not just those two things that got mixed up with each other, but also his leftist activities.

Çutak had very little time for attending classes, so he wasn't really keeping up with the courses. This meant that he had to go to school for longer than he had intended. When he started at the university, he was just starting that first photography studio with his brothers. After that, came all of those other jobs. "Why not a stationery store," he said, "and why not a bookstore?" And suddenly they were opening Beyaz Adam.

He was already in college when we married, and he was still in college after we'd brought two children into the world. He was studying zoology in the science department and was also enrolled in the philosophy department, but, in the end, he couldn't manage both. It was only in 1985–86 that he was able to finish zoology, and that was because it was his last chance—if he didn't finish then, they were going to throw him out.

The story of how he got into college is also quite something. In 1972, the year he finished high school—well, that spring, I'd said yes to him, so his head was in the clouds, of course. So much so that when he went to take the university entrance exam, he forgot to take his registration papers with him. And it was I, again, who noticed those registration papers and recognized them. I ran straight to our directress, Digin Makruhi. Grabbing her bag, she jumped to her feet. We ran and ran and ran all the way from Kumkapı to Istanbul University. We were drenched in sweat by the time we got there, but how were we going to find him in that huge university? It's as big as a city. We were asking everyone we could find. And the clock was ticking. At this point, Çutak was pleading with them, saying, "Please take me into the exam. If they don't bring it in, you can cancel my exam paper." I mean, that was how sure he was that I was going to find those papers and bring them in to him.

They say Çutak had the devil's luck, but I don't like to think that he got what was special about him from the devil. Nevertheless, he was able to use those special powers of his on the officials and get into the exam—and finally we located the right building. We knocked on the door and handed the registration papers to the official. And he passed the exam. He got enough points to get into zoology, so that is what he studied.

HAGOP MİNASYAN

Hrant went straight from high school to college. His outer appearance changed somewhat. The fashion then was for wide-cuffed trousers and long hair, so he started dressing like that, too. So he looked like a typical student. And he was a student, but he didn't go to school very much; he was too busy earning a living. Whenever it came to his mind, he'd drop by and see me. We'd have tea together. He'd always be weighed down with books. Mostly left-wing books . . . He began to read a lot in those years. He didn't speak much. His mind always seemed to be on other things.

ARARAT

My father got a place in the zoology department, but he also attended classes in the philosophy department. It took him a long time to finish because he also to make a living—it wasn't because he wasn't interested. You never saw him happier than when he talked about zoology and biology. In his world, nature never stood still. When he expressed his views on life, he often spoke of nature's ferocity. You can find examples of this in his political writings. He liked using nature as a metaphor.

At home, we'd watch a lot of nature documentaries, and then he'd get all excited, throwing his arms around while he told us things.

If he'd been able to live in a democratic country, he would have been interested in studying science or the philosophy of science—that's what I've always thought, anyway. He was always very excited to hear about advances in science. He got so excited at the news about the first cloning experiments that for days he talked about nothing else. His science books from his university days are still sitting in his library. If he got started on the universe, or the concept of time, or philosophical propositions like the theory of relativity, there was no shutting him up. For him, the philosophy of science was like a long-lost lover.

DELAL

My father loved to read, and the one constant in our house from as far back as I can remember were the piles of books. I couldn't say if he did or didn't like studying zoology and philosophy, but he was always bowled over by the latest advances in space technology, for instance. On Sundays, we would always spend time watching documentaries about the animal world. His ideas on education and success were very different. What he considered a must was not a classical education, because not everyone had a chance at this, but to feel the desire to read, and learn, and grow.

HRANT

It's that time of year again. The results of the university entrance exam have been published, to the elation of some and the needless sorrow of others. In an age in which "success" has become a relative concept, we must also look at our "assumed failures," because hidden inside the harrowing experience of failure are the seeds of true success. And that is why there is no need for our quiet hatred of the crushing failure; it is enough to acknowledge it. In the young, you can awaken the determination of the "tiger that pulls back before it jumps."

But how are we to explain to the young that exam results are not the only measure of success? As for those of us who sat for these exams when they were first brought in during the 1970s, how many of us ended up pursuing studies in areas we'd never once considered?

My own first degree, for example, was in the science faculty. It didn't give me a career—I never became a zoologist or a biologist. So was this success? Or was it the time I spent studying philosophy that proved me successful? If that's how it is, then what if I had given up secondary school in my final year, saying "What business do I have here?"

What I say to the young is this: if you live in a society without a shared understanding of what success is, you have as much a right to fail as you do to succeed. So when you get to the day when they're publishing the exam results, don't eat yourselves up. Instead, keep your mind open and apply yourself to the moral struggle to bring society's views on success back in line with reality. Believe me when I say that it is here where true success begins.

HÜLYA DEMİR

I was friends with Hrant in college. I was studying in the philosophy department of the University of Istanbul when he transferred to us from the department of zoology in the faculty of science. He didn't come to class much. A group of us there were very active, very keen on philosophy. Classmates were always borrowing our notes. We had this sort of back and forth with Hrant, too—or, rather, he would ask, and we would give.

Actually, he was never Hrant to us; his name was Fırat. We had no idea that he was Armenian. We knew that he had a family, but he never introduced us. Our friendship was limited to school. To me, Hrant was like a big brother or a father. This was partly because of the age difference, but it was also just his character. His arms were always open, as if he was about to throw them around someone. He had those broad shoulders, and I always had this feeling that if I began to fall, he'd catch me. Just being with him made me feel safe. Even then, he could touch people with his words—Hrant loved people. He'd look deep into them because he wanted to understand them.

In those years, we were all leftists. We knew that he was a leftist, too, but I can't remember which faction. We were the school's leftists, and he was our older brother.

MASİS KÜRKÇÜGİL

By the time Hrant was in college, he'd almost become my adopted son. For ten years, he was struggling to make a living at the same time he was struggling to keep up with his studies, and there was the leftist struggle on top of that. We did not discuss our differences of opinion on left-wing politics, but I did play a part in getting him to read Marxist theory. Our differences rose out of questions provoked by internal dispute, but over time they grew deeper, moving in the direction of socio-political analysis.

By the mid-1980s, Hrant's formation was more or less complete. And it wasn't limited to Marxist literature; he had read everything that there was to read, from Turkish political history to literature. As someone who witnessed his intellectual development over time, I can say that Hrant's real education took place outside of the university. He genuinely succeeded in educating himself. He was a student in the school of life.

HÜLYA DEMİR

He loved philosophy. We had such interesting discussions in class, and he would always enjoy being there. Even in those crowded lecture halls, he would stand out. He particularly liked our philosophy of science professor. He dominated class discussions and, after a while, the exchanges grew so deep that the rest of us could not understand a thing. He never stayed at school for long, though; he'd never come back with us to the canteen, for example.

The strangest thing is, when I think back on those years, I cannot recall ever seeing him smile. He was always very serious. He seemed preoccupied. He had financial responsibilities; there was always something he had to take somewhere, and somewhere else he had to go to pay someone. One day, we went to a friend's wedding in Kadıköy. Afterward, we paid a visit to Hrant's bookstore. He was also selling secondhand books there. To us, it was a treasure trove, and we bought quite a few books. Beyaz Adam was just starting up at the time, and he was always so busy. Sometimes he could come to class very tired, and he'd tell us how he envied us because we did nothing but study. There were various groups at school, and Fırat was also friends with my friend Zihniye.

ZİHNİYE CAN

In those days, we'd go to a coffeehouse called Medrese. We'd go there early in the morning and drink tea and talk until it was time to go to class. On the rare occasions when he came to class, Fırat would join us there. It was a lighthearted atmosphere, with lots of laughing. But he was always very quiet. I remember very clearly when we spoke about his marriage, because I was very shocked to find out that he was married with two children. There was a big age difference between us, but I was still shocked. "Aren't you ever sorry for marrying so early?" I asked once.

"I adore my wife," he replied. "I adore my children, too. I cannot imagine life without them."I shall never forget these words.

ARARAT

Even though he loved the philosophy department a great deal, eventually he had to give it up. He told us it was because of an argument he had with a professor, who wanted his students to stand up and recite their lessons like they were still in high school. My father refused, so that's why he left.

ZİHNİYE CAN

I don't remember Fırat having any argument like this at school. We only studied together during my first year, if you can call what he was doing studying. It was the 1984–85 academic year. My understanding was that he left school because he had to do his military service.

One day, we were sitting on the stairs, talking. "I have to go into the army," he said. "They're taking me in, whether I finish college or not, so I might as well focus on zoology and get my degree." He was very sad about this. And once again, I was shocked. He was a big brother to us, but he also had troubles that no one else his age had, like military service. He disappeared so fast that we didn't even get a chance to say good-bye.

I knew he was short of money, but that was not something we'd ever spoken about. He didn't share his troubles, ever. I knew him only as Fırat. He hid his name, and the fact that he was Armenian, from us, but we were all leftists. There was no need for him to hide! I only found out that Fırat was Hrant when I saw him years later on a TV program. It was a program about Turkey's Christian minorities. I was not so much surprised as crestfallen. I thought we were close, so it hurt me that he felt he had to hide his Armenian identity from us.

RAKEL

One day, we received a notice from the faculty: either you finish, or we're taking you off the register. Whatever he did, he was going to have to do his military service. We had a friend whose nickname was Bozo. He died later in a car accident. He was a mathematician, a graduate of ODTÜ, the technical universitu. Bozo moved into our house, and, for fifteen days they studied together, day and night. I would take them tea and coffee. I remember how the Latin names perplexed them. "I'm going to get myself that diploma," he kept saying, "and frame it and hang it on the wall."

Over fifteen days, he took fifteen exams. He'd go off in the morning and take one exam and come back in the afternoon to study for the next. Such determination. He graduated, but I'm not sure he ever went in to collect his diploma. All I know is that the next minute, he was in the army.

Part V

The Dissident

13

The Swallow's Nest

HRANT

I first went to Tuzla at the age of eight. One year followed another. That place became our summer camp. We orphanage children had made it with our own hands. Like swallows, carrying sticks and grass to build their own nest.

I gave it twenty years of my life. I met my wife Rakel there. Together, we grew up there. When we married, we were there0, too. And also after our children were born.

After the September 12 coup, the camp's director, Küçükgüzelyan, was taken into custody, charged with "training Armenian militants." This charge was unfounded. None of us were reared as Armenian militants. Both the camp and the orphanage were then left without a director, so a number of us friends got together to save them from closure.

RAKEL

Before my husband was taken into the army, something happened in Turkey, and we all—our family, our friends, everyone—saw with our own eyes what the military really was. Oh, the things we lived through after the September 12 coup. During the period of martial law that followed the coup, they arrested Hrant Güzelyan, the director of Tuzla Children's Camp. They accused him of making religious propaganda, on account of his being a minister. They said he was rearing militants for ASALA, on account of his being Armenian. These were the heavy charges that they took him in for. Someone had to take responsibility for the camp. The children couldn't be left stranded.

We'd been continuously involved with the Tuzla Camp from the time we were children ourselves. We'd put our years in. After getting married, we'd gone there every summer to help out Dr. Güzelyan. Çutak worked as a counselor, and I did everything from keeping the children clean to feeding them. It wasn't work we didn't know. So we decided to take responsibility for the children, and we went back to Tuzla to take charge of the camp.

HOSROF

When Küçükgüzelyan was thrown into prison after the September 12 coup, our terrified Armenian community abandoned him.

Once again, it was Hrant who stepped forward. He went to visit him in prison, he made sure he had what he needed. The case was still in court when he was given a temporary release, and, suddenly, to everyone's surprise, he was out of prison. And it was Hrant, again, who took him in. He was there for him, as always. But Küçükgüzelyan had been worn down by what he'd been through. While inside, he'd been badly tortured. He found a way to get out of the country. And he never came back.

ARUS TECER

My wife and I are among the Armenian children raised by Hrant Küçükgüzelyan. We spent our winters in the orphanage and our summers in Tuzla Camp. Like Hrant, I met my wife there. We went off to work, and, as you see, we never became ASALA militants or terrorists. Whatever we have achieved in life, it is thanks to Güzelyan.

Years later, during the military regime, when our director could no longer bear the pressure that had been put on him and left the country, Hrant took over as director of the Tuzla Camp. Here, he took care of impoverished Anatolian children and saved them from ruin. And Rakel stepped into the shoes of our Morakuyr, who was very old by then. She looked after the children.

HRANT

Our dear Isguhi Morakuyr was responsible for the care of the girls in both the Joğvaran and Tuzla Camp. In the days of the September 12 military regime, the soldiers made many visits to inspect and search the camp. Whenever that happened, Isguhi Morakuyr would take all of the children into her room so they wouldn't get scared, and together they would sing hymns. When the army commander heard these sounds coming down from above, and asked what they were doing, I would be the one to answer: "The children are praying, asking God to protect them." The commander was a good man. He would cut the search short and take his men away.

Isguhi Morakuyr was one of our unsung heroines. I hope it doesn't sound like boasting, but after Güzelyan left, keeping the doors of the Gedikpaşa Armenian Church open became a badge of honor for us. I remember that for five long years, winter and summer, we would travel from as far as two and even three hours away to gather together in that church. The congregation was made up of Isguhi Morakuyr, my wife, and the church janitor. I was their preacher. So what did this preacher have to say to his congregation of three? I mean no offense to myself or to God. Even if we had only ourselves to listen to, we were doing whatever we could to keep the doors of that church open. God wasn't blind, after all. He could see our struggle.

EFRİM BAĞ

When Gedikpaşa Protestant Church was left without a minister after Küçükgüzelyan left the country in the wake of the September 12 coup, Hrant gathered us together and set up a board of seven people. We appointed Hrant as director. We repaired the school and the shops around it. With one hand, Hrant was trying to keep the church open; with the other, he was running the Tuzla Camp.

OHANNES TECER

During the September 12 regime, they sealed off the Gedikpaşa Protestant Church and its orphanage. They took the children to Tuzla Camp so they weren't left stranded. They kept them there winter and summer and sent them to a Turkish primary school nearby. And that is when Hrant and Rakel moved to Tuzla to care for those children.

In the years that Hrant was in charge of the camp, he invited me out a few times. He would wake up before everyone else, and, at the crack of dawn, he would water the whole garden. You never saw anyone as happy as he was when he was working there. In the winter, when it got cold, Rakel would get the children running and take them outside for gymnastics so that they could warm themselves up. They didn't even have wood for the stove. They would gather up twigs and use those to try to get warm. There were almost a hundred children at the camp. They all worked together; they were always there for each other. If we have many in our society who have achieved things in life, it is thanks to Hrant Küçükgüzelyan, who built up the orphanage and this camp from nothing, and also thanks to Hrant Dink, who kept it going after he left.

HRANT

It was not without its incidents, our life at Tuzla Camp. Once, after his sheep damaged our garden, we went over to speak to our neighbor, farmer Yusuf. He came back with his hunting rifle and a few friends and threatened us from a distance. The recklessness of youth. While I was chasing after him with a stone, he fired and scattered his shot all over me, and I fell to the ground. I'll never forget how innocently, sheepishly, Yusuf gazed at me when I was called to the police station so I wouldn't lodge a complaint. So, of course, I told the police chief that I wouldn't be making a complaint. If I had, I am sure that the little man would have spent several years in jail. And it was good that I hadn't been blinded. Rakel remembers it like it was yesterday, taking the shot out of my eyelids with tweezers.

RAKEL

How could I ever forget that? That was another task that fell to me. Where could we have found a doctor? And we had nothing to anesthetize him. His eyes were streaming from the pain, and, yes, he made a bit of noise. But then, he said that the farmer was in just as wretched of a state as we were, so he gave up on the idea of lodging a complaint.

By then, the responsibility for Tuzla Camp was entirely on our shoulders. We were married in '77, and, a year later, our daughter Baydzar was born, and a year after that, our son Arat. The children at the camp were our children by then, too. Only a year and a half had passed since we'd opened Beyaz Adam, but we made the decision to live in Tuzla during the winter and summer. Five hundred meters from the camp was a broken-down house from the Küçükgüzelyan days. We pooled together some money and bought this house. Tomo and Haço joined us, and we all began to live in that house together.

YETVART TOMASYAN (TOMO)

One day, Hrant came to me and said, "There's this house in Tuzla; come, take a look." We went and took a look, and then we bought the place. This place was a little lot, a fifteen-minute walk from the sea, with a one-and-a-half story shanty house sitting in the middle of the property. Things had become very difficult for us in Istanbul, and we wanted out. The September 12 regime was giving us a hard time. At times like this, as you know, it's even harder if you're Armenian. They were raiding houses, arresting our friends. Everyone was on edge. It would be good to get away from Istanbul. And anyway, Hrant wanted to be near Tuzla Camp, which he was running then. My business partner, Haço, had just married a Turkish girl. When his family wouldn't accept her, she came and joined us, too. We spent a month fixing up the place as best we could and moved in. We were living on top of each other. There were many of us in our place, and because we had the elderly people, too, we had the look of a family. Our place was where we all ate and drank. The children grew up together in the yard, and when one of them grew out of their clothes, we handed them on to the next.

MARİ MAYRİG

There were six children in all at the house. There was a pink bag filled with toys, and we'd dump it into the middle of the floor. We were on the middle floor, which was the biggest one, so the children would come to us to play. They were easy children. I don't remember any of them giving me any trouble.

Rakel also had Hrant's parents to care for. Hrant had taken them in, too. Hrant was a good husband and a good child. He was also a good father. He was almost like a friend to his children. But, of course, he loved all children. Hrant was a father to orphans; he was a father to the homeless. He would go off to the Karagözyan Orphanage, gather together a few of the orphans, and bring them back to the house. You'd look, and there wouldd be five more children in the house. And Rakel would clean them up and give them food and drink. Sometimes, they'd stay the night, and the next day Hrant would take them back. And this was when Rakel was still a child herself. That's how it was in those days. They'd both grown up looking after children, and they never stopped.

YETVART TOMASYAN (TOMO)

We lived year-round in Tuzla. We had to go into Istanbul to work, of course, so we'd commute by train. Hrant had just opened the bookstore, and he was trying to get it off the ground. We never knew what time he'd be getting home.

When he worked late into the night, I'd have trouble getting him to leave the store. He wasn't good at keeping appointments. He had no concept of time. It never occurred to him that he might be keeping people waiting—he'd just say, "I'm on my way," and then you'd wait an hour.

MARİ MAYRİG

Our life was very cheerful. Hrant had an organ in that house in Tuzla. I think he must have brought it out from the orphanage. It was a tiny little organ, old, with pipes. He'd sit in front of it and cry, "Come on, now, Rakel, get started!" He had a very good ear. He could play a song by ear after hearing it only once. And Rakel had a lovely voice. She sang everything from Armenian hymns to Turkish folk songs. Hrant and Rakel would curl up in each others arms and sing. It would go on all night.

We lived there together for two years. In Tuzla Camp's last year, a group of seniors were brought in. Apparently, Surp Prgiç Hospital was undergoing a renovation. They did not have a place to stay so they came with all their staff out to the camp. Eventually, the camp was closed down, I think . . .

HRANT

One day, a notice arrived from the General Directorate of Foundations. It seemed that, since 1936, foundations run by minorities had had no right to buy or take possession of property. It was against the law. So the deed to the property was to be canceled, and the property returned to its previous owners. This is what it said on the court document they pressed into our hands—and they did what they said. With their cases and their implicit and explicit sanctions, they managed to seize the camp and return it to its original owners. We put up a fight, but we lost. What could we do? We were up against the state.

And now what was I to do? Look back on the labor of my childhood and say, "Well done?" or "For the love of God?"

Oh, humanity! I have a complaint to make. They threw us out of the civilization we built with our own hands. They seized the home in which we raised 1,500 children. They destroyed our nest.

If they ever made another orphanage there for poor children, whoever they might be—if they used it as a camp for children without means or children in distress, I would give it my blessing. But as things are now, I cannot. Because the Tuzla camp for poor children—our Atlantis civilization—now lies in ruins. They even removed the well where chirping children once drew water. And the building—its teeth have fallen out, its cheeks are sunken, its shoulders sag. The earth is barren, the trees mournful.

As for my own rebellious nosedives, they are as sharp as the swallow's when the nest it built with such care is destroyed with a single blow. And yet hopeless . . .

14

The Ballad of the Prisons

HRANT

Either I loved danger, or danger loved me. But I was extraordinarily innocent.

RAKEL

Try as we might to stay out of the way during the September 12 regime, it finally found its way to us in Tuzla. First, they arrested Çutak and Brother Orhan (Hosrof). And then, after years of taking us to court, they seized Tuzla Camp. Those were very hard times, indeed. I have a very clear memory of the day they were arrested.

That day, Çutak went upstairs to Tomo's place. His brother Orhan (Hosrof) had returned from Beirut and was staying with us, but that night he was in Istanbul. He had the car. We needed the car, too, because my husband needed it to take me to the doctor. That's why he went upstairs—to ask if we could use their car.

While Çutak was upstairs, I heard some noises. I looked out and saw police and soldiers and what have you, all standing outside our door. They had their guns out, and in their midst was Brother Orhan. I froze. I can't remember how Çutak got downstairs or what he said to them. They searched the house inside and out and went off with a lot of books. But not just books. On their way out, they picked up Çutak and his brother, too. As he went through the door, Çutak threw me a look as if to say, *Don't you worry about a thing*, and off he went with those armed men. How is it possible not to worry? I was suffering from a bleeding at the time, and my health was in ruins.

The next day, my father-in-law took me to the doctor in Istanbul. They put me in the hospital, where I spent a few anxious days. We had no news from him. If anything happened, what was I to do? To whom could I go to claim my rights? I was up against the army. That was one problem. And, also, we're Armenians. My father-in-law stayed with me, bless him. I can trust him. I convinced myself that he would go off and track our Çutak down and then come back and tell me the news.

HOSROF

I was late getting on the road that night. There was a curfew, so I was rushing to get back to Tuzla in time. Suddenly, I was stopped by the police. My car had Dutch plates. I was just back from Beirut. And I had a foreign passport. They asked me where I was going. I gave them my Tuzla address, but I didn't tell them that Fırat Dink was my brother because I didn't want to draw him into this. "I'm going to see a friend," I said. I didn't speak in Turkish, which probably this aroused their suspicions.

They escorted me to the house. During their search, they found left-wing books. In those days, left-wing books were banned. So they arrested both me and my brother. I remember that they took us to Tuzla Infantry School. Or was that the second time? I've erased all of that from my memory, so I don't remember it very clearly now, I'm afraid.

MARİ MAYRİG

The two brothers were arrested while we were all living in Tuzla.

It was because of Hosrof, I think. But when they left the house, they took Hrant with them, too. Rakel was bleeding badly at the time, and the doctors admitted her to the hospital. The children were at the house, and Rakel was in the hospital. And when she got out, she was trying to find her husband—the whole thing was a nightmare.

I took care of all of the children while all of this was going on. But we had no idea what was going on. Tomo was furious. "What kind of nonsense is this?" he kept saying. "He knew there was a curfew, so why was he out driving so late?"

YETVART TOMOSYAN (TOMO)

When the soldiers and the police raided the place downstairs, we were in our apartment upstairs. We were about to drive into Istanbul, but before we could, they came and took Hrant away. And Hosrof, too, of course. As if it weren't enough to get himself arrested, he brought the authorities to our doorstep. They took off with the men downstairs. Meanwhile, we're upstairs, not making a peep.

Hrant's father and I went to Samandıra, outside Istanbul, because we knew that there was a military barracks there. In those days, this was the middle of nowhere. At the time, there were no such things as visits. The army was running the country. You just waited at the gate and pleaded with the guards, begging them to bring you some news from inside.

If I remember correctly, they arrested these two twice. The first time, the brothers managed to get them to buy the story that they were friends. And Hosrof had a foreign passport, so no one knew that they were brothers. But after they got out, they couldn't keep their mouths shut. I mean, they didn't say anything inside, but when they got out, they started telling everyone how they'd fooled the army. Then the camp janitor informed on them, saying that the two men weren't friends but brothers. This time, they arrested them and threw them into prison. They spent three months in there, I recall . . .

Those were the days when ASALA was assassinating Turkish diplomats. Because Hosrof had just come in from abroad, they suspected an ASALA link, I think.

Our friendship never recovered from this episode. After Tuzla, we didn't see each other as much. There wasn't a particular reason; it was just that we'd been through too much. We had two children, and they had two children . . . and we ended up looking after them all. Plus, Hrant's parents; it threw our lives upside down. And then, all of this happened where we were living. The police and the gendarmes had found out where we lived, so from then on, we were living on tenterhooks. It's not easy being Armenian in a military regime. And now our house had been raided. Everything was very difficult . . . so very difficult.

RAKEL

The first time they were taken in, Ararat was one year old. We went in to see them. The child pulled back, scared—they'd cut off all of his father's hair. "My son, can't you recognize me?" he said sadly. Or was that the second time? I can't quite remember because almost as soon as they released them, they took them back in again.

The second time, we had no news of them for a week. We were terrified. We went from one prison to the next, trying to find them. There were so many people dying from torture in those days. Who could be held accountable?

But we kept looking. We looked through the lists, and we couldn't find his name. We left notes, asking them to contact us if he was there. Then, my father-in-law and I got on a bus. We had the two children with us, and we were out in the middle of nowhere. I prayed silently: *Oh, Lord, did you protect them as they traveled along these roads?*

Finally, we reached Samandıra, at the end of the earth. They brought out another list, and, once again, their names weren't on it. So we thought that maybe they kept their names off the list so that no one could visit them. So we say, "We don't want to see them. We just want to know where they are. They're here, aren't they?"

I wrote a note and gave it to the guard. And I got a note back that said Fırat Dink has been here for x number of days. Oh, our joy! He was still alive; thank the Lord!

We rushed home with the news. And then the waiting began. They'd move him from the cells to the barracks, and then we would be able to see him. I was very ill. After all of that heavy bleeding, I came down with hepatitis. I could barely move a muscle. But it's at times like these that you find out who your friends are. You look up, and the person you least expect to see has come to visit. And the people you expected to be there at your side have run off in a cloud of dust. It's at times like these that you can separate your friends from your enemies. Or maybe I don't mean *enemies*. I mean the ones who don't show their friendship.

Dr. Küçükgüzelyan, for example, was a friend. He'd only been out for a short while at that time, but he had no qualms about coming to fetch us and taking us to see Çutak. He was a man of courage. We already knew that, but it's still important not to forget such things.

HRANT

In the immediate aftermath of the September 12 coup, they were raiding houses one by one, taking people in, and locking them up in whatever place they could find. One of these places was in Samandıra in Istanbul. They'd turned a military barracks into a prison, and military toilets into cells. These cubicles were less than a square meter in size, and they were all in a row. They'd covered the toilet holes with wooden grilles. So this was where they locked up the all the people they brought in—whoever they could find.

It had been exactly eight days since they had brought me in with my brother. Now and then, they would take us upstairs for interrogation. After giving us our share of what they had to offer, they would take us right down again and lock us up.

Night and day, we were subjected to psychological torture. The soldiers made us sing military marches constantly. Every half an hour, a new guard would bash against the door, shouting, "Sing the march, you bastard!" The march they made us sing most often was the "March of Independence." Think about it: these men imagined that they could teach us patriotism by making us sing the "March of Independence" while we were locked up in those toilets. If you didn't start singing, they'd unlock the door to give you one hell of a beating. After you'd survived a few beatings, you got some seniority, and the guards who came in next would give you some slack. Inevitably, they preferred to pick on the newcomers.

HOSROF

They took us in, handcuffed. They were about to put us into our cells like that. And when I say "cell," it was this narrow makeshift room that used to be a toilet. You could either stand or crouch, that was about it. Just as they were about to open the door, one of the soldiers cursed our mother—as if we had not been humiliated enough. Now they were swearing at us, too. Well, Hrant didn't hold back, and with his hands cuffed, he headbutted the soldier. So the soldier laid into our boy. Then they threw us into two adjacent cells. Our first day at the military prison in Samandıra had begun with a beating.

Night fell. Then, through the gap of the door, I saw something glimmer in the dark. To my amazement, I saw the soldier who had beaten up my brother extending a lit cigarette into the cell.

HRANT

Then they brought in a new group of prisoners. Almost all of them were Armenians. They packed them into the cells next to me. When the soldiers called out their names, I found out who they were.

What I remember best of those days were the magnificent concerts of the "toilet choir." The minute they heard a soldier approaching, some of them would yell out, "Commander, shall we sing the march?" And then they'd start singing and yelling the national anthem at the top of their lungs. Those toilets had never witnessed a choir like that, I'm sure, and they never would again. Of course, I'm not saying this to belittle those people, but shame on the people who decided to teach us the "March of Independence" in those toilets. And shame on the mentality that gave them the idea . . .

NECDET KOÇTÜRK

After the September 12 coup, they gathered up people viewed as suspicious and locked them up in detention centers. These were different from prisons. Prisons were where they sent people after questioning if they believed them to be guilty. In these detention centers, they could question people under torture for fifteen days with the permission of a prosecutor. This was an arrangement brought in by the military rule. Don't bother trying to ask for the law . .

So they put wooden slabs over the toilets and turned a row of toilet cubicles into cells. Before torture and after torture, they kept us in these cells, handcuffed. This was a way to break the ones who weren't talking. When we were staying in these cells, they'd serve us meals in this little place under the stairs. That was the only time they took off the handcuffs.

HRANT

The last time I ever saw Manuel Vartabed was in his cell there. Fate had brought us to the same place for different reasons. And it wasn't just us. There were so many other well-known figures from the Armenian community. They had brought us all in for groundless or invented reasons and subjected to us to unconscionable suffering.

They released some of the others after torturing them and interrogating them a few times, but they really had it in for Manuel Vartabed. They tried him in a September 12 military court on the basis of coerced confessions and sentenced him to fourteen years.

They claimed that he had been organizing against Turks in Jerusalem, given a dog the name of Atatürk, and other trumped-up charges of this type, playing with this luckless priest's life. And, for a long time, he kept hoping that His Eminence Patriarch Şnorhk would find a way to save him, but to no avail, because the leaders of September 12 wanted all non-Muslim groups, like all other groups, to sacrifice some of their own. So here it is, another dossier for the day when the democratic forces of his country call to account those responsible for September 12.

Manuel Yergatyan is dead, but his name has yet to be cleared.

NECDET KOÇTÜRK

The barracks were mixed. You had socialist youth in the same barracks with men selling black-market Marlboros. Paying no attention, they put Fırat and his brother Orhan into our barracks. They were viewed as normal prisoners because they never spoke about politics. And, of course, we had no idea that they were Armenian. These were the days when ASALA was front-page news. It wasn't for political reasons they'd been arrested, after all. When you put it all together, it made sense that they would not reveal their Armenian identities and avoid talking about politics.

HRANT

The transition between being locked up in a cell and being locked up in a barracks is something that only those who have been through it can really appreciate. After eight days of being locked up in that cell, they took my statement and then sent me off to the barracks. Between the time you spent sitting all alone in that cell, not knowing what is to become of you, and the time you spend in the barracks, surrounded by people, there is a stretch of time when you feel very, very strange. There you are, listening to the bloodcurdling screams floating down the stairs from the room where they take the statements, and somehow you're still hoping that it will be your turn next. Because now, at last, you know what's going to happen to you upstairs. Just a little touch of *falaka* (whipping the soles of our feet), and then they'll string you up and leave you hanging for a little while. And then some electric shocks. And that's all! So if you manage to get through all of that and give your statement and sign it, you're all set . . . And off to the barracks. It's like you're out of prison, now, because you're no longer alone. At last, you're surrounded by people again. After sitting in the darkness of the cell, it's like seeing the lights of a village sparkling in the distance. The cell becomes synonymous with death, the barracks with life. At least until they throw you back into that cell . . .

NECDET KOÇTÜRK

The torture there was extreme. I have faint memories of Fırat being taken back to the cells, but after that, I lost touch with him. He was most certainly tortured. There was no getting out of those cells without seeing torture.

HRANT

During the September 12 period, they worked hard to violate my human dignity. The guilty party was a man who, after forcing me to the floor,

crushed my fingers under the heels of his shoe while singing folk songs: my torturer. He must have heard me singing folk songs nonstop in the barracks, and now he was having fun with me. I had belted out a pained rendition of "Spring Has Come to the Mountains of My Homeland." This, I shall never forget. Isn't it beautiful, how your own burning desires can flow into a simple folk song? It's the ballad of the prisons, the ballad of the lonely . . . especially the lonely.

NECDET KOÇTÜRK

After keeping us inside for three months, we were released for intervals of three or four minutes. When I got outside, it was raining very hard. I saw them just in front of me. They were clinging to each other like kittens, soaked to the skin and swaying from side to side as they walked down the hill. I'd been tortured before my release, so I was having trouble breathing. I tried shouting after them, but I was not loud enough for them to hear. I could walk only very slowly, so it took me a long time to catch up with them. I'm not sure if I joined them or if they joined me. What I do know is that when they took me in, my mother had pressed a blanket into my hand. They'd tried to take it away from me at the police station, but I'd managed to keep it. They'd wanted to take it away at the detention center, but I'd kept it again. And I'd guarded it closely the whole time I was in prison. So now it was this blanket that I spread over our heads as we three walked on through the torrential rain. We were on a mountaintop, and the earth was bare . . . not a soul to be seen.

That walk made its imprint on us. It became our history. This was the beginning of our friendship, and, in later years, we told it to each other so many times that we never forgot it.

RAKEL

At last, one day the phone rang. "We're at the Tuzla police station," he said. "Heat up the bathwater. We're coming home!"

I fairly flew upstairs, shouting, "Mayrig! He's back. Çutak is back!" At least, I think that's what I said. I was so overjoyed that I could hardly think. By the time he got home, I had calmed myself down a bit. But he was in very low spirits. He'd lost weight. His mind wandered, and he would jump out of bed at night. He'd sit on the edge of the chair and fix his eyes on the same point for hours. I would sit next to him and pray.

On the third day, I said, "Come on, let's go to Istanbul." He left me at my father's, and he went to his bookstore.

My father insisted on taking me to the doctor. "My girl," he said, "your skin is bright yellow." We went, and the doctor diagnosed hepatitis. My father was the only one who could see that I was ill. I couldn't see myself, after all. And it saddened me that Çutak was not in a position to see anything at all.

He was shocked when he heard. They put me into the hospital. And that was how my illness became his recovery. Occupying himself with the children, coming to see me in the hospital every evening, worrying about me the rest of the time—all of this helped him forget his own troubles. That's how he got out from underneath them. I remember thinking that this was God's work.

15

The Company of Suspect Soldiers

HRANT

I have suffered a great deal of discrimination on account of being Armenian. One such instance was while I was doing my military service. In 1986, I spent eight months at the Denizli 18th Infantry Regiment. At the swearing-in ceremony, all of my friends were promoted to the rank of petty officer. Only I remained a private.

I was a grown man with two children, so perhaps I shouldn't have let it get to me. But the truth is, this act of discrimination hurt me to the core. While all of the others went off after the ceremony to celebrate with their families, I spent many lonely hours crying behind a tin shed. I kept pacing up and down and scraping my key along the slotted tin wall of the shed so that no one would hear me crying. Back and forth I went, walking and crying . . .

AUNT SİRANUŞ

One day, Nvart was visiting. Two sisters, sitting together in the house. We looked up, and there was Hrant. "I'm off to do my military service," he said, and he began to cry. A grown man, already a father. He had Baydzar and Ararat. But tears were rolling down his cheeks. We got upset, too. That was how sad he was when he went off to the army.

RAKEL

As soon as he passed his university exams, my husband went off to do his military service. He had graduated from college, but he was not made a reserve officer; they made him complete his service as a private. I wasn't able to visit him. I was pregnant with our daughter Sera and I had nearly lost her, so I wasn't allowed to travel long distances. My husband came to visit us once on a week's leave, and that was all, but this was for Sera's birth. We experienced happiness and sadness at once.

They assigned him to the "company of suspect soldiers"—this was where they put the ones considered to be a threat to state security. The humiliation weighed very heavily on him, but, even there, he had friends who loved and respected him.

OLCAY HALULU

Hrant and I did our military service together at the 187 short-term Denizli 18th Infantry Regiment. There were 150 of us. We enlisted in December 1985, and were discharged in July 1986. When we were in the army together, his name wasn't Hrant but Fırat Dink.

We met during our month of basic training. He was vibrant and full of life back then, too. He was tall and thin, but he had a mighty stride. We immediately warmed to each other. Our conversations grew steadily deeper, extending into political issues, continuing until the day we were discharged.

We university graduates were offered a shorter period of military service if we agreed to serve in the infantry. After a month of basic training, we all took the oath with our hands on our weapons and became drill sergeants.

Hrant was the only one who did not. I do not recall anyone else being left out like he was.

Hrant's company was known as the "company of suspect soldiers." I don't know why they put him there. I never questioned it back then. Perhaps he was seen as suspect because of his ethnic identity. People could be seen as suspect if they had a history of left-wing activity, had evaded the draft, or were criminals. But Hrant had never been convicted of any crime! In fact, he had never even been charged with anything.

What occupied Hrant's thoughts most during his military service was how he would respond if he were one day punished or treated with violence. He was afraid of being beaten up during his military service. He was afraid because he was afraid of himself, of how he could react. But in any event, that never happened.

HRANT

After all of my army friends were commissioned as officers, only I remained a private. The commander of our regiment called me in and said, "Don't be upset. If you have any problems, come to me." Those words still grate on my mind.

They separated me; they marked me as suspect. They would not put me on guard duty or give me arduous duties. In one sense, they made things easier for me. All I had to do was put in my time and then go home. I should have taken some comfort in that. But I couldn't. They had violated something that matters far more than rank—they had violated my human dignity. Once again, I was made to feel what it meant to be Armenian.

OLCAY HALULU

One day, we bunked off exercises, and we were sitting in the sun, talking. Hrant knew a lot about film culture. This was not long after they'd started

Cinema Days in Istanbul. We agreed that if we could hijack a helicopter, we could get to the Emek Cinema in Beyoğlu in time for the 3:00 showing of the film *Stranger than Paradise*, and then fly right back.

In those days, they had shows in Anatolia that they put on for us soldiers: topless shows. "Open evenings," they called them. So once he and I went to one of these evenings together, and it was so awful that we left right away. We also put together an amateur humor magazine called *Mock the Regiment*. Hrant even left a copy in a plastic bag on the table where the high-ranking officers ate. In those days, porn magazines were considered suspect, so they were sold in plastic bags. That's why he did the same with our humor magazine.

That was what kept us going in that place. Irony and jokes. But military service wasn't a joke, of course. Everyone gets very isolated in the army, and they become introverted. That's the insane side of being in the army. Hrant was like that, too. Sometimes he'd fold himself up like a piece of paper. Other times, we talked to each other about the ones we loved. So I heard all about Rakel. And Malatya, and his relationship with his father, and the orphanage, and the things he'd done with his brothers, and the Armenian Children's Camp in Tuzla . . . He'd put so much work into that. It was one of the great tragedies of his life when they seized the foundation's land.

HOSROF

It was while my brother was in the army that the everlasting legal wrangling over the Tuzla Children's Camp finally came to an end. I was handling the court case in his absence, and we tried to stay in touch by letter. They were absolutely determined to close the camp. By the time Hrant returned from the army, it had officially been seized. I know he was utterly devastated.

HRANT

My dear brother Orhan,

I feel as if I am stabbing myself in the back. I keep telling myself that it might have worked out differently if I'd been there. Maybe then they wouldn't have dared . . .

Now these lands are out of bounds for us. Put this into your head. Just concentrate on making money. This is the only way forward for us. I am sick and tired of struggling with these filthy people. Let's make a bit of profit. We've given everything we have, our money and ourselves, in pursuit of empty pride. But for what? Is it worth it? Even so, there's no surrender! Let's stay wise, cool-headed, and cordial so that we don't cede the world to these pimps.

I'd be grateful if you could send me a tracksuit and shoes and a little money.

Your brother.

RAKEL

We exchanged lots of letters during that period. He would write to me, and separately to the children. We knew our letters were being read, so we couldn't be as relaxed as we would have liked. But we still tried to voice our longings. The children were just learning how to read. I wanted them to write to their father, too. Sometimes they tried to get out of it, and I would have to find ways to make them do it. Sometimes I put a copy of a Nasreddin Hoca book on the table. At the end of the letter, they would take a story from it and write it down. Sometimes, two of them would choose the same story and have an argument. I still have a few of those letters.

HRANT

My darling wife,

I received your heartfelt letter. Lately, I have been feeling very low. Those people in Istanbul have taken advantage of my absence, and at this distance there is nothing I can do to stop their disgusting opportunism. My arms and legs are tied, and I'm furious. Please believe me when I say that I have never in my life felt this helpless. But whenever I receive one of your letters, I forget my troubles. Let the rope snap, I think. I have a wife and children who love me very much, and this is enough for me, I tell myself. I've made my best effort to pull myself together, and now I'm feeling a little better.

From here on in, Rakel, I'm leaving everything to God. Let it be as he decides. It is for him to stop injustice and mete out punishment, and for us to put our trust in him and pray. Every day, every moment, I am praying. For you, and also for me. This gives me strength. I can't speak to you too warmly on the phone because there are people all around me, and that makes it hard to speak comfortably. I gave a letter to a soldier going to Istanbul to deliver by hand. It was a letter filled with longing. Did it reach you? I wrote to you about our children, about the time we climbed to the top of Kınalıada, the time I kissed you in Maçka Park, and Makruhi's house and all our other sweet memories. I lived through them all again as I was writing. And in truth, I am still living them! And so that is how things are with me, my one and only, my darling sweetheart, my only love, my wife. Dear God, how I long to embrace you and the children, and hold you tight! Do the children ever ask about me? Do they ever cry? You go ahead and cry, Rakel. Don't be ashamed. Because, believe me, I sometimes cry, too. But tears don't make a person smaller. On the contrary, it exalts them. When I'm crying, I feel very happy to be crying, and to be crying for you. You and the children are my flesh and blood. Believe me, everything you feel, I too feel at the same moment.

Your Çutak

ARARAT

I have missed you very much. Look after yourself, Father. I am trying not to upset my mother. I am trying not to hit Baydzar. Father, I can't think of anything else to say. But I'm writing as much as I can.

Your loving son, Arat

HRANT

My son, my little lion.

I have written you a poem. Let's see if you like it. Let's see if you can learn it by heart . . .

One day I was born.
Now I'm alive.
I have toys.
I play with them.
But tomorrow,
When I'm born again,
I'll make those toys myself.
And when I'm born again after that,
I'll throw them away
And live the game for real.

BAYDZAR

My dear father,

I can't tell you how much I've missed you. Father, dear, I keep forgetting to send you my picture. I'm so so sorry. But this time, I am definitely going to send it. I got the toys you sent me, and I like them very much. I am working very hard at school. I am trying not to fight with Ararat.

Dear Father, today Mother made a stew. I ate a whole plate because I know how much you like it. Ever since the letter you wrote to me on February 6th of 1986, I've been eating every meal. Father, I would like to thank you for all the things you said about my report card. I'm going to continue being this successful. Father, dear, I haven't been writing many letters lately. I would like to apologize for that. Father, dear, I want to write you a story. I'll write it now. "Nasreddin Hoca went to the lake one day . . ."

RAKEL

My darling Çutak,

Today, Arat put on his trousers and swaggered around the room, laughing and saying "I've finished my military service." Meaning that you were back . . . and Delal kept calling him "bald daddy" and laughing.

So this how things are with us. Maybe you asked them to kiss me for you. I say "maybe" because they will neither tell me what they write or what they read, so I have to guess. Then they did a two-pronged attack, and you can guess the rest. And, of course, all three of us are waiting for a fourth to join us. I keep saying that I don't want us to waste time sighing, but I've run out of strength. We miss you terribly.

My little Çutak, I can already feel our child kicking. And I look very different. When you come back, you are going to see me differently.

I wanted you to know so that you don't find it too strange. I've missed you so much.

Our children are sound asleep now. It's half past midnight. In a little while, I'm going to bed, too. Before I forget, let me tell you that we received your story, and we loved it. We always love your stories, and this one you wrote beautifully. When I told them that you had written the story, the children were so surprised. And they said, "You mean we can write stories, too, if we want to?" it? And I said, "Of course you can." And that is how they came to understand how stories are born.

Good-bye for now. God is with us all. Do not worry about us. Look after yourself. Don't let yourself get upset.

Your Rakel, who loves and misses you very much.

Part VI

The Businessman

16

Beyaz Adam
(The White Man)

HRANT

What I want more than anything is to settle down into a disciplined life. This is not to say that I had never wanted this before. If it's almost the new year, and all of the shop windows are decorated. If, among my presents, I find a showy pocket phone directory or an eye-catching pen, that longing comes right back. I am full of a greedy desire to use these accessories to bring some order into my life. But how? Where is it that order ends, and I begin?

I never learned to use any of these things properly. The directory ended up in the telephone booth, the diary in my torn jacket pocket, and my watch on the sink in the public toilet. And as for my pen, who knows whose desk I left it on? And then I console myself by saying, "So who says you have to lead an orderly life? Think about who you are and how you got here." And soon I am back to my old habits, and the life for which I was "predestined" . . .

OLCAY HALULU

I really got to know my army friend Hrant, or Fırat, after he got out of the army and became a businessman. It was 1987. One day, when I was out of work and out of sorts, I wrote him a letter, and he did not leave it unanswered. "Come on over," he said. "I'll pay your fare."

When I got there, I found out that he and a number of other friends from the military were setting up a publishing house for children's books. The name of the publishing house was Beyaz Adam. He already had a bookshop by that name in Bakırköy, and he was running "our" publishing house from a rented property across the street. This little place had an office for Hrant, because he was the owner. And, believe it or not, there was talk of running something else out of there, too. In those days, there was a German magazine called *Burda*, and it had a Turkish edition. Hrant had made an arrangement with them, but not with the magazine we all knew. They distributed with these magazines paper patterns that they called "masters." so that housewives could sew them at home. Our friend here had organized a partnership of sorts for these masters, so they were sending these special patterns for everything from clown outfits to flashy evening gowns to this little shop of ours. It wasn't long before they were piled up everywhere. But there was no stopping us by then. So we had all of these university-graduate partners wandering around, peddling these things. Meanwhile, Hrant sat in his office. The business was his brainchild, after all. But in the end, we were able to sell only ten of these masters. We were stuck with the rest.

OŞİN ÇİLİNGİR

If you ask me, Hrant was never a good businessman. He was too much a creature of emotion. A person who makes instant decisions based on his emotions can never be good at business. He wasn't good at management, and he wasn't good at being a director. Of course, all of these judgments are retrospective, made long after he had set himself up in business. On the other hand, his ability to create a business from nothing was truly staggering. He might have been a terrible businessman, but he was a very good entrepreneur. Usually, people think something through and then they do it. With Hrant, it was the opposite. First he'd do it, and then he'd think it through.

OLCAY HALULU

We had this other book business. The graphics were wonderful, but you'd have to be an adulta to color them in. They weren't suitable for children. We printed thousands of copies of three different coloring books, and they piled up in the corners of the shop. We couldn't move those, either.

Then we had this brilliant idea of publishing a weekly city guide to Istanbul. That winter, we had five days of heavy snow, and transportation was at a standstill. While we were trying to get this guide started, another publishing house came up with the same idea and brought it into life. This was when our people were on the point of giving up the business.

I have no idea how these partners of ours even managed to break even, but by now they'd opened up a branch of Beyaz Adam in Kadıköy. Some of us moved over there. A year or two later, that shut down, too. In 1988, I moved back to Beyaz Adam in Bakırköy.

Hrant never got stuck on anything. If something didn't work out, he never got upset—he just moved on to the next thing. How he clung to life! At one point, we opened a secondhand bookstore a little down the road from Beyaz Adam. That was a small place, too. We brought in all of our old books from our homes and piled them up. Then that place closed, too. It didn't even have a sign showing that it was a secondhand bookstore.

Hrant was very hardworking. He was the boss, but he helped out with everything. I saw him carrying plenty of merchandise around the store. The store had a very narrow entrance, after all, and it was three stories below ground. Once, when we were lugging those big bundles of books, he said, "Physical fatigue is good for you. When you get home at night, you can sleep easy."

I can't remember how I slept that night, but he'd rented me a place in the Istanbul suburbs. He was paying my rent, and if I needed anything more, he'd take out his wallet. We weren't paid proper wages, but I didn't ask for any, either.

NECDET KOÇTÜRK

Hrant and I were in the same military prison during the September 12 regime, but our real friendship began after I started helping out at the bookstore. When the schools opened, they'd lock the cash registers because it was so crowded. Sometimes they even had to lock the doors. At times like that, Hrant asked for help from his friends. And we'd all come running, Turks and Armenians alike. So, on a day like that, he called me and said that he needed a man he could trust. I rushed to his side. I did a good job on the cash register. He was so pleased that it got to be a regular thing. I had my own engineering business, but at the beginning of the school year, I wouldn't just work at the shop. We were so thick by then that I'd stay over at his house.

MİKHAİL YAĞBASAN

I had a front-row seat for everything that Hrant Ahparig did from the time he started Beyaz Adam in 1979. There were days when he did his own carrying. There were days when he couldn't pay his bills and faced eviction. He took on big responsibilities. He went through very hard times, but he got out from under them by the sweat of his own brow.

During the September 12 regime, he was obliged to move to Tuzla. He'd travel to the bookstore every day. He went to prison and came out again, but it didn't bring him down. He was even more determined about his work. So he called me back in, asking for my help. Around that time, he finished college and went off to do his military service. Meanwhile, the bookstore kept going. I worked with Hrant Ahparig until 1987, when my father gathered the whole tribe together and moved us to Brussels.

After we went abroad, his brother Yervant went to work at Beyaz Adam for good. He started to run the business. What I'm trying to say is that Hrant Ahparig didn't have an easy time setting up his little empire. The secret behind Beyaz Adam is Hrant Dink's courage. And—I don't want to boast—our unconditional support. But without his courage, our support would have amounted to nothing. He never lost that courage . . .

YERVANT

My brother did many kinds of work over his lifetime. If he got fed up, he'd put on his jacket and leave. When he left, he never did the books, never worked out the accounts. He had a different attitude about money, after all. He'd loan someone some money, for example, and he'd never ask himself if that person was going to pay him back. When I took over the books at the bookstore, I was liable for every check I signed, so I had to put all of this chaos into some order. Actually, I'm not a particularly organized person, either, so it was Brother Oşin who picked up after me. A lot of work passed on to us.

OŞİN ÇİLİNGİR

I came in as manager in 1989. The bookkeeping and the bills were in a bit of a mess, and that was why Hrant asked me to come in and help. When I began, their credit-worthiness was zero. The place was swimming with bounced checks and demands for payment. Things were so bad that companies were refusing to send them books. But the Dink brothers were tirelessly enthusiastic.

When I started work, Beyaz Adam was both a stationer and a bookstore. Over time, the stationery section got smaller and moved upstairs. Meanwhile, the bookstore grew and grew. Thanks especially to Hosrof's efforts, they expanded into language-instruction books. And that's how they began to grow.

HOSROF

We worked very hard, and we put our profits back into the business. With books in foreign languages, scholarly works, professional publications, and so on, we were soon filling seven stories. We'd become one of the biggest bookstores in the city.

All of the creative thinking came from Hrant. He would set it up, and we would run it because he had no idea how to manage a businessor money.

The first Beyaz Adam lasted for thirteen years. Then the landlord kicked us out, and we moved to our second location. That was in 1994. Then they kicked us out of there, too. In 1999, we moved into our third location. All of this took a lot of work. Our father had left us nothing, and no one else had, either. Whatever we borrowed, we paid back. We had problems after moving into this building, but somehow we pulled together a few loans. We paid these back, too. When I look around me today, I wonder how many families are struggling with nothing as we did.

OŞİN ÇİLİNGİR

Beyaz Adam was our bread and butter. It wasn't just the brothers working it, it was a place where whole families worked and earned their keep. We were all like one big family there. We'd talk and shout like a family, and share our bread, and whenever the store was quiet, we had a lovely time together. I left in 2005. The brothers continued working it together, with Yervant taking charge of running the store and the money. Hrant's son, Arat, was putting a lot of work in, too.

ARARAT

I've worked at Beyaz Adam all my life. I would go straight there from school and help my uncles, and sometimes I even did my homework there. One of the older boys working there once pointed at the textbook I was sitting on and said, "Could you give me that *Logic*?" That's when I first heard the word "logic."

Everyone in the family worked there. My mother, my Aunt Zabel, my Aunt Haygan, and us children, we all worked there. But it was my uncles who actually ran the business.

My father wasn't very good at business. He had the soul of an entrepreneur. He'd get an idea and throw it out there. For him, Beyaz Adam was home. When it got hot, he'd take off his shirt and throw it to one side. He'd sell books wearing only his undershirt. He was a very easygoing man; no one ever got on his nerves. His office was a shambles. He had a sofa in there, and a television, and a round dining table. He ate in there, and something he took naps in there, too.

In September, when the schools opened, everyone in the family came in, and we worked and worked. Even during the ten years when he was running *Agos*, my father joined us every September. He would even stop writing his columns. He'd work the cash register, but he was always mixing things up, and I would sort things out. Once, he hadn't put the money into the till, but he couldn't remember where he had put it instead. He'd put it in his bag and left with it. We figured it out later.

OŞİN ÇİLİNGİR

Hrant wasn't interested in accounting, and whenever he tried to involve himself, he couldn't make any sense of it. That's the way it was. But this was Beyaz Adam spirit. For instance, he came in one day with a new idea. When he saw that it worked, he made it permanent. One of his brilliant ideas was offering resources that helped students with their homework.

He was the one who got it going, and then I joined in. Over time, we had gotten things so well organized that we were providing ready-made sets of book excerpts. After things were computerized, we were handling ten or fifteen thousand assignments.

HRANT

Beyaz Adam made a profound difference in the way I lived. I was already someone who read a great deal, and now reading was my job. Bakırköy was an area that was open to development, and that's why I chose it.

Then I tried out an interesting new idea, and I think it was something that Istanbul benefited from. As you know, teachers give their pupils homework. And to do their homework, students have to go hunting for resources. They'd search through books; they'd go to libraries. They'd come to us, too. A child would come in and ask if we had a book on such-and-such a subject. And I would say, "Yes, we do." But it didn't sit well with me, selling a huge book like that to a child. What if he couldn't afford it?

I was still mulling this over one day when I suddenly said, "Stop. Let me make you a photocopy." The child went off and told his friend, and then his friend was there, asking for the same thing—and then it was his friend, and that friend's friend. And suddenly we saw that Beyaz Adam

127

was no longer a bookstore but a sort of library that had found a way to give schoolchildren what they needed.

I wasn't making any profit from this, and it was more than the sweat of my brow that went into it. It was also the sweat of my brain. But, once again, I was the one who profited the most from this business. I turned myself into a manic researcher and also one of the happiest men in the world. I could hurtle from one subject to the next every five minutes, each time making a new child happy. And, in a way I could never have hoped for, it ended up being a big advertisement for the business. I became known for this work, first in Bakırköy and then across the entire city. Thirty years earlier, the bookstores of Istanbul were not doing much, so when someone from Malatya put this much work into it, the city took notice. Over time, I was able to turn Beyaz Adam into one of the biggest bookstores in the city.

OŞİN ÇİLİNGİR

This whole thing came out of Hrant's desire to help people. It was a habit left over from his days of being a mentor and helping children out with their homework. And it came from his time as director of the Tuzla Children's Camp. For Hrant, it was a rule to help anyone who needed help. If it was a material need, or if someone asked him for a loan, he'd hand it right over; if he didn't have it, he would find it, and then he would forget he'd ever given the money in the first place. In a spiritual sense, he was supporting us all, too. You'd go to him with your troubles, and he would take time out to listen, and then, no doubt about it, he'd find a solution.

ARTİN YASULKAL

Things Hrant never asked for for himself, he had no trouble asking his friends for on behalf of others. He made extraordinary sacrifices as if it were the easiest thing in the world.

People who weren't close to him didn't know it, but he was a true friend to the down and out. People have talked about the holes in the soles of his shoes when he was lying on the pavement after he was shot. As if he were a man in need . . . It rubbed me the wrong way when I heard that. Hrant was not a man in need. On the contrary, he was someone who gave to others in need.

He had holes in the soles of his shoes because he was also someone who didn't look after himself. It wasn't because he was poor. To escape Rakel's notice, he would slip his shoes on at the door and race out. Hrant would give all manner of material and spiritual help to those in need, without other people noticing. It wasn't enough for him to help them. He would bring them to work with him. He would put a few coins in their pockets and make them feel as if they were working. He would do this for the down and out as well as for the handicapped.

OŞİN ÇİLİNGİR

If an old person had to go to the hospital, he'd go with them in the car. If he met a homeless person on the street, he would bring him to the bookstore and give him something to eat. There was never a time when we didn't have and the poor and the handicapped there. Hrant would welcome them all in. This could be hard to handle, especially when the schools had just opened, and we were all running around like mad. But would Hrant listen?

He was truly the friend to the needy. He never put people into categories. But then, over time, he cut himself off from Beyaz Adam. Leaving his brothers and me behind, he went off to Antalya with a clear conscience. There he set up a new business with the same enthusiasm. He didn't know anything about the jewelry business, but that didn't stop him from opening one. He spoke languages he didn't know with the tourists and sold his wares. And then, before you knew it, he had learned some of those languages. Then, suddenly, he went into the leather business, and after that the carpet business. He didn't know anything about these businesses, either, but somehow he taught himself.

RAKEL

Çutak would go to Antalya during the tourist season. Between 1988 and 1996, he went there every summer. And whenever I had finished all of my work and school was out, I started going down there with the children to join him. I'd help out in the store a little and have a little holiday, too. Actually, the business in Side started out small, but he kept it going for eight years. The climate there was hot, so the tourist season was long. He would stay, and, when the schools opened up, I would take the children back to Istanbul.

ARARAT

When my father first went to Antalya, his cousins were there. First, they worked together, and then they expanded the business. They opened up different stores for selling carpets, bags, leather, and copperware. They had a whole street in Side to themselves. My father helped run all of the businesses.

My father learned German there, and he began to speak English—neither of them well, but he had a flair for conversation. He was very generous. He never carried a wallet; he'd just stuff money into his pockets as if he might need to take it right out again. He would order food for the tourists, throw his arms around them, kiss their cheeks, and make instant friends. And that was how he turned himself into an Antalya tradesman.

He went down and started working there because he always needed to be doing something new, and maybe also because he wanted to expand his range. But, in the end, he didn't make much money. The Antalya period lasted eight years. In the last years of Antalya, he started writing book reviews for the Armenian newspaper *Marmara*. By then, he was probably tired of being a businessman. Around the same time, he also began working with Tomo Ahparig to found Aras Publishing House.

YETVART TOMASYAN (TOMO)

It was 1993. Mıgirdiç Margosyan's book *The Quarter of the Infidels* had just come out in Turkish and was attracting a great deal of attention. So, around that same time, Hrant and I sat down one day and talked about founding a publishing house that would bring Armenian literature into the Turkish language. "That would be wonderful," I said, "but I just don't have the time."

A month later, he came back and talked me into it. And that is how we founded Aras Publishing. Hrant would never put money into such ventures; he put in his work. He knew a lot of people in the publishing business, and he called in all of his connections.

He was no good with money—that was Hrant's problem. Our mistake was that we put him in charge of the money. He took care of the Aras accounts for two years. He was so careless that I was tearing out the hair I didn't have. Then, in the summers, he would go off to Antalya with wife and children. He was selling things to tourists there. When he was getting ready to go that year when we were starting the publishing house, I lost my temper and said, "Why are you leaving everything to me?" And then he got angry. We got angry at each other, and then look what happened—I was left with the business, as you can see.

MIGIRDİÇ MARGOSYAN

Hrant, Tomo, and my brother Ardaşes came to me one day and said, "Let's start a publishing house. You're our old teacher and mentor. Come and take charge of it." In those years, there was no knowledge of Armenian literature in Turkey, so our aim was to reach out to Turkish readers with original works and translations.

Hrant was one of the founders. We set ourselves up in a tiny room. We were making very slow progress. Hrant got bored with this tempo, and he lost interest in the publishing house. If there were three of us in there, we had no room for a fourth anyway. Additionally, we were all struggling to make ends meet—maybe Hrant more so than the rest of us. So he started putting in less time. And then, in the summer, he went off to Antalya. Two years had passed by then. We even discussing shutting the house down, but in the end, we decided to keep going.

But no one could hold Hrant back. His next idea was for his *Agos* project. It was all he could talk about. In the beginning, I wanted to help him, but my friends were nervous about it. If Hrant didn't have it in him to commit to a little publishing house, he was never going to succeed in starting a newspaper, or so they said. In the end, Hrant gathered together another group of friends, and they founded *Agos*.

YETVART TOMOSYAN

When we were setting up the publishing house, Hrant always had the last word. We didn't publish books that he didn't like. But still, the publishing house didn't satisfy him, so he left.

Later, when he decided to found *Agos*, he came back and asked for help. The truth of the matter is that we couldn't trust him enough to give him any support. During its first year, I didn't visit *Agos* once. Hrant was angry at us for abandoning him. Later, I'd go to see him more often. If you want the truth, he and I were always squabbling, always arguing, but I never let anyone criticize him to my face. And if I criticized him, what was the point? He never listened to anything I said. But whatever he did, he was always my child.

We started Aras Publishing with Hrant's enthusiasm. We took it as far as we could together, and then he went his own way. He gathered together a new group of people with the same enthusiasm that he had, and he continued on his way. By the time the first publications came out, Hrant already was on a different path. A great path, very great . . .

17

The Gambler

OŞİN ÇİLİNGİR

Hrant got some of his father's gambling genes. And he loved playing cards. And horse racing . . . But he was different from his father. He never played for money. He wasn't interested in the money, but in winning. That was his attitude toward life itself, I think. He approached it like a gambler. You could see it when he was setting up a new business, or when he was bringing out the paper, or putting himself forward as a leader—there was something in the way he did these things that called to mind a gambler ready to lose everything. He staked everything he had on those businesses he started up from nothing, like when he started up Beyaz Adam and turned it into one of the biggest bookstores in the city. He did it again when, knowing nothing about the newspaper business, he set up *Agos*. He came to be one of our most important intellectuals, not just inside the Armenian community but in all of Turkey. Winning, yet again. When he was defending his cause, he put everything on the line, including his life. He lost his life, but still he won. Was it just him, though? We won, too. Not just Turkey's Armenians. We all won. Thanks to him, we won.

Hrant's philosophy of life was grounded in emotion. When he was choosing what horses to bet on, he ignored the facts and looked instead at their names and other signs to build up an idea of who they were. Even before these horses had gone a hundred meters, he'd begin to shout and cheer. If his horse was ahead, he'd already be declaring it the winner, watching the rest of the race with enormous pride. Most of the time, he lost. Hrant didn't play horses for money, though. His real passion was for picking six winners in a row.

ETYEN MAHÇUPYAN

Hrant had a passion for gambling. Only those who'd seen him gambling were in a position to understand his passion for politics. When he was playing poker, he was like a burning man plunging himself into a crystal spring. We never played in Istanbul, but when we went abroad, we'd play roulette. He'd go into a trance and join in with people whose languages he couldn't speak. But the whole time he was playing, he kept speaking. And if he was on a winning streak, his joy knew no bounds. He played just one number at roulette: the number 17. There was an interesting story about that, which he told me later.

In the days that Hrant was a businessman, he had debts, and every day there were promissory notes. In those days, his younger brother Yervant was frequenting a hotel casino, and he was playing every day. One day, Hrant and Hosrof went to the casino to get him to stop, but then suddenly all three of them were at the tables. Then they looked around and realized that this was not the way it was supposed to be, so they stopped and hightailed it out of there.

But then, one day, Hrant was closing up his store. There were bills that he had to pay the next day, and he had 2,000 liras in the bank. He took out the money and went off to the casino. He put it all on 17, and he won. He put everything down on 17 again, and again he won. Now he had this big pile of money in front of him. He raced off to the phone and called his brother and said, "Come and get me out of here." And he must have gotten there in time, because the next day they were able to pay off all of their debts.

And another story: We went to Singapore together. While we were there, we both bought cameras and mobile phones for ourselves. "I can win back the money at the casino," Hrant said. And he did. He had that kind of luck.

Our craziest gambling story is about a dog race. This was when we went to Australia. We went into this place, and the moment we walked in, we saw a TV screen displaying a number of dogs. Hrant took one look. "This is a 2-4 race," he said. This meant that he was going to bet on two dogs to come in first or second. He gave me the money and asked me to go and place the bets. And can you believe it? He won! What he noticed on that screen, what he said was going to happen, happened.

OŞIN ÇILINGIR

His real competitors at the track were his brothers, Hosrof and Yervant. At the track, they'd leave behind their usual way of treating one another and compete in earnest. The one who was playing for real was Yervant. He knew everything about breeding, performance, and the jockeys, and he factored all of that in. Hosrof went on hunches. He was the best at handicapping and guessing winners. Hrant was the worst player of the three. He was the dealer, too, and whenever they they played cards, Hosrof and Yervant would join forces against Hrant. And they'd always win outright! But I never once saw Hrant stack the deck.

During the *Agos* years, when he got to know Etyen Mahçupyan, it did not just mark the coming together of two minds but also a return to the races. Hrant had at last found the right partner.

ETYEN MAHÇUPYAN

When Hrant found out that I played the horses, and especially when he saw how seriously I took it, he was very pleased. In the first years, he didn't join in much, but after 2005 he became a genuine aficionado.

He played on his hunches. He had a good memory for horses. He usually judged them right, but winning was another question. He knew some really crazy horses, and, when they ran, he would always want to place bets on them. Those horses would generally win. We'd talk first, and then we'd place our bets. We usually did this by phone. We even played the time went to Bodrum together on vacation, and we managed to watch the races on television every afternoon. A few times we went in on bets together and won.

When he won, he would call me early in the morning and say, "So, my child, do you happen to need any money?" Hrant and his family had a strange relationship with money. You could almost call it a lack of a relationship with money. After a time, I grew to accept this. At the end of the day, the pleasure was in playing together. We never won sums big enough to share, anyway. If we had, we probably would have shared the winnings. Sometimes we teamed up in pairs, and sometimes it was each man for himself. The aim was to make each other angry and have a bit of fun.

NECDET KOÇTÜRK

With Hrant, the gambling was not gambling so much as it was challenging life itself. He played to win. He loved all games of chance, and if he happened to spot a tombala man on an island ferry, he could never hold back from playing. In casinos, he played roulette. His lucky number was 17. Once, he played that number five times in a row and won.

He didn't know much about cards, but he loved making wagers. We got so close that we were spending almost every weekend together. On Saturdays and Sundays, he'd always call to arrange some fun. I'd go over to the bookstore, and we'd play cards. From there, we'd go to the racetrack—we'd play the horses, have a meal, and make a day of it. Sometimes, we'd make our bets in the bookstore. The television in his office was always on, and we'd watch the races there.

ATİLLA ANAKÖK

I was the third member of the group. If Hrant didn't have anything happening, we'd get together on weekends and play for hours. This continued until the very end. He learned from us and eventually mastered poker. He played with passion. Necdet deliberately stacked the deck to wind up Hrant, just so they could argue. The real fun was in that. It was part of the game. When he lost, he got angry. He would scream and shout in the middle of the game. But once the game was over, he'd forget all about it and rise from the table in fine spirits. If he won, he'd go straight over and pay the bill. He had the biggest heart in the world.

His brother Hosrof was usually our fourth. Hrant never spoke politics much with us. We were friends from when we were leftists, but we didn't talk politics. He had other friends with whom he could talk politics. When he was with us, it was like he was clearing his mind, enjoying the flavor of friendship.

NECDET KOÇTÜRK

He didn't play cards for money. Even if we were playing for money, at the end of the game, the winner would order food for the losers. He was lucky at poker. When he won, there was no shutting him up. And when he lost, I noticed something interesting. It's hard to describe, but something would come over him that I'd seen in his mother. Something like a momentary trance. It was as if he was gritting his teeth and trying to pull himself through whatever he was feeling. It felt as if he were going to lash out at anyone who happened to talk to him at that moment. The expression on his face would change. It was as if he were suppressing something very big, very violent.

ETYEN MAHÇUPYAN

Hrant had this big dream: to be an international gambler, to get "all dressed up" and stride in and out of casinos. An old fantasy from his childhood, no doubt. He imagined being a man like Maverick—dressed in a tuxedo, a chain watch in his vest pocket, and wearing a wide-brimmed hat—so that when he walked into a casino, all of the great players would recognize him and whisper into each other's ears: "Hrant has arrived!"

He would sit down at a table, place his bet, and win. There would be an uproar, and everyone would be talking to him, and then—bam!—three days later, he would turn up somewhere else and win again, and there would be another uproar. And again, the whole city would be talking about him. And so he became a legend. He'd describe this fantasy about Hrant Dink, the legendary gambler, in a most cinematic fashion. And as he did, he became the boy he once was. In the end, he did become a legend. Of course, it was a very different legend!

NECDET KOÇTÜRK

Hrant loved arguing while we were playing cards, and when we went out fishing, but not to score points—whatever he did, he threw himself into heart and soul. And when he won, he did the same.

It happened, too, when we started going with our families to Kınalıada for the summer. First, he was inviting us to stay over every weekend, and then we thought, *No, this isn't right*, so we found our own place out there. He always wanted to spend time with me, even if it was just to drink tea. On weekends, when we went fishing, we'd sit there with our fishing lines for hours, saying nothing. In fact, he wasn't a very talkative person. It was enough for us to be together. My wife, Müge, used to say that Hrant was my "second wife" because I spent all of my free time with him.

MÜGE KOÇTÜRK

One day, I looked around and saw that Hrant had, for all intents and purposes, become the "second wife," In the winter months, they spent all of their weekends together. And then, as if that weren't enough, we got a house out on the island, and they started spending every evening together. If we went out with the families for a stroll along the sea, Rakel and I would look after the children. They would go out fishing or play cards. His brother Orhan and Attila spent a lot of time with them, too. They were so happy when they were together that it was almost flowing from their eyes. If I said that they never wanted to be apart, I wouldn't be exaggerating.

But with me, he was always bickering. As far back as Antalya, I could see how macho he was. He was an Anatolian man through and through. He guarded Rakel jealously. He didn't even want her wearing jeans. I told him to his face what I thought of that, which managed to upset him. And he was always losing his temper. Once, he even broke a chair that he was sitting on, he was so angry. But he still knew how to touch my heart. He respected the fact that I was religious, and he would call and wish me well on holidays. There was even one summer when we were staying with them during Kurban Bayram. At my request, we went out early in the morning to buy a lamb. He was Christian, and I was Muslim, and together we sacrificed a lamb.

But in any event, when they were out on the island, spending time together, these men of ours forgot that we even existed. Rakel and I . . .well, we'd long since given up on Valentine's Day, but we thought that they should at least make some sort of gesture on Mother's Day. So we let them know. The next Mother's Day, Rakel invited us over for supper. These two came in together, and they hadn't even brought a bunch of flowers. That made me really angry, so I turned to Rakel and said, "Istanbul has two pickaxes, and you and I found them."

And what did Hrant say next? He turned to Necdet and said, "Then you be the axe, son, so that I can be the handle, so we can stay together."

One summer evening, Necdet and I were alone together, for some reason, and we were walking along the shore. Hrant came off the ferry and rushed over to us, saying, "I gave you four days with your husband. Tonight, he's mine!"

And that was the last straw. "Hey, what's that supposed to mean? Are you his second wife or what?"

That didn't faze him at all. "Yes," he said. "Exactly." And from then on, that is what I called him: the second wife.

ATİLLA ANAKÖK

He had this straw hat. He'd put it on, and went out to the sea. He'd sing to himself, very softly. This would go on for hours. If, after many mackerel, he caught a big fish, he was as happy as a child.

He was the one with the most luck. He didn't know how to tie knots, so he'd have someone else do that for him, but he was certainly very lucky. Once, the one they called "black eyes" even caught a huge bonito. The work of a master. He loved fishing, and he loved playing cards. He also loved eating watermelon. Oh, how happy his eyes were then!

ĞAZAROS ÇERKEZOĞLU (GAZİ)

Hrant would call me "fisherman," and when he was angry, "bear," but my real nickname is Gazi. In the summers, on Kınalı, we were together every evening. So, let's say that we all got together in the evening. Normally, we would all go home for supper, and there the day would end. But then Hrant would turn up, and all bets were off. He'd pick up the phone and pretend to call Rakel, saying, "Listen, I have just one thing to say. I'm not coming home tonight!" And then he'd turn to us and say, "Oh, come on now! What kind of men are you?" and try to make us angry. And then we'd crumble, and people would start saying, "Hrant, could you call my house for me?" And he wouldn't turn them down!

If you're talking about weekends, he spent his days fishing in his boat and his evenings playing cards with us. We'd find time to eat, too. "You're the one responsible for the fish, fisherman," he'd tell me. And if there weren't any fish, it was my job to make macaroni and sauce in a big pot. We'd eat and drink, and then Hrant and I would saunter off to play cards. If you wanted to get Hrant angry during a game, all you had to do was pair up with Dr. Avedis.

AVEDİS DEMİR

There was nothing Hrant couldn't make me do. One weekend, we went out in the boat to fish. We cast our lines right in front of the Kınalıada pier, and we were catching mackerel. He was expecting his son, his son's wife, and his grandchild on the boat coming in from Bostancı. Suddenly, he said, "Come on, let's jump into the water."

"I'm not wearing a swimsuit," I said.

"Never mind," he said, "I'm not wearing one, either."

He took off his shorts and jumped into the sea, with me right after him. So there we were, swimming in our Skivvies right in front of the pier. And he was shouting, "The water's beautiful, isn't it?"

And I said, "Hey, listen! The ferry's coming any minute now, and your son is on it with his family. We're going to disgrace them."

"So what?" he said as he danced in the water . . .

Hrant was the loveliest man you could ever meet. He loved laughing. He loved throwing his arms around people. He'd give them such heartfelt hugs that he almost cracked their bones. And when it came to kissing cheeks . . .

Because we were both so gregarious, people used to say that we were alike. But he was the one. He would call, and I would come running. "Wherever you are, come right over. We're going out fishing," he'd say, and then he'd start cursing. Actually, he didn't have a foul mouth. Cursing was his way of showing that he was an Anatolian. It was also very good-natured. The island fishermen loved him. Wherever the fish were, they'd tip him off. He was good at fishing, Hrant was. Every time he threw the line, he caught a fish. He treated me like his cabin boy. He treated his brother Hosrof like that, too.

GAZİ

The first time he took out his motorboat, he didn't tell Necdet or Atilla. He went out in high spirits, early in the morning, and went out to the sea. Had he learned about boats in Malatya? He caught a few little fish, but he was in no state to eat them. After a day in the sun, he was burned to a crisp. We didn't see him for quite a few days after that.

We'd go out fishing together in his motorboat. We could call it a "motorboat," but it really was a rowboat with an outboard motor, and it it was always breaking down on us. He would shout and cry when he had to fix it, so usually he had someone else do it. As for the noise he made in the meantime, it was impossible to describe!

HOSROF

Necdet, Atilla, and my brother bought this boat together. The following summer, he asked me to go in on it with them. He was the one who brought me in. They knew how to work the fishing lines, so my job was cleaning the boat and gathering mussels to use as bait. That's how I came to be called the "cabin boy."

In 2006, they said that we needed captain's licenses. The four of us were going to take the exam, and we decided that whoever got the highest score would be the captain. I was already the cabin boy, so it was going to have to be one of the other three!

There was a handbook for the exam. I did a little studying. My brother said that we already knew all of the information, so he never opened it once. When we walked out of the exam, Necdet, Attila, and my brother were all making fun of me. This went on for a month because we had to keep waiting for the exam results. Then, one day, I came out to the island. They were all in the coffeehouse, as usual. "No way you passed the exam," they said. "You're still our cabin boy."

We went to an internet café with Necdet's son to get our results. I looked, and I saw that I'd gotten 96 out of 100. My brother was in a state. And, of course, there was no way that they could stop me from teasing them, not after that . . .

But I never got to be the captain. By this time, we had come to the end of the summer of 2006. And we never went out in the boat together again . . .

Part VII

Family Man

18

Three Apples Fall from the Sky

HRANT

April 23 was a high point—a most honorable moment—for a nation emerging from decades of strife. This was the day that these words rang through the National Assembly of Turkey: "The sovereignty unconditionally belongs to the nation." And the April 23 Children's Holiday is the legacy passed on to the children who represent the present and the future. It was perhaps the day that the Turkish Republic looked forward to the most.

The darkest day for the Armenian people, now spread all across the globe, is April 24. In the early hours of April 24, 1915, Istanbul's Armenian intellectuals, writers, artists, teachers, lawyers, and deputies were taken from their homes one by one. They were taken away, never to return. This was the starting date of the historical drama that would, within just a few days, spread across the entire Ottoman Empire.

How we are to understand this is beyond me, but if you are both Armenian and Turkish, you throw yourself wholeheartedly into the April 23 celebrations, only to partake in such great sadness the next day. How many of us must endure such dilemmas on this earth? It's hard to understand, and hard to explain. All I can hope for is that no one should ever have to live with such a dilemma again.

I adore April 23. It also happens to be the day that my wife and I got married. We married very young. Why did we choose April 23? I can no longer remember. Maybe it was because we were still children ourselves. Or perhaps it was because we entered the nuptial chamber on the night that binds April 23 and April 24 together. And that was when we conceived our first child. Which side of midnight, though? The April 23 or 24? We can never know. Maybe it wasn't on the 23rd or the 24th. Maybe, at that moment, it was April 23 and a half.

RAKEL

Only God knows if we conceived our daughter that night. Our first child was born on March 8, 1978. We called her Baydzar. In Armenian, it means "light," "brilliance," and "enlightenment." It was Çutak's paternal grandmother's name. During the September 12 regime, we had to get the children birth certificates. Ararat was born by then, and he didn't have one, either. We were delinquent in that regard. And Çutak said, "These names are too Armenian. Let's make things a little softer."

So Baydzar became Delal, and Ararat became Arat. Delal was my mother's name, after all. It was a Kurdish name, and I loved it. It means "the precious one." At home, we call her Baydzar. How happy we were when she was born. She was God's first gift to us.

DELAL (BAYDZAR)

My earliest memory of my father is from our years in Tuzla. We had an organ. I remember his big man's feet pumping its pedals, and his veined hands traveling over the keys. He used to play that organ in the camp dining room. I don't remember his face, just the organ and his feet, and his enormous hands.

My father's hands were very big, and you could see all of the veins. When he came back from the army, he had put on weight, and those veins had disappeared. I remember how shocked I was the first time I looked at his hands again.

Another thing I remember from Tuzla is the games he played with me and Ararat. My brother was still a baby then. And, of course, I remember all of the things I did to get rid of Ararat . . .

RAKEL

Ararat was born on September 6, 1979. In those days, there was no knowing the sex of your child in advance. But it was clear that Çutak wanted a boy— so clear that when Küçükgüzelyan was driving us to the hospital from Tuzla Camp, he said, "If it's a boy, call him Ararat. For Armenians, Ararat means 'greatness,' so let your son carry that greatness forward in his name."

That night, I was still in labor, so my husband went back to the camp. Early the next morning, they called him and told him that I'd had a boy. They all remember how loud he shouted, and how he lay down on the floor of the dining hall—that's how great his happiness was.

ARARAT

My earliest memories are of Tuzla Camp. I remember Karabaş, our dog. He spent the winters with us, and in the summer he was the playmate of all the children in the camp. I was the youngest child there. The older ones looked after me. I was never the "director's child," I was just one of the children. My sister, too. Even when we were very little, my father made sure that we understood that.

Even in the later years of our childhood, we were never really aware of going through hard times. We didn't ask for much, anyway. That was how we'd been brought up. My mother would always cook us lovely food. Maybe our clothes were more modest than our friends', but that was all. Because we didn't have expectations, we never felt poor, just as we never felt wealthy.

DELAL

Even when we were still at Tuzla and I was very small, I felt that there was something different about my father. The father I remember was very big and different from everyone else. There was something special about his mannerisms and the way he spoke. At Tuzla, no one cared that I was Hrant Dink's daughter. All of the children wore the same T-shirts and the same shorts. Our house was in Tuzla, but in the summers we stayed at the camp and slept there.

I don't remember the time when my father was arrested; they probably they tried to shield it from us. But I knew there was something strange about us, and that we weren't a normal family. I could tell this from the way our family elders spoke.

ARARAT

My father's relations with the family elders were good. Aunt Siranuş was his favorite. He could joke with her. He'd tease her by calling her "girl." That's the way he showed his love to us. He teased the ones he loved.

DELAL

After Tuzla, my father opened up a toy store on Kınalıada one summer. It sold beach balls and things like that; that's probably why I remember it. The first house I remember clearly is the apartment that we rented in Bakırköy. My father put bookshelves up on the walls. He had many books, and he was always reading. I don't remember his student days, only that he went into the army as soon as he finished. Because he was always reading, I have no sense of when his education began or ended.

In our house, there was always respect. My father was always joking, always cheerful. He loved teasing us. He was very affectionate, and he spoiled us. He would carry us on his shoulders. That's how he carried me when I was little. We would ride on his back. When I talk about it now, I can feel his warm head under my hands, and his warm hair . . . right now . . .

But he could also be authoritarian. He was less so later on, but when we were little, he was more strict. We would do all sorts of nonsense to our mother, and we wouldn't listen to what she said, but when our father came home, we got quiet right away. We had chores that we had to do before he got home—setting the table, drawing the curtains, and turning off the television by a certain time, things like that. Our mother would warn us. My father never gave me a beating. Ararat got quite a few, though, most of them from my mother. He was a very naughty little boy.

ARARAT

I never got a beating from my father. Once, when I was eight or nine, he hit me with a newspaper, and there was one time that he hit me when I was little, in Tuzla. I don't remember this, but my mother told me that he did. But I got a lot of beatings from my mother.

My father never came for parents' evenings; that was my mother's job. He never asked about my homework. He knew what class I was in, and that was all. I remember him coming to my classroom once when I was in primary school. I even remember that we were in class, expecting an inspector, so when my father walked in, all of the children thought he was the inspector and stood up.

My father never got angry at me about school. I never worked very hard, but my marks were good. In middle school, I was the top student out of all of the boys. In high school, I had to repeat an exam once, but that was all.

DELAL

When I came home with my report card, they never looked at it that carefully because they knew I had all Excellents. My father wrote a children's story once. Ararat and I did the drawings. "If you do them well, we'll get it published," he said. He'd play chess with us. When they were doing the logo for Beyaz Adam, he asked me and Arat for our opinions. He was always doing homework for the schoolchildren who went to the bookstore. He never did it for us, but he'd give us the resources. He brought us toys. When I learned how to count, he brought us a toy that was still very rare at that time. How happy I was! When we got our first color television, it was a struggle to keep us from watching it all the time.

My father was always open to learning new things. What he learned changed him. He was always developing. He was very glad that I was good at school, and he learned with me. The moment he learned something from me, he'd try it out, and if he failed, he'd say, "Fine, that's enough."

ARARAT

My father went through many changes over his lifetime. As he matured, he changed. In the beginning, when life was tough, he was more of a disciplinarian. He was more possessive with my mother. It might have been mixed in with jokes, but my father was a jealous man.

DELAL

But if you ask me, it was with Sera that my father changed. When he came back from the army, he was different. He'd become a gentler man. He came back to the house on the morning that Sera was born. He sat me and Arat next to him, and said, "I'm calling your sister Sera. Do you like that name, too?"

RAKEL

Sera was born on August 5, 1986. She was our late present. Before he went into the army, I was unable to answer my husband's desires. He'd always loved children, and he wanted us to have a lot of children. But because of my health problems, I'd had to say no. And that was why, when Sera was born so many years later, she was such a gift to us. Çutak was in the army while I was pregnant. When Sera was born, he got a week's leave. He took the girl into his arms and gave her a name. I knew the names Tara and Sara from the Holy Book, and I loved them. "Sera falls softer on the ears," my husband said.

I was a little older in my third pregnancy; I was twenty-seven already. Our financial situation was a bit easier. We were very happy when Sera was born.

SERA

I'm the youngest in the family. Life was getting rosier when I joined them, and that's why there's so much I don't understand or know. I wasn't there with them in Tuzla, and I didn't correspond with my father when he was in the army. In other words, I was always the baby, but if only I could talk about all of the serious things I witnessed, if only I had those vivid memories. If only I didn't have such a poor memory! My father had a phenomenal memory, and not only for what he had lived through but also for what others had lived through. How I loved listening to my father! He had a very warm voice, and it made me feel safe.

When I think of the photographs from my childhood, I see a few different frames. Before he started *Agos*, we always went to Antalya for our vacations. That's where I learned to ride a bicycle, and where I learned how to love animals, and that was thanks to my father because he loved animals so much. Every summer, there'd be another animal that we were looking after: cats and dogs and even donkeys. There was nothing my father wouldn't do for our donkey, Bozo. He would talk to him, and share his drinks . . .

DELAL

He and Bozo had a very strange relationship. They'd fight. The donkey would be standing there, rearing its head and kicking, and if my father got close enough to slap him once or twice, the donkey would bite him—take his leg right into his mouth. Then it would start braying. Sometimes, he would get the donkey to drink beer from tourists' glasses. And then it'd be braying all night. When Father was in the village buying the donkey, he said, "This one looks like my friend Bozo," and that's how he gave that kind man's name to the donkey.

SERA

I was crazy about my father when I was little. I even wanted to sit on his lap when he was driving, and I got my way! I remember listening in amazement as my father spoke German to the tourists. Every child has a hero, and mine was my father.

I remember once in Antalya when he got very angry with us. When we were only this high, my cousins Zepür and Maral and I went to a hotel without telling anyone and ate a meal like grown-ups do. And our parents were in a panic, looking for us everywhere. When our evening was over, and we went home, my father was very angry. His punishment for us was that for three nights, all three of us had to stay where he was working, a café/bar called Rachel.

ARARAT

Rachel was the name of the jewelry store that my father opened in Antalya. When he moved to the new place, he continued with the same name. "Rachel" was the foreign version of my mother's name. We'd all go to Antalya for the summer. We'd work there and help him out, but it was also a bit of a holiday for us. My father would go swimming with us, if he had the chance. He was a good swimmer and could hold his breath for a long time. He'd dive in, and we'd start to get worried, wondering when he was going to come up, and when he did, he was way far away. He was like a cormorant. My father loved skinny-dipping, too. Especially when he went fishing and went way out in his boat, he couldn't stop himself from stripping off his clothes and diving in.

DELAL

I didn't like my father's Antalya years very much because during the long winter months, he wasn't with us. It was nice to have a lovely place to go for our summer vacation, but, for me, Antalya meant spending less time with my father. During the last years in Antalya, he would sit down after lunch and write things in Armenian and send them off to the *Marmara* newspaper. That's where my father began to change . . .

In 1996, when he founded *Agos*, I had started college. After class, I'd go to the paper. I was happier seeing my father there. The moment I got there, he would give me something written in Armenian, and he'd say, "Put that into the computer." The first issue wasn't even out yet . . .

SERA

When my father started the paper, we stopped going to Antalya for the summer. I was in the last year of primary school by then. In my childish mind, I was furious. The only thing I could think was, *If it weren't for* Agos, *we could go to Antalya.* And now what I think is, *If it weren't for* Agos, *my father would be alive.* That's a very sad thing to say, though, because *Agos* was the best thing my father did in his life. By starting *Agos*, he believed that he was doing something good for his homeland, which he loved very much.

DELAL

My father was never shy about expressing his love, and even when we had guests for supper, he would launch right into the story of how he courted my mother—how he fell in love at first sight, and how she kept her distance. My father was deeply in love with my mother to the very end. He would write her poems. When he called for her, he would say, "O Rakel . . ." This was something from Kurdish. He also called her *Hanım*. Sometimes, to tease her, he'd say, "Hey, wife!" He loved to tease her.

RAKEL

Çutak was always full of laughter at home. He had a very loud laugh. He wasn't witty, but he loved joking around. We'd tease each other. One thing I say a lot is "pah!" It's something from Kurdish. When I hear something impossible, it's the first thing I say. It's like saying, "Wait a minute now—it's not like that at all!" He loved that word.

Of course, there were times when he got angry. Me too. But it never lasted long. Sometimes we apologized to each other, or we would make peace without needing to say anything. We never hung on to resentments; we would just embrace and make peace. Never once did he say a mean word.

DELAL

My father believed in love. True love. On this, we saw eye to eye. I was still in middle school when I started going out with someone, and I went right to him and told him. He'd always said, "Tell me everything. We shouldn't hide things from each other."

I'll never forget it. One summer, my boyfriend was going far away, and I was at home in tears. My mother was at her wit's end, so she called my father at *Agos*, and he came straight home. He sat down next to me, put my head on his lap, and said, "Cry, my girl, cry. It's by crying that it will pass." Then, he asked, "Do you feel that you belong to him?" And I said, "No, it's nothing like that." He felt relieved after that, because in his book, love was feeling like you belonged to someone.

When I went out with a Turkish boy in college, my parents were very anxious, but they pretended that it was fine. Finally, I couldn't take it anymore. I went to *Agos* and said to my father, "It's not right, the way you're acting. Let's talk about this openly."

And he said, "You have to live through everything in life, but when it's your children . . ." But before he could finish his sentence, his eyes filled with tears. And I was in shock. Then, he sat me on his lap, and we embraced and kissed.

He was saying things like, "My girl, down the line, your children would suffer terribly ." When I said that I had no plans to marry him, how quickly he relaxed! I was a grown girl by then, but there I was at *Agos*, sitting on his lap. I was his little girl, but I was also a friend to whom he could talk about anything.

HRANT

My niece got married recently. My wife asked if we were going. "Allah, Allah," I said. "How could we not? She's our niece, and as almost like a sister." So then I asked her why she was even asking such an awkward question, and so timidly. And then it came out: "She's marrying a Turk."

The family was split between those who were in favor of going and those who were not. But I had made my decision already, so I said, "Come on, then, let's get going. This is our girl we're talking about."

The wedding table stood at the edge of a pool with a view of the Bosphorus, and in answer to the registar's question, the young ones cried a joyful "Yes!" And they were kissing each other throughout their entire dance.

But then, I looked at my Uncle Armenak, and he was crying. I looked at our people, and the boy's people, and most of them were crying. It was hard to tell who was crying from joy and who from grief.

I didn't cry that night. I didn't dance, either. I took out a loan on the future. On those who would marry in years to come. If they all succeeded in owning their identities and passing that legacy on to the children, and living happily ever after, then I'll come back and dance. If not, I'll go back to stand beside that pool and cry in the same place where I saw my uncle in tears.

ARARAT

My father gave great importance to the family. For him, it was a very delicate subject. His main concern was that Armenians would decrease in number and then vanish. That was why he didn't want his children marrying Turks. This is a viewpoint that had come down to him from my grandfather Siament. You might think it politically incorrect, but it was simply their desire to see their own culture continue, that's all.

You see, Father had a special relationship with my grandfather Siament. My grandfather would sit on the sofa with one leg pulled in. My father would crouch next to him. And they would talk and talk. Actually, my grandfather wasn't very talkative, but with my father, it was different. Even if he'd started out as the "unwanted groom," my father had changed that with his determination.. He had earned my grandfather's respect. When they were together, my father would use his idiomatic Turkish. This was probably out of empathy. My father admired my grandfather. What he saw in him was the continuation of the story of Armenian legacy.

DELAL

At home, he would ask me to get him a glass of water. Not Ararat, but me, because I was a girl. And I never complained; I would go and get it for him. Then, when I went to study at Boğaziçi University, I found out about feminism, and one day I discussed it with my father. From that day on, he never asked me to bring him water. He started getting it himself.

We weren't brought up in an ideological household. My father was a leftist, but he never talked about politics with me. But at the end of the day, we grew up in a house with enough books to fill a library, and even when I was little, he was giving me Nazım Hikmet books to read. He never talked about 1915. I'm not even sure when I first heard of it. It was probably the time that Isguhi Morakuyr told us what had happened in her village. Later, when I was in college, we were researching the Ottoman women's movement, and I saw the date April 24. This was a piece of history that I could feel in my own gut.

Once, on my father's desk at *Agos*, I saw some pictures. I picked them up right in front of them, but we didn't speak. I never asked him about this subject. After all, if we were all feeling the same pain, why would we talk about it? Is it possible to describe pain?

ARARAT

There wasn't much politics discussed at home. Unless something very serious had happened that day, we didn't mention politics. As for the Armenian question, maybe that amounted to 10 percent of what we talked about. Why talk about the injustices visited on the foundations? Or who did what to the Armenians in 1915, or what we did to them? No one talks about such things in other Armenian homes , as far as I know. But people know it. I don't remember when and from whom I learned it, either. From no one, I guess.

But my father did talk about other things: the natural world, the concept of time, the universe, and other scientific subjects like that. He was always fun to listen to. He'd be looking at a nature documentary, and he would get all excited and shout out, "Arrrrat, Arrrrat, come and look at this!" And then, when I got there, he would act it all out with his whole body. He had a very wide range of interests. Sometimes he would talk for hours about philosophy and literature and art.

HRANT

Rakel is very devout. Religion fills all of her needs. Religion takes up most of her life. For me, it's not like that. But we honor our cultural traditions, and we always observe them. Rakel and I never talk to our children about her faith or my views. What we want most for our children is for them to grow up to become good, honest people with a sense of right and wrong.

ARARAT

My father's attitude toward religion was also interesting. In his youth, he had worked at the Patriarchate, and when he was working as a mentor, he preached and read passages from the Holy Book to children. But his own ideas on religion were different. So, for example, when my mother interpreted events in daily life through the writings of the Bible, he would complain, saying, "Can you be serious?" If my mother kept it up, he'd say, "Do I make you listen to communist propaganda? Then don't make me listen to religious propaganda!"

He did not recognize the Patriarchate as the leaders of the faith. "It's just a bunch of chairs over there," he'd say. "What do they have to do with religion?" He said that faith was a personal matter. He wasn't religious, but I am sure there were moments when he took refuge in religion. He wasn't your normal atheist or positivist. For him, the questions were more philosophical.

HRANT

At our house, crowds are our medicine. Every holiday, every New Year, we all gather together here. I love crowds. They always bring out the joy in me. I'll sing. I'll dance. I'll show my joy, and I'll show my sadness. I tend to warm to people from the heart, not the head. I wear my heart on my sleeve. My heart is my weapon.

Of course, I don't always get up and dance. There need to be a reason for it. It needs to come in and of itself. At my son's wedding, for example, I danced on the tables. To live to see your child get married . . .to see all of the love returned . . .what lovely things these are! We have to do those days justice, enjoy them to the utmost. If you're sure of your feelings, why hold them back? No one—neither social stigma nor social mores—can restrain me when things turn out so right.

ARARAT

My parents' relationship was a great inspiration to me, and I was very struck by their love for each other. And I didn't want there to be a large age difference between me and my children. I wanted to be a young father so that I could understand my children better. I was still in college when I got married. I had a job, at least! I was working at the bookstore. When I told my father I wanted to get married, he was very happy. The only thing he asked me was if I was sure.

DELAL

One day, Arat came and told us that he had decided to get married. Karolin was already coming to the house a lot and was already one of the family. I was surprised that Karolin wanted this, thinking, *How is she going to make anything of this boy*? They were very young to be getting married, but my father didn't object. We all came together, and then we went to her family to ask for their blessing. I had quite a good time there. And at the wedding, the one who had the best time was my father. He and my mother jumped right up to danced the *halay*, and they stayed on that dance floor all night. Even that wasn't enough for my father—he was so happy that at one point he even got up on the table.

ARARAT

When I was choosing a university, I didn't have a clear preference. I asked my father for his thoughts. He turned to his friend Necdet. "You're good at numbers," he said, "and you draw well. Why don't you choose architecture?" So that's how I ended up in architectural school. I enrolled the same year that I finished high school, but it took me a very long time to get through it. By the time I graduated, I was married with two children.

SERA

I worked hard to get into college, but I didn't get enough points on the entrance exam to get into the department that I wanted. I was in despair, and registering for a department that would accept my score, when my father swooped in to save me. He told me that he had found a department that admitted students on the basis of aptitude. Together, we looked into visual arts and visual communications design in the School of Communication. He knew me better than I knew myself; he knew what I wanted before I did.

In high school, I never stood out, never was appreciated, but in that school, that department, I became an honors student. For this, I have him to thank. He may have seen me at my graduation ceremony in 2009, but I never got to wrap my arms around him and thank him.

DELAL

My father never tried to impose his will on us when it came to universities. I know he was proud that we were studying because he liked people pushing their limits and working hard. What he felt at my graduation was joy at seeing the fruits of that hard work.

We studied at Armenian high schools, because that is what my father wanted for us. Political pressures had resulted in these schools being economically and academically weaker than desired, so those responsible for pupils who succeeded were given great importance. When I got into Boğaziçi University, my father took me by the hand, and together we went back to my primary school to thank my teachers. "If there's any success here, it's your success," he said, and with these words he honored them. Doing well in college and pursuing a doctorate—I took these things seriously, and my father shared every bit of my enthusiasm.

HRANT

Today, I wish to share with you my pride in one of my little ones. Last year, we sent my oldest daughter Delal to the United States to pursue a doctorate in chemical engineering at Purdue University in Indiana. This branch of engineering has come to have relevance to a key area of medicine and developed a computer program dealing with cancer cells.

On the eve of her departure, we gathered together family and friends for a good-bye meal. It was a lively evening—we sang, and I was drunk with joy. It was in those high spirits that I called her "my little lamb." And then, I said, "When mothers and fathers send their sons off to the army, they jump around, dancing and waving their arms. And now I shall do the same, but when I jump up to dance, it is to encourage you to grow and to serve humanity. And you have my full trust."

And now my little lamb has become a serious scientist. And her drunken father is very proud.

DELAL

I really lost it over that article. He had brought us up to be so wary of privilege, so it made me furious that he wrote about my "success" in his newspaper.

153

Even though I knew that underneath it was childish fatherly pride, it still upset me.

Every time I came home for a visit, my father would meet me at the airport. Once, when he and my mother were taking me back to the airport, I said, "You have more white in your hair—is it me who's aged you?" I was joking, but how sorry I was to have said this. Sorry a thousand times over. He got so upset.

"Have I aged that much? My darling wife, have I aged? Is there really a lot of white in my hair?" He turned to my mother for reassurance. But, as he did with every other beauty in his life, he came to celebrate the fact that he was getting older. Like when he first started getting a belly and tried to pull it in, he'd push it right out when my mother said, "*Aman*, Çutak. Don't make it look bigger than it is." He was obstinate. But he never got a chance to grow old . . .

HRANT

As I approached the threshold, I had some sense of the anxieties that might come with aging, but I never imagined that I would ever be able to cry, "Hurray for getting old!" That, however, has become my daily slogan. Yes. It's "Hurray for getting old," because you cannot truly see your children settling into marriage unless you do. And if, like me, you live to see them continuing the family, then you really have reason to rejoice.

The first joy was the birth of our little granddaughter Nora. At a time when the children were leaving home and standing on their own feet, and Rakel and I had begun whispering, "Is our nest emptying out?," little Nora was the miracle that proved to us that our numbers were again increasing. It felt as if we were all returning to the hearth. They say that grandchildren are different. They are right.

KAROLİN DİNK

Arat and I went into the hospital at six in the morning on the day Nora was born. As the hours passed, the hospital filled with family, but still our father hadn't arrived. I kept thinking that he must have been held up at work. Nora was born just before three in the afternoon. Everyone was overjoyed, and people were coming and going and calling on the phone. By now it was evening, and my father-in-law still wasn't there. Then, a big vase of flowers arrived. He had sent them, and they arrived before he did.

Time passed. People started leaving. The room emptied out. By now, it's night. And finally, he arrived. He sat across from me, asked me how I was, and didn't know what else to say. I remembering laughing about how fidgety he was. And I said to myself, *He's excited, too.* And I still have the card he sent with the flowers: "To my daughter, Karolin, hoping you make a rapid recovery . . ."

HRANT

Just after the birth of our granddaughter Nora, our daughter Delal was awarded her doctorate. For four years, Delal had been living alone in the

American Midwest, far from the big cities, and working on her thesis, and we rushed to join her, straight from the room where Nora had been born.

I took all of the girls in the family to their big sister and cousin's splendid graduation ceremony. I wanted them to see it, and be influenced by it, and follow in her footsteps, increasing in number . . .

It is hard to describe how fulfilled I felt as a father during that ceremony. It is my sincere wish that God grant all those bringing children into the world the chance to live to enjoy the same privilege.

DELAL

During the last years at *Agos*, he was different at home. The stress was getting to him, and he was usually tired and preoccupied. But still, every once in a while, he'd be his old lively, joyous self. When he brought the younger girls in the family—Sera, Zepür, and Maral—to America for my graduation, he was in his old high spirits. His delight was infectious, and he spoiled us so, piling on the presents. He did all this in a spirit of defiance, almost. Rejoicing in the face of all of the tension and anxiety that we were going through.

The anxiety dated back to the first time my father went on television, and it grew with every day. We were battling with very mixed emotions. All children love their fathers as fathers, but it was during this period that I came to know my father as a person, and to love him as a person. This began in the 2000s. That night on *Political Arena* when he asked, "How long have we stayed under one tree long enough to eat its fruit?"—how very right he was! But that was the first night I feared for my father. After that live broadcast, the phones didn't stop ringing. Voices saying things that you couldn't believe. So there was joy, and pride, and anxiety, all rolled into one . . .

ARARAT

When my father spoke on television, I would stand right in front of the screen, my heart beating like an animal's, sensing danger. My fear was what they might do to him for saying the things he was saying. My father had a crazy side. Anger, courage, or fear—whatever he felt, it was more than what others felt; it was extreme. He refused to accept injustice, and he wouldn't stay silent. He wouldn't suppress his anger, and he wouldn't bend. The way he was at home is how he was everywhere. He was quick to get upset, and quick to calm down, but at the moment when his temper flared, he could do things without considering the consequences. And because I knew that, I couldn't stand still, let alone sit still, while I listened to him.

It went on like this for years. Toward the end, he somehow learned how to rein in his temper. Even so, after those programs, I didn't say much to encourage him. It was only a few times that I said to him, "You spoke very well, Dad." My father loved being complimented, but he never got it from me. I never told him that I was proud of him. It felt artificial, saying things like that. Later, I kept thinking how much I wish I'd said it, but I didn't.

DELAL

I saw that something was changing, but what I was beginning to feel was fear rather than amazement. I was always proud of my father, he never did anything I thought was wrong. But I was also afraid . . . I knew my mother felt the same. We tended not to talk about it. If we'd voiced our fears, how could we have carried on as if nothing was wrong? My father was anxious, too. How could he not be, knowing what had happened in the past? He was anxious, but he continued on his path because it was the only just path.

From the first time he appeared on television, he chose his words very carefully. He spoke with an inner confidence, conveying his concerns in language that was always calm, never offensive. My father loved the old legends, and he loved telling epic tales, and he related his own history in those same tones. That was why he could reach people. Because he knew he could.

ARARAT

My father had a number of concerns about the world. Politics was just one of them, and if he focused on politics, it was because he considered it to be the best and most concrete starting point. He had a mission in life that came to him from the conditions in which he had lived, and it influenced his every thought and action. My father didn't look at the world the way people thought he did. He saw, and he believed. He was intensely aware, but he brought such a dedication to his work, almost like a missionary. I was always in awe of this, and I often wondered how, when he was so aware of how things were, he could keep building up new reserves of strength. If you look at those who think about history and those who make it, what you find is a history of two types of people. What always amazed me about my father is that he found a way to combine those two types inside one body. As keenly aware as he was of the obstacles that he was up against, he was still committed to action.

SERA

When my father was on television, fear would overtake me, and I would stand up. Not to watch those programs, not to read *Agos*, but to flee from the truth. All I really wanted was for my father to come home from work, for me to run the door and hug him, and for him to rub his unshaven face against my cheek and kiss me. So, yes, that's all I ever wanted. But it wasn't an option to flee those realities, those truths.

When they started threatening my father, when they opened those cases against him, I would quake with fear, and I would wish that I could be with him because he was the only one who could calm me down. He told me the things I wanted to hear. He would try to convince me that nothing would happen to him, which was what he had convinced himself was true. I did a lot of crying at home, and, of course, my father spent a lot of time talking to me.

When he said that he might have to leave the country, I cried a lot then, too. That time, he cried with me. "I can put up with anything," he said, "except seeing you cry." After that, we hugged each other. What I found most amazing about my father's nature was his courage and the power of his love. I was always amazed that there could be a person like him on this earth.

Later on, we spoke again about the possibility of leaving, but we couldn't make it happen. This was our home. Where else could we live? In the end, we weren't able to pack up and leave. And so we lost our father. We were severely punished for loving our country so much.

It was toward the end of December in 2006, and there was a party to celebrate the tenth anniversary of *Agos*. My father and I danced. I have a photograph of that dance, and sometimes I look at it and imagine myself back there, with my arms around him. My father was so elated that night, and he was singing all of these songs. But I will never forget how he looked when he sang that sad song: "I am on a long and narrow road, day and night I walk, I don't know how, day and night I walk . . ."

DELAL

I was at that celebration, too. I was back from Brussels for Christmas. But that's not the night that felt like a farewell. The night I cried my heart out, the night that felt like a farewell, was that last New Year's Eve that we spent together. We always celebrated New Year's Eve as a family, at home. That night, we went to a party because he'd promised the host, who was a friend from abroad, that we would come. The dinner was at an association in Pangaltı. He took me with him, but he didn't talk much in the taxi; instead, he called all sorts of people to wish them a happy New Year. That was normal for my father on special days, but, right then, there was something about it that didn't feel right. At the dinner, he was quiet; he didn't speak much. What were we even doing there on New Year's Eve? That was what I couldn't understand.

Then, we went home. The celebrations continued at the house. He decided to play Father Christmas for Nora. He never wanted to miss anything with Nora. At home, he found his joy again, but there was still something in the air that I found strange.

HRANT

As with every new year, I feel the pressure of time, and change, and speed. All of the mixed emotions of previous years come flowing back: change divided by time, to be multiplied by speed, and I think, "It works out to zero." It works out to zero. I can never factor speed into time.

Good God, to see that time has changed with such speed! Thank God that I have my eighteen-month-old Nora to come to my rescue. In spite of all of the silly hyped-up educational toys we've bought for her, she is faster than I am at playing with technology. Wherever there's a button, Nora's finger is there to press it! Now it's the refrigerator. Now it's the oven. It's not just in the technology arena that I can't keep up with her. She runs faster than me, too. She's growing fast and learning fast, too. She has all of the privileges. She has our full and undivided attention. In the old days, we'd go to visit my son. Now we say, "Let's go see Nora." And if my wife calls me to give me the good news, she doesn't mention my son or his wife, she just says, "Nora and company are coming over." She's so privileged that she's started calling me by the name only my wife has ever used for me—Çutak. She's hurled herself headlong into our marriage.

So, friends, don't miss out on your grandchildren. As we face the New Year, let us drink to their health. Let us raise our glasses and do whatever in our power to ensure that they are happy and never suffer pain. In the words of the Armenian poet Tumanyan, "May the children live, but not as we did."

SERA

We always draw lots at New Year's, and that last time, I was the one to buy my father's present. I bought him a wallet and a belt. When I gave him the wallet, I said, "The only photos you can put inside are ours and Nora's!" We put Nora's photo in right away, but I didn't have a chance to give him mine, and nineteen days later, I lost my father. He had that wallet in his pocket . . .

DELAL

I spent the first week of January in Istanbul, and then I went back to my job in Brussels. But I took that strange feeling with me.

It's so hard to speak about it . . . It brings back the taste and smell of my pain as I speak, but at the same time, my words don't come close to describing it. I'm a stranger to my own words. I can't find a way to heal. Every day, I look for my father. I miss him so much . . .

SERA

We were a happy family. My father gave a lot of importance to holding his family together. Our life was very colorful when we were all together. Now, all I see in my life is black. The only color in our lives comes from Nora, who my father loved so much, and Nare, who he never got to meet. My father was gone by the time Nare was born. The rest of us were at the hospital. Our eyes kept searching for him, as if he were going to come dancing down the corridor, singing, "Nora, Nare, hey, Nare!" But he never arrived. Our Nare was born into blackness. But Nare had a surprise for us, because as she got older, she had some gestures that reminded us so much of my father. We never mentioned it to each other, but maybe we all had moments when we hugged Nare as if she were him.

HRANT

Soon, a second grandchild, Nare, is coming. In fact, I have begun to sing her name early, because her father wants a different name. He's made up this name, Karuna. By adding an *a* to the name Karun, which in Armenian means "spring," he's invented a new name for a girl. "And so she'll be Karuna," he says.

If you asked me how I made up the name Nare, well, it comes from the ancient Armenian name Nareg. Take off the g, and it becomes a name that will sound feminine to modern ears. Actually, I didn't invent this name. It's a name you hear a lot in Armenia.

But I haven't surrendered. I am still holding on to my father's (grandfather's) rights in my determination to call her Nare. I am prepared to enter into all manner of intrigue and cunning. I have even composed the tune. As I dance in, loving Nora and Nare together, I shall sing, "Nora, Nare, hey, Nare."

ARARAT

"Daddy, you're happy!" While you are swinging your father's cradle, in comes a little sprite, pirouetting toward the breakfast table, fluttering her butterfly wings, to say, "Daddy, you're happy!" and what are you to think but that this is a message from God? So then, you leave the dream world in which you have seized every opportunity to take refuge, and you think, *Why are you intruding on our happiness, and what is this child trying to say*? When at last you understand, there is a lump in your throat: today is Father's Day, and for the first time this little child is trying her best to congratulate you, and you are a son having breakfast on his first Father's Day without a father. And all I could think to say to Nora was, "My father could beat your father."

Even in primary school, I never liked the way that my friends would boast about their fathers—when I had real stories to tell. I'd keep thinking, *Hey, you, I have a father, too, you know, and my father . . .* But I kept my mouth shut. I waited my turn. It seemed to me that there were better things for a son to do than talk about his father. And I know that you, too, wanted me to do more than talk about my father. If sons didn't defeat their fathers, how would the world go on turning? That is yet another thing that the murderers took away from us—his children's right to defeat their father.

When I brought my child to my father's house on the fiftieth day, what I longed to say was, "Father, now I am carrying two—look, here is Karuna." But my father was not there, just my father's vote. Which name was it to be: Nora or Karuna? The one you'd chosen, or the one I'd wanted? Well, you won. From the moment the doctor handed us the fruits of our labor, when I was cradling Nare, fresh from the womb, the first thing I saw was you—through the prism of my tears, I was rocking my father's cradle. *Oh dear*, I thought, *how will my father's nose look on a girl?*

The first time I looked at Nare, I looked in anger. I was, I think, angry at everything that had come in the wake of our loss because it was all making it so much harder to turn back time. But there she was, looking back at me, pure, innocent, and alive. And I felt a strange mixture of anger and love, and a knot in my heart, reminding me of you, but also reminding me that I have lost you. Death knocked on our door, and then it ran away. And now, every day, it's life that knocks on that door. It's Nora's little bare feet, and Nare's gurgling. Your grandchildren deceive you with your brothers, and I deceive you every day with life.

I can't even remember if I ever did anything for you on Father's Day. Certainly I remember giving you a few little things, and wrapping my arms around you to kiss you, and your beard brushing against my cheek, and my fingers fiddling with your eyebrows, and the cleft in your chin, and every line on your face. But I cannot remember going straight up to you and wishing you a happy Father's Day. We never had much time for such clichés in our family—just the usual expressions of love and respect, and of thanks. Some of my friends have told me that when they reached a certain age, their fathers took them to that famous place in Karaköy. Just think. There are fathers like that. But no, you never took me to a brothel. Much later, you said, "Come along with me; you're old enough," and you took me with you to the Şişli Courthouse: we were still being prosecuted.

These days, I've lost all hope of going back in time. After all, that was what we talked about during our last serious conversation. I'd been struggling and failing to grasp Einstein's theory of relativity, so I'd asked you. And now it seems that this was the last of our wonderful conversations about the universe. Now, very slowly, I'm getting used to the idea. When Nora and Nare run around the room, they will never trip on your long eyebrows. They will never talk to you about the universe. If only I could shout out to you, with all of those clichés. If only I could shout out how proud of you I was on the day you "couldn't hide your tears from the cameras." As your eyes filled with tears, I said to myself, "There he is, my father, a man stripped bare." At your graveside, a hundred thousand people honored you as a martyr. And now I am back there, standing alone, and honoring you as my father. Amen.

19

The Dink Brothers

RAKEL

They were a breed apart, those three. They lived in each other's pockets. Nowhere else could you find loyalty that deep. This is how at ease they were with each other: they would curse themselves, and even curse their mother, and then they'd realize what they'd done, burst out laughing, and throw their arms around each other like the children they still were.

I was only sixteen when we got married. Çutak's brothers were living with their father at the time. Once we were living all together in one house, they became my brothers, too. As the Lord says, "You shall leave your mother and father to become one with your husband. This will be your new family." And so these brothers were now my flesh and blood.

Now my loyalty was with them, and that was all there was to be said. I made them my brothers. They had been in my life since the orphanage. And then, after we got married, it was my job to cook for them and do their laundry. I would even look under their blankets to see if they'd left their dirty socks there. There was, at last, a woman in the house, and I wasn't going to let them keep their old habits, was I?

HOSROF

We three had no family; our mother and father were always apart. It would be more accurate to say that we never lived with them. We, who'd never had a family life, then tried to create our own families. That's why Hrant was strict with us. There were even times when he felt it just to give us a slap or two. If we succeeded in making a family of ourselves, it was not because we each did our share—it was mostly because of our big brother. He became the father of our family. As with every family, we had our troubles and quarrels, but there was one way we were different: nothing could separate us.

YERVANT

Hrant was the father of the family, of course. Not just because he was the oldest, but because he protected us. He was always there—the father standing over us, shielding us from harm.

When we were little, our mother was the one who fed us and kept our bottoms clean, and even she could not care for us all of the time. Once we

161

grew up and suddenly our big brother got married, Rakel was the one who "kept our bottoms clean." Rakel became our second mother. Then their first child was born, and this child was our child, too. It wasn't just my brother who had multiplied, it was all of us. And that's how it carried on. Seven children in all, and two grandchildren. Nine in all, yes? Whatever any of us needed, we found. There was never any talk about what was my share and what was yours.

ZABEL

Before marrying Hosrof and coming into the family as a daughter-in-law, I already knew Hrant Ahparig. He'd been a counselor at the Kınalıada Children's Camp. He was the strictest and most authoritarian of them all.

He would order his brothers around. He never paused to think that maybe he shouldn't scold them in front of their fiancées because that might hurt their pride. So, for example, I worshipped this man who I was going to marry. It really bothered me to see Hrant treating his brothers the way he did. But I never said anything, because Hrant Ahparig was the patriarch. We respected him, but we feared him, too. His brothers and his brothers' children were sacred to him.

He was the backbone of the family, but the three brothers would have such terrible fights. "Have you ever once treated me like your big brother? Have you ever even called me 'big brother?'" That's what he said to his brothers once. Bellowed. And the younger ones would yell right back: "Is that what this is all about? Are you treating us like this just to hear us call you 'big brother?'" And the amazing thing is that, even with all of his authority, he never got them to call him "big brother" once. Not until the January 19, 2007. That's the first time I heard them call him "big brother."

HAYGAN

The brothers were unbelievably close. When they got together, it wasn't possible to know if they were fighting, or just talking, or playing games, or sharing something important. It was just a lot of yelling and shouting. And they brought us into their warm embrace. We three families became inseparable. When we had children, it just carried on.

One summer, we were all in Antalya. At the time, Hrant Ahparig owned a car—a white Murat. We'd all pile into that car and go to the beach. One time, we squeezed in seven children, three wives, Hrant, his mother and his father, and then there was his cousin Satenik. How we managed to get thirteen people into one car, I cannot even begin to imagine right now. That same day, when we were coming back from the beach, there were tourists standing outside his shop. First he got out, and the rest of us followed, and we just kept on coming. Finally, one of the tourists could no longer restrain herself. "Who are all of these people?" she asked. Hrant turned around and, in German, said, "Alles meine Frau und Tochter." All of my wives and daughters. We'd become his harem.

LUSİN

They were like the elements. One was air, one was water, one was earth. It was as if they were physically connected to each other, from head to toe. That's why we seven children all feel as if parts of us are missing now. We just can't manage to make a whole.

HAYCAN

The thing about my uncle that I shall never forget is the same thing that no one else in the family will ever forget, either. When I was in the last year of primary school, I was, like all of my classmates, crazy about arcade games. Back then, we had no computer games to play at home. So, one day, I got it in my head to go to an arcade. Time passed, but I didn't notice. Then, suddenly, I heard my uncle's voice behind me: "Haycan!" He didn't say it harshly, but my first instinct was not to find out what was happening but to run. I ran and I ran until I was in the underground market, but I can't tell you how I got there. When I was little, there was no one who could run down a street as fast as me. As I was running, I kept looking over my shoulder. My uncle was running after me, dressed in his raincoat, with that golf hat he always wore and his hands in his pockets, and crying, "Haycan!" I was still running, but at the same time I was asking myself, *How can my uncle run this fast* (because I'm young, and he's old)?

But anyway, we were still running—me in front and my uncle behind—and it was after ten o'clock at night. How I got home, how I locked myself in our bathroom, I cannot tell you. I'd won the race, but I was scared to death. I never got punished, but I also never went anywhere ever again without having to hear about it.

MARAL

How lively my uncle was. How joyful. I remember him always laughing. He had such a wonderful smile. The child who most resembles him is Delal. Delal has my uncle's soul, almost. She's very hardworking, but she can be wild, too!

As for Ararat, he's unbelievably brainy. And very deep. He's the big brother I respect the most. When he married Karolin, we girls were so upset. Sera, Lusin, and I literally went into mourning. I remember sobbing and sobbing. No, it wasn't because we didn't love Karolin. When they were just dating, we didn't mind at all. But when they decided to get married, things changed. In the end, the three of us decided to wear black to the wedding. And so we did . . .

When Uncle Hrant saw us all decked out in black, he couldn't believe his eyes. "What do you think you're doing? Are you in mourning?" he asked. But I think he was secretly amused by our mischief. Inside, he was chuckling, I think. What I mean to say is that we were very happy with my uncle.

ZEPÜR

During our first summers on Kınalıada, we'd always stay at my uncle's. And he was the first one to accept that we were growing up. He was the first one to let us go to the nightclub. And if my uncle said yes, no one else dared say no. Don't ask me how someone can have a father who is not her father. My uncle was the father of our whole family.

LUSİN

I shall never forget the New Year's Eve we spent together. When I began to grow up and asked to go out with my friends instead, he said, "You'll spend plenty of New Year's Eves without us." So I would stay at home, sulking. But when the party at home got going, I'd forget all about the outside world. First, there was a huge meal. My uncle would sit at the head of the table, with one brother at each side. He'd take turns teasing them and teasing us. Toward midnight, my uncle would go missing, and *Gağant Baba* would arrive.

I think I was in middle school when Father Christmas brought me a book as a gift. That's when my illusions were destroyed. We sold books at the store, after all. How easy it was: take them down from the shelves, wrap them up, and give them to the children. The moment we figured out that the packages held books, we stopped even reaching out for them. Ararat was the only one who opened his present, and when he flicked through the pages, he found some money hiding in it. All I remember after that is the screaming and squealing as we ripped open our presents. That night, he gave us the best present ever. It wasn't the money. What my present showed me was his emotional intelligence.

By that age, I knew that my uncle was Gağant Baba, but I carried on believing in him. Right up until 2007 . . .

HAYCAN

During the years when he was setting up *Agos*, we saw much less of my uncle. It was during these same years that he started to go a little gray. Whenever I went to see him at *Agos*, I'd always find him in his office, staring at his computer. I didn't want to disturb him, so I'd wander around the room quietly, looking at the books on his shelves, waiting for him to see me. After a while, I would give up and go talk to the other people in the office. Then, my uncle would come out of his office to give me a roasting, saying, "What's all this? You come all the way here to chat up the girls and you don't even come in to say hello to me?" And I'd say, "But I was wandering around your room for ages, and you didn't even notice." He'd refuse to believe me and give me another roasting.

One day, I'd gone to visit my uncle again, and while I was waiting, I was talking to the other people in the office. My uncle walked in and, in a loud voice, said, "Haycan. How's it going, Haycan?"

And I said, "Everything's fine, uncle."

He stood there for a second or two, and then, as he turned around, he said, "Let me eat your balls." That was his way of showing his deep affection for me! I can't tell you how embarrassed I was. But it's a moment I'll remember for the rest of my life.

LUSİN

One thing I never understood was how my uncle seemed to know about everything. Yes, he had that way about him. For instance, once I lost my identification card, and I didn't tell anyone, but he knew. It wasn't just him. All three brothers were uncanny like that. They had a mystical side to them. I was always seeing them do things like this.

In the autumn of 2006, when I went on vacation to Kaş, was another time. It turned out that the friend I went to visit there lived in a house owned by a friend of Uncle Hrant's from the army. As time went on, I found out that just about everyone else there was his friend, too. I've thought of Kaş as an enchanted place ever since. I've never felt alone there, because every time I met a new person, we seemed to be more of a whole. Just like our family. Everything my uncle and his brothers touched grew. It was almost as if they had a pact with God. They were God's children.

HRANT

We three brothers brought only seven children into the world.

We were able to educate all seven at Armenian schools until college. We understood how important it was in life to maintain our mother tongue and culture.

This year, Maral graduated from Getronogan. Next year, it will be Sera and Zepür's turn. It's a shame that they will be the last.

At Maral's graduation, my friend Tomo and I were fretting again about the same old problem, saying that our biggest mistake in life was not to have had more children. It wasn't right, making do with such a thin harvest. But now the most important thing was to take pride in what we had.

Part VIII

A Sad Farewell

20

The Lost Letter

AUNT SİRANUŞ

My sister's name, Nvart, means "rose" in Armenian. She was named after a flower, but there was nothing flowery about her life. She was very troubled, my sister. Life had dealt her a hard hand. And so had her husband.

HOSROF

My father loved my mother, but my mother had no such feelings. She may have at the outset, but after what she went through, those feelings were dead.

My mother did not know how to read, but she was a very intelligent woman. By nature, she lived inside her head, closed off to the outside world. My mother's only reason for living was her children, but she didn't have the means. In those days, the most secure life for us was at the orphanage that fed and sheltered us. But whenever she was able to look after us, she did. And she was authoritative with us. We three brothers were not afraid of life. But when we were growing up, we were afraid of our mother. She might have been poor, but she was very honest. We may have grown up in an orphanage, but we always had love and respect for our mother.

YERVANT

My mother' family was very close-knit and tied to its feudal traditions. My grandmother, Ahçik, was the matriarch, and her word was law. And my Uncle Haygaz was the family's protector. Actually, my mother's family was always there for her. Had she wished, she could have gone back to her family in Malatya and led an easy life. After we were given to the orphanage, my Uncle Armenak went back to Malatya, and he took my mother with him. But she couldn't stay there; she went back to Istanbul and found a house close to the orphanage.

This was the beginning of her struggle to survive, alone and illiterate, in the big city. She had done this by choice, so she wasn't a downtrodden woman. It's interesting—she would cry about us, but nothing else could make her cry. So, really, when we're talking about my mother, we're talking about a woman who sacrificed her life for her children. And a woman who lost her mental faculties on their account.

HOSROF

When we were a little older, we started feeling great anger toward our father. Even so, he was, aside from his gambling addiction, a very good man. He didn't take much interest in us in those days, thinking that our needs were met by the orphanage, but later, when we were struggling to make our way in the cruel outside world, he helped us however he could. He took us into his house. So, after that, our feelings for him softened.

YERVANT

We were often angry with our father. We didn't exactly respect him, but in spite of everything, we loved him. He was our father. "Father" is a word that means a lot to a child, and if those expectations aren't met, then your father becomes just one of the people you love, and that's that.

My father never lost hope of getting back together with my mother one day, but my mother had no interest in this. It must have been when I was in middle school. I was living with my mother. My father started coming and going, pretending that he was there to visit me. Every time he did, my mother would scold him, but he wouldn't give up. Sometimes he would press money into my hand and send me off to her house. First, my mother wouldn't accept it, but one time, my father's excuse had some logic to it. He was giving her the money to put toward the children's needs. I was finally able to persuade her, and she accepted the money. All of this was a sign that my father was beginning to pull himself together.

One day, I got very ill. My father heard and came over in a panic, banging on the door and crying, "Let me see my son!" My mother let him in to avoid embarrassment. First, they had a fiery argument, and then a more moderate discussion, and then they started to speak to each other again. Later, my father came back with his arms full.

After this episode, I started inviting him inside whenever he visited on weekends. My mother could say nothing. These comings and goings increased in number until all of the relatives had heard. My Uncle Haygaz came to Istanbul from Malatya, and they had a very long talk; he probably convinced her to give him another chance. My uncles and my father would come to the house for coffee, as custom dictated, and the two families would gather together and discuss the matter and bring it to a satisfactory conclusion. Everyone came that day. Everyone but my father. He'd got lost in a card game at the coffeehouse and forgotten this meeting that could have changed his life.

RAKEL

He was a softhearted man, my father-in-law . . . When we were married, he was the only one who opened his arms, and his home, to us. Çutak still had resentments from the past, but, even so, there was never a single scene during the time we lived together. Çutak was never affectionate with his father, the way he was with his Aunt Siranuş and his Mari Bibi, but he also knew that his father was the only one who had opened his arms to us. It was four years before we could afford to move out of that ramshackle house in Feriköy and move into our own home—the first home we could afford to rent, in other words. And when we moved into that house, we took his father with us. We couldn't leave him there!

He also lived with us while we were at Tuzla Camp. Nvart Hanım was with us then, too. But they never talked to each other. By then, of course, Nvart Hanım wasn't speaking to anyone.

ARARAT

I don't remember seeing my grandfather around the house, just outside. I'd see him wandering around Bakırköy. He was always buying me *döner*. Sometimes he'd drop by to take me out. He loved me very much, and I loved him very much. He was tall and slender. He was handsome, my grandfather.

I never got much of a chance to see my father and my grandfather together, but whenever my father spoke about him, I could always hear the love in his voice. When the three brothers were talking among themselves, they'd talk about his habits. When they played cards, they'd mimic him.

DELAL

My grandfather had his own house. In the morning, he'd stop me on my way to school and give me pocket money. Even if I got upset or refused, he would still give it to me. I knew he and my grandmother weren't together, and that there were tensions between them.

He was always coughing. Then, one day, when we'd gone out for a meal after a ceremony, we received a phone call and found out that he had died. He'd suffered a heart attack while alone in the house. I remember feeling angry, wondering why he'd had to die so alone. It was an anger without a clear target.

HOSROF

We'd taken him to the doctor the week before. The doctor had given him pills to lessen the risk of a heart attack. We were looking in on him every day. That day was Sera's baptism ceremony. "Check in on him before we go to church," my big brother said. I went in, and there was my father, sitting in his chair. He was in his pajamas. His pills were next to the television. He hadn't been able to reach them. I thought he was asleep. This was the first time I'd seen death, and it was only later that I understood what I had seen.

YERVANT

By now, my mother had lost her mental faculties. Before this, she had come close to burning down her house. They said that the stove had caught fire while she was cooking meat.

HOSROF

My mother thought only about us, and she was terrified that something might happen to us. So strength meant everything to her; she would put all of her faith in it. And when my brother and I were arrested in Tuzla, her illness became more apparent. She fell in love with Kenan Evren, the most powerful general of the September 12 regime, believing that his strength would save us. Before that, she was in love with Küçükgüzelyan. As the director of the orphanage, he was the most powerful person there—a man who had been father to hundreds of children, including us. There is probably no need to say that these infatuations were platonic.

AUNT SİRANUŞ

Then, when they went to live in Bakırköy, Hrant took her in for good. In those days, she'd come to see me everyday. "I'm disturbing you," she'd say. "Please excuse me."

And I'd say, "Please, sister, please come in." Who else was going to give her their time?

And then she'd say, "Come on, now, sister. Let's go see the children."

Her mind was gone by then. We'd go off to Beyaz Adam—the old store. She'd stop at the pharmacy on the corner of the *meydan* and spend a long time peering around her. "Take a look, would you?" she'd say. "Are the police going that way? Could they do anything to my children?"

"My dear sister, the police go past here all the time. Come on, now, let's go into the store. Look, there's nothing to be afraid of," I'd say, and I would take her into the store. And the children would kiss their mother and tease us a little, too, and then we'd go back. She could think of nothing but her sons. Something was going to happen to them. Someone was going to hurt them. She kept saying that, and then something did happen . . .

ARARAT

My *yaya*—my grandmother—was just a normal person to me; I never found her behavior strange. I loved her very much, and she loved me. She loved all children, really. But she was absolutely devoted to her own.

No one was good enough for them. For my mother and the other wives, she could be a difficult mother-in-law. She complained a lot, and sometimes she even swore.

But the things my yaya did that others found odd didn't seem odd to me. She would sit with her head bowed, swaying back and forth. She would stay there thinking, and maybe thinking about who was plotting against her, for hours on end.

DELAL

She'd tell us stories, but because she swore in daily life, the characters in her stories swore, too. My mother would get very angry with her for that.

Her stories were both shocking and entertaining. And maybe that is why I remember them so well.

She stank of Maltepes. Her fingers were yellow from nicotine. At home, she sat inside a cloud of smoke. Arat and I would hide her cigarettes. When it looked like she was about to find them, we'd race off, each one blaming the other, as she came after us.

She deteriorated physically toward the end. She stopped looking after herself. She'd scrape the floor with her slippers. She ate normally, but she complained about not being able to eat. And sometimes she would say, "If I died, it would set me free."

RAKEL

She was not a well woman. She was once admitted to the Bakırköy Psychiatric Hospital. She stayed there for a month. She went often to the doctor, who had her on various medications.

Nothing satisfied her, and she was always complaining. For me, this led to a lifetime of spiritual struggle. I knew the Lord's word. The truth of the matter was that I found her contrary character unacceptable, but nonetheless I had to accept her. So that was why I withdrew into my own world, where I battled with the word of God. "Your battle is not with the armies you can see, but those that remain invisible," says the Lord. So I looked to the army inside me, and I battled with it in my internal world. And this battle will never end.

When my mother-in-law was with us, I was like a robot. I was cut off from everything, and in my internal world. Such fear inside me. If there was fear inside me, that meant that there was a part of me that belonged to the devil, and I'd think, *I have yet to vanquish him.* "Take this fear away from me and go," I'd tell the devil, because I am the child of Jesus, and you have no place here. This was how I battled with myself. These were my internal conversations. And this is how I managed to keep going for many years.

AUNT SİRANUŞ

When Nvart first got out of hospital, she came to me. I gave her a bath. She spent one night here, and then she got up and went back to Hrant's house.

One day, I had just gotten back from the village. She called me up and told me that she'd twisted her ankle. "Please come over, sister," she said. "I've been waiting for you for three days now." So I went straight there. Vartanuş was going to see her, too. We met in the street and went up together.

Nvart was in her room. "This morning, I woke up," she said. "I looked down from the balcony, and I almost jumped. But then I thought that if I fell on top of a car, I wouldn't die, so then I didn't."

"Oh please," I said, "don't do anything like that. Look, if you did anything like that, they'd throw your children into jail." I said this in all innocence, to scare her. Then we put her into the bath. We gave her a good wash. We dressed her. We clipped her nails. Rakel was at home, but she had to go to Arat's school.

"I have some business to see to," I said. "Let me go and take care of that, sister, and then I'm taking you back to the village." I put her into bed, and I tucked her in. I left the house. I had just turned the corner when she threw herself off the balcony. If I'd known that was going to happen, would I have even left the house? I was planning to come back that evening to take her away with me.

AUNT VARTANUŞ

"Let me set myself free from this life," she said. "I want to jump, but Hrant would get worried. He would be upset. I had Maral write a letter for me, saying that no one should be upset."

And I said, "Don't talk like that." My sister-in-law Siranuş was there with us. Nvart hadn't had breakfast. We got her a bottle of milk. We had her drink the milk. We put her back into bed. Then she got up, and my sister-in-law said, "I'm coming back this afternoon and taking you to the village." I heard Rakel saying that she had to go out, too. Then we left.

RAKEL

That day, the little girls were with me, too. The aunts came over. We ate something together. At one point, she'd told Aunt Siranuş that she was going to kill herself. Commit suicide. Aunt Siranuş got very upset and came and told me that this is what she had been saying. And I reassured her, "Don't worry. She's said this so many times already." Then, the aunts left the house.

About ten minutes later, I went into the bathroom to get ready to go out. I was brushing my teeth when the doorbell rang. She was closest to the door. *She'll answer*, I thought. The doorbell rang again. No one was opening it. She was the one who looked after the telephone and the door, so if she hadn't . . . With that thought, I went flying out of the bathroom. She was nowhere to be seen. Through the door, I could hear our downstairs neighbor. "Rakel Kuyrig," she was crying, "please come down right now!"

As I ran down the stairs, I already knew what had happened. I began to pray. *Oh, Lord, what am I to do? Help me, please*, I begged. They're probably already blaming it on me. A crowd had gathered around her. They're looking at me, and I'm praying . . .

MARAL

I had just learned how to write. That morning, we were at Aunt Rakel's. I'll never forget. My yaya was wearing a white undershirt that day. She came over to me, gave me a paper and pencil, and asked me to write something down for her. It was just one sentence: "My sons never once did me wrong." She had me write this for her because she didn't know how to read or write. So my yaya's last words were written in my childish hand. I wrote them without knowing what they meant. Later, we got a phone call. It was during that phone call that I first heard the word "deceased." I didn't know what that meant. I went to Sera and Zepür and said, "Our yaya has deceased." They didn't understand, either.

I remember the sentence that my yaya had me write for her very clearly because so many people asked me about it. And, for years, I repeated it. But we've never been able to find it. The police came and asked about it and did a search, but we couldn't find it. Had my grandmother given it to me, and I put it somewhere? Or had she put it somewhere? I don't know. But I remember seeing my childish words on that paper.

AUNT SİRANUŞ

I came back and there, in front of the house, it was doomsday. Zabel must have heard, too, because she was rushing toward the house but saying nothing. I found Hosrof at the door. His face was ashen white. He tried to bar my way. Then, finally, I got through, and there was Hrant, with his face in his hands, saying, "Mama, how could you do this to me?"

DELAL

My father never hid his sorrows. I remember his silence. This silence went on for days and weeks. I remember feeling angry at my yaya when I saw the state her children were in. How could she do this to her children?

RAKEL

After this happened, my husband buried himself in silence. He wouldn't talk to me. This went on for months. And I waited . . . It was very hard, of course, but I prayed, and I waited.

HRANT

My mother's name was Nvart. If you asked me to describe her, I'd begin with her smell. But there's no way to describe it. It's a mother's smell. There's nothing else like it.

My mother killed herself. She threw herself off our balcony. From the sixth floor.

I was at work that day. In the middle of the day, we got a phone call telling us to come straight home. I knew something bad had happened. I flew out of the store and began running. Our house was very close by. I looked and saw people gathered around the front of the house. Someone was lying in the middle of the road, covered in newspapers. I lifted the newspapers, and there I saw my mother. Covered in blood . . .

Book Two

Baron Hrant

Part I

Looking

21

Hrant's *Agos*

HRANT

The birth of *Agos* was shaped by the conditions in which the Armenian community was living. The newspapers published in Armenian were no longer enough for us because the majority of Anatolia's Armenians knew only Turkish and thus had no access to the Armenian press. This meant that communication inside the Armenian community had broken down. Also, the Armenian community, which until now had been a closed community, wished to open up to the outside world.

Furthermore, we needed to defend ourselves in that outside world because there they were telling a different story about us. At the time, the word "Armenian" had become a curse word. Some people linked us with the PKK (The Kurdistan Workers' Party) and others with ASALA (The Armenian Secret Army for the Liberation of Armenia). And we Armenians were hiding in our houses like worms, listening to what they said about us on television and doing nothing. Privately, we railed against these lies, but we did not raise our voices. But now the time had come to make a stand . . .

One day, the Patriarch Karekin Kazancıyan II called me in to see him. He showed me an article of the sort I was just describing from that morning's *Sabah*. It was accompanied by a photograph in which Abdullah Öcalan was standing next to a priest, and below it, it said, "Proof of the PKK–Armenian alliance!"

They called me and a few friends into the Patriarchate Council to ask what we could do to counter these lies. I gave my views, saying, "It's time for you to end your silence. Do a press conference." This was a risky business, but both the domestic and international press attended, and the press conference was a great success. After this, we said, "Why stop at a press conference? Why not bring out a newspaper?" That's how we got the idea for *Agos*.

One of our main aims was to open the Armenian community to society at large. To be a window and a door.

ANNA TURAY

The road to *Agos* began in 1994 at the Patriarchate. At the time, Turkish press relations were being run by a deputy of Patriarch Karekin II named Mesrob Mutafyan. We were a small group of volunteers who had come in to help them.

One was Hrant. He was lively, courageous, radical, and also rather rough. In the beginning, he even seemed a bit boorish to me, but after a few meetings, I came to see how forceful he was in his thinking. I was there from *Cumhuriyet,* so I had good professional connections, while Hrant was very enterprising. In a short time, we established close relations with Turkey's leading intellectuals and journalists. We began to educate them about the Armenian community. Once we were working effectively as a press team, we slowly came around to the idea of starting a newspaper in which our voices could be heard. It wasn't just that the Armenian community wasn't properly understood by the Turkish public—we weren't communicating properly among ourselves, either. And just as we were not communicating with other non-Muslim groups inside Turkey, we had other problems with the Armenian diaspora. This was particularly the case for Armenians of Anatolian origin. To achieve all of this, we needed our own newspaper. At the beginning, Hrant had proposed a weekly magazine. We agreed to make it a weekly publication but in a newspaper format to make it easier to read.

LUİZ BAKAR

Since 1993, I have been the press secretary at the Armenian Patriarchate, though in fact I am a lawyer. Hrant and I were both on the press commission. He was writing book reviews for the *Marmara* newspaper under the pen name Çutak. He'd always had close relations with the Patriarchate. He'd tell me that he'd loved Patriarch Şnorhk Kalustyan enough to call him father. He was also very close to Patriarch Karekin II. He was even closer to the patriarch's deputy, Mesrob Mutafyan, who was the public face of the Patriarchate. The idea of a press commission was one they developed together. And the same went for *Agos.*

HARUTYUN ŞEŞETYAN

I'm actually an engineer, but I was the fourth member of the press commission. The Patriarch's deputy, Mutafyan, called me into the Patriarchate, and that was the first time I met Hrant. Hrant was a brash, swarthy, and courageous Anatolian lad. He was very plain-spoken, very natural. It could be said that the idea of *Agos* was first broached in the Patriarchate, but only because that was where we happened to be at the time. Mutafyan called us together as a press group, and the idea emerged as we were talking.

When we were discussing possible names, Mutafyan thought we should have a name like *Selam* or *Merhaba,* or perhaps the Armenian *Parev.* Then our journalist brother Rupen Maşoyan, who had been listening to us in silence, suggested *Agos.* The newspaper rose out of this type of intellectual consensus. Hrant Dink, Anna Turay, Luiz Bakar, and I were its founders. Sarkis Seropyan took charge of the pages to be published in Armenian.

SARKİS SEROPYAN

I am actually a heating technician. I was just getting ready to retire when a proposal came from Hrant. "We're bringing out a paper. Would you like to be in on it?" he said. I agreed at once: first, because I liked the idea of this newspaper; second, because I trusted Hrant. If this wild boy put it in his mind to do something, it always happened.

The word *agos* is a village term shared by Armenian and Turkish, and it means "the furrow opened by the plow for sowing seeds." Hrant liked this very much, but he still did a referendum. He chose a moment one morning while the girls who came in as volunteers to clean were still dusting and cleaning the windows. Hrant called these young ones together and asked, "Should your newspaper be called *Parev* or *Agos*?" Everyone knew what *parev* meant. "What does *agos* mean?" they asked. Hrant explained, after which they said, "It should be *Agos*." I'll never forget it. Hrant had them raise their hands, and he did a referendum.

DİRAN BAKAR

I'm a lawyer. For years, I'd been involved in lawsuits concerning the minority foundations. When *Agos* was still under discussion, Hrant said, "That's enough, let's not delay any longer. Let's bring out this paper as soon as we can." After that, things became more serious. That evening, we met with the other founders. We still hadn't found an executive editor. I looked at the time, and it was past midnight, so I said, "All right, I'll be the editor. Put my name on the masthead."

LUİZ BAKAR

The legal documents were still being prepared. The first pieces were just coming in when Hrant suddenly announced that the newspaper was coming out. We couldn't believe him "Enough is enough," he said. "I'll take responsibility for this." The newspaper needed to get going, and, by the skin of our teeth, we did it.

SARKİS SEROPYAN

We had the courage of the ignorant. As I said, we had a *khent* as our leader. We rented a third-floor apartment in an old building and went straight to work. Six months later, in January, we put out a pilot issue. We distributed it for free. In April, we brought out our first real issue.

Those early months were one long scramble. Everyone was arguing with everyone else. And each time, in the end, Hrant turned out to be right. He was very farsighted, and he was good at getting the lay of the land, and his analysis always turned out to be correct.

ANNA TURAY

Luiz Bakar had good relations with the most prominent members of the community, so she was in charge of advertising. Because she was a lawyer and kept abreast of all cases involving the community, she made good headlines with the news he brought from court. Harutyun Şeşetyan took care of the finances.

We decided that rather than make one person responsible for raising money, we would share it among us. Later, we were able to support the paper with a subscription system. In the beginning, we printed the paper at the plant of my own paper, *Cumhuriyet*. For a while, we paid nothing; they were very helpful to us. The founding partners—Hrant, Luiz, Harutyun, and I—all put in our own money. At our meetings before the launch, we talked at great length about who should be editor in chief, but no one wanted to take this on. We all had other jobs. In the end, Hrant put himself forward. We also lacked a lead writer. Then, one day, without any prompting, Hrant wrote a column for page 7. He signed it as "Leapfrog," a nickname from his ball games with Ümit Kıvanç. That's where he got the name.

HRANT

Many people have asked me why I sign my column "Leapfrog."

Well, it arose from my own life one day, all on its own. We were finishing the last page of our first issue, and Nuran cried out to me, "Hraaaaant! Come on, now, and decide what you're going to call your column so we can put this page to bed." While she was shrieking, we were a short distance away, making penalty shots into a goal—three arms wide—with a paper ball made from sheets of our pilot issue. We'd been pinned to our chairs all day, and now, like all children, we wanted to play. And at one point, we said to each other, "So, what do you say? Let's play leapfrog." You know, that game we all played when we were little. But Nuran wouldn't let us. Tugging our arms, she was calling us to another game: playing journalist. She sat us down in front of our computers. "This is where you can play leapfrog," she said. And then, once again, she asked me what name I was going to use for my column. And then it came to me. Leapfrog.

It's a lovely game, leapfrog. You bend down, and your friend jumps over you, shouting "Hooop!" Under normal circumstances, he could jump much farther using your back as a support than he could on his own. It's fun playing with a lot of people, too. You bend and they jump. They bend and you jump.

Playing journalist at *Agos* was something like playing leapfrog. We let others jump over our backs. We supported each other, just like we tried to support our community. "Come on," we said. "We'll bend down, and you jump over us. Let's cover distances we wouldn't be able to cover on our own."

ÜMİT KIVANÇ

It was in 1996. That was when we met. Hrant was someone who knew what he wanted, but didn't know how to do it. What he wanted was what something I wanted, too, so I came to his aid. I said that I would design the paper and stay on through the first two issues. I think I must have spent four, four and a half, months at *Agos*. Everyone there was new to the job; no one had the experience. Work that should have taken two days took four or five. We were working until midnight, and then we were taking all night. Even when we were going through the various logo choices, we were already squabbling. That's how stubborn he was!

In most things, I am a fastidious professional. This wasn't a game. We were starting a proper newspaper, a newspaper that both friends and enemies would be watching. Obsessed as I was with precision and perfectionism, I found myself standing up in fury at an emergency management committee meeting one morning, faced with a demand that would ruin all we had done to date. When this man, not seeming to take in the bitter truth that our paper would not be printed if we did not get it in by a certain time, pinched my cheeks and said, "Oh, you can do it, my friend."

I said, "My son, you're not an urbanized Armenian, you're a Turkish peasant!" That's what I said to him at the end of the first month. Later, I started calling him the "so-called Armenian." I even introduced him like that a few times: "Meet Hrant Dink, the so-called Armenian!"

ANNA TURAY

Ümit was a very difficult man. He spoke without thinking how his words might sound. In fact, at the very beginning, I put off introducing them. I was afraid they might eat each other, and that was why, once all of the articles for the first issue were ready, I took them over to Ümit Kıvanç. Beginning with the logo, he laid out the whole paper, page by page. After that, Ümit and Hrant met and got to like each other very much, but their slanging matches were beyond belief. Especially playing on the cliché, "the so-called Armenian genocide," used by the Turkish state to deny it ever happened, and calling Hrant the "so-called Armenian."

HRANT

We were genuine. We played our game with enthusiasm, enjoying every moment. We respected fair play and we supported each other. Not once did any of us land by mistake on another's back, not once did we crush the person we jumped over. Did we reveal any flaws, make any mistakes? Too many to count. Everything we did, we did with the innocence and enthusiasm of children. This applied to our good deeds as well as our mistakes.

ANNA TURAY

During the first years of *Agos*, our main preoccupation was working out the paper's political line. The conservatives who counted as the Istanbul Armenian establishment did not welcome the newspaper. In the community's Armenian daily, *Jamanag*, they didn't even mention the launch of *Agos*: this was because we were challenging the status quo. They were also uneasy that most of the paper was in Turkish, because this, too, upset the conventions of a closed community. There was no end to the gossip about us—everything from rumors about our being a state organ to rumors about our secret backers. When we started publishing, there were many people who said that *Agos* wouldn't last.

HRANT

The first problem we ran into was the antagonism of the conservative Armenian press. They predicted we'd be gone in six months. Some papers didn't even report the paper's launch. For some people, publishing in Turkish was a backward step. Meanwhile, we struggled to explain that by using Turkish, we hoped to do good things for our community.

Agos **began with an initial capital of $28,000, and this we achieved with the money put in by our friends, the founders of** *Agos.* **The founders were not just those who put in their work and gave us the benefit of their experience, but also those who pulled together that capital. And I am happy to say that at no point did** *Agos* **seek or receive financial support from outside donors. We managed to keep going on our advertising and circulation.**

Others tried to peg us as the voice of the Patriarchate, whereas all they gave us was moral support. And that was how it continued.

One man who provided continual support was Patriarch Karekin II who, despite so many people urging him to stand in our way, described *Agos* **as "God's Easter gift to the Armenian people." Standing at his side was his deputy, Mesrob Mutafyan, arguing that we needed a newspaper in Turkish and stressing the importance of reaching Armenians who could not speak Armenian.**

ANNA TURAY

It was important for the paper to be mostly in Turkish. With most of Istanbul's Armenians having emigrated to other countries, our community was now composed mostly of Armenians who'd come to Istanbul from Anatolia. Because most of our schools and churches in Anatolia had closed their doors very long ago, most of these newcomers could not speak the language. What's more, the existing publications were in Armenian, and they spoke to a closed community. We were aiming to be a young and dynamic newspaper that could reach everyone and that was attuned to current and world affairs and developments in the Turkish press.

HRANT

The history of Armenians migrating from Anatolia to Istanbul goes back thirty or forty years. Previous generations of Armenians living in Istanbul could speak and write Armenian as fluently as water. So what were the wretches coming in from Anatolia to do? They'd had to struggle to survive. And where were the schools to help them save their

language? Where were the churches that would bring them up to the level of Istanbul's Armenians?

Nevertheless, the first thing they did when they got to Istanbul was send their children to school. But did anyone ever factor in the adults who didn't know Armenian? Did they follow the logic of the dead being gone, so it's best to look after the living?

At the moment of launching *Agos*, and even as we continued, we encountered an astonishing degree of deflection and defamation in certain circles, and this raised interesting "what ifs." The Armenian language was in these circles both capital and commodity, and by and large, there was no wish to share it.

One reason why the number of people speaking and writing Armenian in Istanbul has sunk to its current levels is exactly this merchant mentality. Show me one capitalist willing to share his capital with others. If you are looking for objective data to support my allegation, you can find it in the number of writers, painters, literary scholars, and journalists this community has or has not produced over the past fifty years. The number, you will find, is zero. It didn't produce a single one. Or, rather, it didn't educate their young to become such things.

One of our aims in starting *Agos* was to serve as a sort of intellectual kitchen for young people; to bring out of our community the social scholars and intellectuals of the next generation.

KARİN KARAKAŞLI

I'd won a short story competition for young people. Hrant Dink came to the prize ceremony, and no sooner had we met than he began telling me about the new newspaper they were starting. Later on, they invited me to *Agos* for an interview. This was when they were putting out the sixth issue, and by the time it came out, I was already working there and learning how to write the news. Ümit Kıvanç was in charge of the layout and training Nuran Ağan, while the editor in chief, Hrant Dink, was struggling to master journalism.

LEDA MERMER

I was in my last year of high school. I heard at school that a newspaper named *Agos* had called to say they wanted to interview students preparing for college. I'll never forget my surprise when I walked in. They didn't even have any office furniture. Whatever you'd have in a normal house, that was what they had. And it was on that first day that the newspaper proprietor and editor in chief Baron Hrant, who was doing the interview, said, "I can see the excitement in your eyes. Would you like to come and work for us?" I found myself working on the layout of the newspaper. There were just two of us in the technical department being trained by Ümit Kıvanç.

KARİN KARAKAŞLI

Hrant Dink was someone with a great faith in young people. He believed that the Armenian community had not given its young people a proper education, and he was asking challenging questions about education in his writings. He was also was trying to make *Agos* into a newspaper for which young people felt comfortable writing. On our three Armenian pages, he gave great importance to news that might interest young people.

He was always tussling with Seropyan, Gobelyan, and Maşoyan, saying, "Come on, now, boys, enough of this stilted literary language. Make up headlines that people can understand."

He had me write a column in my primary-school Armenian. In the beginning, I really struggled. Then I started taking language and literature classes, and I saw that, with encouragement, you could achieve anything. Later, I wrote a column for *Agos*'s Turkish pages. After Diran Bakar left, I was in charge of the editorial section for years. Hrant was able to see in people gifts that they didn't know they had, and he knew how to bring them out.

ARİS NALCI

I am currently the news editor at *Agos*. I first met Baron Hrant in 1996, when I was still a high school student. They called from the paper to say tha tthey wanted to do an interview with us, and off we went to that ratty office. Hrant Dink himself did the interview.

When I was in high school, I didn't much like reading Armenian newspapers because of my experience in school. Armenian was an ornate language that was hard to teach, and the books they used were old. It was the lesson we liked least. What you knew of your mother tongue was whatever your family spoke at home, so Armenian newspapers used the same language that they used in class. They couldn't say the word "Patriarch" without adding a paragraph of adjectives, and that paragraph would stop any child from reading further. My Armenian started improving when I went to work at *Agos*.

When Hrant Dink and I met again many months after that first interview, he remembered me right away. At once, he pressed a camera into my hands. Off I went into what they called "the archive," which was really the editorial team's kitchen. To make a long story short, it's thanks to Hrant Dink that I became a journalist.

SARKİS SEROPYAN

Even though we had become so close, Hrant still addressed me using the formal "you" in front of others. He even added the honorific *Baron*. In Armenian, *Baron* means "Sir." Actually, it comes from the French, but the Armenian custom of addressing male teachers as Baron began in Istanbul. It wasn't long before Hrant, too, became known as Baron at Agos. For the young people working with us, there was no other form of address possible. The only exception was Karin. She was younger than the rest of us, but because she was so mature and so hardworking, she was soon Hrant's "right hand."

KARİN KARAKAŞLI

In the early days, *Agos* managed to bring the generations together to create a family atmosphere. Over time, Hrant brought in most of his books from home into the newspaper.

Our first place in Dolapdere had a floor space of 60 square meters, and the furniture consisted of a dining room table that Luiz Bakar had acquired at a foreclosure sale. *Agos* never had an office atmosphere—not at the beginning, and not later on, either. Hrant turned every space he used into a home, and that was how he treated it.

Then we moved into the top floor of an office building in Pangaltı. It was mostly sweatshops in that building. The elevator was always breaking down under the weight of their bales of cloth and our newspapers, so we'd have to go huffing and puffing up seven flights of stairs. We also had a little mouse there. We called it Mıgır. It had a habit of coming out on Wednesday nights and sliding across the floor, chirping. There were also pigeons roosting on the windowsill opposite.

When we got fed up, all we had to do was go out to the big balcony in the front, but Hrant would get very angry at us if we sat on the sides. Later, I found out that this had to do with his mother's death.

In the winter, water would come in through the ceiling. We'd sit there wearing hats and gloves. We all had electric heaters at our feet, which is why some of us scorched our chairs. We had carpets on the floor. Hrant had even brought one of the big ones up on his own shoulders. He was the one who made it feel like home there. He was the one who called the woman in charge of the kitchen Anna Mayrig. It was very important for him that we had food cooked for us on the premises, that we all had enough to eat.

ANNA MAYRİG

When I went to work at *Agos*, it was still early days. I spent ten years of my life there. I saw the good days and the bad. It was like a home. He'd even eat breakfast there. If he was happy, he called me Anna Mayrig, and if he was angry, it was, "Anna! Come in here, girl!"

When he was angry, he'd shout at us all. He'd roar. I'll never forget the morning when Leda was a little late. He punched the door so hard that he shatter the frosted glass. Then he slammed his door and shut himself up in there for hours.

I was in charge of the tea, the coffee, the food, everything. Once a week, he even sent me off to get his shoes shined. He'd walk around in socks until I got back. He'd send off the girls to buy him trousers and jackets and ties and things like that. Then he'd take some water from my teapot and shave and get all dressed up, and go off to his meeting.

When visitors came, he'd ask me to make coffee. He didn't drink coffee himself because it upset his stomach. He drank a lot of tea, but even this he drank light. He wouldn't eat bulgur. He called it chicken feed. He liked the egg dish *menemen*. If I made rice with chicken, I would serve the meat to the young ones; he asked me to keep the bones for him. He'd take them out one by one and gnaw them. Mostly he ate dishes with potatoes, but what he liked more than eating the potatoes was dunking his bread in the sauce. When he was finished, he'd carry his own tray back into the kitchen.

LEDA MERMER

Baron Hrant would stay up all night, working at in that ratty office. It had stone floors except in his office, where there was wall-to-wall carpeting. He'd sleep on the floor. He did a lot of all-nighters in this office, too, but not on the floor—in his chair. And there was this blanket that he wouldn't be apart from. When he was very tired, he would wrap himself up in that blanket and lie down on the floor. He also had a wardrobe bag with shirts and jackets in his office, in case he decided to go somewhere at a moment's notice. He'd shave at *Agos*, and sometimes he even took a shower there. He wandered around in socks and slippers. He always had the television on in his office. He'd watch the news channels. And in the afternoons, the horse races . . .

KARİN KARAKAŞLI

We only became aware of this horse-racing thing when we moved to this building. Even if the most important guest in the world had just arrived, he'd come into my office to fill out his form. I had my own office here, finally. He'd joke with me, saying, "This matchbox is just about the right size for Karakaşlı." His own office was always very dark. I called it "the cave," because sometimes he really would retreat into his cave. Everything in his office was old and made of wood. Hanging over the door were the cowbells I'd brought him from Switzerland. Every time you opened or closed the door, they tinkled. Hanging on his walls were Anatolian paintings given to him by an Armenian artist who had dropped by on his way through. And there were also photographs of clerics who had served the Armenian community, such as Patriarch Şnorhk; of famous writers, such as William Saroyan and Hagop Mntzuri; and of an old Armenian grandmother. And everywhere, statues of horses. The bookcases were bursting with books. The whole place would be a shambles, but when the paper was put to bed on Thursdays, Hrant would see his chance and do a big spring clean.

LEDA MERMER

There weren't many men working at *Agos*. As time went on, new female colleagues joined us. We'd finish the issue toward midnight on Wednesdays.

After sending it off, Hrant would pile us all into his car and, one by one, drop us off at home. He saw this as his duty. Maybe because he was accustomed to carting around bales of books, he always drove a station wagon. In the early days, his car was pomegranate red, and the car he got next was navy blue. But usually it was so dusty that you couldn't tell what color it was. Inside the car was a shambles, too. He wouldn't lock the doors, and he drove erratically.

Most of us lived in Kurtuluş, but a few lived in Bakırköy. Hrant was our personal driver. When it was cold, he'd wrap a scarf around his head, and then he'd look like a Kurdish *peshmerga*. Once, we'd left the paper very late, and near Kurtuluş, we were stopped by the police. Only girls in the car. And Hrant at the wheel. The police asked for our identity cards. They asked us where we were going. And what did Baron say? "The girls and I have just finished work, and I'm taking them home." And he said it so naturally that the police just said, "Fine." Afterward, we all burst out laughing. We laughed all the way home.

One interesting thing about Baron Hrant was that he was color-blind. If he started confusing red with green at traffic lights, it was our turn to tease him, of course . . . and we'd have so much fun, we'd forget how tired we were.

HRANT

Come, let's play the "color Game." As it happens, I'm color-blind. What can I do? What God gives, his slaves must accept. I can't for the life of me tell green from red, and that is why, for a very long time, I was unable to get a driver's license. I kept failing the sight test. And when confronted by a book putting those shades side by side, showing a shape or a number, I would mix a fish with a bird, and call a tree a house.

I remember putting my foot in it by saying, "What lovely green eyes you have," when complimenting my hazel-eyed beloved wife. And I cannot forget how much fun my children had with me, asking, "What color is this? And this?" Every time I mixed them up, they'd burst out laughing. It was no different from the commotion my coworkers make when we stop at traffic lights when I'm dropping them off at home.

ANNA TURAY

Hrant ran Agos like an amateur. He was dedicated, but his amateurishness was tiring. Months had passed, and still he hadn't set up any systems. Whenever I had time to spare, I'd rush over to *Agos* from *Cumhuriyet*, but there was nothing I could do to bring order to the chaos. Hrant and I started arguing. "You all leave me here to do the work alone, and then you come by on Wednesdays to pass judgment," he said, and he was right.

Hrant chose to hand the editorial department over to young people with no experience. He gathered around him a team of amateurs just out of college and, over time, he trained them. In the meantime, he trained himself, too. One of these young people was Karin Karakaşlı. Karin knew several foreign languages, and she was well-educated and hardworking. She did everything from writing columns to running the editorial office. She was Hrant's right hand. And in the 2000s, when Hrant became one of Turkey's most prominent figures and couldn't find the time for *Agos*, Karin carried the paper alone for a long time.

KARİN KARAKAŞLI

In the chaos of *Agos*'s early years, we began to grope for some sense of the paper's identity. We could say that Hrant was looking for an identity for himself as well as for the newspaper. With this in mind, he set out to define the values of the Armenian community. He looked at the way the community lived, discussing its religious feasts, its history and culture, its arts, and its language.

For Hrant, another aim was to challenge the negative perception of Armenians in Turkish society. Beginning with the hostile accounts of Armenians in textbooks, he asked courageous questions about the extent of prejudice in Turkish society as a whole. It was the first time that an Armenian in Turkey was doing this.

HRANT

I am sure that most of you have a lovely minority story from the past that you like to tell now with nostalgia. When the time is right, I have no doubt that you tell these stories with sighs. "My father's master was an Armenian . . ." "Our neighbor Mari Yaya's bean dish *pilaki* was so good we'd lick our fingers . . ." "My army friend Kevork and I were like blood brothers . . ." I am sure that you all tell personal tales like these every day.

We are so used to how unaware you are to how these tender nostalgic caresses of yours can feel more like slaps. And we are also used to the fact that you still see us like your antiques. That you even make a hobby out of us. However, this superficial curiosity is, in the end, an act of selfishness.

The real question is this: 'Why did they disappear?'

KARİN KARAKAŞLI

At the same time that Hrant was reminding his own community of its Armenian identity and shaking it up as much as he could, he began to address Turkish society as a whole because the nation had forgotten that this identity even existed. In the beginning, when he set out to speak to them about the Armenian issue, he never asked about what happened in 1915. He talked instead about Armenians' contributions to Turkish cultural values. He described what it was like to live in Turkey as an Armenian, and why. He used his own experiences and observations as a starting point.

HRANT

"Solitude cannot be shared." So said the poet Özdemir Asaf. An open-air theater is my stopping point today. They're putting on a big music festival. And what a lovely name they've given it: *A Lyrical History.*

The program has everything, and all of its music has roots in this country's history. Every tune resonated with the culture of those who played it, playing as they marched by. Turks, Greeks, Jews, Circassians, and so many others, sharing their diverse cultures in the same garden and gracing the same stage. It's hard not to feel excited.

But there's a sour pit in my stomach as the program continues, for this garden has no room for us Armenians.

What a shame! How could they not know those tunes that we all learned by heart? Or the great Armenian composers? Was it that they couldn't find anyone to sing their songs? I feel like shouting out, "Even I could have sung them for you!" Everyone around me is so happy. But me? I'm all alone.

By now, I am walking around angrily. Verses and songs pouring from my lips of their own accord.

What can we do? Must we start from the very beginning with those who have erased us and relate the whole history of Armenian music, theater, architecture, and our great service to all of the arts in this country? We shall, of course, without ever losing our tempers or our enthusiasm.

But first, let's come together to share the loneliness of lyrics.

KARİN KARAKAŞLI

Turkish society knew nothing about its Armenian minority and nothing about the ways in which Armenians were discriminated against by the Turkish state, and that is why they got away with it.

One of the biggest problems facing the Armenian minority was the state seizure of property. And for Hrant, this was also a personal issue. With its seizure of Tuzla Camp, the state policy toward minority foundations was there for all to see. He campaigned to make visible the violation of what he called orphans' rights.

DİKRAN GÜLMEZGİL

I attended the Karagözyan Orphanage Primary School. For ten years, I have been the director of the Karagözyan Foundation, which runs the orphanage that gave me shelter when I was a child.

I had a dream: to regain the land and property that had had been confiscated by the state and to restore what the foundation rightfully owned. When I came to this post, there was a parking lot and an open air market on thefoundation's property. For twenty-five years, it had been standing there, crumbling. First, we took our case to court, but the mafia and so forth gave us a hard time; in the end, though, we were able to evict them.

We had long meetings with the tradesmen and came to an agreement. In 2006, after six years of struggle, we were finally able to take back our property. Hrant's *Agos* was with us all the way. Their news pieces and articles researching the legal dimensions of the case informed our struggle.

HRANT

The case opened by the Karagözyan Foundation to reclaim its property paved the way for our line-by-line examination of the countless cases opened by the foundation's General Directorate against minority foundations over thirty years. Dear God, how had all of these cases concluded as they had? How could the state allow it? How did our community leaders become this helpless? How was it that no one stood up and asked for justice? It's not the way people think . . .

"It is noted that entities with non-Turkish legal identities can no longer own property. Because legal entities are stronger in relation to real people, and their right to property had not been limited, they posed various threats to the state, giving rise to a number of objections . . ."

The above lines came from a decision made by the Supreme Court of Appeals against the Greek Hospital in Balıklı. Later, it was used as the legal justification for the expropriation of property owned by Greek, Armenian, Jewish, and all other minority foundations. So, this is it: the decision that led to twenty-five years of seizing property owned by numerous minority foundations!

The crucial issue we wish to point out here is not the interpretation of the law. Our quarrel is with the designation of those confirmed as citizens of the Turkish Republic on their identity cards as non-Turkish. Isn't this a form of separatism? How could they have permitted it? Are Turkey's Armenians and members of other Christian minorities citizens of this country or not? This is the real question. According the Court of Appeals, we're not—we're foreigners. But, then, what is the meaning of the words that we, too, recite every morning in school: "I am Turkish, honest and hardworking . . ."

Now, just imagine what would happen if someone from one of these minorities came out and drew on this decision to assert that he was not Turkish—the powers governing this country would scoop him up, throw him in jail, and make him crawl on all fours. Am I right? So what gives them the right to discriminate in this way? And how is it that our highest court of justice, which exists to pass independent judgment, could unanimously decide on this interpretation? Who is going to resolve this contradiction for us?

DİRAN BAKAR

Hrant and I gave everything we had to the struggle on behalf of the foundations whose property had been seized, this being one of the Armenian community's largest concerns. We worked shoulder to shoulder. Whenever one of these cases came up, I would go straight to Hrant. He would report on the cases, drawing upon our legal observations. But even this wasn't enough: he would write about it in his own columns.

The 1936 declaration presented a very complicated issue. Toward the end of the early Republican era, in 1936, when the Foundation Law came into effect, minority foundations were asked to make declarations of their property. So, in other words, if someone died and left their property to a foundation, the deeds would carry the foundation's name.

Later on, there was uneasiness about this arrangement. Because they did not want the foundations to expand, they made it difficult for them to acquire new property. Following a 1974 Court of Appeals decision, permission to will or donate property was removed. And so it was that they opened up cases against all minority foundations—Greek, Jewish, and Armenian—and seized these properties. The interesting thing is: this Court of Appeals decision made during the military regime following the March 12, 1971, coup made this unlawful arrangement retrospective. This impacted all property acquired between 1936 and 1974. This was how they managed to take away the Tuzla Camp where Hrant had spent his own childhood and to return it to its former owner.

We lawyers had been fighting against this for years, citing case law and statutes and arguing that it contravened the Lausanne Convention, but the turning point was when, with the help of *Agos*, the general public became aware of this great injustice. *Agos* chased the stories, did an inventory of the victims of the 1936 declaration, and supported the foundation directors seeking redress. The one who did all this, the child who did all this, was Hrant. When he spoke about these things, there was no legalese, no murkiness, and no confusion because he could take the most bureaucratic matter and show how it affected normal people in the course of their lives.

KARİN KARAKAŞLI

The newspaper was slowly establishing its viewpoint. In the 1997 elections of the directors of the Armenian foundations, Hrant Dink and *Agos* made their voices heard. With its news reports on the elections and its interviews with candidates, the newspaper was in election mode many weeks in advance. It was not enough to take the pulse of the Armenian community; sometimes the paper was the very manifestation of that pulse. Infected by Hrant's enthusiasm, everyone started swarming in to the newspaper. What began as interviews became, after a time, sermons that he was preaching to himself. During those first elections, everyone working at *Agos* witnessed and shared his enthusiasm, be it through his laughter or his bursts of anger.

HRANT

The newspaper staff has begun to call me "boss" recently, even though I do nothing but bend over backwards for them. I knew from the outset that I would have to take on the job of editor in chief. And whoever makes the decisions, holds the power. This can be a dangerous thing. Even if you anticipate it, even if you know how serious it all is, like it or not, this

is where you end up. When you make the final decision, those working with you surrender their freedom to become your subjects. You say two words, and then it happens. And one day a sly friend shakes you up with the slogan of the day, scribbled a little piece of paper: 'You are our father, whatever you say, we shall do.'

LEDA MERMER

Baron Hrant didn't like it when people didn't agree with him. And it was hard for him to agree with them. In later years, when the editorial and technical service meetings were brought together, I started attending them, too. That's when I found out how things were . . . Baron Hrant would ask everyone for their views. You're right, he said, and then he'd have his own way. Actually, hardly anyone came out against him. But still he'd put things to a vote. He was democratic but after his own fashion . . .But he also had a very harsh side to him. Everyone was terrified of it. Maybe it was the ones who took it most seriously who got into those shouting matches. The biggest arguments were on Wednesdays, when we were putting the paper to bed.

There were some terrible outbursts at the editorial board meetings in August 1997. After one such meeting Anna Turay and Yetvart Danzikyan left the paper. And that Friday, for the first time, Hrant didn't come in to the paper.

ANNA TURAY

I left Agos because of personality differences and concerns about its approach. The newspaper was becoming a power base. I had come here to do journalism, and I did not want the paper to become a base from which to run the community . . . In my view, that's unprofessional. Furthermore, I felt that the democratic consensus we'd enjoyed at the outset was changing. Our arguments were becoming more personal.

I definitely severed my links with Agos. And Hrant, of course, never came to me to ask why. I respected his position and I left. Now, when I look back, it all seems so very sad . . .

HRANT

Most of my friends tell me that Agos is generally considered to be synonymous with Hrant Dink, and that this is not a good thing for a newspaper.

This criticism does have merit . . . It may have not been what I wanted, but this is what happened. It's been quite a job, bringing Agos' aims and principles into being, and setting them into motion; it called for a special kind of dedication, stubbornness and courage, and from the beginning, this responsibility fell to me. I must admit that I'm better suited temperamentally to working alone than I am to working in a team. That said, I never wanted to be a manager. I never would want to sit at the head of any institution anywhere. That is why, at the outset, I resisted the idea of being the editor in chief. Managing wasn't my forte. It's not what I'm best at. I would work hard, and I would be creative, but I was not a good manager. In the end, I wasn't able to relay all this to the friends with whom I embarked on this mission.

I was desperately eager to get *Agos* started and established as soon as humanly possible. I was willing to putting aside all of my other businesses to work toward this ideal. The others were not in a position to do the same. Under these circumstances, I was obliged to put myself in charge. As I said, there was no other choice, and, like it or not, I became the "head" of *Agos*.

If only I could be a good manager. If only I could still be working with the group of friends who founded it; if only we were all still working together at *Agos*. I could say that I was sad to have failed to make this happen, but let me also confess that I felt no remorse about those who left. Because I am the sort of person who goes his own way and says what he thinks, the people with whom I work are always changing. And, anyway, that was the one principle that we had from the very beginning. The doors of *Agos* are always open. People can enter, and they can leave . . .

KARİN KARAKAŞLI

Agos wasn't like a newspaper—it was like a dervish lodge. You never knew who was going to come in next. From the beginning, it served as an unofficial information center. All kinds of people would come in: students working on their dissertations, journalists on assignment, reporters from foreign newspapers, and people saying, "Could you help me, brother? My grandmother's village was once Armenian. Could you have a look at it for me?" Autistic children would come and help us pack up the papers. It was a refuge for all sorts. Homeless people from Armenia. Women who'd been left to live rough lives with their children. And Hrant's old prison friends were never far away, either. *Agos* was a place where good-hearted madmen honored the mad spirit of Hrant himself.

ARİS NALCI

There were always a lot of mad people at *Agos*. It's still like that. You have to be mad to work here. Which of us could you call clever? Whoever you were, Hrant would find a job for you. When I first arrived, there was Azniv Kuyrig, for example. She was older than all of us. She had no husband and one child. She'd been through a depression and didn't speak. She and Arman would spend hours together in the archives, clipping newspapers. There were others like that, too. If I call them mad, it doesn't mean they had no brains, because some of them were very smart indeed. Baron Hrant was always yelling at Arman, saying, "Is this how you go through these papers?" But he also knew that Arman was never going to leave. We knew this, too. He's still the backbone of our archives section, and he runs it however he sits fit.

SARKİS SEROPYAN

It didn't take long for us all to get worn down by Hrant's Khent-ness, because it was colossally difficult to work with him. I was sorry when our first friends left, but we had to keep going. "Look," he'd say to me, "you'll see. There will be a Before *Agos* and an *After* Agos. People will come to think of *Agos* as a milestone."

Hrant didn't make many mistakes, but this was one of them. People don't say Before *Agos* and After *Agos*. They say Before Hrant and After Hrant. Because he was the milestone."

HRANT

There was a time when it was impossible to imagine an Anatolian neighborhood without its mad people. In Anatolian culture, there was at least one in every neighborhood or village. In Malatya, ours was named "Crazy Gaffar." The tradesman's joker. The housewives' harmless bully. The good child's friend, and the bad child's monster. He'd stone those who stoned them and play tricks on those who played tricks on him.

If you talk to the older generations of Malatyans, I am sure that they will all remember him with the same affection. What they'll mention first is how he'd "put everything out in the open."

Listen to how the merchants of the time would boast about him, as if he were their own creation. "We'd take the wretch and dress him up nice. He'd take a long look at himself, and don't tell him to hurry up. But it wasn't for nothing. What we really liked to do was to make him rip the clothes off. 'Oh, look, Gaffar, that's a shroud you're wearing.' We'd say that, and he'd rip it all off. And he would be left there, in only the skin he was born in. But Crazy Gaffar—he was stark naked, and off he'd go. All through the neighborhood, in full view of women and girls. The women would chase him off with stones.

So now you're asking me, *Why are you telling us this story about Crazy Gaffar*? I don't know, but all I can say is that when *Agos* celebrated its second birthday, Crazy Gaffar came back into my mind. That's all. Because don't some people think that *Agos* is the madman of the Armenian community? The truth is that this was a label we actively sought out. Haven't we been playing the wise fool for two years now? And did we not somehow manage a few successes?

I know what you're going to ask next: "Fine, but what does that have to do with Crazy Gaffar tearing off his clothes?" Well, how much can *Agos* achieve as an "activist newspaper in a stagnant community?" The truth is that we are happy with our name. Even if the community is stagnant and maybe a little dead, when we raise various subjects, and they shout, "That's enough! No more interfering; no more criticism!" and try to put some of their shrouds on us, what can we do but follow in Gaffar's footsteps? But let it be known that if anyone ever tries to trick us into wearing a shroud, Wwe'll tear it into shreds and roam around in our innocent nakedness, right until the very end. We're open to madness, but our madness is illuminated by reason, and it comes from the heart. As long as they don't try to turn us into Gaffars.

22

From the *Agos* Perspective

HRANT

The man whose work you are reading in this column is not a writer. Until three years ago, he had no involvement, close or distant, with the world of journalism. He read a great deal, but that was as far as it went. His writing was full of grammatical errors, clumsy sentences, and corrections that were not correct. Generally, he wrote as he spokebecause he didn't have much in the way of a literary style. He knew nothing of writing technique, having never studied it in school. Just to look for this column is to understand how very modest it is. You can find his column on the page where they run the continuations. And isn't this the page where they squeeze in things that can't fit onto the front pages? Every week, he sketches a few thoughts into whatever empty space is left. There have been many weeks when there has been no room left at all.

When you take all of this into account, then it makes perfect sense that he writes under the name of Leapfrog. You know how they say that there are places where madcaps can do their own thing? Well, this is an expression custom-made for the man whose work you are reading in this column.

Those close to this man know all of this only too well. They know that he is the soul of recklessness. In his relations with other people, there is no middle ground. If he loves them, he loves them with all his soul. If he hates them, he hates them to the marrow. If he happens to run into someone he considers a soulmate, it doesn't matter how solemn the occasion is, and it doesn't matter if the room is crowded, nothing will stop him from kissing that person to his heart's content . . . over and over.

KARİN KARAKAŞLI

By the time we were entering our third year, the newspaper had become some sort of civil society hub. Foreign journalists came in to speak to Hrant, as did representatives from political parties and civil society organizations, and I ended up becoming Hrant's interpreter for English and German. It was astonishing to me to see how easily he established a rapport with each and every visitor, be they journalists or diplomats. Suddenly, he'd plant one hand on the person's knee as he confidently explained himself. No one who came to see him left without having been profoundly affected.

One of Hrant's inventions was the page entitled "From the *Agos* Perspective." In certain issues, he reserved the last page for special reports, using the logo of a man taking a photograph. We had the bright idea that he had chosen for this logo a man with thick eyebrows like his own, and so we had a lot of fun with him.

Hrant would invite the directors of our foundations to use this space to exchange views on our social structures. Thus, Agos affected the first serious mapping, from its own perspective, of the Armenian community: the Patriarchate and the churches, the foundations and the associations, the hospitals, the schools and the graduates they turned out . . .

Agos's first big test was the election of the new Patriarch because it was overshadowed by a long history of state minority politics.

LUİZ BAKAR

Following the elections for our foundations, we were faced with another election following the death in March 1998 of Patriarch Karekin II, who, with the support he gave *Agos*, carried a special importance for us. It wasn't long before election fever took us over. Two candidates emerged: the first was Şahan Srpazan, and the second was Mesrob Srpazan, with whom we had worked closely when we were setting up the paper. *Agos*'s candidate was, of course, Mesrob Mutafyan II. We threw ourselves into his campaign heart and soul. And I can say that it was during this election that we first became aware of our own power.

SARKİS SEROPYAN

From the perspective of the Armenian community, the 1998 elections for a new Patriarch were very difficult. Bearing in mind that they had to be bishops to be eligible, there were just two candidates. But when the Turkish state became involved, putting its weight behind one of these candidates, those in the Armenian community with close links to the state came out against Mesrob Mutafyan. At this point, things became complicated, of course. Once it was clear that the state was taking sides, the elections were thoroughly politicized, after which there was no stopping Hrant! The injustices he had seen in the course of his life had yet to be accounted for, so he just kept going. With the help of *Agos*, he was able to help Mutafyan to a degree he would never see again. And it was while he was playing a key role in the election that he also displayed the Armenian community's dirty laundry for all to see.

HRANT

Minorities are not simply left in the hands of the officials at the Minorities Bureau of the Security. It is well known that certain members of our community utilize their connections with various state organizations as capital within the community. And so it was that a person I had never

met, but whose name I had heard many times, came to pay me a visit at *Agos*. "So you're Hrant Dink, are you?" he said, and then he launched into his speech. "Look here, now. I read you, and I like you, so if you ever run into any trouble with the state or the police, please come straight to me. I can solve it immediately, don't you worry." Politely, I demurred. I haven't exchanged greetings with him once from that day forward.

My esteemed readers, there is a very big difference between belonging to this country's majority and belonging to its minorities in that—even for the smallest matters—we must deal with an agency inside the security services known as the Minorities Bureau. So you're looking for a director to head your foundation? You must pass through that bureau. So you're holding an election, or working for an association, or applying for a passport? In all of these cases, that bureau will be your first stop.

So now it is being said that these people are playing an important role in the election of a new Patriarch. Now if these people hope to use the radical right press to frighten the community and do what they wish with the ballot box, what shall we say to them? They are free to carry on. For our community might witness all of this with fear and a little sorrow, but when they reach the ballot box, and in that little room where they stand alone, they can put right all of the insults of this campaign with the vote they put into that box. It is really that simple.

SARKİS SEROPYAN

Until the 1998 Patriarchal election, our subdued community had not been accustomed to airing its internal disputes in public. When a newspaper like *Agos* aired those disputes in Turkish, there was widespread consternation.

And then we looked and saw that some people in the Turkish press were suggesting that the Turkish state was opposed to Mutafyan's candidacy. We noticed that one of them was the editor in chief of *Hürriyet*.

HRANT

In his *Hürriyet* article entitled "The Armenian Community's Difficult Election," Ertuğrul Özkök claimed that the state was "in possession of several negative reports on Mutafyan." These reports were said to be critical of his overly warm relations with Yerevan and various pointed remarks he had made about the Armenian issue.

We are familiar with this sort of aspersion. What they all have in common is that they neglect to tell us who has made the denunciation. If we looked into these denunciations, we are pretty sure that we would find a very small number of names behind them, by which I mean just a few members of our community.

In the aforementioned article, there are passages addressing the Armenian community that exceed their purpose, offering veiled threats.

In summary: "There is good reason why minority communities let themselves be guided by the sort of people who shy away from disputes with the state. This is needed not only for their own but also the country's peace. One must not insist on an attitude that one can do whatever one likes vis-a-vis the state, as this would open up wounds between the community and state that would be difficult to close again."

SARKİS SEROPYAN

All of this revived ancient fears inside the community. Following this, the circles inside the community with links to the state launched a campaign of threats and negative propaganda. There were whispers; there were rumors. But in spite of all this effort, Mutafyan won in the end. And there was something else just as important as the election results themselves, and that was that the Turkish Armenian community voted in the largest ever numbers. It was thanks to the vigorous efforts of *Agos* that this was achieved.

DİRAN BAKAR

In November 1998, *Agos* faced its first unexpected recall order for its 130. issue. The reason was an article by Yervant Özuzun criticizing the Wealth Tax from fifty seven years ago. It was clear that *Agos'* entry into minority politics was beginning to cause concern in high places.

It fell to me as the executive editor to go in to the prosecutor's office to make a statement. Hrant and I found ourselves in the State Security Court, charged with "openly provoking in the people hatred and enmity with regard to race and ethnic difference." There, we offered information on the 1942 wealth tax, which had applied only to non-Muslim citizens. We spoke of how wrong and how unjust it was: instead of taxing everyone according to what they earned and owned, it was, we said, a measure to discriminate against some citizens on the basis of race, class, and religion. We spoke about the camps, especially the camp known as Aşkale, where Greek, Jewish, and Armenian citizens unable to pay these high taxes were sent to do forced labor. We argued that this measure had resulted in a loss for all of Turkey. Our defense must have made its mark, because the judges made a unanimous decision to acquit us.

HRANT

All of those people who gave *Agos* three months to live, and then six months, and then a year—how disappointed they must be.

The man writing this column will never forget the phone call from the person who wrote so many of his own columns about him, or the day that this person said, "Six months from now, you'll get what's coming to you, and where will you hide then?"

But the man writing this column paid him no heed. He continued along the road he knew to be just. And the paper kept going, safe and sound to this day. Recently, as you know, *Agos* was tried in the State Security Court and acquitted. The man writing this column says, "This acquittal is proof that *Agos* has come of age, or, in other words, it was the most serious test of its will . . ."

SARKİS SEROPYAN

After *Agos* was given its recall decision, Hrant began to openly attack those in the community who were operating as state informers, saying, "I know how the game works, and I know who you are." As soon as Patriarch Mutafyan was elected, he started cozying up to the very people who'd run the slander campaign against him. And so they profited from what they had done during the elections. It upset Hrant greatly to see Mutafyan honoring these people without once calling them to account for their actions.

HRANT

On the evening of the day that he was elected Patriarch, Mesrob Srpazan and I cried with joy, but it proved to be our last embrace. That same day, I noticed him giving favor to the group that had opposed him during the campaign. I expressed my misgivings in my column, saying that "today is not the day to express our joy in winning, but the day to comfort our sorrowful brothers."

From that day on, I took care not to show myself too much in the company of the Patriarchate elders. By then, people were talking too much about the influence that *Agos* had wielded in the election and starting to say things like "Hrant Dink is to all intents and purposes the community's secular Patriarch." The Patriarchate elders might take exception to such utterings, and so it seemed best to know our place and retreat into our corner. It seemed better to let him choose his own circle of advisors and for us to keep our usual distance and retire to our newspaper. So we would go to see them only if we had been invited, and we attended as journalists, nothing more.

EFRİM BAĞ

I served for three terms as the director of the Kumkapı Meryem Ana Church (Church of St. Mary of Blachernae in Kumkapı) Foundation. We supported *Agos* from the beginning, and, in the Patriarch election, we supported Mutafyan. In those days, there were no divisions. I shall never forget how, on the day Mutafyan was elected Patriarch, Hrant fell to his knees in Meryem Ana Church, saying "Thank the Lord" as tears flowed from his eyes. But what's done is done: immediately after the election, our Patriarch changed, whereupon Hrant began to criticize the way the Patriarchate spent its money. Things everyone had been witnessing in silence for years, Hrant was now discussing openly. He wanted the community to "secularize,"—to separate the church directors and the school directors. He wanted transparency. He went so far as to suggest that all of the donations collected for our schools should be put into one pool and distributed from there; in this way, even if the schools received relatively little, they could cover their educational expenses. He said this because our community had always had its wealthy foundations and its poor ones.

We were already speaking about these things, but when Hrant started writing about them openly in his newspaper, the Patriarchate and its circle became uneasy. Rumors about Hrant began to make the roundsbecause he was breaking taboos . . .

HRANT

Opening up taboo subjects is hard enough, but it's even hard to keep these discussions from slipping into other channels. And now, finally, *Agos* was ruffling feathers by questioning the order of things and making suggestions abhorrent to those who put religion at the center of our inward-looking community—namely, that our foundations should be transparent in their dealings and less tied to our church. These parties then kicked up a fuss, going so far as to claim that in saying that our churches and schools should be separated, so that the priests look after the churches and laymen look after the schools, this Hrant Dink is actually entering into a power struggle with the Patriarch.

As always, they made their first moves in a most insidious way. They started a whispering campaign—always the most powerful means of communication in a closed community—which they supplemented with privately circulated emails in which they branded Hrant Dink an informer who was trying to bring down the entire community.

I have raised three children, and now they are all grown, and they protect their honor at least as much as I do. I have always stood up for a society in which they, and my wife, and my brothers, and my close friends, and my comrades can hold their heads high, and that is what I shall continue to do in future.

ARARAT

Transparency and secularization stood at the heart of my father's dispute with the Patriarchate. My father wanted education to be secularized, and he argued that the church foundations should no longer be in charge of the schools. But this was never seriously debated in such terms. Inside the community, it boiled down to a dispute between Hrant Dink and Mesrob Mutafyan. It was seen as a power struggle.

I would never say that my father was the Armenian community's secular leader. Many in the community admired him because he was saying things no one else dared to say. But there was also fear, and that's the long and short of it. The things he said made people uneasy. The Armenian community did not fall in behind him, whereas a leader is someone who has followers. My father was a lonely man because he was a revolutionary. With what he said and what he wrote, he tried to transform our society, but our community shrank away in terror. They weren't used to people standing up and saying what they thought. They were afraid of standing up for their rights—afraid that this might lead to strife. The foundations, for example: the entire community had a responsibility here, but my father was the only one who spoke about it in public. And so, little by little, he became a spokesman for civil society. He became a spokesman because no one else was speaking. If only there had been, because it was a state of affairs that made the Patriarchate circles increasingly uneasy. And this was the second dimension of the dispute between Hrant Dink and the Patriarchate.

DİKRAN GÜLMEZGİL

Hrant's candor created uneasiness in large segments of the community because, in one sense, he was trying to bring a new order to the community. Those who were doing wrong feared that Hrant might find out and expose them. Even if the people behind the Patriarch secretly agreed with Hrant, they didn't support him in public.

With time, Hrant began to argue that the Patriarch should not have the last word on every matter and that the community should "secularize" and become "transparent". We also thought that the Patriarchate should no longer act as the single authority. We wanted a civil board to take on the Patriarch's burden. Whether the Turkish state was going to let that happen was another question, but, in any event, it hadn't come to that point yet.

HRANT

The Armenian community of Turkey does not have a representation issue; its one and only issue is secularization. Before there can be a new sort of organization to bring about this secularization, there needs to be a change in mentality. In effect, this society has plenty of civil organizations already; however, they do not present themselves as such. From the hospitals to the foundations, from the associations to the sports organizations and choirs, we see secular structures in place. But the problem is that none of these can speak, make statements, invite guests, or organize events without first gaining the permission of the Patriarch. These are civil organizations without civil status. And so the question is not about civil or spiritual representation. It is a question of mentality.

LUİZ BAKAR

As the Patriarchate's press secretary, I was not convinced by Hrant's case for secularization, and I was totally opposed to his call for transparency. Finding the Patriarchate's expenses excessive, Hrant called for all of these expenses to be clear and transparent. New tricks for old dogs, in other words! This led to strained relations, and after a heated argument in 2001, I left *Agos*.

DİRAN BAKAR

We were continuing along the path we had set for ourselves when the paper had its second confiscation order. In 2001, around the time of the foundation elections, *Agos* faced a confiscation order for the second time. The order was prompted by an article Hrant had written under his own name.

HRANT

If April 23 is one of Turkey's best-loved dates, April 24 must be the date that it loves least. The first is the date that was agreed on by our National Assembly and entrusted to our children and our future, while the second is the symbol of the Armenian genocide, which is Turkey's biggest problem with the outside world.

April 24 is the focal point of the Armenian world's systematic efforts to influence public opinion. It is acknowledged as the "darkest day" in Armenian history. Wherever they might be in the world, Armenians make banners and take to the streets, for on April 24, 1915, and especially in Istanbul, Armenian intellectuals, writers, artists, teachers, lawyers, doctors, and members of parliament were taken, one by one, from their homes and, with the exception of just a few, were never to return.

What some call the "Armenian genocide," and others call the "Armenian relocation," and the official history of Turkey terms the "Armenian Deportation" began a few days later within the borders of the Ottoman Empire.

The only Armenians who keep quiet on April 24 are the Armenians of Turkey. They can neither take to the streets nor build monuments in honor of their ancestors. There are very good reasons for this. Above all, they are afraid; they are timid. Beyond that, there is the anxious desire not to weigh their children down with dark memories.

And though they are mortally offended to hear the word "Armenian" used as a curse and to see the Anatolian Armenians blamed for an endless succession of mass graves—but never a single one in which the skeletons are acknowledged as their own—they dare not even speak of the victims of April 24, lest they offend the society in which they live.

But this does not mean that they have "abandoned their ancestors to the past and forgotten them." They undertake to continue their legacy every day that they live and to protect their language and culture. As long as they have the strength, they will continue in this courageous task.

KARİN KARAKAŞLI

In this article, Hrant was quoting from an Armenian source that described the arrest of Istanbul's Armenian intellectuals on April 24, 1915, and their removal to Ayaş, never to be heard from again.

He ended it by saying, "If all across the globe, April 24 is commemorated by Armenians and foreigners alike, and if nothing happens at all in Turkey, then perhaps this is where we should begin. When Armenians and all other Turks can gather together in our own meetings of remembrance to show our respect for the pain and suffering unleashed on that day, then we shall have moved much closer to a resolution. When we have arrived at the point that we can celebrate April 23 together and commemorate the 24th April as one, the Armenian issue will have ceased to be an issue."

HRANT

On account of my article entitled "One Day . . .April 24," our newspaper was once again given a confiscation order by the State Security Court, and, once again, I was called to give a statement. We didn't even report this, so as not to cause our readers anxiety. Nevertheless, I sensed something strange behind this confiscation order. After all, the same article appeared during the same week in the weekly *Aktüel*, but in that case there was no confiscation order whatsoever. The truth is that I felt there was something going on under the surface and that the community's little mice had been keeping themselves busy.

The next day, when I went in to see the prosecutor, there was no need for me to even speak. The prosecutor understood things perfectly and found no grounds for prosecution. He removed the confiscation order. Then, without having me say a word, he wrote my statement, signed it, and said, "It is such a pity that we keep seeing these things happening to the press, but don't worry." With that, he sent me off. What can I say? We managed to avoid getting eaten by the rats, and that was the positive side.

SARKİS SEROPYAN

This is how our community is, you see . . . Because we have been kept down so long, we have our snakes. Instead of standing up to a man, they try to bring him down by going behind his back—informers, in other words. Hrant knew them by sight, and he kept track of them. After being pardoned for the second time, he said, "Never mind, my friend. Don't let it get to you. Continue on your way. Let's look after our own business."

KARİN KARAKAŞLI

The first rift between *Agos* and the Patriarchate lasted a very long time—from 1998 to 2007. Sometimes it was a quiet parting of ways, but from time to time something would happen that would escalate things.

But Hrant's interest was not limited to the Armenian community. During this same period, he became involved with Turkey's leading intellectuals and welcomed them into *Agos*. While progressive and democratic writers and scholars came to take an interest in Armenian identity and minority issues, he became similarly concerned with Turkish issues. And, gradually, a group of these intellectuals became part of the *Agos* staff.

BASKIN ORAN

When they were setting up *Agos*, Hrant asked me to write for them. At the time, I was writing for another paper, so I wasn't able to accept the invitation, but as a gesture of goodwill, I sent a piece to the first issue. Then, in 2000, I called Hrant at last. "I am saving the top righthand corner for you," he said, adding, "but I can't pay you much." I was shocked, because it never occurred to me that he was going to pay me anything.

In those days, I was teaching in the University of Ankara's political science department. Even so, we would speak on the phone every day and exchange views. I also gave him critiques of the paper. The only thing he didn't want my views on was the Patriarchate. That was one subject he wasn't going to let me critique.

After I joined the cadre of *Agos* writers, I wrote only one piece to which he objected. I'd sent in a piece that was sharply critical of the Armenian diaspora. I was railing against them as a single entity because, in those days, that's how I thought of the diaspora. He picked up the phone and told me that it wasn't going to have the effect I desired, but if I insisted, he was going to put the piece in as it was—whereupon I softened the style a bit. We came to an agreement.

TANER AKÇAM

We were in close contact while Hrant was setting up *Agos* and also afterward. Then, in 1997, I was forced to leave Turkey to return to my academic career in Germany. One time, when I came back to visit, Hrant invited me to write for *Agos*, adding, "But, hey, I'm not going to be able to pay you much." I agreed at once. We called my column "Now and Again" because I couldn't write regularly. This made Hrant very angry. Even the last time we saw each other, he said, "If you don't start writing regularly, I'm going to kick you out, you hear?" At the time, he thought it very important that he had opened the paper up to me. "My friend," he said, "there's not another paper in Turkey that would publish you. So when I take you on, I'm taking a risk." And so it was that I became *Agos*'s first non-Armenian writer.

I wouldn't take any money for my columns. Instead, he covered the cost of translating some books I needed from Armenian. From Germany, I went to work at a university in America. But the farther away we were from each other geographically, the closer we became. We kept each other informed on important subjects.

ŞAFAK PAVEY

I began to write for *Agos* in 1997, at Hrant's suggestion. Even before that, in the summer of 1996, not long after I'd had that horrible accident that left half of my body lying on the train tracks, he was asking me to write for him. Although I didn't accept right away, as soon as I had pulled myself together a bit, I began writing for him. My column was called "Notes from Abroad" because I was receiving treatment in England at the time. Until 2004, when I became responsible for UN External Affairs in Teheran, I wrote for *Agos* no matter where I happened to be in the world.

AYDIN ENGİN

Hrant was asking me to write for *Agos* from the very first issue. Because I was working for other papers, I wasn't able to do so for the first few years. His newspaper was a brave community newspaper, which shook the timid, silent Armenian community to its very core. But his own demeanor there was just terrible. Hrant was an "artisan." He was an old-fashioned boss with no use for modern systems and management, and the place had the most unbelievable collection of helpers, assistants, and apprentices.

He was in charge of everything, and only he could make the decisions. I lost count of how many times I told him how wrong all of this was and how he should give the young ones responsibility for some decisions and let them take the initiative. But he wouldn't listen. Only later, when Hrant became known as the Armenians' "voice of courage" and began to travel abroad a great deal, did he begin to move in this direction. But he still remained a law unto himself.

MASİS KÜRKÇÜGİL

Agos was a phenomenon, and it was Hrant who made it so. Without Hrant, there would have been no *Agos*. But it's also a miracle that he was able to do it at all. As far as I know, there is no other minority newspaper remotely like it. There he was, talking about the community's baptisms and weddings, but also discussing the banned socialist poet Nazim Hikmet and then taking sides in the Patriarchate election as well as supporting a socialist party in Turkey's general elections. No one could have conceived of such a paper, and how much Hrant himself foresaw this, I cannot say. But there you are, he did it.

Agos became an orchestra. Hrant was a maestro who gathered together people you could never imagine together and brought their voices into harmony. I imagine that even the singers were shocked by the music they created together. If, for example, you asked our heating technician, Sarkis Seropyan, if he'd ever imagined a newspaper running Professor Baskın Oran and Professor Taner Akçam side by side, I am sure he would say that he hadn't. As for the young ones on the paper, they had no idea what was going on. And the readers— the paper they bought was not the one they expected, so there's that, too. As I said, *Agos* was in every way a phenomenon—because Hrant himself was a phenomenon. Agos was not the sort of paper that a clever man would ever bring out. Only a wild man could do this . . . a *khent*.

HRANT

We published the first issue of Agos in *Zadik* (Easter) of 1996, on April 5, 1996, but we never observed that as the anniversary: it was always Zadik. Whenever Easter falls in any year, that is the day on which we celebrate

the anniversary—on the day of the resurrection. Or, to put it differently, we equated our own birth with the resurrection. And so, here we are again. Easter has arrived, and we are celebrating our tenth anniversary as we enter our eleventh year.

We are proud to have been able to achieve a number of the goals that we set for ourselves over this decade. We have been particularly successful in bringing the Armenian community's internal issues to the Turkish mainstream press, thereby gaining the attention of the political and academic worlds as well as society at large. By now, there is no issue that Turkey's Armenians have not been able to air in the public domain.

Another of our successes is to have taken the word "Armenian," for ninety years used as a curse, and given it true meaning and respect. If Turkey's Armenians can wear their identity with pride today, it is, in my view, thanks in large part to *Agos*.

As for the window that Agos opened between Armenian and Turkish society, it did not just allow those inside to look out—it also allowed those outside to look in. We did not just present our own concerns to the Turkish public, we also made Turkey's concerns the concerns of Turkish Armenians. At the end of the day, we came to understand one thing very clearly: that we shall never create heaven just by solving our own problems.

If today the Armenian question has ceased to be taboo, if it can now be talked about, and if there is a significant number of people in this country who have begun to question history and to see certain realities, *Agos* has played a part in this, too. We have never drawn back from taking political positions when we've thought it necessary. We have a right to play a part in politics, too, and we knew that without engaging politically, it would never be possible to transform society. It was with this knowledge that we offered our views on the opening up of the border between Turkey and Armenia.

It was with this knowledge that we were always in favor of Turkey entering the European Union. It was with this knowledge that we spoke out for democracy and freedom of expression.

So there it is: my little summary of the past ten years. We are not going to say how fast time has flown, because it hasn't.

There were difficult days, but we got through them. There will be more difficult days to come, but we'll get through those, too.

Let's confess that none of the troubles coming in from the outside, and none of the pressure put on us, was as wounding as what we went through internally. But let this be our credo: however much they try to exclude us from our community, we shall, to the same extent, remain inside. Let the world know that *Agos* rose from the bosom of the Turkish Armenian community and will remain forever in its embrace.

Hoping that things continue to improve . . .

"Krisdos haryav i merelots." (Christ rose from among the dead)

23

A World Called *Agos*

HRANT

In *To Love is to Touch*, the anthropologist Desmond Morris relates how, in this ever more crowded world, we have ceased to touch each other and to see how dangerous this untouchability can be. In his lengthy discussion of what a humane gesture a friendly slap on the back can be, and how much value it can carry, he goes on to describe it as an act of love: "Touch is our most fundamental sense. It is sometimes known as the sense from which all others come. What a shame it is, most especially if we don't even notice it happening, but the less we touch each other, the greater the distance between us."

We agree with Morris: to touch and be touched, that's love. So if you love something, I mean really love someone, we have this to say: don't shirk away from touching or being touched by others. Don't be afraid. Reach out and touch someone!

AYDA TANİKYAN

When Hrant and I met for the first time since his graduation from middle school, he was already a man with a cause and the editor in chief of *Agos*. And I was the director of the private Barsamian school in Nice. But now we were sitting together at a table in the Çiçek Pasajı, flying through the years, turning the past into yesterday. Because my return to Istanbul had been reported in *Agos*, he and his classmates had organized an evening for me. We all gathered together at a restaurant called Boncuk. From then on, every time I came back to Turkey, I would pay a visit to *Agos*, and we would discuss everything, negative and positive, that had come to my ears from the Armenian community, and everything else, too. He was saying such things that there were times when I felt so proud that it took my breath away.

During one such visit to *Agos*, he told me that he had been invited to Cannes to the showing of Atom Egoyan's film, but he was not sure whether he should go or not. I said, *insisted*, that we could fly there together. And maybe I helped him make up his mind, because we did fly to Nice together. That was how I met his son, who had come to the airport to see him off. "Your son is even more handsome than you are," I said. He was very pleased to hear that.

"The boy wants to get married," he said.

And I said, "What did you expect? Like father, like son. Everything in a hurry. Just like you."

In school, Hrant was never one to show his feelings. But when I first visited the *Agos* office, aged almost, he lifted me up and told everyone, "Here she is! The great love of my life!" Of course, I love all of my students, but I shall love Hrant forever.

AYŞE ÖNAL

We were rudderless, marginalized leftists who had been all but crushed by the September 12 coup. I would see Hrant at left-wing gatherings, and we would greet each other, but I didn't know his name. I thought he was someone like us; I had no idea that he had a family to support. How we became friends I cannot quite remember, but one day, he said, "Do you know what you and I have in common? You have the face of a suffering woman, and I have the face of a suffering man."

That made me angry. "What are you talking about?" I said. I felt like he was telling me that I wasn't good-looking. But after my daughter Şafak was in that accident, I came to understand what he meant. There was pain in our faces, and sadness, too. We both came from poor families. When people saw us, they'd say, "These people are not from Istanbul, but Anatolia."

Hrant was a genuine Anatolian. He'd never let anyone pay for him—never let rich people buy him meals, for instance. The moment he saw me, he'd know if I had money or not, and after we had parted company, I would find a wad of money that he had secretly put into my pocket.

The compassion in our friendship came from Hrant. In those days, leftists didn't show love or warmth toward each other. Such things seemed almost rude. But when Hrant was talking to you, he couldn't stop touching you. If he was standing up, he'd put his hand on your shoulder, and if he was sitting, he'd put his hand on your knee. He would throw his big arms around you and squeeze you hard. It was never taken the wrong way. The only woman in his life was Rakel. He loved Rakel more than anyone in the world. Orhan (Armenak) Bakır came second, I would say. Whatever he talked about, however irrelevant, he would always mention his name.

Hrant couldn't resist the ones he loved most, particularly the children. He was absolutely distraught when my daughter had her accident, but he couldn't bring himself to visit her. When Şafak was still undergoing treatment and still in her wheelchair, they came with some Easter eggs that Rakel had colored, and that was the first time that Hrant was able to look her in the eyes.

He and my daughter loved gossiping about me. Hrant thought I was chubby, and whenever I came to *Agos*, he'd say to Anna Mayrig, "Don't give this one another bite." He liked that I could take a joke. Our friendship wasn't about politics. Whether or not he could take me seriously as a woman journalist—that I don't know. But I can say this openly: I was Hrant's closest, and only, female friend.

ŞAFAK PAVEY

He was my fairy-tale father because if anyone could dream up their own father, they would want that father to be Hrant. He was a very close friend of my mother, Ayşe Önal. When I was a child, he entered my life through the stories of Saroyan, and he never left it. How much I learned from my fairy-tale father! Before I knew it, his children were my siblings, and his family was my family.

Then he made me a writer in his *Agos* nest. In 1996, there was that accident that left the whole left side of my body on the railroad tracks, and that same summer, he got me writing, this fairy tale father of mine. Because he always wanted things to end happily ever after.

After the accident, he found a doctor in Israel to attach a prosthetic leg. While I was undergoing treatment, my doctor sent me back to Turkey for two weeks. When I got back, he was going to attach the leg. But during my time away, he died of cancer. He did everything he could for me until his dying breath. When I found out about this, I wrote down what I had been through and gave it to Hrant. And that was how we got going. "From now on, I'm giving you your pocket money," he said.

His biggest concern was finding a husband for me! By calling me "our girl" he took me under his wing. Even in his relationship with Rakel, there was something fatherly. Before his daughter Delal went to America to get her master's degree, he hired a talented artist to do her portrait. One day, when I went over to visit, he was standing in front of that portrait, sobbing his heart out. And this was even before his daughter left!

In Saroyan's stories, there was an Armenian father. I had a sense of that father in Hrant's voice, and in his hands, and in his relationships with children. The photos on the walls of his *Agos* office said so much about my fairy-tale father's world. They were all black and white. One was of a mother and daughter fallen on the death march; another was from the 1900s of a big Armenian family in Anatolia. Then, William Saroyan, with that big moustache and that big hat. And right next to him, a smiling Hagop Mntzuri. There was also a portrait of the Patriarch Şnorhk and a portrait of Karin Karakaşlı, taken by Ara Güler.

KARİN KARAKAŞLI

At all the most important moments of my life, I found him standing at my side. You will hear much the same from everyone he loved, really. You'd turn your head, and he'd be there. He'd become family. But when it came to his own troubles, he would go into his shell. He was like those animals that lick their own wounds. There was a lonely place inside him that no one could reach, a noble silence shrouding the thing that truly troubled him. And this was why when he got upset, he wouldn't go to anyone for comfort. He'd just shut himself up in his office and pace the room for hours. His face would go blank, blank enough to cause you fright, and you could only touch him if he had first given you permission.

At my first interview, I remember not understanding what he meant when he said, "This is not an office. This is where I broaden your world." So he was a person I came to understand over time, by working at his side. He had dreams—big dreams—and he showed how dreams could come true. With him at your side, you grew stronger, because he believed in you before than you did yourself. He found the best of you and brought it out. He would break into a huge smile and wave his arms. I have never known anyone to take such innocent pleasure in the achievements of those he loved.

Many young people—Turkish and Armenian alike—benefitted from this special gift of his. Some worked at *Agos*, and some did very different kinds of work, but there was a great deal of Hrant in the identities they forged for themselves. He became the great tree of the forest, giving shade to the new shoots. It was with him that we discovered we were a forest, after all.

GARO PAYLAN

During my years in middle school, when ASALA was very much in the news, threatening letters advising us to leave the country started come to our house. Half of our relatives did leave the country, never to return. And at the same time, my mother started calling me Kaya outside the house instead of Garo. She started calling herself Serpil instead of Sirarpi. In the summers, when I went to work at my father's shop, I discovered that he was no longer Avedis, but Halis.

So when I first became acquainted with Hrant, and *Agos*, what impressed me most was this: his name was Hrant, and he was standing up to the people who used the word "Armenian" as a curse. The day after I read his column on Armenian identity, I went in to work. I reached into my drawer and took out my business card with my real name, Garo Paylan—the card we gave only to foreign visitors—and I put in on my desk. Then, I took the cards that were already on the desk—the ones carrying the name Kaya Paylan—and threw them into the wastepaper basket.

Until that terrible day when we lost him, I found Hrant Ahparig at my side many times. It was because he was there that I was able to keep going. It's still like that, even now.

PINAR SELEK

I'd been out of prison for a week or so. A European parliamentarian who'd been following my case wanted to meet with me, and so I did. I was waiting for just one person, but two people arrived. Hrant had found out that this politician was going to meet me, and he'd come along. It was as if we'd been friends forever. Sometimes he answered questions directed at me, and then he'd throw me a glance, as if to say, "Isn't that the way it is?" Then he and I spoke. He mostly wanted to know about prison. He listened intently.

That first time we met, he invited me to visit *Agos*. He met me at the door. He took me from desk to desk, introducing me to everyone. We had lunch, we drank coffee, I read our fortunes from the coffee grounds, and we talked and talked. I am a chatterbox. But he wasn't bad, either. I remembered how interested I was in hearing what he had to say. I felt at peace, but tears were coming to my eyes. I could feel him taking me under his wing. And what a lovely feeling that was.

Sometimes he invited me over, and sometimes I just dropped by. My case was in the news at the time, and he felt deeply for the injustice I was suffering. But Hrant and I spent very little time talking about the case itself.

As soon as I finished my study of the history of war and peace in Turkey, I took it to him. He took it and read it and came back saying, "But, Pınar, my dearest, we've never made peace in this country." I used his words in my title: "We've Never Made Peace."

ECE TEMELKURAN

It began like this: we were sitting in his office at *Agos*, and Hrant said, "So, for example, what if you went to Armenia?" Adding, "I can set everything up for you." He picked up the phone, and—how strange it was—it was the first time I'd watched Hrant speaking Armenian.

I went to Yerevan, and I came back. And this time, he said, "So come on, then, you've earned yourself a meal."

Later, I found out from Karin that when Hrant read my series, tears had welled up in his eyes, and he had said all sorts of wonderful things about me when I wasn't there. So off we went to eat, and this time, he said, "The next place you should go is France." Once again, Hrant set everything up. Once again, I did a series of pieces. Both of these series were unprecedented in Turkey.

Then, Hrant and I went out for a *rakı*. That evening, another door began to open. For the first time, he used another tone with me. He told me about his personal connection to the issue. He talked about Rakel. And how he fell in love. He told me about a long story he'd written, only to lose it when his computer crashed. Listening to all of this, I came to understand that the Armenian issue was something that brought my friend great pain.

And then he started on America. "You must go to America, too," he said. "I'll arrange everything this time, too. And then you'll have to turn all this into a book." When they killed Hrant, I gave up on the idea of going to America. I felt destroyed. And then, thinking it was a way of keeping the promise I had made to him, I set off down the road again. I went to America. I could still feel Hrant with me. That's why the Turkish title of my book became *The Depths of Ararat*.

FETHİYE ÇETİN

I met Hrant Dink years before I became his lawyer. He astounded me with his courage, and he also had a lawyer's grasp of the case law around minority issues. His office at *Agos* wasn't your normal sort of office, and he wasn't the sort of editor who just sat there at his desk. He would sit across from me, knee to knee, and, as we spoke, he would somehow end up with his hand on my knee.

When my grandmother died, I told my lawyer friend Luiz Bakar that I wanted to put a notice in *Agos*. The notice began with the words, "Her name was Heranuş," and I went on to say that I was hoping to make contact with the Armenian relatives she had not been able to locate during her lifetime. This was in February. The notice went out, and before I knew it, Hrant was on the phone. "So many readers are calling in," he said. "Women are crying on the phone." It was after my notice went out that we became friends.

A few months later, he called me when I was on my way to work. "Come straight over to *Agos*," he said, "so that you can speak to your relatives." I went there right away. First a ferry, then a taxi, and then, somewhere along the way, I jumped out of the car and ran the rest of the way. Hrant met me with his arms outstretched. We hugged each other and began to cry. Earlier that day, my relatives had called *Agos* from America. Hrant had logged their numbers. In any case, he was going to make sure we spoke.

I couldn't say a word on the phone. Hrant spoke in my place. I was one big jumble of emotions. In the end, we were able to reconnect with my grandmother's sister, after so many years. Hrant brought out some chocolate and some Armenian cognac, and we celebrated together.

Later, when I began to think about writing down this story, he gave me the courage to do so. The first article about the book came out in *Agos*, too. In a sense, *My Grandmother* was a book that brought to life what Hrant was fighting for. It was a book that, with its personal story, utterly demolished official history. For how can someone who is family also be your enemy?

RAGIP ZARAKOLU

I knew Hrant from our leftist years in the aftermath of the September 12 coup, but I knew him as Fırat. These were the days when he was setting up Beyaz Adam. My wife Ayşe (Zarakolu) was working in Turkey's only progressive distribution company, so she worked with them to fill their need for not only textbooks but also for left-wing publications.

The September 12 junta used the ASALA attacks as an excuse to keep a close watch on all Armenians. Fearing repercussions, many Armenians emigrated at that point. For an Armenian to open up three branches of a bookstore during this period called for courage, because the September 12 regime was the enemy of books. At a time when they were burning the books they seized from houses and prisons, and throwing them into the sea, Hrant and Ayşe came together in courageous solidarity.

Then we at Belge Publishing brought out *The Armenian Taboo* by Yves Ternon. This was the first book to be published in Turkey on the Armenian genocide, and it caused an earthquake both inside this country and in the diaspora. I remember that, after distributing the book in the space of one day, all of us working in the publishing house bid each other farewell. Knowing that people would be too afraid to come in and buy the book, Hrant organized for the book to be distributed inside the community. Even as the prosecutor was trying to arrest Ayşe, we were, with the help of our left-wing comrade Taner Akçam, able to meet Vahakn Dadrian, and it was while the prosecution was still going on that we published his book, *Genocide as a Problem of National and International Law*. This book, too, was banned. They gave Ayşe a very stiff sentence, something like two years in prison, for Ternon's book.

While these trials were never covered in the Turkish press, Hrant's *Agos* followed them closely. I was an *Agos* regular from the very beginning. And also, because of my very long beard, the staff at *Agos* liked to call me *Vartabed*, the Armenian word for "priest."

In 1997, when we were celebrating our publishing house's twentieth anniversary, Hrant said this to Ayşe: "We are very much in debt to you because you brought out the fire we'd hidden inside us." This moved us very deeply. After that, we lost Ayşe, as you know.

Years later, when, with the efforts of our friend Eren Keskin, director of the Human Rights Association, his solidarity was honored with the Ayşe Nur Zarakolu Thought and Expression Award, it was Hrant's turn to become emotional.

HÜLYA DEMİR

I was friendly with Hrant in college, in the days when he was Fırat. Then, I was at Belge Publishing, and we were publishing books on Turkey's minority issues. Later, when I was working at the Human Rights Association, I continued to take an interest in this subject. One day, we organized a meal. People were talking about someone on the guest list who was a leftist also working on minority issues. He was Hrant Dink, joining us from the Armenian community. And, of course, I did not make the connection.

And then, who should walk through the door? Our Fırat! I remember shouting: "Who's this Hrant then? Who's Fırat? Who are you anyway?" But he just threw his arms around me, like he always used to do, and gave me a big hug. Meanwhile, I was shouting, "Why did you hide your true identity from me?" And he told me that we'd talk about it later. But we never did.

We did renew our friendship, though. One day, he invited us to his place in Bakırköy. Rakel made us an amazing meal. Etyen Mahçupyan and his late wife, Elâ, were there, too. And also Oral and İpek Çalışlar. This was just around the time when Hrant was becoming famous. The conversation was all about politics. And, somehow, it was the men who did all the speaking. The women sat apart and did not join the serious conversation. I remember how annoyed we were about that. And, as you know, İpek is a feminist. She got very angry that evening.

While Hrant was deepening his friendship with my husband, Rıdvan (Akar), he was relegating me to the little girls' table. No matter how hard I tried, he wouldn't talk politics with me. Somehow, in his eyes, I was never able to grow up.

İPEK ÇALIŞLAR

Was Hrant macho? Of course he was. But he was very protective of women, too. All of his closest friends were a lot more macho than he was. And perhaps it was because the political issues of the day were so grave that he gave less importance to women's issues. If he had lived, he would certainly, I think, have reached a point where he would have seen these as being among the most important issues facing us.

I met Hrant at *Agos*. First I was a devotee of the paper, and then of its editor in chief. Whenever I listened to Hrant, my mind would do somersaults, as if caught up by a great wind; I'd feel like some sort of Indiana Jones. He knew things we didn't. It was from him that I learned about so many forgotten and suppressed events.

Hrant's great heart beat as one with Rakel's. Whenever he spoke of her, the tone of his voice would change. On the first night, he invited us to his house, and we met a happy, beautiful woman who was in love with her husband. What a lovely meal they made for us. Over the years, our friendship deepened. We heard many stories about the Tuzla Children's Camp, where their love story began. At the dinners they hosted at Boncuk, the famous Beyoğlu *meyhane*, we'd look over our shoulder, and there would be a famous Armenian singer. Or an Armenian violin virtuoso. It was here we heard the great *duduk* player, Jivan Gasparyan, for the first time. And then there were those unforgettable nights on Kınalıada, when Sarkis Usta's son Ğazaros made us midnight macaroni and we danced the *zeybek* and shared endless stories from childhood.

FEYHAN ORAN

I first met Hrant at a symposium I attended in Istanbul with my husband, Baskın. From the moment we met, he addressed me as "my dear Feyhan," and I felt as if we'd already known each other for a long time. This was part of his nature, this ability to be intimate. He'd embrace you so hard that he almost pulled you into his chest. Every time we came to Istanbul, we got together. In the beginning, he'd invite us to his office at *Agos*, which already felt like home. Then, he'd take us home to Rakel, who would make us the most splendid meals. There were also those evenings of male bonding at Boncuk, with me as the only female among them.

Every time he phoned the house, after he was through talking about weighty matters with Baskın, he'd ask to speak to me, and he'd say, "Is this man giving you a hard time? If he ever gives you are hard time, I'll kill him, you know!" That was the running joke between us.

Hrant was all emotion, from head to toe. I always enjoyed seeing him at academic conferences. While everyone else read their papers, throwing around big words, he would tell a moving story. That's how he touched people's hearts. Some people are hardened by the pain and suffering they've endured. Hrant was just the opposite. He was someone who was trying to make sure that others did not suffer as he had; he had a fine and gentle spirit that reached out to the poor, the oppressed, the powerless, and everyone he loved. He had no time for wrongdoers.

There was one day in Ankara when Hrant and Baskın appeared on Hulki Cevizoğlu's television programme, *Nutshell*. Mehmet Gül of the MHP (Nationalist Action Party) was on with them. It was extremely tense and unpleasant. Hrant was going to come to us that evening, but he couldn't. "Let me walk the streets alone for a while," he said. But if he had heard at this moment that, Mehmet Gül, for example, was receiving, let's say, death threats, he'd have been the first to come running. He had faith in goodness, you might say. He wasn't very religious. "I do believe there is a higher power, but I don't know its name," he would say. But, beyond that, he had nothing to do with organized religion, be it Muslim or Christian. But if I were able to give him a religious title, it would have been "Prophet."

CENGİZ ÇANDAR

It was the first years of *Agos*. Ayşe Önal had brought me together with a Lebanese journalist. There was one other person at the table. He listened to us for hours without saying a word. I thought he was Kurdish. Then the Lebanese journalist left. The man I'd taken for a Kurd turned out to be Armenian. It was the man I'd been hearing about. Hrant Dink! Within minutes, we were exchanging jokes and needling each other as if we'd known each other for ages. Big hugs and kisses when we said good-bye.

Physically, Hrant was "as big as a mountain," to use the old phrase. He had a sort of majesty that gave people confidence. If he said, "Let's get going," there was no way of saying no. I got to know him better over the years. He was the most genuine person I ever met. What you saw was what you got. A straight arrow. Utterly true to his ideals. To be close to him was to be purified. And that was probably why people were drawn to him.

The last time we saw each other was at a panel discussion organized by the Human Rights Association, where we were both speakers. Perihan Mağden spoke after Hrant, and, at one point, she said, with her sharp ironical wit, "Actually, there is no such thing as an Armenian issue in Turkey. There is a Hrant Dink issue, and that's it!" We all couldn't help bursting into laughter. Hrant was sitting there next to me, looking forlorn and abandoned, a pained smile on his face.

I always saw Hrant as a sort of mythic hero. He made me think of Prometheus in the legend of Sisyphus. Here was a community that had dwindled to just tens of thousands, and to honor its place in the country's past and then to bring it forward, to connect it with the present in the spirit of love—this was a mindboggling enterprise, and he had taken it all upon his own two shoulders. And he tried to do all of this hand in hand with Turks. But how delightfully reckless he was, as he walked through the streets with his precarious burden.

ETYEN MAHÇUPYAN

Hrant loved the streets. From his earliest years, he'd been someone who never knew when he would be going out into those streets, or when he'd be coming home, or, sometimes, if he'd even have a home. But he wasn't a street child so much as a child of the street. Or rather, he was a lord of the streets, someone who tried to bring some order to them. For him, *Agos* was just another street. Here again, he tried to shape it in his image.

Neither of us was ever able to remember where it was we first met. Then, one day, he invited me to *Agos* for an interview. After that, our friendship grew closer.

I'm not sure how it happened, but during those last years, he was my clos-est friend in the world. It almost felt as if our friendship was not something we had willed; rather, it was a pleasure that had been bestowed on us from on high, and that was how we chose to enjoy it. We would walk the streets for hours, talking about everything under the sun. When we spoke about deep things, time seemed to stop. There would be long silences, and then he would say something. It might be about the Turkish-Armenian border. It might be about his mother's tragic death. We got to know each other in the rapid flow of life. Or, rather, while walking. There was something Tom Sawyer-ish or Huckleberry Finn-ish about us, with a hint of Steinbeck . . .

He was a warmhearted man, fast to make friends, but he had strong defenses, too, and it was only very rarely that you could get past them. Despite all of that sociability, there was part of him that was always alone. And when he *was* alone, such sadness. But to let you see this, he had to know that he could go into his shell in your company.

On the other hand, other people brought him joy. He looked at people the way a botanist might look at flowers. He never got tired of looking at them. He liked making an impression on them and showing them the way because he was curious about them. He knew how to rope people in. In that sense, he was a flirt. He flirted with men, too. He was an emotional man. He could bring out emotions even in people who seemed not to have them. He cured people. Once you were in his fold, it was impossible not to notice his healing powers.

Like everyone else who got to know him, I felt my heart grow bigger during our years together. What with our age difference, and the difference in our characters, I was the "elder brother," and, like so many firstborn children, I was a bit introverted, reticent, and antisocial, but over time, I became more like the "little brother." I took on some of his ease and self-confidence, and— most important—his impish sincerity. But just as my heart was beginning to grow, I lost it.

ELİF ŞAFAK

Some people are like rainbows. They let their colors sparkle from afar but are impossible to touch, impossible to reach. Other people are like oases

and impossible to understand from a distance—only when you get closer do you come to appreciate their riches and their depths. Hrant was like that. He loved people. He loved this country. He embraced it with all of his heart. Its culture, its stories, its melodies and songs . . .

When I first met him, many years ago, what struck me most was the power of his emotions. We had coffee at *Agos*, his paper, his world. As he spoke, his eyes welled with tears.

This was around the time when he got his passport. He was going to be able to travel the world for the first time. He was as excited as a child. He was so curious. So emotional. He could stand in other people's shoes and cry for them. Whoever was in trouble was his friend. If everyone could come to the same table and get to know each other, they would all come to love each other—that's what he believed.

JEAN KEHEYAN

I met Hrant when I came to Turkey to write a report on the Armenians still in Anatolia for the French newspaper *Liberation*. From the very first words he spoke, I knew that, despite his young age, Hrant was going to be the big brother I had never had. Before meeting Hrant Dink, my views on Turkey were basically reductive. Even at our first meeting, he was able to persuade me, with the seriousness and cogency of an academic, and drain my mental universe of its cultural black-and-white ink. And thus he lightened, if only just a little, the legacy passed on to me by my orphaned parents the moment they were sent away with refugees' passports bearing the stamp that they must never return.

And so it was that I began to visit Turkey frequently. It might sound like a contradiction, but Istanbul felt like home. This was thanks to Hrant. With his extensive knowledge of the complexities of the Armenian issue, he was an extraordinary guide both for his Turkish brothers and his brothers in the diaspora.

In the beginning, I had a hard time accepting this thoroughly honest man's beliefs, but it wasn't long before I realized that I could make good and straightforward connections with Turkish society. And, furthermore, I saw that this would be possible because there were in this society people who could found newspapers that spoke of what had really happened to the Armenians and how they had suffered, and that there were people who could keep these stories alive by putting them in writing.

And so we vowed to continue to work together and to devote our lives to this struggle. He became my big brother and I his *cano*, his dear friend.

CEM ÖZDEMİR

When it came to understanding Turkey's past and contemporary minority politics, Hrant was my compass. I first met Hrant when I came to do a piece for *Die Welt*. When I asked if I could also speak to Patriarch Mesrob

II, he took me out by ferry to the Patriarch's residence on Kınalıada. But he didn't go inside. He preferred to stay in the yard of the Patriarchate's summer residenceplaying with the children in its summer camp. At the time, I had no knowledge of his dispute with the Patriarchate, nor did I know that he had grown up in an orphanage and loved children more than anything else in the world.

I shall never forget bringing Yaşar Kemal and Hrant Dink together for the first time. The great author began by telling us about the Akhtamar Church in Van, about which he'd written a piece in the 1950s for *Cumhuriyet*. At that time, the church had been left in an appalling condition by a society not wishing to remember who had once worshipped there. Having seen that its last remains were being dug up, Yaşar Kemal launched a campaign in *Cumhuriyet* that led to the church's being saved.

That day, these two Anatolians—one Armenian and one Turkish—had a long and intense conversation. They were like twins who'd been separated at birth. They forgot I was even there. Then, Yaşar Kemal turned to me and said, "Such unspeakable suffering these people have been through!" And Hrant said, "You're right, brother, you uprooted us well and truly!" Yaşar Kemal's answer was short: "He's telling the truth!" he said. When they parted company, they embraced each other with emotion. And Yaşar Kemal said, "I'm very taken by this crazy boy. Thanks for bringing us together."

Hrant is a continuation of the great tradition of Anatolian humanism, as previously manifested by Mevlana, Yunus Emre, and Hacı Bektaş Veli. No one like him will ever come again to this land where he was sacrificed.

MÜGE GÖÇEK

When Hrant and I met at the University of Michigan, I was disarmed by his warmth and openness. I even said, "Listen, do you have any brothers? If they're anything like you, I want to meet them," at which he burst into great peals of laughter.

It was interesting to watch Hrant in academic circles because he wasn't interested in concepts so much as the secret meanings and positions they concealed. What I found most moving was his humane approach with even the most bigoted, prejudiced people, and his ability to engage them in conversation. He was the physical embodiment of the humanist approach.

Later, I went to visit him in his own world: at *Agos*. Hrant was also the one who introduced me to his beloved Baron, Sarkis Seropyan, and arranged for him to accompany me on my trips to Anatolia to investigate the Armenian presence. In so doing, he enriched not just my research but my entire world. Hrant was a man who loved the Anatolian soil, and he loved everyone who shared that love with him. And by bringing them together, he caused that love to multiply.

That last summer, we met on Kınalı. That was the first time I saw him with his wife and grandchild. How at peace he was with his true loves!

That summer, I invited him back to America. "Bring your family," I said. "Stay as long as you like."

I shall never forget his answer: "Now, how could I do that?" he said. "If I stay out of Turkey for more than a few days, I turn into a fish out of water. How I pine for my country, my home! Just look at the Armenians of the diaspora. They can't stop pining for it, either. So how could I ever manage outside my country and my lands?"

HASAN CEMAL

Hrant and I first met each other in July of 2004. It would be more accurate to say that we hugged each other. Ayşe and I were drinking *rakı* in Bebek, and Hrant arrived with Rakel. "There's something I must do," he said in his great and joyous voice. "Come here so I can give you a hug." The reason, I think, was that several days earlier, I'd made space for his interview with Neşe Düzel.

A year passed. Then came the fourth scholarly conference to bring together Turkish and Armenian historians to discuss the Armenian issue, this one being in Salzburg. The conference, which took place in a castle, brought together the foremost experts on the subject. I recall that Taner Akçam, Müge Göçek, and Ferhat Kentel were among the Turkish scholars in attendance. We were part of a group of journalists from Istanbul who had come as observers. One of us was Hrant Dink, the editor in chief of *Agos*.

For me, the most important part of that trip was getting to know Hrant intimately in the space of a few days and coming to love him. Hrant and I took long strolls along the lakeshore in the evenings. When he was speaking with his usual enthusiasm, he would always find a way to rise above our usual slogans and clichés. He influenced me deeply with his sincerity, also forcing me to rethink the Armenian issue. As I wrote in my book, *1915: Armenian Genocide*, I knew that I, too, had to break those taboos around the Armenian issue. It was Taner Akçam who unlocked my mind, and Hrant who unlocked my heart.

DİLEK KURBAN

I knew something about the Armenian issue. My grandfather would tell me what he'd heard from his own father: how the rivers of Dersim had run red, how the Armenians had been forced off their land, how the house in a village in Bingöl that my great-grandfather moved into after leaving Dersim had once belonged to an Armenian. I knew all of these stories, but I'd never really dwelled on them.

Hrant and I crossed paths at Columbia University. What struck me most was how amazingly Anatolian this Armenian man was. He seemed like some sort of miracle to me. It was from him that I found out that the Armenian name of my grandfather's village meant "little lake," and also that the Armenian community had a special affection for the Alevis.

After returning to Turkey, I became an *Agos* regular. After all, anyone interested in minorities ended up there. I shall never forget the conference that he and I organized on minority rights. While waiting at the elevator on the first day to go to lunch, we were still deep in conversation. When the elevator arrived, it was very full, but I was quick to say, "Let's get in, too." When we got in, the elevator creaked, so Hrant got out. And there he was, outside the lift. With the rest of us inside. As the door closed, he bowed his head, and with a smile that was half sad, half mischievous, he said, "This is the way it's always been, after all." On the day Hrant died, that was the first image that came back to me. Once again, we had stayed, and he had left.

NİLÜFER GÖLE

As Hrant related his painful stories from real life, he was trying to awaken our memories, little by little. As he whispered into our ears, he was reminding us that that Armenians had lived in these lands.

We first met when *Agos* asked to interview me. The interview turned into a two-way conversation. I had just returned from eastern Turkey. We began by discussing Kars and Ani and their environs, and then we moved on from Turkey to Europe.

I didn't become friends with Hrant when I met him; rather, I met him because of the amity I already felt for him. Real friendship means knowing the value of the person who has welcomed you into their home. It means acknowledging his or her grace and generosity. While he was alive, Hrant gave us the chance to heal ourselves. He wanted people of conscience to listen to the voice of the Armenians and thus free us of the blindness emanating from the history of Turkish identity.

And for Armenians to free themselves of their legacy of hatred by speaking with Turks—for this was what he did himself. He opened up conversations between different peoples, different faiths, and different countries. He created bonds of affection, organized meals, created spaces for reflection, and established networks that crossed borders.

Hrant also came to the New Year's supper I gave every year for my friends in Istanbul. The last time we saw each other was on January 1, 2007. He was very troubled that night, very preoccupied, and we were not able to protect him. He was always the one to embrace and protect us; he made as all feel we as if mattered. That evening, I think I made some sort of awkward effort to let him know that, but it was wholly inadequate. None of us did enough.

TANER AKÇAM

After the September 12 coup, I left the country for political reasons and didn't return for a decade. During this period, İletişim Publishing published my book, *Turkish National Identity and the Armenian Issue*. The first Armenian friends I met through İletişim's Fahri Aral decided to introduce me to someone they called the "crazy boy." "He's a bookseller," they said. The crazy boy turned out to be Hrant.

My strongest memory of Hrant is how he and his Armenian friends decided to baptize me. "This is usually done with wine," they said, "but we're going to do it with *rakı*." The baptism took place in church, and it was very crowded. There was dancing, and there was food, and we all had lots of fun.

By now, I'd started visiting Turkey a lot. If I didn't go by the paper to see Hrant every day I that was there, he'd get angry. He would sit me in his office for hours and do whatever he could to detain me. The night before I left the country, I would always go to Hrant's house. The plane would be leaving very early. Neither of us would sleep. We would stretch out in the TV room in the back and talk until morning. Hrant would have the channel changer in his hand, and he'd flick from channel to channel all night long. And there on the table would be Rakel's bible . . .

Toward the end, we were back at *Agos*. They had opened another case against Hrant on account of his having used the word "genocide" in an interview with Reuters. And I had written an article in *Agos* saying, "I use this word every day, so you should open a case against me, too." Which they did, and whereupon I flew in from America. After giving a statement to the prosecutor, I went to visit Hrant with his lawyer, Fethiye Çetin. It was the first time I had seen him this uneasy. This was not the Hrant I knew. I told him he should go abroad at once. "You know," he replied, "Whenever I go abroad, I miss my country so terribly."

ÜMİT KIVANÇ

For almost ten years, I had taken a secret pride in the fact that I had played a part in *Agos*'s becoming a good, clean paper. But for a long time, I'd had nothing to do with it. Most of us who had held it together in the early shoestring days were gone, but the newspaper was still coming out, still going from strength to strength.

I'd turned my back. *Agos* was there, and Hrant with it. They were both alive. Now only one is.

It is hard to understand how someone with a desktop as messy as Hrant's could walk so straight down a murderous political path. Perhaps we can think about it like this: He never planned things in detail; he acted on what he felt and believed, and this is why he radiated so much energy, to a degree that would be hard to replicate.

After we lost Hrant, people spoke a great deal about his sincerity. This I understood in the way previously described.

When Hrant and *Agos* were in life together, Turkey was a richer place, and it could have become richer still. But now, just one has survived.

We are doing our best to keep *Agos* going. It's as crowded here as ever, but there is one sound missing. One laugh we no longer hear, one shout no longer ringing in the corridors, one man no longer filling the whole room.

And how do we experience this absence? I can't describe it. It's Hrant's stubborn spirit, still there.

Part II

Touching

24

An Armenian in Turkey

HRANT

In the time of the deportations, when the edict went out, saying, "Prepare to leave your homes," everyone went into a panic, saying, "What are we going to take with us? What are we going to do?" But the village elder is in a different world. He shows no panic whatsoever. He's sitting down, repairing the threshing sledge. "Come on, now. It's time to leave," they cry. "You're not going to be able to take this threshing sledge with you, so why are you still sitting there, repairing it?"

"That may well be," he says. "If we have to leave, then we're leaving. But we planted those crops, and someone will certainly be here to harvest them. And whoever that is, they'll need this threshing sledge. Do we want this man coming here and finding it broken?"

I also have a friend named Ferman. He's from Bitlis. Throughout his life, his family has suffered in exile for historical reasons. Now he has a summer house in Marmara Ereğlisi, and it's right on the shore, and there's a garden, too. The problem is, there's not a single tree in this garden. He dazzles his guests with his tomatoes and peppers, his sunflowers and corn. But I feel guilt a thousand times over for asking him, "Why don't you plant one tree, at least?"

"I'll never do that, my friend," he said, and with that he related his story of exile. "If I planted a tree, how long would I have to wait before I could eat its fruit?" he asked. "I can grow tomatoes in no time at all. I harvest them, I eat them, and it's finished." So there you have it, our state of mind . . .

AYŞE ÖNAL

It must have been '95 or '96—Agos wasn't out yet. We did a television program entitled *To be Armenian, Jewish, or Greek in Turkey*. That was Hrant's first appearance on television, and, on that occasion, he told his story about Ferman. He reminded the Turkish people that Armenians once lived on these lands, too. Appealing to their consciences, he made them cry. Usually when we made programs like this, we expected hate mail and obscenities, but that evening, an unbelievable number of people called to congratulate us. And they all asked, "Who's that man?"

ORAL ÇALIŞLAR

It was in '98. Hrant wasas a guest on the program I was doing in those days, entitled *Our Media*, together with other representatives of Istanbul's minorities to discuss the issues facing minority journalists. But the program on which he really began to shine was ATV's *Political Arena*. The topic was "Minorities: Lost Colors," and it featured our fellow citizens from the Greek, Jewish, and Armenian minorities. It was on this program that Hrant spoke for the first time about how the September 12 military regime had confiscated the Tuzla Camp. He spoke with his usual sincerity, and everyone was deeply moved. The weighty subject of the Minority Foundations became a human tragedy. The Turkish viewers, who knew nothing about this subject, were shocked. The Armenians, meanwhile, were crying.

HRANT

I am an Armenian. I have carried this burden since birth. I inherited this identity from my mother and father, and I also have the duty to pass it on.

According to the 1923 Lausanne Treaty, we minorities were told that we shall manage our own schools with our own money. If we needed help from the government, we would receive it.

What I wish to explain here is this: My two brothers and I grew up in an orphanage. One day, they took us to an empty lot in Tuzla. The church had bought the land, had paid for it, and had been granted government permits, and this became the summer camp for the children of the orphanage. We all worked there. We were children, but we still planted trees, built buildings, and turned the place into one big camp. The trees grew taller, and so did the children. It was there I met a girl who was an orphan like me. I married her. We settled there with our children. For me, it was a nest, a refuge, a shelter. I grew older, and then my wife and I became the camp's directors.

Then, one day, a yellow envelope arrived. We opened it, and it was a ruling by the Supreme Court of Appeals. Minority foundations were banned from acquiring any property beyond that which was listed in the 1936 declarations. It seemed that they had given us the permit by mistake. We now had to return the property to its previous owner, this piece of paper told us. They threw us out of that place. And now it is a wasteland.

What good is history to me now? What matters is what I'm living through today. But, still, I have this hope. Let me make one other thing clear: In a democratizing country, in union with all those who are fighting for democracy, sooner or later we shall succeed in our efforts. And this will not be to import democracy but to rise to the occasion like the men we are and create one that is truly ours. This is what I mean to say.

MARİ MAYRİG

Ah, well, of all the Armenians watching that program were reduced to tears. We all cried. We could not believe our ears. We all picked up the phone that night and told others to turn on the television. Because of what had happened to us, we were, as a community, thoroughly intimidated. We were afraid even to talk among ourselves, never mind going on television and speaking. Hrant was not just speaking—he was speaking beautifully. There was no cowering, no shuffling of feet; he was simply speaking of the issues that most concerned him. What I mean to say is that his voice was strong. His back was straight. He held his head high. And we old people, we swelled with pride, while the young ones said, "He's saying exactly what I've been wanting to say." We were taken by surprise, and we were pleased.

After that, he began appearing on television more often. His voice never faded. And that is when we began to be afraid. Some people were afraid for Hrant: "They'll harm this boy," they said. Others feared for themselves. "This boy is talking," they said, "and it's going to backfire, and when it does, it will backfire on us."

AVEDİS DEMİR

Hrant was the only person who dared to say all of the things I wished to say as an Armenian. It wasn't just the Turks whose consciences he touched—he taught Armenians a great deal, too. For Hrant, Armenian nationalism was no different from Turkish nationalism. His mission was to save both peoples from the scourge of nationalism. He became the translator of our emotions. "You want documentation?" he said. "Well, I am that documentation." And the moment he said that, the force of all of the stories I had heard from my forebears gave way to one single force: a man named Hrant Dink.

Hrant's greatest gift was his ability to touch people. He'd reach out and either put his hand on your shoulder or put his hand on your knee, and that was how he was able to go on talking. We all knew this, all of his friends, all of us. We knew that he could touch people's hearts if he talked to them one on one. Only later would we discover that he also knew how to do the same thing for large groups.

ORAL ÇALIŞLAR

In the years that followed, Hrant did a lot of television. And, over time, he trained himself. He became even more persuasive. There was the time he appeared on a program on Channel 7 with me and Etyen Mahçupyan to discuss the Armenian issue with three ambassadors from the foreign ministry. And here's what was interesting: though Hrant could be harsh with those close to him, the persona he presented on television was soft and persuasive. And this was how he was able to use gentle language even when debating the likes of Kemal Kerinçsiz, who is currently being tried for conspiring to bring about a coup, and the ultranationalist Mehmet Gül, and, in so doing, to occupy the higher ground.

ŞİNASİ HAZNEDAR

It was in 1999 that we began to hear people talking about Hrant Dink on television. Those were the years when Turkey was becoming increasingly polarized. Trabzon, meanwhile, was a stronghold of nationalism. So we launched an initiative called the Trabzon Empathy Group. We were reaching out to the country's leading intellectuals. Those were the days when there was lively debate on joining the EU. So we invited the rising star, Hrant Dink, to speak to us on this issue. I think it was the first time he attended a conference having to do with Turkish politics as a whole.

HRANT

Our city of Trabzon is known for its conservatism and even its fanaticism. So when they came and asked if I could speak on language and ethnicity at one of the panels they were organizing on "The Questions of Harmonization to the European Union," I can't say that it didn't bring me any anxiety.

Framing my talk with the EU accession process, I spoke of the importance of learning to live together. This was the first time that the people of Trabzon had ever heard the thoughts and positions of a Turkish citizen who was openly declaring his Armenian identity. And that was why, when some began to heckle me, crying "Explain Karabağ!" and "Explain ASALA!", I met them with empathy. But that did not stop me from giving the answers I needed them to hear. Taking this approach does seem to bring down the temperature pretty nicely during tense encounters like this. And I do think we achieved this.

The answers that my friends and I offered had enough of an effect on the audience that we gave each other a standing ovation at the end. And at times like this, there is no need to hold back our heartfelt tears. Actually, when we were applauding each other, we were really crying on each other's shoulders.

ALİ BAYRAMOĞLU

This was the first event I did with Hrant. For Hrant to go to Trabzon at that moment in time was a splendid act of defiance. If you consider its nationalist impulses on minority issues, Trabzon was hostile territory. To invite an Armenian to come to speak was to exacerbate tensions even further. There was serious heckling during Hrant's talk, but he kept his tone gentle and succeeding in touching people's hearts. The talk had begun with catcalls, but it ended with applause. I remember, at the airport on the way in, he had told me that he was apprehensive, but, when we left, he was very pleased.

I also remember the two of us taking a walk through the city. Wherever he went in Anatolia, Hrant was always looking for traces of the Armenians who had once lived there. He could recognize the symbols on the walls of old houses. He would point them out one by one and explain them. For all those years, I'd been a university lecturer, but it was not until I was there with him that I found out what happened to the Armenians of Trabzon in 1915. He told me how people had been huddling in the *hamams*, only to be slaughtered. We walked around the streets of Trabzon for many hours, discussing the Armenian question.

In later years, I often thought back to that meeting. When Hrant was speaking in Trabzon that day, Ogün Samast, who would kill him eight years later, must have been a child of eight or ten. And I keep asking myself if he was one of the children who surrounded us in that bookstore, or if he walked those same streets . . .

HRANT

There were more than fifty of us from Istanbul, Ankara, and Izmir as guests of the Diyarbakır branch of the Human Rights Foundation. As the city's population increased, so too had its poverty. The state of emergency, having become the city's everyday reality, could be felt even in its air, which was as heavy as lead.

The panels went on for two days, in packed rooms, with continuous live coverage on local television. We are all at our best when we act in innocence, and I kept that in mind when I went to speak to the people of Diyarbakır. I kissed the hands of those older than me and kissed the young ones on their eyes. I described what Anatolia was like a hundred years ago. I recalled the riches created by those who had settled its lands. I spoke of the colleges that this region had then, with instruction in seven languages, and of the wine and silk industries that were the source of the region's wealth. I painted a picture of what it might be like here today, had it not been for those painful events. I told them the story of our grandfathers, who had refused to hurry when the deportation arrived, choosing instead to repair a broken threshing sledge because "someone will be coming here to harvest this crop." And then I asked, "Where is that threshing sledge now, I wonder? First, let us find it, and then, let us repair it."

In my speech, I suggested that even after all of the painful events of the past, most Armenians did not, as some had tried to suggest, wish the Turks and the Kurds to be enemies. Speaking as an Anatolian, I explained why it was wrong to nurture a society with Armenian trauma. And, once again, I pledged to do whatever I could to help the peoples of Anatolia find the will to live together again in peace, almost making the sign of the cross.

SEZGİN TANRIKULU

In 2000, having decided, as the Diyarbakır representative of the Turkish Human Rights Association, to hold a conference also involving the Human Rights Foundation, I invited Hrant. In his talk, he spoke to the Kurdish people as an Anatolian Armenian, and he pledged to work for peace. He made a deep impression on us. It was here that I realized for the first time how close we were in our thinking and in the problems we had to solve. After 2002, when they started opening all of those cases against him, I was serving as head of the Diyarbakır Bar, and I followed those cases closely.

ALİ BAYRAMOĞLU

It was in 2002 that Hrant was first prosecuted for "insulting Turkishness." Once again, we pulled together a group of intellectuals—journalists and scholars—and went to Urfa. Hrant was with us. It was a wide-ranging meeting in which we covered everything from secularism to Kemalism, the Kurdish problem to identity issues. In the talk he gave there, Hrant explored what the term "people of Turkey" might offer, beginning with the pledge that all schoolchildren learn by heart and quoting various lines from the national anthem, he described the emotional dilemma that all Armenians of Turkey had to confront. Even if they spend their whole lives reciting, "I am a Turk. I am honest and hard-working...", there was no room for an Armenian in the concept of Turkishness.

HRANT

When I touched on the concept of Turkishness at the Urfa panel, it was in response to a question. This was the question someone asked me: "Do you Armenians say the same pledge as the rest of us in your schools? And, if you do, how does it make you feel to recite, 'I am a Turk, I am honest and hardworking...'"

In my answer, I was not speaking for all Armenians, but just for myself. "Yes," I said, "we recite that same pledge in our schools. I can no longer remember how I felt when I was a child, reciting this pledge, but this is how I feel about it now: I am honest and hardworking, but I am not a Turk. I am an Armenian of Turkey."

When I said this, I had no intention of insulting Turkishness. I simply wished to explain how I felt. When Atatürk said, "How lucky are those who can call themselves Turks," his idea of the Turk was all-embracing, but later, as it took on racist, ethnic overtones, it lost all connection with the original concept. After all that I have suffered in the name of national unity, how could it be possible for me to be comfortable seeing myself as a Turk? No matter how many times we recite, "I am a Turk, I am honest and hardworking..." we Armenians are still seen as the "other." And this is what we must swallow with our daily bread: the relentless pronouncements by Turkist Turks who claim that we do not belong here. What we

need now is a new concept that can make us feel that we are all equal citizens of the Turkish Republic.

As we launched into a discussion of the term "people of Turkey," I offered my own question. "Please," I said. "Tell me. What are we to make of this line from the national anthem: 'A rose for my heroic race.'" It could well be said that Mehmet Akif Ersoy did not mean the word "race" to cause the sort of offense it does to me today, and that he used it as a synonym of "people" to keep the rhythm. But that is now what offends me about this word. Race, as I understand it, is a biological term that acts at the same time as a sociological term, and when the two terms are operating in tandem, they set out to divide all people, and all living creatures, into categories. They do not set out to bring people together. And that is why a national anthem that mentions race is not setting out to unify, but to discriminate, thus encouraging that most violent form of discrimination: racism.

ALİ BAYRAMOĞLU

In this particular talk, Hrant broke a very big taboo. Even more important, he was not just criticizing Turks but questioning stereotypes and breaking taboos from the perspective of an Armenian. This was a first. In due course, when Article 301 came into effect, he was the first to be prosecuted. But that did not faze him one bit. And now, he was making a name for himself. He continued to travel across the country, racing from one meeting to the next.

HRANT

Here we are in Malatya. Our first stop is my birthplace, the ancient neighborhood that is home to some ten Armenian families and that some call the Salköprü and others the "Armenian Quarter." I walk around the four walls of its fine old church, but in vain, for there is no way in. This sacred space from childhood is closed to visitors, its walls and windows blocked with stone.

The residents of the neighborhood are of the opinion that closing the church to visitors has saved it from further vandalism. The neighboring *muhtar*, meanwhile, says that he did make an effort to have the church restored and made into a museum or a cultural center, but without success—this despite the fact that, even though it is very small, there is still an Armenian community in Malatya. If only it could open its doors again, as a church.

As we continue walking through the streets, we see that the high walls of the Armenian cemetery have been undermined and then brought down by the roads that the municipality has built on three sides. Another building that the council has destroyed: the sanctuary at the cemetery entrance, where a funeral's last rituals are performed. What is there to say? Is there anything left to say?

ZEYNEP ORAL

In July 2003, we took part in a panel in Malatya entitled "Democratization and Multiculturalism." This was Hrant's first visit back to his own roots to retrace his childhood. He couldn't stop talking—he was as elated as a child! Suddenly, we came to a street. He walked in front. All at once, he stopped. We caught up with him and stopped, too. He was silent, so we stayed silent. It's one thing to feel something, and another to see it. What we saw hurt our eyes before it hurt our hearts. Before us stood an ancient Armenian church, its doors and windows blocked with stone. Once upon a time, it had been the finest church in the area, and now it was in ruins.

We held our panel in a packed room. While Hrant was describing what multiculturalism looked like from a minority perspective, there was tension in the room. The residents of his birthplace couldn't understand him. You know how it is: prophets are never appreciated in their own lands.

Then we went up into the mountain villages. Here, Hrant cheered up again. He started talking again, talking all day long. That evening, a village *muhtar* served us supper on his roof. As we sat there under the stars, we carried on talking. And, oh, the folk songs that Hrant sang for us in that deep voice of his. Before us stretched the vast Malatya Plain and, in our hearts, there was the hope of a better Turkey . . .

ALİ BAYRAMOĞLU

Hrant was someone who could touch a stone and heat it. One touch was all it took. When he touched you, or embraced you, it was impossible not to feel love. All he had to do was walk into a room, and he generated warmth. Whenever he spoke, he touched people's hearts. The way a musician might, or a poet . . .

And if he pressed something hard, he could set it on fire. If he called the state into account, in the name of the people, he could set it on fire. If he called upon the collective conscience, he could set *us* on fire. If he questioned the authority of a particular community, be it Armenian or leftist or whatever else, he could set us fire yet again. He just had this way of setting hearts on fire.

HRANT

I came from the left, though I must confess that the leftist mentality had little time for questions of identity. "What do we need identity for? We're all the same. It's true: we're all brothers. Did such things bother us when we were young? We were all neighbors, and we all lived together happily." That's all well and good, because now we are paying a high price for those happy days. Because those days when you were living as good neighbors, those days when we Armenians were making our lovely meatballs and bean dishes, you remember as so sweet, but they were, in fact, very painful days. One by one, we were dropping away. But even as they insisted that we were all brothers, all the same, they failed to notice that they were losing the ones who were different.

If you see difference as a source of richness, you create one kind of society. If you see it as a danger, you create another.

When we speak about Alevis, or about headscarves, we are talking about identity. Almost everything we talk about in Turkey is about identity. Class struggle and identity struggle go hand in hand. But class struggle cannot resolve identity struggle. This is the case all the world over. The time has come for the left to take this on board and embrace it as a fundamental principle.

AYDIN ENGİN

While Hrant was trying to win over even the nationalists, he did not pass up the opportunity to speak as a leftist to those socialists who refused to engage with questions of identity and give them a good scolding. And he was the one who told Turkey how lame the Turkish left was on the Armenian issue. He showed how the left chose to ignore it. According to him, you were not a leftist if all you did was talk about class struggle and stand up for the proletariat. You also had to stand up for all groups that Turkey discriminated against—first and foremost, the minorities. Because for Hrant, being a leftist was, above all, a question of conscience.

HRANT

I have no trouble understanding the nationalist mindset. I can hear what they say, and I can guess how they'll act when we meet. What choice do they have? They were raised to see the "other" as the enemy; it's in their blood. So I can either refuse to talk with them, or I can talk with them and try not to press their buttons. But here's the funny thing: even if you haven't pressed their buttons, if you go on television as an Armenian and a fully fledged fellow citizen, you can, without saying anything of note, still drive them crazy!

But, never mind, this still does not stop me from saying that I find the rightist mentality easier to deal with. I say this because, on the other side, there's a group, a group you sometimes think you belong to. Mostly they pass as leftists, sometimes even as democrats. Only when they are truly put to the test do they drop their masks. And this is what we've seen recently, in all of these discussions about the Armenian question. Listen to them now, and you can hear how hard they are working to explain away the wealth tax and pretend our catastrophe never happened.

There is one central issue that this nation's democrats have yet to consider adequately. The official line on the Armenian question is clear, and parts of it make sense. But, now I ask you, who on the left has written on the Armenian question from the founding of the republic to today?

The recent debates on this taboo have become the true test. The nationalist position is clear, and it does not surprise us. The ones that really fail are our so-called leftists and our democrats.

ALİ BAYRAMOĞLU

In the early years of the new millennium, Hrant was taking on all of Turkey's major issues. From the bottom of his heart, he believed that each and every one of these problems could be resolved through democratization. To a large degree, his conviction was reinforced by the dynamics of the time. And so, at this point, there was no difference between him and us. Even so, and as we all knew, Hrant had made his name by representing the sensitivities of Armenian identity in *Agos*. Here, the crucial issue was how to establish a link between this sensitivity and democracy. This is very important. Hrant is talking about Armenian identity as an insider, but he can also speak about all other identities, everything from Kurdish identity to Muslim identity. Thus, he was able to show us what it meant to be a true democrat.

ETYEN MAHÇUPYAN

As far as Hrant's political trajectory is concerned, I saw him as a man who'd gone from leftism to nationalism, and from there to becoming a democrat. But as he traveled this route, he stayed connected to the ideas he'd acquired along the way and remained committed to them. As for his political position during the last years, they were so close to my own that I could have signed my name below his every column. As he went through this transformation, Hrant was influenced by us all—by Mehmet Altan, and Cengiz Çandar, and Ali Bayramoğlu. He became a staunch democrat, but he also remained true to the political sentiments he had developed around Armenian identity. Of course, Hrant influenced us as much as we influenced him. He was the one who put the Armenian issue back on the national agenda. For example, I, as an Armenian, did not see this as the burning political issue. Hrant changed my mind, too.

Of course, it's important to mention here how important the scholars were. The historian Taner Akçam's books were starting to get translated into Turkish around this time. The historian Halil Berktay was, after all, one of pioneers, one of the first to challenge official history in his writings.

Additionally, the Kurdish issue had become a key issue in the media. There was a new democratic mentality coming to the fore, a new form of opposition. When groups with different identities began to put all of their concerns into the same melting pot, we saw a new sort of democratic thinking come into being. Doors opened in both print and broadcast media, paving the way for a living debate on identity. And through those doors came Hrant, with his warm, sincere voice. And he made the Armenian issue into something that people could hear. By now, he occupied the far-seeing perspective of a multicultural world of multiple identities. During those last years, he was no longer just talking about the Armenian issue. He spoke out for the Alevis and the Kurds. He was on the side of the girls wearing headscarves when universities refused to admit them on account of their headscarves.

ALİ BAYRAMOĞLU

It's extraordinarily difficult to be a non-Muslim in Turkey because you carry around with you a strong sense of being "other." On the other hand, Muslim values and Muslim symbols play a powerful part in the Turkish mindset. And when this mindset dominates, non-Muslims cannot feel at peace. Hrant was someone who lived inside this reality and was also trying to transcend it. This was not an easy enterprise—not at all. It was important, while speaking out for a Christian Armenian identity, to refuse to see the Muslim woman's headscarf as a threat and to speak out for her rights. Etyen did the same, of course, as a non-Mulsim intellectual, but Hrant, with his newspaper, and his outbursts, and his positions, was an activist. And to take such stands as an activist was even more important.

MUSTAFA KARAALİOĞLU

In addition to fighting his own fights, Hrant entered into the Islam and secularism debate. Here, he positioned himself clearly as a democratic intellectual. We appeared together on many television programs. And though I came from the Islamist camp, and he was the spokesman for the Armenian minority, I finished his sentences and he finished mine.

I'll never forget the time we appeared together on a program that was making a lot of noise about "Christian missionary activity." And he said, "Listen, everybody! Turkey isn't 99 percent Muslim—it's 99.9 percent Muslim. Why are you still so afraid of Christians?"

Hrant was a unique thinker who respected and drew from not just the ideas of liberals and the left but also from devout Muslims. He was an intellectual who spoke of the breach of human rights with regard to the headscarf issue: of political bans: of the "reactionary scare" cooked up by the military regime, and of secularist paranoia, which has in recent days become almost an ideology—and all of this far more forcefully than your average Muslim. He raised his voice loud enough to condemn those who had brought in the headscarf ban as "modern bigots."

HRANT

How must it have felt to go to your daughter's graduation and not to be admitted on account of wearing a headscarf? I shall leave that question to the mothers. At that moment, I was the father, and it was as big an earthquake for me as it was for her. And when that mother was pulling at her daughter's gown and saying, "Come along, girl. If they won't take us in, let's just leave," well that, in effect, was to save her from the earthquake.

I don't know why, but at that moment, I felt ashamed of myself. It occurred to me to take that mother's headscarf and ask my Christian wife to wear it, and then, after we had barged into the hall, to cry out, "Go ahead! Throw us out, too, why don't you?"

These secularists who rail against those who are trying to bring religion into politics, maybe they're the ones who are doing just that. Secularists should distance themselves from these meddlers who are so occupied with what these matrons wear on their heads. Otherwise, this concept that they label bigotry will abandon the devout and come to plague their own side. In the end, our secularists will be exposed as "modern bigots."

ETYEN MAHÇUPYAN

Hrant was our nation's last wandering minstrel. He did not carry a saz—he never touched his last saz, the one that his children gave him as a present—but whenever he spoke, he knew that he was singing a folk song, and what he wanted most was for everyone to join in with him, for each to bring out the saz in his or her heart. Like all the minstrels who came before him, Hrant had no book. He had his words, and those words were inspired by his encounters along the road.

HRANT

At last, the sun is rising! And now, the peoples of this land can say good morning to each other in their own language. Mine is in Armenian. "*Pariluys.*" *Pariluys*, oh beautiful land of mine.

And even if our state radio and television stations are only doing so for the sake of appearances, there are publishers bringing out works in Anatolian languages, while Leyla Zana and her friends, veterans of the struggle for Kurdish identity, are being released from prison.

Meanwhile, Jivan Gasparyan, the great *duduk* player, has brought the music of peace to Turkish television audiences. For the first time ever, they have aired a film about the Armenians' most painful days.

Pariluys, oh beautiful land of mine. *Pariluys.*

Without a doubt, none of this is going to resolve the problems that were taboo and insurmountable for so many long years, but it does offer us something more important: a chance to escape the claws of history and move beyond the suffering that has held us captive for so long. On one side, we have those who say, "An end to the cease-fire, a return to war," and on the other, we have those who say, "No, we've had enough weapons, blood, and tears." It has never been so important for Turkey's intellectuals to stand together.

The moment has come for the intellectuals of the East and the West to move fast. We must roll up our sleeves and forge a unity of conscience the likes of which we have never before seen so that we can bring about the peace we all desire. The name of our ship is *Democracy*, and it has embarked on a path of no return.

"*Pariluys*, my dear Turkey. May your day be full of light."

FERHAT KENTEL

At the time Hrant was just starting up *Agos*, he was a member of both the New Democracy Movement and the Helsinki Citizens Association. In the years that followed, he took part in all meetings concerning the democratization process. But what was even more important was that he carried the Armenian issue with him to all of these platforms.

We worked together on the Minorities Commission at the Helsinki Citizens Association. When he spoke of what it meant to be a minority in Turkey, and when he described how the minorities had been stripped of their property, these revelations brought guilt to us all. We learned about the Armenian issue from Hrant, and, deep inside, we felt what it meant to be an Armenian in Turkey.

DİLEK KURBAN

In 2005, I was asked to organize a conference on minority rights for TESEV. As a person from Dersim, I knew plenty of Alevis and Kurds, but I had never met a non-Muslim. And, of course, it was Hrant who came to my aid. When I made contact with those I hoped might participate, all I had to do was say his name. At the two-day conference we brought into being together, we heard from scholars recounting in detail how, step by step, Turkey's minorities had been dispossessed. But the most memorable talk was the one in which Hrant offered his insider's perspective.

HRANT

Minorities have served as the main target of the state and of every succeeding government since the founding of the republic, and throughout that time, the government has been consistent in their efforts to reduce them in size. Sometimes this has meant reducing their numbers, while, at other times, it has meant reducing their assets. If you reduce their numbers, the question of their assets is left unresolved. If you reduce their assets, the question of their numbers is likewise left unresolved. Thus exposed, they become easy targets for the state and also for the society whose views it has manipulated.

This policy of reduction is a management decision and a political choice. In this country, the late Ayşe Nur Zarakolu was tried for publishing Yves Ternon's *The Armenian Taboo*. She was tried for inciting the people to hatred. She was acquitted, and we should note the grounds: "There were no longer enough Armenians in the country to incite significant hatred."

Going back to the 1970s, when the Cyprus issue was heating up—there arrived a decision to reduce the assets of minority foundations, and, in its judgment, the Court of Appeals had the gall to classify us minority Turks as foreigners, and they confiscated our foundations' property.

So, let's see, how did the Turkish Republic explain this policy of reducing its own population? It framed its discussion in terms of security risk. In so doing, it presented the injustices done to the minorities as legitimate and necessary, and it continues doing so to this day.

We just celebrated the fiftieth anniversary of the riots of September 6–7, 1955. Even today, fifty years after those painful, undeniable events, when our country was seeking admission to the EU, forget apologies—we have yet to see a single state or government official offering so much as two words of sorrow. In summary, there is one question I believe to be more important than all others in Turkey today, and we must keep asking each other how to answer it: "We reduced these peoples' numbers, and we seized their assets. What did we gain by that, and what did we lose?"

ETYEN MAHÇUPYAN

It was April 2005. Hrant was charged under Article 301 for a single sentence in his celebrated series in *Agos* on Armenian identity. At the same time, he and I had been invited together to the Turkish National Assembly. The occasion, organized jointly by the Assembly's EU Membership Commission and the Foreign Affairs Commission to discuss the Armenian question, brought together around thirty ambassadors and deputies. This was the first gathering of its kind, and it opened up the possibility of dialogue. It was with this knowledge that we agreed to speak there.

HRANT

We were a people who had lived on Anatolian soil for three thousand years, and one day we were no longer there. We lost all connection with that land. A people's culture is inextricably linked with the lands in which it is rooted, and when it loses those roots, it ceases to exist as a people.

This is the main reason why the Armenian diaspora continues to search for its roots in 1915 – because it was never able to set down roots elsewhere. The Armenian people believed that their forefathers were done a great injustice and that this injustice has yet to be acknowledged. So, tell me, is this not an honorable position? I stand before you, asking this question of the peoples of Turkey.

When I have visited the Armenian world, and when I have spoken with the diaspora, what I asked them is this: "If a Turk denies the genocide, do you wish to prove him dishonorable?" The man standing before you believes that genocide is a grievous crime and knows it to be racism, but he also believes that his own ancestors could never be guilty of racism or genocide. Is this not also an honorable position?

In my opinion, both sides are capable of seeing the other's position as honorable.

So, yes, the ruling and opposition parties have offered us an opening, but we need more than just an opening; we need a new approach. Say, for example, that the director of the Turkish Historical Institute makes a statement saying that "if the Armenians know the location of any mass graves, they should come and show me where they are, and I'll open it up." By saying this, he is making light of the Armenian people's suffering. Nothing can come from a discussion about skeletons. That is why what is more important than looking at history is deciding how to look at history. And to decide that, you don't need documents, you need ethics and a conscience.

Beyond approach, there is a second issue: we must separate history from politics. Let us not try to resolve our historical disputes before resolving our political ones. Let us not say to Armenia, "First, let's talk history and establish what happened, and when we've done that, we can establish relations." Because you can't begin talking until you've established relations. First, let's resolve our political relations with Armenia and at once move to normalizing relations between the two peoples.

In the past, Europe colluded in the efforts of these peoples to destroy each other; today, we ourselves must try to forge our peace. This project offers the most responsible way forward and is far more important than parliamentary genocide resolutions.

ORAL ÇALIŞLAR

For Hrant, the normalization of Turkish-Armenian relations became a mission, almost. To move this forward, it was crucial to hold meetings inside Turkey, where the Armenian issue could be discussed in the way that it was now coming to be discussed abroad. One day, he came bouncing in, saying, "Something wonderful is going to happen in September! We're going to have a meeting on the Armenian issue in Turkey! This is historic! This is a first!"

HALİL BERKTAY

The ninetieth anniversary of 1915 was in 2005. After meeting for years at the University of Chicago and the University of Michigan, we scholars thought the time had come to organize a meeting inside Turkey. Together with our friends in the history and social science departments of three major universities, we formed an organizing committee. Our aim was to speak out as scholars of conscience against Turkish official ideology of denial. Of course, all hell broke loose, so we postponed the meeting to autumn.

At that point, Kemal Kerinçsiz and a far right group known as the Grand Union of Lawyers Association—names that had first come to our ears in the cases that were being brought against Hrant—petitioned the courts and succeeded in stopping the conference. But we stood firm. The intellectuals attending the conference lodged complaints with the president, the prime minister, and his ministers, drawing attention to the threats posed to freedom of expression and the prosecutions against the author Orhan Pamuk, the professor Baskın Oran, and the journalist Hrant Dink.

MURAT BELGE

It was a very strange situation, actually. Everyone, including the President of the Republic, was discussing the court order to stop our conference, which was entitled, "Ottoman Armenians in the Last Years of the Empire." In the end, the justice minister Cemil Çiçek caved in; having previously accused the conference organizers of "stabbing us in the back," he suggested that we hold the conference in a different venue. So we took the conference to another university and held it there. On the first day of the conference, when an ultranationalist gang outside Bilgi University tried to push through the doors, raining eggs, tomatoes, and curses down on us—well, after all of the tensions we'd lived through, all they did was add a bit of salt and pepper to the proceedings. Twenty-five years earlier, they would have shot us or bombed us.

Hrant was on the organizing committee, and throughout all of this, he had one thought on his mind: to make this conference a reality. And the speech he gave there brought tears to the eyes of everyone in the room.

HRANT

The essence of life is in the relationships that living things form with their habitat. This is the case for all living things—for plants and for animals, and for human beings. They can exist only in their habitats; they cannot survive otherwise. Even if you carry them off on a golden tray, you are still severing their connection with the place where they once lived; you are severing their roots. That's what happened during the deportations. A people that had lived on these lands for 3,000 years, rooting their culture and their civilization in these same lands, were expelled from them, sent to wander to the ends of the earth. Some died, some stayed, some dispersed. So there you have it: Armenian identity in a nutshell.

Let me finish with a true story:

One day, I received a call from an elderly gentleman in a town near Sivas. "Son," he said, "we've been looking for you, and now we've found you. There's an old woman here, and she must be one of yours. This woman has consigned herself to God's mercy. If you can find her relatives, tell them to come and get her, and if you can't, let us say our own prayers over her and bury her here."

Her name was Beatrice, and she was seventy years old. She was visiting from France.

I made a few calls, and in ten minutes I had tracked down her relatives—at the end of the day, we all know each other, because there are so few of us. I went over to the relatives' store and asked them, "Do you know anyone who meets this description?"

The middle-aged woman in the shop turned around and said, "She's my mother." She went on to tell me that her mother lived in France and that she visited Turkey three or four times a year and went straight out to her village. As soon as I told her what had happened, she immediately set out on the road. I asked her if she was going to bring back her mother's body. "Dear brother," she said, "that's what I'm trying to do, but there's this uncle here who keeps trying to talk me out of it." Still weeping, she handed the phone to her uncle. I got angry at this uncle. Why was he making this woman cry?

"My son," the uncle said, "I didn't say a thing. I told her, 'My girl, she's your mother; she belongs to you. But if you ask me, you should leave her here. To be buried here. The water has found its way to its crack,' I said."

And at that moment, I was undone. Undone by this old Anatolian expression, this old way of looking at things. Yes, the water had found its way to its crack.

It's true. The Armenians really do have their eyes on this country, this land, because this is where our roots are. But do not worry—they do not want to take this land, they just want to come back to this land, to sink deep inside it . . .

25

A Turkish Armenian in the Armenian World

HRANT

There are Armenians living in every part of the world, but the center from which they radiate is Anatolia. This migration, which began in 1850, initially motivated by economic reasons and sometimes by personal choice, became mandatory with the 1915 "deportation order." And, before long, Armenians were living in exile all over the world.

In the years of the republic, those who survived found their way to Istanbul and, with time, moved on to settle all across the world.

The Anatolian Armenians now inhabit a space as wide as the world itself. They call it the diaspora, but in their minds they are still living in Anatolia. In other words, the diaspora is their "world republic of Anatolia," or even their "global version of Anatolia."

ALİ BAYRAMOĞLU

Hrant was a man who grounded his political thinking and political positions in his own practice. To achieve this, he paid close attention to what was going on around him and what he felt. After all, the stories he told were about his own experiences. He was able to develop his utterly unique ideas about the diaspora after getting a passport and beginning to travel abroad, where he was able to reach and touch diaspora Armenians. This was confined to the last five years of his life because, for a very long time, Hrant was not able to get a passport. This matter troubled him a great deal. He said that a security investigation had barred him from having a passport. This may well have come from the fact that he had once been a leftist and was still a politicized Armenian.

HRANT

I have never in my life killed a man. I was never judged to have been a member of an [illegal] organization. And I have never been found guilty of tax fraud. Every time I have been taken to court for political reasons, I have been acquitted. I have never been given a sentence. And never has a court ruled that I cannot travel abroad. But, apparently, I am a suspect person. However, no one has ever told me why.

In the face of this injustice, I must confess that I am not in a position to complain about where that leaves me. At the end of the day, this is my country, and that is more than enough for me. I have never once suggested to my lawyers that we should seek redress at the European Court of Human Rights. Until now, I have simply confirmed my patriotism and told myself there was no need to go abroad. If I was going to have to go that far to get a passport, then, the hell with it! If the state is going to give me a passport, then fine. If not, that was fine, too. I wasn't going to go begging. And that was where I left it.

AYŞE ÖNAL

Hrant was very upset that he couldn't get a passport. What troubled him the most was that his daughter was heading for America for her doctorate studies, and he was not going to be able to visit her there.

The rest of us—all of us who had been prosecuted and sentenced and sent to prison during the military regime—had by now managed to get passports. But they still weren't letting him have one, you see.

At first, Hrant felt just upset about this, but over time he started getting very angry. "If they won't give me one, then I'm not going begging," he said. Then, suddenly, a passport landed at his feet. I happened to be at *Agos* that day. I was once again arguing with him about the position he'd taken when a courier came for Hrant. He opened the envelope, and then he handed me his passport, saying, "So there we are, then. Now I have one too!" As if this was the real joke!

GERARD LIBARIDIAN

I knew that Hrant did not have a passport and had been unable to travel abroad. We wanted him badly to come to our workshop at the University of Michigan. Of course, by this time, I was no longer in the Armenian government and was teaching at the university. I called my old interlocutor at the Turkish Foreign Ministry, Candan Azer, with whom I had started the negotiations on behalf of Armenia for the normalization of relations between Armenia and Turke between 1992 and 1994. I told him that they were making a big mistake, that Hrant was a bridge builder and the best asset for Turkey/Armenia relations. I spoke to him for twenty minutes or so and did not let him say a word. And then I said something like, "Candan, you have to give him a passport. Whether you do it for me as a personal favor and/or for Turkey, you have to do this. I have paid a price for dealing with you; if need be, consider this the price you pay for all your intransigence." He said nothing, and we hung up. Then Hrant got his passport. Now it is possible that others intervened too; I cannot know that. But I checked with Candan later when I saw him in Istanbul, and he confirmed that indeed he had intervened with conviction and had been able to have the ban lifted. I never told Hrant this story.

TANER AKÇAM

When Hrant finally got a passport, he found an opportunity to travel to America. At once, I invited him to a meeting at the University in Michigan at Ann Arbor. He had virtually no English and so was unable to contribute much to the meeting. With the help of a translator, he was able to follow what was going on. But of course he made the most of it, once again. He did lots of interviews with the participants and then he ran them, one by one, in *Agos*. At the open session he organized after the workshop, he was the spokesman. Speaking in Turkish. This first meeting in Ann Arbor was for Hrant a window that opened up to the world.

BASKIN ORAN

I traveled with Hrant on his first trip abroad to the Armenian conference held at the University of Michigan in March 2002. The plane was empty, and we sat side by side. The first thing he told me was that the day before, he had gone out to the airport in his corduroy suit and handed his new passport to the security officer. When this person told him that he was fine and could pass through security, he said, "No—I'm flying out tomorrow. I just came today to find out if there were going to be any difficulties."

Through the flight, we talked. And then, when the meal was served, he asked me if we paid up front or later. And, once again, we laughed, of course. But there was a lot of pain in that laughter. Shame on those who denied this man a passport for so long.

HRANT

For two weeks now, I have been with the diaspora Armenians of America and Canada. And, once again, I am beguiled by the mysterious enchantment of understanding things by seeing them. Once again, I am reminded that neither listening nor reading can yield such riches. Nothing but seeing! It's been one long line of firsts for me. And maybe it is something like staying at home until the age of fifty and then finally sensing one's sexuality to be overwhelmed by these powerful feelings . . .

I am still on this dizzying tour. From Chicago to Detroit, and then on to a four-day meeting at the University of Michigan, and from there to Canada. And from there on to New York, Boston, Chicago . . .

Of these meetings, I want to speak of the scholarship undertaken at the University of Michigan at Ann Arbor on Turkish-Armenian relations at the turn of the century.

The first to arrive in town, on the morning before the workshop, was Cengiz Çandar, and on the afternoon of the same day, it was Baskın Oran, his wife, and me. Taner Akçam was among those who did a lot of the legwork for our symposium. For two days, he was driving to and from the airport, picking us up one by one and taking us back to Ann Arbor.

In particular, I want to mention Fatma Müge Göçek, the head of the sociology department at the University of Michigan and the organizer of this meeting. Responding in a scholarly manner to the provocations of some Turkish attendants of the concluding session, she ensured a smooth ending for the conference. The same held true of Ronald Suny of the University of Chicago, Müge Hanım's highly resourceful ally, who lessened the tensions with his wit.

FATMA MÜGE GÖÇEK

In March 2002, we welcomed Armenian and Turkish academics and intellectuals at our second Workshop on Armenian Turkish Scholarship (WATS), and among them was Hrant. The reason for this was that while the diaspora and the Armenians of Armenia were well represented at our workshop, we had no Turkish Armenians. The absence of a Turkish Armenian perspective in our discussions was keenly felt.

Hrant's contribution to the meeting was very important—as I had guessed it would be—particularly because it was the first time that diaspora Armenians were able to enter into a dialogue with a Turkish Armenian.

RONALD SUNY

In 2000, we'd held our first workshop at the University of Chicago, bringing together Turkish and Armenian historians and social scientists to discuss the 1915 genocide. At our second workshop in 2002, hosted by Müge Göcek and Gerard Libaridian at the University of Michigan at Ann Arbor, we decided to hold an open session at which we invited journalists as well as scholars. Among those who joined us from Turkey was Hrant Dink, editor of *Agos*, the Turkish Armenian weekly newspaper.

Hrant was a true patriot. He dreamed of a Turkey in which Turks, Kurds, Armenians, Jews, and Greeks could live together in peace. The only thing he couldn't bear was the denial of the painful history that these peoples had shared. This was why he took a critical stance against the society he lived in.

The talk he gave at this workshop moved us all deeply. He spoke in a language very different from the one to which we were accustomed in the academic world. He expressed even the most complex issues in words that came straight from the heart, and, with these words, he brought us all together.

BASKIN ORAN

On the Turkish side there were scholars asking, "What did we do? Who did it? They were the ones who did it to us?" Meanwhile, on the Armenian side, we had some of the most radical names of the diaspora. With one exception, no one there assumed a stance openly holding Turkey to blame. Discussions were balanced, in deference to the difficulties presented by the subject and the constitution of the workshop itself. Even Professor Hovannissian, who was known for his radical views, chose his words with the utmost of care, saying,

"I'm tired of talking only about negatives. Let me take this opportunity to talk about the good things." With that, he shared his knowledge of the Turks who had helped the Armenians during the deportations. There were lengthy discussions, but no raised voices.

On the other hand, the Armenian contingent took every opportunity to use what conference organiser F. Müge Göçek called the G-word, a term that the Turkish participants were unwilling to use. What struck me about the diaspora was this: they were always talking about 1915, never touching on the present, and when they mentioned the Armenians of Turkey, they counted them as part of the diaspora.

The most important contribution came from Gerard Libaridian, the architect of the rapprochement politics put forward by the former president of Armenia, Ter Petrosyan.

GERARD LIBARIDIAN

I think the value of my presentation was its topic: state relations between Turkey and Armenia since the independence of Armenia in 1991. As advisor to Ter Petrossian and, for a while, also as First Deputy Minister of Foreign Affairs, I happened to have been the main person in charge of Armenia-Turkey state-level negotiations from 1992 to 1997, so I offered in a simple narrative those facts as well as a perspective.

On the other hand, Hrant's participation in the workshop, whether in the group or in smaller informal settings, was, I thought, cathartic. You see, a good part of the controversy on the genocide and its denial had emerged as a result of the issue having become rooted in the identities of the Armenian people, especially the diaspora and the Turkish state, and what the latter taught its citizens—hence the synergy between identity and academic battles. Hrant tried what had not tried before: he attempted to reconcile two identities, that of a citizen of Turkey and that of an ethnic Armenian with strong memories of the past, one with Anatolian roots.

CENGİZ ÇANDAR

On the last day, Hrant and I summarized the workshop proceedings at an open session and answered questions. What was interesting here was the provocative stance taken by the majority of Turks in attendance. But the diaspora representatives at the previous sessions had done their bit, too. They painted such a negative portrait of Turkey that those of us who'd come from Turkey began to doubt, from time to time, that they were discussing the country where we lived. Hrant, meanwhile, listened to the conversation intently, aggrieved at the way the diaspora representatives described Turkish Armenians as "unfortunates fallen into the claws of the Turks" and showing them no importance. He took it and took it until finally he said, "Look, wherever you pass your days—in America, or Canada, or France, or Argentina—you live there as if you're from there. It's only on April 24 that you become Armenians. But we live every day as Armenians, and only on April 24 is it asked of us that we forget we are Armenians. So there you have it, the difference between us."

MÜGE GÖCEK

This is what Hrant said to the diaspora Armenians at the meeting: "We are living in our fatherland, even if it is by the skin of our teeth, and that is why our priorities are different. Our aim is not to have the genocide recognized, as yours is; what we want most is that Turkey democratize. Only if it is democratized can we make things right for Armenians in Turkey."

This was the first time that the diaspora Armenians had ever met an Armenian like this. Also, when he said that what we wanted from Turkey in terms of land was enough for a man to be buried under, he brought about an entirely new opening in the debate in the diaspora about land claims. And he said all of this in plain and modest language, showing to us all how good he was as a preacher. We scholars were very influenced by him, while Hrant was very influenced by what came out of our workshop. It was with great enthusiasm that he joined our workshops in Minnesota and Salzburg, and he always gave us his support.

GERARD LIBARIDIAN

As the organizers of the second workshop, we were very pleased by Hrant's participation. Hrant was not an academic scholar, but he certainly turned out to be a giant of an intellectual. He had thought deeply about our issues and searched not only with his mind but also with his soul.

What made Hrant a unique personality was his determination, his moral courage, his refusal to attack back, and his infinite patience and tolerance. In the gentlest way, he was challenging the underlying assumptions of both institutionalized camps consisting of those Turks and Armenians who had found a comfortable niche in their identity politics, on occasion determining the contours and limits of scholarship. He was challenging those who fed on each other's rhetoric, as if they needed each other.

I think Hrant's temperament and ability to bridge different worlds were critical to the creation of a level of discourse that made it possible for his project to continue and develop.

CENGİZ ÇANDAR

During this, his first encounter with diaspora Armenians in Ann Arbor, Hrant managed to reach out and touch everyone he met, with no exceptions. Among us were some of the giants of Armenian historiography, Vahakn Dadrian and Richard Hovanissian. Vahakn Dadrian, author of *The History of Armenian Genocide* and an acknowledged authority on this subject, took every opportunity over this three-day workshop to offer fierce criticisms of Turkey. But even he was moved by Hrant's warmth.

HRANT

While in Michigan I had a chance to meet Vahakn Dadrian, and I have no doubt that this encounter made its mark on me. Outside the sessions, we had discussions that went on for hours. We were able to bring all of our differences of opinion right out into the open. When I asked him, "If you were in a position to choose, what would you prefer: that Turkey acknowledged the genocide, or that, in advance of that, Turkey democratized?"

At first, he didn't answer. "Come back to the house," he said. "We can talk it through there." I did not make him wait to hear my own view: I told him that my first and essential choice was for Turkey to democratize, and I pressed him to visit me in Turkey.

VAHAKN DADRIAN

Before meeting Hrant Dink, I already knew about *Agos*, which I was reading. It was because I had been following this publication through its earlier years, appreciating its civilized and balanced line, that I'd formed a certain image of Hrant in my mind. It was during this conference on the Armenian issue that my image was confirmed. A year after the University of Michigan workshop, Dink would join us at our third workshop at the University of Minnesota, once again showing his serious and balanced engagement with the Armenian issue.

HRANT

From America, we went to Canada, and in both Toronto and Montreal we were able to meet for the first time with Canada's Armenians. At meetings, we shared our views on Istanbul's Armenians, the diaspora, Armenia, the Turkish–Armenian dialogue, and similar topics with rooms filled to overflowing.

Truthfully, the degree of interest took me by surprise. Did everyone share my views? Certainly not, but I do think that we all had an influence on each other. And this was enough, for now . . .

Then, at the insistent invitation of the Turkish Armenians in the Australian cities of Melbourne and Sydney, we put our passports back in our pockets and set out once again. We held our first meeting in a large hall in one of Sydney's sports clubs. They called it a conference, but it would be more accurate to say that I was presenting more as a journalist, bringing them news from Turkey. In Sydney, Turkish Armenians were often belittled by various Armenian nationalists who'd settled there as benighted or even "Turkified" Armenians.

By explaining how we stood up to the injustices visited on Armenians in Turkey, and how we wished to open a dialogue to open up between Turkey and Armenia, I tried to convey the distance Turkey has traveled toward democracy. I described how an important section of Turkish society is showing a genuine interest in the truth about the Armenian genocide, and I offered examples from the media and academia. My talks helped to raise morale. And so we came to the end of yet another tiring but happy day.

During the two weeks we spent in Australia, we managed to visit all of our schools and speak to their pupils. This is what happened in one of them: One of the teachers had drawn a map on a piece of cardboard and was teaching the students where they came from. Some were from Syria, others from Iran, Baghdad, and Lebanon. I reminded her that something is missing on this map, and I and tell the children that they all come from Anatolia.

TANER AKÇAM

Hrant gave a great deal of importance to his links with the diaspora. To set up these connections, he traveled from one country to the next to let them know how Turkey had changed. He was very troubled by how little the diaspora organizations understood about the new Turkey as well as by their general lack of interest. "Why can't they understand how important Turkey is if the Armenian issue is ever to be resolved? It's here where things will be settled," he would say. Because he saw democratization as the ultimate aim, he wanted the diaspora to give this movement its support.

HRANT

After Australia, we went to Los Angeles. But it's not really Los Angeles. It's more like "Los Armenos." There were almost half a million Armenians living in this part of California. A hundred thousand of them have come here from Armenia.

I am able to meet and address these people at two meetings in Los Angeles. Like a stork I carry news from us to them, and them to us. And in both directions, longing.

At another point I was fortunate enough to attend a meeting with the leading writers of the Armenian diaspora press. Krikor Şenyan, for example: this great journalist, known by all sides for his impartiality and for his courage in standing up against injustice, even to the point of risking his life, carried with pride the scars of a deathly beating at the hands of the Tashnags.

TANER AKÇAM

Hrant did not like the way the diaspora set out to resolve the Armenian issue as a third state and seized every opportunity to criticize this. And that is why he had as many enemies inside the diaspora as he had friends. But Hrant himself had no trouble with the diaspora; he came out against the Tashnag's hard political line, but that was all.

It was interesting, watching Hrant's dealings with the diaspora. The diaspora neither knew nor understood today's Turkey. As Hrant described to them the Turkey of the year 2000, the diaspora would remind him of what happened after 1908. They saw Hrant as this strange creature who reminded them that they were so caught up in history that they'd got stuck in it. There were even some who suspected him of being an agent of the Turkish state.

HRANT

For a number of years now, Turkish and Armenian historians, scholars, and intellectuals have been gathering together in various American universities; the third of these gatherings took place in Minnesota. About fifty people were in attendance, and the atmosphere was altogether different from before. Gone was the reticence that both sides had shown in previous years. Relations had begun to normalize.

At this year's meeting, alongside the historical discussions, there were opportunities for each side to explore their opposing attitudes and viewpoints, presenting papers on issues such as identity and "the other."

It was everyone's shared wish to establish similar workshops in both Turkish and Armenian universities.

TANER AKÇAM

Hrant and I were again together at the workshop held in March 2003 at the University of Minnesota in Minneapolis-St. Paul. He was very influenced by these workshops, and he kept saying that we had to organize a conference like this in Turkey. His dream would come true at last in 2005, with the first Armenian conference in Istanbul.

During these conferences in the United States, Hrant established very strong personal ties with the representatives of the diaspora. This was extremely important, because Hrant was uniquely equipped to open up channels for change with the people he met.

It was like this: As recently as ten years earlier, even though there were many Armenians living in the United States who wished to visit Turkey, the vast majority feared what might happen to them if they did. There were even those who said, "I have an Armenian name on my passport. If I went to Turkey, would they arrest me?"

Among these people and inside the diaspora as a whole there were those who were well known and also at a level to influence Turkish-Armenian issues. "You send those people to me," Hrant used to say. And I would initiate relations and then give them Hrant's and *Agos*'s addresses. Hrant would meet them at the airport, settle them in his office at *Agos*, and begin to talk. In the evening, he would take them to an Armenian *meyhane* called Boncuk and continue there. And it might seem hard to believe, but every one of these people returned to the United States saying that their fears about Turkey and the Turks were gone and that their views changed. Hrant had, in effect, turned himself into some sort of prejudice-breaking machine.

HRANT

For a while now, I have been traveling in the Near East with a group of friends of different leanings and from different walks of life. We have amongus Islamists, communists, liberals, and Christians. Some of us are politicians; others are journalists, writers, and professors. To date, we have visited Iran, Syria, Egypt, and Jordan. Wherever we have gone, we have met with politicians and academics, with members of the ruling party and the opposition, and with ordinary people. Our aim is not to view the East through Western eyes but to understand each place on its own terms.

NURAY MERT

In June 2003, a small group of leftist, Muslim, and democratic intellectuals embarked on an initiative we called the "Eastern Conference." Hrant was part of this. Our aim was to respond to the American invasion of Iraq, to establish links with intellectuals in neighboring countries, and, in so doing, to broaden the horizons of peace and freedom for those living alongside us. This was our pipe dream! We went to Syria, Iran, and Lebanon. In all of these countries, there was a world familiar to Hrant—especially in Aleppo and Beirut were there Armenians who'd gone from here to there. Because he thought that they weren't ready for us, he left us out of his first meetings. He played the pioneer.

ETYEN MAHÇUPYAN

During the Eastern Conference trips, two distinct perspectives emerged. One group opposed the United States, while the other group wanted to distinguish the region's pro-democracy groups from the others. Hrant was in the second camp, but this was not overly important for him, because he had joined this group primarily to track down families that had been banished to Deir-ez-Zor in 1915. Through these trips, he was literally going out to hunt down Armenians. Usually, he would contact them on his own, returning with his address and phone books and his tote bags full of books.

NURAY MERT

Sometimes, he reminded me of a child struggling to find a way to bring together two sides of an estranged family. In 2004, we went to Armenia with Hrant as our guide. This was an exhilarating but also somewhat strange encounter. We surprised those we met, and we also made them uneasy. In fact, we were an imposition. But we felt fine because we had Hrant at our side, and he was our brother as well as theirs. Wherever we went, Hrant was at home, but he was at the same time something of an outsider, like all Armenians, whether still living on their own land or spread out to all four corners of the world.

ETYEN MAHÇUPYAN

Hrant was beside himself with joy in Armenia. Even if he felt caught in the middle sometimes, this made little difference; the important thing was that

Turks and Armenians were coming together and making direct contact. To see them approaching each other on the human scale was for him the sign of a long-awaited miracle. I remember him as unfailingly happy, smiling, and energetic. He was overjoyed to be able to go to Etchmiadzin to visit Karekin II, Catholicos (Patriarch) of All Armenians,

In Yerevan, there was a meal one night during which a group of musicians were playing. Hrant requested a tune. They began playing "The Black Sea Was Churning," but with Armenian lyrics—despite the fact that the lyrics of this song were by the Azeri poet Ahmet Cevad and the melody by the Armenian minstrel Sayat Nova. We were all shocked. While Hrant was singing "The Bride from the Mountains," the group sang along in Turkish. His joy at that moment was boundless. This was what coming together meant for him! To discover that what you thought was yours alone also belonged to the other, and to learn to understand what that meant.

HRANT

That the Eastern Conference's last journey would be significantly different from the ones that had come before was evident from the outset. Until now, we had visited neighboring countries that were largely Muslim, but now we were going to a country that was thoroughly Christian. Furthermore, this country was Armenia, and as our own country had no diplomatic relations with it, the borders were closed.

What all the Turkish intellectuals agreed upon was this: there was a wall dividing the two countries, and it had been woven by history, and to scale it was not something that would happen between today and tomorrow. But was it just history that made it so heavy? No. What was most important was the heaviness of today. The most important reason for Armenia's current stance is its lack of trust in Turkey. It is epitomized by the negative politics conducted since Armenia's independence, which is layered and refreshed by the sense of insecurity coming from history.

In recent times, we intellectuals of Turkey have been discussing two fundamental issues along with the proposed approval of Turkey's accession to the EU on December 17. One is to find a common language on the subject of history, but the more important issue is the establishment of diplomatic relations with Armenia and the immediate opening of the border.

ETYEN MAHÇUPYAN

The decision to begin the process of Turkey's accession to the European Union was to be made on December 17, 2004. Hrant firmly believed that the accession process would be greatly aided by several measures to further the democratization of Turkey, with the Armenian issue being at the fore.

At just around this time, we received an invitation from France to meet with the Armenian diaspora. The organizer of this gathering was Jean Keheyan, one of most distinguished French dissidents. This was to be a new experience for us both. Together with Ali Bayramoğlu, we set out for Marseilles to come together for the first time with the Armenians of France.

HRANT

The date for Turkey's EU negotiations was approaching. The French Armenians had launched a "no" campaign in opposition.

They had just one reason for opposing Turkey's accession to the EU: "Turkey's refusal to acknowledge the Armenian genocide." I, on the other hand, had many reasons for wanting Turkey to become part of the EU. First, I am a citizen of Turkey, and I want to be European like they are. Second, I am a member of a minority, and I want to live with the same freedom and security as they do. Next, I am thinking about my brothers and sisters in Armenia, and if Turkey is admitted to the EU, then Armenia itself will have a better chance of entering, too.

At the present moment, there is no issue in Turkey that is more important than accession to the EU. Not even the prospect of actually joining it.

As the current discussion ultimately demonstrates, the values we describe as European are not absolute because we are talking about European values that are only now struggling to absorb a multiculturality that includes İslam. With this matter yet to be resolved, it is very difficult to know what tomorrow will bring and what transformations lie ahead. Even if in future years, when we have reached that point, if it turns out to be a disaster, let's not stop ourselves from celebrating right now because this is the most beautiful part of the process.

And it was from this perspective that the meeting called by Jean Kehayan, that bold dissenting voice from the left, was so important. For the first time ever, we were going to meet with the Armenians of France to discuss Turkey's accession to the EU. But before we could even get there, there was an outcry as the hardcore Armenian activists of Marseilles did whatever they could to urge people not to attend. Their main target was Jean Kehayan. His superlative column in *Liberation*, in which this fearless democrat spoke out with such eloquent brilliance against the dominant position of French Armenians, coming out in favor of Turkey's entry into the EU, was enough to incense the hard-core Armenian activists. Oh, how they railed against Jean . . .

JEAN KEHAYAN

The efforts to pass a genocide-recognition resolution in the French National Assembly was essentially driven by those deputies who represented areas with strong Armenian communities. For them, the issue had nothing to do with the bitter historical burden that we Armenians carry; it had to do with votes. And it was at a time when another such proposed resolution happened to coincide with the most heated moment in the debate about Turkey's entry into the EU that Hrant came, at my invitation, to meet the Armenians of France in Marseilles. And it was during his first meetings with the diaspora that he found himself up against the harshest activists behind the "no" campaign. In his speech, he spoke with a confidence and charisma that could move mountains.

The leaders of the Armenian diaspora, having turned the genocide into a sort of industry, were well aware of the significance of this first great gathering, and that was why they did everything in their power to stop people attending. They even went so far as to organize a rival event on the same evening.

HRANT

What saddened me the most was that the historian Yves Ternon did not attend the meeting. It was a shame, because had he attended, I would have been able to tell him about all of the cases that had been opened against his book, *The Armenian Taboo*, following its translation into Turkish, and the struggles we went through to keep the book in circulation, and all of the changes we had seen in Turkey from that day to this. As for Ternon's reason for not attending—"I refuse to sit at the same table with Turks"—well, the truth is, it broke my heart twice. First, he is wrong to refuse to sit with Turks. There is quite simply no way to effect a solution without entering into a dialogue with Turks. But the reason he broke my heart a second time was that he ignored the fact that two of the people coming from Turkey to attend the meeting were not Turks, but Turkish Armenians.

ALİ BAYRAMOĞLU

This meeting was Hrant's first encounter with the Armenian diaspora of France. Many of those who utter his name with such love today then saw his presence as a shadow over the world they'd created, and they voiced this opinion openly. Even after the talk Hrant gave in Marseilles had made its great impression, the majority of the French Armenian Federation remained vehemently opposed to him. I was the only Turk in the hall where the meeting took place. Hrant spoke in Armenian. He spoke like a politician, first standing and then sitting down. As he spoke, he thumped the table from time to time and raised his voice. I did not know Armenian but I could tell from the tone of his voice and his body language that he was castigating the diaspora for its obsession with the past and its policy of perpetual enmity against the Turks.

HRANT

Like all other countries in the world, Turkey is changing. It's changing very slowly, but in the end, it still counts for change, so what a shame it is that you are unable or unwilling to see this change. It may be that it frightens you because it means you would have to change, too. Perhaps you are the ones who are not changing and who resist the very idea.

There is a significant contradiction in your stated position, and this has to do with not knowing what you want. If what you want is for Turkey

to acknowledge the genocide, then you shouldn't come out against the democratization of Turkey; instead, you should be supporting it. But if you oppose the engine that would drive that democratization—Turkey's entry into the EU—you are in effect standing in the way of its democratization and perhaps the chance for it to own up to its history.

And here is what this shows: it may well be that you fear the day that Turkey acknowledges the genocide . . .

JEAN KEHAYAN

I was no stranger to Hrant's views on the narrow-mindedness of the Armenian diaspora in France. When I made my first visit to Turkey and went to meet him, he convinced me, too; he was instrumental in dismantling the sterotypes I'd brought with me.

And in Marseilles, Hrant asserted that , as a Turkish Armenian and a Turkish citizen, he deserved the same rights as those enjoyed by all citizens of the EU. He argued that the official history of Turkey, founded as it was on the lies about the 1915 Armenian genocide, would not begin to founder until the day arrived when it could be freely debated. "It falls to us to correct the historical record," he said, "for if we fail to do so, Turkey will remain in thrall to this fearful skeleton in its closet and never be able to enter the modern age."

At the meeting that night in Marseilles, Hrant, Etyen Mahcupyan, and Ali Bayramoğlu stood up to that dark opposition with great intelligence. They informed the audience that that democratic future of Turkey and Armenia lay in the hands of people who thought as they did.

HRANT

Wherever they happen to live in the world, and whatever else they dream of, every Armenian's most fervent wish is that Armenia thrive and survive, bringing happiness to those who live there. But even though this is your dream, too, you jeopardize it by opposing any effort to establish friendly relations with Turkey, or to open the border.

Whereas an opening of the border would be the first step in the normalization of relations between the two nations, leading to an amelioration of their problems and an increase in cooperation, let us not forget how this would contribute to the peace and security of the entire region; all of this would in turn bring stability to Armenia. What your policy demonstrates is that you are driven by emotions alone, leaving reason to one side. The time has come for you to ask yourself which kind of neighbor would be more reliable: a reasonable Turkey inside the EU, or a Turkey that has been excluded from it.

ISABELLE KORTIAN

Hrant Dink was an iconoclast. He shattered taboos and brought prejudice and discrimination out into the open. He was the first in the Armenian world to see the recognition campaign as a game between the winners and the losers and to stand up against it. He openly questioned the legitimacy of the positions taken by various sectors of the Armenian world. Until the end, he criticized those in the diaspora who venerated the lost victims of 1915 while using Turkey's EU accession as a political football. But at the same time, with his honorable deportment, he shattered the diaspora's prevailing stereotype of Turkish Armenians as "prisoners or turncoats."

HRANT

My impressions from the Marseilles conference can be summarized as such: The Armenians of France were vehemently against Turkey's entry into the EU. They viewed Turkey to have been in thrall to a regime that has not changed over the past 150 years and will never change in the future, and they fear its absorption into the European Union. They see Turkey's recent moves towards democratization as some sort of trick to hoodwink the Europeans. Their trump card is the Article 305 in the Turkish Penal Code, which may give ground to the argument that the mention of the Armenian genocide is a crime.

A number of them believe that Armenia has nothing gain from the opening of the Turkish–Armenian border, while Turkey could benefit considerably.

When it comes to the recognition of the genocide, however, there are diverging views. The great and silent majority believe that if Turkey recognized the genocide, it would bring them peace of mind, and that this would be enough. However, a radical group of activists holds that this would not be enough, and that it is also necessary to demand restitution. That said, even these activists recognize their dream of reclaiming land as empty, for it would be impossible to implement. Most certainly this group would have been undone when Armenian President Koçaryan declared that "Armenia had no claim on Turkish territory."

ETYEN MAHÇUPYAN

While we were in Marseilles, the Tashnags wanted to speak to us outside the meeting, so we went with Hrant to see them. We were shocked to discover how harsh and bigoted they were. Even at that first meeting, we had begun to think that we could complement each other. Neither of us wrote our speeches. Mine spoke to people's minds, and his to their hearts.

A good speech is one that allows the speaker to develop his thoughts along the way. When Hrant spoke, he followed his feelings. This was effective in a number of ways. To speak well, one has to put oneself to the test. Hrant's speeches may have seemed emotional on the surface, but those feelings were securely and intelligently grounded. The listeners could see this. Hrant was a politician from the day he was born, and he knew how to bring audiences into the palm of his hand. He had a power to affect people to an extent that is rarely seen.

In the end, we have become the "diaspora duo." Together, we set out to take the diasporans by surprise and shatter their received ideas, and we succeeded.

HRANT

Throughout all of this, the questions we asked ourselves were this: Who were we? Why was it that certain things had begun to revolve around us? How did it happen that we journalists, we news reporters, had turned into the news? Why did everything we said make headlines? Why were both foreign and domestic news reporters seeking us out and interviewing us? What was going on? Were we being swept along by a force greater than our own will?

These questions were hidden inside the details of what we'd been going through. Let me say this much: a group belonging to the harshest representatives of the diaspora came to me after my speech and said, "Until today, we looked at you and your friend Etyen with some suspicion, but now that we have seen how sincere you are, in your words and in your thinking, we confess that we were mistaken," and these words of theirs sent me off into the corner to shed tears. But so be it. Like it or not, we Turkish Armenians were fated to shed these tears. But the days of pillage and plunder are over. By dint of our will, we would change our fate.

ETYEN MAHÇUPYAN

Hrant liked saying, "Until today, the diaspora Armenians did whatever they did without consulting Turkey's Armenians, but from now on, they're going to have to." That was his great dream—that they would listen to what Turkey's Armenians had to say. He took this dream all over the world with him and made the most of it.

In all of his dealings with the diaspora, Hrant's chief aim was for them to come to a proper understanding of contemporary Turkey. In his thoughts about how the future might unfold, he was also tactical. And so there were politics. When speaking to an audience, he was fully aware of the fact that a speech without their involvement would be apolitical.

Once he'd created a space in which the audience could engage with politics, he knew there were things he could change. This wasn't just a theory; as he spoke, he would bring that audience into his speech. There were two key moments in which he would do this. First, he would ask, "In your opinion, do you think Turks know what happened in 1915?" Then he would ask, "Do you think Turkey should join the EU?" When he asked this question, he would stop and look at them, smiling. And then would come this question: "In your opinion, which is more important? That Turkey acknowledge the Armenian genocide, or that Turkey democratize?" He would ask this question in the same tone of voice you might use when telling a child a fairy tale. In his voice was the reassurance, "I don't mean to harm you."

When Hrant was with the diasporans, all he said to his audiences was, "Look at me." And when they looked, they remembered him. There he was: "the Armenian of the century."

ALİ BAYRAMOĞLU

We traveled from Marseilles to Paris by train. On the train, he began to sing the song, "Sare Gelin" ("The Bride from the Mountains"). He was singing it half in Armenian and half in Turkish. You know how Turkish workers going off to Europe will see a plain and then remember the Ankara steppes and then start singing a folk song—well, that's what he was like. He was the most Anatolian of us all. He was someone who missed his country, who longed for it.

In Paris, he took us to a tavern to hear an Armenian singer. There, he played our host with the greatest pride. He sang all night. When we left, he said he wanted to walk. It turned out to be a long way. In the end, his shoes started hurting him, but he didn't mind; he just pushed down the heels of his shoes and kept on walking. And on he walked, wearing one of those caps he loved to wear so much, with his jacket thrown over his shoulder. We were in Paris, but everything about him was Anatolian.

ETYEN MAHÇUPYAN

Because I don't have a very good memory, I cannot say exactly which date we went to which meeting together. What I remember of those trips are snapshots and how I was feeling at the time. So now when was it that Hrant and I shared the same bed? Was it in Marseilles, or was it in Paris? We were staying in this old and shabby hotel. That night, when he went to bed, he didn't turn off the light. Did he turn it off at home? Or did he always sleep with the light on? Was this a fear left over from childhood? I have no way of knowing. But he snored all night. And we'd been listening to him all day long. And now, with this snoring, it meant that he never shut up, day or night.

HRANT

I was abroad for almost a month. In a number of European cities and also in Yerevan, I attended meetings on the Armenian issue. Etyen Mahçupyan was with me for most of these. We began on April 5, 2005, at the Turkish National Assembly, moving on to the European Parliament in Strasbourg, with our final stop being at an international conference in Yerevan. In between these points, we also attended meetings in London, Frankfurt, Stuttgart, Salzburg, and Berlin.

RONALD SUNY

In April 2005, Hrant joined us at the workshop we held in Salzburg. A large group of journalists and intellectuals had joined us from Turkey. Among the participants were also representatives of the diaspora from France and Beirut. We'd begun this workshop as a small group, wishing to open up a dialogue between diaspora and Turkish intellectuals, but now that our work had now begun to disseminate, the workshop had greatly increased in importance. The last meeting Hrant attended was at the University of California at Berkeley on 5th March 2006, and with him came Ragıp Zarakolu. I was impressed by his command of English at that meeting, because until that day I had only ever heard him speaking Turkish and Armenian.

ETYEN MAHÇUPYAN

After all of these encounters, Hrant was a known quantity in the diaspora. So you could say he had entered the world stage. He made frequent visits to Armenia. I accompanied him twice. When he was there, he was clearly much happier than he was in the diaspora. It was in every way evident that he was proud that Armenia existed. The Armenians took their pleasures seriously. But he also saw how poor and run-down Armenia was, and that saddened him deeply.

Hrant always held that Turkey and Armenia should initiate diplomatic relations, but he didn't warm to the idea of the West putting pressure on them to open up talks. What he tried to do, as a Turkish Armenian, was to serve as a bridge between the two countries. He never turned down an invitation from Armenia: he attended every meeting to which he was invited.

HRANT

There has been a string of conferences in Armenia bringing together Turks and Armenians with diverse views along with participants from other countries. I attended the international conference held in April 2005 with Baskın Oran, Murat Belge, and Taner Akçam. When Baskın Oran uttered harsh words about the Armenians, the room nearly turned to ice. The answers Oran got in return were every bit as harsh. But Baskın made the trip, voiced his criticisms in the middle of Yerevan, got his answers, and went home happy. The world didn't come to an end.

FEYHAN ORAN

That meeting in Yerevan was very stormy. At one of the sessions, Baskın made a protest, saying, "Don't use the word 'genocide;' it's this word that stops people listening to you, even though you are in the right." And with that, the complaints grew more vociferous. Even Libraridian entered the fray, taking the microphone to protest in Turkish, "That's just not acceptable, Baskın; that's just not acceptable!" At that point, Taner Akçam emerged from the ranks of the observers to say, "I don't agree with Baskın. In my opinion, we should be using this word," after which things really flared up. In the end, Hrant spoke. He said a few things in Armenian, and things calmed down.

Hrant took care of all those who'd come to the conference from Turkey and got everyone to mingle. I shall never forget the historian Dadrian—on the last evening, he came up to me and asked, "Do you know how to make *tulumba tatlısı*? And *kuru köfte* and *mantı*?" He even hummed the Turkish song he'd learned at school. Hrant hugged him the way he hugged us all. "My friend, you must come to Turkey," he'd say. "Come and see it for yourself, and you'll see how different it is from what you think."

GERARD LIBARIDIAN

By then, I was no longer part of the government in Armenia; in fact, I was in opposition to it. Still, I thought that my presence may bring a balance to the proceedings, along with Hrant's.

By then, Hrant had become a towering figure, one that could not be easily categorized, one who was a real definer of issues. But such personalities who do not "belong" to anyone are more of a threat. Thus, the powers that be automatically target them, either to co-opt them in their own schemes or to destroy them. The co-optation of Hrant Dink into various political programs began even before his assassination. Parties to the conflict—states, political parties and others—tried to show that Hrant was proving their point. Of course, Hrant welcomed any opportunity to compel people, states, groups, and individuals to think beyond the limits of their comfort.

SAMSON ÖZARARAT

Hrant had made a name for himself in the diaspora; he was now someone to whose words people gave weight, and he had paid many visits to Armenia. His greatest gift was that he could speak with everyone and anyone and connect with them all. He tried to tell each side about the other side. There were those who understood him, and those who didn't. But whether they did or not, they all respected him.

Because I had many dealings with him in my capacity as Armenia's representative of Black Sea Economic Cooperation organization, I was able to watch him perform on many occasions. He did not hold back from making uncompromising criticisms of Armenia, the lopsided relations between the diaspora and Armenia, or the deficiencies of Armenian democracy. None of this was welcomed.

TANER AKÇAM

Throughout that trip we took to Armenia to attend that conference, Hrant was very happy. He took it upon himself to be our eyes and ears. He was the one who decided what we did, where we went, who we met, and which television channels we appeared on. Murat Belge and I appeared on a live TV program. He was our interpreter.

Giro Manoyan was the foreign relations officer for the Armenian Tashnag Party, which everyone in Turkey demonized. Giro was Hrant's close friend. On the eve of April 24, the Turkish journalists said, "The Tashnags are going to stage a show in which they will burn the Turkish flag." Hrant went and spoke to Giro, who, when he went back to the Tashnag Youth Association, persuaded it to desist from burning the flag in deference to those who had come to attend the conference. That's what Hrant was like, you see. Every step he took, he brought the Turkish and Armenian sides closer together. With his very presence, he brought them together.

But one day, we were having a heated conversation in a restaurant. A couple sitting at the table next to us sent us a bottle of wine. Later, they got up and joined our table. They turned out to be the US Ambassador to Armenia and his wife. There followed a long and heartwarming conversation. The subject, of course, was how to resolve the Turkish-Armenian issue. Hrant was elated, and he couldn't stop speaking. And the end of the evening, I said to him, "If I were Turkey, I would make you honorary consul." I could tell from the way his eyes sparkled that he was thinking, *But I'm doing that already.* He really did consider himself Turkey's envoy to Armenia and Armenia's envoy to Turkey.

ETYEN MAHÇUPYAN

In September 2005, we were again in Australia, at the invitation of our Armenian friends. This was Hrant's second visit. Rakel came with us, too. He'd arranged in advance some meetings in both Melbourne and Sydney. This was a very interesting journey, too.

So that all of its minorities could observe their own cultural traditions, the Australian state had allocated large spaces for them to do so—sports pavilions, coffeehouses, walking paths, and picnic grounds. Our encounters with the country's Armenians also took place in these gigantic arenas.

Picture this scene: the Armenians who have immigrated to Australia are spread across this picnic ground, barbecuing meat on their braziers, in clouds of smoke, while Hrant and I walk among them. There are hundreds of people, and Hrant takes an interest in each and every one—almost like a populist politician. He'd met these people when he was here before, and now, one by one, he remembers their names, he's asking them if their spouses are in better health and how the children are doing in school, and and the like. What an unbelievable scene. And then, at the meeting in the middle of this picnic, Hrant gave a speech that was worthy of a political leader. His confidence spread out across that entire meadow. When he introduced me to the 500 or 600 people he'd been addressing, he said, "Don't worry, this man has brains enough for us all, and I,"—he paused here and beat his chest—"have enough heart." This was the first time he said this. After that, he repeated it quite often.

They say I was the one with the brains, but the decisions he made on his own were always right, so he had no need to advertise my brains like that. What I think is that he said it in order to bring more heart into our relationship. He believed that I would become more Armenian, become a more outward-facing man with the strength to carry all of this and move forward. He thought he was changing me, transforming me, turning me into his comrade. And he was right . . .

HRANT

Over the past few months, I had been touring the diaspora, and by the end I had come to see that so far we have not been hitting our heads against the wall.

This time, I was with Etyen Mahçupyan, visiting the Armenian diaspora on the distant continent of Australia. For two weeks, we have attended a series of meetings in Sydney and Melbourne. We have been meeting with various groups in the Armenian community and debating the issues.

What we have found surprising is that the most welcoming of these groups is the one commonly thought to be the harshest: the Tashnags. The Tashnags are going through an important transformation. Until now, these people who thought it would have been degrading to utter the word "Turk" wish to enter into a dialogue with Turks. They have come to look kindly on a Turkey inside the EU and on the possibility of their joining them there. It goes without saying that they do not yet trust Turkey sufficiently. There are, after all, any number of examples they can give of Turkey's democratic deficit.

But there is also this: they are even more shocked to see a proponent of democracy like me saying that we needed to put this deficit in context to better understand it, and this helped them to begin to make sense of the complexities of Turkey today.

ETYEN MAHÇUPYAN

Hrant and I took many journeys around the Armenian diaspora. Our discussions got stuck on two different issues. The first was whether or not Turkey would change. Our interlocutors, convinced that Turks would never come to accept their "other," were reluctant to be persuaded otherwise. The second point concerned Turkey's Armenians. They asked why, after all they had gone through, were they still in Turkey, and why we were still living with the Turks. Whatever we said, they behaved as if they had not been persuaded. Undoubtedly, what was behind this stance was the huge longing that they could not face up to: the longing for their country. After living without having their own state for such a long time, they had based their identities and their very existence on their culture and on the land that had nourished that culture. When you uproot a culture, you turn it upside down because without the land there is no water and no wind, there are no trees, and—of course—no people.

When we figured this out, we took care to speak gently; we were aware that it would be hurtful to say that when an Anatolian leaves Anatolia, they are no longer the same person. What need was there to taunt them with the lives that had been stolen from them? Even if we pulled back from such discussions, especially in the course of these meetings, we would be confronted, little by little, with bashful questions in their efforts to remember Anatolia. After telling us what village their fathers and grandfathers had come from, they would begin to ask questions about Turkey today. Anatolia was what bound us together, but with a furtive passion that could be neither voiced nor admitted, almost like a secret and forbidden love. When they spoke of the good relations they had enjoyed with Turks in the old days, their faces would light up, and they would even feel called upon to say that these nostalgic scenes would never be repeated because they had convinced themselves that there was no going back into the past, and no chance of ever enjoying a close association with Turks.

We, on the other hand, declared that we wished to live in Turkey not because of the land's air or water, but because of its people; we told them that our closest friends and comrades were Turks. And they would look at us with doubtful eyes and suggest that we spoke like this to console ourselves.

After taking all of that trouble to persuade them, and seeing that we had made some headway with most of those in front of us, we would return happily to our hotel. We felt almost as if we were turning rusty keys one by one, taking an entire society outside for an airing. Our optimism didn't flag, not even for a day.

HRANT

For a very long time, we lived together on the same land, and we share a common memory. But now, we have turned our common memory into monologues, with each side singing its own tune. But if we set about turning our monologues into a dialogue, then we could rebuild our shared memories, and then we'd have no time to waste on persuading foreign parliaments to pass laws. This is my belief. In this way, there would no longer be any need for apologies or statements of denial. After all, wouldn't the dialogue be an apology in action?

History's pages belong to the past, while the blank ones are for what is still to come. From the perspective of Turkish–Armenian relations, what matters most is our common destiny that can link what has been passed on by previous generations with what we ourselves wish to hand down. Our forefathers have filled many pages with what befell them in the past. The real question is how we shall fill the blank pages awaiting us.

Are we going to act like those responsible for the great catastrophe of the past, or are we going to learn from our mistakes and write the next chapters of history in a way befitting civilized people? This is the greatest responsibility we face.

Part III

Seeing

26

The Road to Recovery

HRANT

As an Armenian of Turkey, I have spent many years speaking and writing about Turkish–Armenian relations. Although I must, to some degree, tailor my words to suit my many and diverse audiences, I have stood firm on two points. The first is the right to take a critical stance with those I address, and the second is not to confuse them. Sadly, my counterparts have often failed to display the same care.

When addressing Europeans, I have criticized the Europeans, only to see Armenians and Turks taking the credit and ignoring their own responsibilities. When addressing Turks, I have criticized the Turks, only to see the Armenians and the Europeans taking the credit and seeking to cover up their own mistakes. When addressing Armenians, I have of course criticized the Armenians, but whenever I have done so, it has been the Turks especially who have taken all the credit for themselves, whether they condemned or praised my remarks. And let me say that I have been much vilified and much praised.

For the most part, criticism and praise have come from the same quarters. They themselves had a hard time knowing whether they were going to criticize me next or praise me. But it can't be helped. When I've found myself in such circumstances, my only concern has been to be sincere. And that is all there is to it.

And so here we are again, with April 24 fast approaching, and the Armenian people grieving among themselves. Once again, they must go in search of those with whom they can share that grief. Every time we meet with Armenians living outside Turkey, they ask "What's going on in Turkey? Are they going to recognize the genocide or what?" And it's hardly surprising that they expect a hopeful answer. When will the Turkish nation understand how Armenians feel? When will they share our pain? What a shame it is that, in the here and now, we cannot tell them, "Soon." That said, we need not tell them, "Never."

There is no doubt that we have entered a new era. On the one hand, we see a new will to face history and democratize, and on the other, we see the old resistance, the old fear of owning up to what happened.

But one thing is certain: this old resistance will not last forever. As it democratizes, Turkey will come to own up to the truth. As it comes to face the truth, it will democratize. But one thing is certain: this old resistance will not last forever. Or if this wait be more like a prayer—and for me it is—that one day, whether Turk or Armenian, one day, our voices will rise up together to a democratic "amen."

ALİ BAYRAMOĞLU

After Hrant had begun his efforts to reach out to the Armenian world as a Turkish Armenian, he began to understand each side much better. And thereafter he was able to base his views on the Armenian issue on a much firmer foundation because he was a man who drew and developed all of his political thought and political positions from his own life experience.

ETYEN MAHÇUPYAN

Turkey's Armenian issue could only be politically analyzed and resolved if considered from a democratic perspective. Hrant was the one who did this. This was the conclusion that Hrant reached, after his many years of reflection and experience. While he was analyzing the deepening of the historical rift from both perspectives, he also developed new concepts. The illness afflicting the Armenians he named "trauma" and the illness afflicting the Turks, "paranoia."

HRANT

We are far away from the day when Turkey and Armenia can overcome the historical dispute, which is the main obstacle dividing them. This is because their opposing views and statements have created a stalemate. What's more, history is not just an issue between countries but between peoples. And this is why these two countries cannot resolve the issue of history until such a time that the Turkish and Armenian peoples have done so. In the end, when those nations reach an accord on history, it is political accord; for an accord to be achieved between two peoples, what we need is not a political agreement but a moral and ethical rapprochement developed over time. In arenas that allow for constructive dialogue, they can first exchange their differing views, and, over time, we can see a normalization of relations wherein deeply held ideas begin to soften. History cannot be resolved, after all; we can only seek to understand it, in part. And understanding is something that can only be achieved over time. It will never happen overnight with an instant state ruling.

If Turkey and Armenia have no relations, it is largely to do with history and with the stances that derive from that history and continue to color their attitudes toward one another in an unhealthy way. As difficult as this is to say, it's important to confess: the Armenians with their traumas and the Turks with their paranoia are suffering from reciprocal forms of mental distress. They each serve as each other's "other," and that "otherness" forms the very basis of their identity.

ETYEN MAHÇUPYAN

As an Armenian of Turkey, Hrant embraced both identities, and in developing his very distinct views, he again drew his ideas from his own sincere beliefs and experiences. Of course, we should not forget the courage behind his analysis. Hrant shied away from applying his ideas about trauma to the Armenian world as a whole, offering his own distinctions. This, again, was derived from his observations and experiences as an Armenian of Turkey with the Armenian diaspora and Armenia itself.

ALİ BAYRAMOĞLU

He toured the diaspora and made strong ties there; he also paid many visits to Armenia, and, as a result of all that, his somewhat idealized vision of Armenia gave way to more contemporary and democratic views on the actual country. If he began to talk about the lack of homogeneity in the country's fragmented political arena, it was because he saw the Armenian polity as surpassing national borders. And whenever he spoke, whichever group he was addressing, he spoke from this place, this understanding.

HRANT

In analyzing Armenian identity, we must first review the ways in which the concept of the "Turk" has played itself out in terms of both history and everyday life. There are, additionally, important differences in the "Turk" as conceptualized by the diaspora Armenians, the Armenians of Armenia, and the Armenians of Turkey. The Armenians of Turkey are still living with Turks, while the Armenians of Armenia are their neighbors, but the majority of Armenians of the diaspora live very far away from them. And it is this distance that makes the trauma they suffer distinct. The homeland of all Armenians everywhere is Anatolia. Diaspora Armenians, wherever in the world they might have settled, continue to carry the cultural traces that belong to Anatolia. Even now, so many generations later, one still comes across those who speak Turkish with their local accent.

It is therefore no exaggeration to describe the Armenian diaspora as the "global version of Anatolia." The diaspora expresses not just the loss of the Armenian homeland. It also signals a geographical disconnection: the sundering apart of peoples who lived side by side for many centuries. It signifies the destruction, to a large extent, of the "territorial integrity" that constitutes a nation. Inevitably, this has gone on to damage national identity.

For two generations now, the Armenian people have been suffering the effects of that damage very deeply. It is one thing to "live" an identity and another to try to "keep it alive." For the last century, the Armenians have been occupied with trying to preserve their identity instead of living it. So today, we can see that in Armenia they are living this identity, while in the diaspora, they are trying to keep it alive.

ETYEN MAHÇUPYAN

After his many encounters with the Armenian diaspora, this was what Hrant saw: Armenians outside Turkey were pushing forward a demand for justice because their ancestors had been expelled from their lands in 1915. It was therefore necessary to accept their anger, as well as their demands for justice, as natural.

At that point, he'd say this: "Those demanding justice for the past must also demand justice for the present. You have to look at Turkish society today and ask what they know, and how much they knew, and what they've been through. For there were also Muslim Turks who stood up against the perpetrators, and who lost their livelihoods, and their lives, as a consequence. It's important to know these things, too." They didn't like hearing this. They'd even get angry.

HRANT

For the diaspora Armenians, the "Turk" is the Turk they left behind at a date in the past. That date is 1915, when they were subjected to genocide; that date is 1942, when they suffered "economic genocide" with the imposition of the Wealth Tax; that date is 1955, when, on September 6 and 7, a new form of vandalism came into play. The "Turk" they have in mind is the one that can never change; they were unable to live together in peace in the past, and they never will.

For the Armenians of Armenia, the Turk is again the Turk of 1915, except that now they are living side by side. Whether they like it or not, they will continue to have to do so.

But the Armenians of Turkey continue to live with the Turk. And while it is an enervating issue for diasporan Armenians, for Armenians of Turkey, the concept of the "Turk" is medicinal.

We can see the differing reflections of this trauma throughout the Armenian world at the annual April 24 commemorations. In the diaspora, we see hardline anti-Turkish commemorations that can go so far as to burn the Turkish flag, while in Armenia, entire families walk in solemn silence to the genocide memorial and lay flowers. Like it or not, the Armenians of Turkey are the strangest. They have neither monuments nor energy with which to mark the date.

Unless the Armenian world finds a way to save itself from the trauma that has been passed from generation to generation, it may not be possible to create a peaceful future. This trauma tells us that we are stuck inside the darkness chapter of our history. What a shame it is that we cannot find our way out of that chapter and back to the present. One might well ask, "Why should we forget those days?" But this is a needless question. It comes from the mistaken assumption that recovering from a trauma and returning to normal is the same as forgetting the past. How can any of us forget his past? And why should we? But if a nation nourishes its present and its past on that dark chapter alone, how can we understand it except as trauma?

ETYEN MAHÇUPYAN

Those in the diaspora said that Turks would never change, that in spite of all the new things that civilization had brought with it, they would remain fundamentally incapable of accepting the "other."

We, on the other hand, said that it was wrong to speak of the Turk as a unified category—that, in recent times, there had been a dynamic of change in certain sectors of society, and that both the past and the "other" were being viewed differently, and that Turkish society was tired of being fooled; for all these, we gave examples. And we said that it was impossible to be a good Armenian without getting to know the Turks.

If the two peoples had managed to live together in peace on these lands for so long, it was very difficult to be yourself without also knowing the "other." And this was why it was wrong, and wholly inadequate, for diasporans born outside Turkey, and rooting their identity there, without ever having met a a Turk, to give lectures on this subject. Of course, the reverse was just as true. It was impossible to be a good Turk without knowing Armenians.

HRANT

Coming now to the Turks' paranoia: the first source of the paranoia Turks feel about Armenians is the question of land. In fact, it is not a very realistic fear in today's world. Above all, the Armenian world itself is divided on the issue. There is without question a longing felt universally by Armenians for the land of their historical roots, but the same canot be said of the demand that the land be returned to them.

The second source of this paranoia is the fear of reparations. Tied up with that is a guilt complex. In the end, what the departed left behind was shared among those remaining. Here, it is enough to point to the silence that followed on from these collective acts. As for the efforts throughout the republican period to erase all traces of Armenian presence, the main reason is this: not to leave anything they could come and point to, saying, "Look, this was once ours."

The historic paranoia that Turks carry to this day is not intractable. All we need to do is to say that there is no need for the Turks to make clear-cut reparations to the Armenians. There are many other, more reasonable, and more ethical ways forward. There can be joint projects and the sharing of information; with these, both the expectation of reparations on the Armenian side and the paranoia on the Turkish side will fade away.

ETYEN MAHÇUPYAN

If you look at Hrant's deep analysis of Turkish paranoia, his approach to politics can be more easily discerned. Here, it is very clear that he was thinking about what might happen next and how matters might be resolved.

In saying that both sides had fallen ill together, and now could heal together, he was indicating a new political aim. This aim was to democratize Turkey.

HRANT

When it comes to the question of owning up to history, most particularly with regard to the Armenian genocide, Turkey has from the very outset chosen hilly ground over a plain. Whatever the conditions of the day, it has kept up its guard. When things get difficult, it has identified those responsible, rounded them up and condemned them. When things calm down, it has celebrated those responsible as heroes and rewarded them with what is left of Armenian property. The day arrived when it made the subject taboo and hid it in the ditches. The day arrived when, in other lands, the genocide became known, and it was left alone on its hilltop.

At first, the story went as if no Armenians had ever lived in these lands. Even Dolmabahçe Palace was built not by the Armenian Balyan but the Italian Bali. There was never a town called "Ani." Now it was "Anı"; "Anı" was its name. Or let's just say they were here, but not that many of them. So let's say they had lived here, but were few in number.

Few they might have been, but they had gone too far. There weren't very many, but they caused trouble. So, when that happened, they were kindly told to leave. And then, well, sadly, a number of them fell ill along the way and died—well, quite a lot of them. And, of course, that was a shame. A certain number died, but a much larger number were killed. And then? Well, nothing, really. There is no *then*. To sum it up, various things happened, but those things were actually . . . actually, those stories are false. Unfounded, after all.

When we speak of the Armenian genocide, the problem Turkey faces is neither one of denial or of recognition. Turkey's main problem is comprehension. The real issue is for the Turkish people to become aware of the historical realities. This will only happen through the Turkish struggle to democratize, because as our peoples gain in comprehension, they will wish to find a new way to study history. And for this to happen, society needs to have democratized.

Outside efforts to call it "genocide" and internal measures to ban the word will not accelerate the process; they will only make it more difficult for the Turkish people to accept the historical facts.

In the end, it's not the case that Turkish society is denying facts it knows; it is simply defending what it believes to be true.

MURAT BELGE

Hrant expressed his bold views on the Armenian issue during his visits to Armenia, too. At the speech he gave at the international conference organized by the Armenian Foreign Ministry in Yerevan in 2005, he asked the Armenians to abandon their negative image of the Turk and to set out to read Turkey properly, with a view to understanding it. Turkish society was not denying a history they knew; they were just repeating back what they'd been taught. To discuss this taboo openly and without penalty was only possible with democracy. To this end, the struggle to democratize Turkey was to be supported, and so too was Turkey's EU membership bid. At that point, the attitudes inside the Armenian leadership were positive. President Koçaryan's statement —"We remember the past with pain, and not with hatred"—was significant. So too was the statement made by foreign minister Oskanyan to the effect that there would be no demand for land, just an agreement on the historical facts.

VARTAN OSKANYAN

The border between Turkey and Armenia is accepted as a political reality in today's international community. So too is the political reality that we live side by side. That Armenia does not pose a security threat to Turkey is another political reality. And finally, the call for relations to be opened between today's Armenia and today's Turkey form a third political reality.

There are those who oppose Turkey's entry into the EU. We, however, support this bid. Let Turkey become a member of the EU so that our borders may open, and so that our citizens may converse openly with Turkish scholars about the genocide.

HRANT

The Armenian world's future is intricately tied up with the future of Turkey. That is why it is in the Armenian world's interest to support democratization in Turkey. And this can only happen through its own efforts, and its own internal dynamics, while external pressure—as history has shown—will do no good at all.

As for the historical deadlock, there is no single party responsible, nor do Turks and Armenians carry all the blame. If you consider all those involved, all their witnesses, you can see that all sides were in collusion. The question was deferred, and then ignored. The world powers had their own archival accounts of what had happened, yet they chose to remain silent and indifferent. That the French, the English, the Germans, the Austrians, and the Americans have persisted in this duplicity for ninety years is the most striking example of this careless indifference. And that is why the string of "genocide resolutions" in third-party countries achieve little more than promoting the rise of Turkish nationalism and further

impeding democratization. So that is why it's so important to be careful in your choice of doctor, prescription, and treatment. If we come out and say, "The parliaments of third-party countries are not the right places for the discussion of the Armenian question because we should be the ones discussing it, and we should be discussing it here," we also need to indicate where we intend to go for treatment.

If we are to solve this problem, will it be enough to establish a dialogue between the two peoples? My answer is crystal clear: Yes it is. In fact, it is the only solution.

VARTAN OSKANYAN

Armenian politics is generally local, regional, and national in outlook. Hrant, on the other hand, was one of the few political thinker-activists who was able to raise the Armenian issue to the international level. Also, Hrant saw the Armenian community as divided into three camps: the diaspora, Armenia, and the Armenians of Turkey. This, too, was very correct. The Armenians of Turkey categorically do not, as some have insisted, belong to the diaspora. They are, by contrast, the descendants of our ancestors who lived in those lands. Whether they're in Istanbul or Anatolia, they are still living in the land of our forefathers. This is something that must be understood and respected. Only when this happens can the Armenians of Turkey find their way to understanding the history of Armenia, and Turkish history, and the present state of Turkish–Armenian relations, as well as its future.

HRANT

The position of Turkey's Armenians is highly important for several reasons. To repair relations between Turkey and Armenia, we need more than words; there are also many things to be done. Because we Armenians of Turkey can claim the identities of both sides, we can serve as litmus paper for a new approach that respects the dignity of both.

At a time when there is no official dialogue between the two countries, there is, of course, a view in certain cautious circles that this is an inopportune moment for Turkey's Armenians to join the debate. Yet it is the lack of an official dialogue that makes our presence and initiative so crucially important. If we exist, then we must exist today; we must use this dark day to rise up in all sincerity and make our standpoint clear.

In the end, we are the Armenians of Turkey; we have no April 24 memorials and no ceremonies to remember it, either, but we have seventeen schools and thirty-five churches, and we still make our lives from the land we inherited from our forefathers, and we continue to base our identity on that legacy.

Our only desire is for Turkey and Armenia, Turks and Armenians, to find a way to live together, once again, in peace.

We are the Armenians of Turkey, and we know our place in the scheme of things; we have everything to offer and we speak from the heart. We stand in the center, and we cry out to both sides: "If you are sincere about repairing relations between Turkey and Armenia, we can help. You are welcome to use us as you wish."

VARTAN OSKANYAN

Hrant believed that the Armenians would achieve nothing by remaining locked inside the past, for both national and emotional reasons, signaling the importance of our paying attention to Turkish history, identity, and democratization. He knew full well that those defending xenophobia, isolation, and all manner of intolerance would in the end fall into their own trap. He saw very clearly that the Armenians, in seeking to protect themselves, had made this mistake and were confusing Turkish politics with the Turkish people.

Hrant also believed in the power of the word. But as much as he might have lived by words, and drawn his strength and courage and even his power from words, he also dodged them.

HRANT

Coming to the definition of the word "genocide" . . .

If a state uproots its own citizens, even its children, its women, and its infirm, sending them off down roads unknown and never-ending, and if, as a result, a large number of them vanish, what words should we use? How can we convey this story to our fellow citizens today and, with it, our humanity?

If we enter into semantics, fussing over what to call it—"genocide" or "emigration":—or if, having failed to condemn both terms equally, we favor "deportation" over "genocide" or "genocide" over "deportation," what shred of human dignity will we have salvaged?

You can call it one name, or you can call it another, but you will not change its essence. Genocide, massacre, holocaust, slaughter, mass murder—none of these words come close to describing what actually happened. And the story of what happened is not just the story of those who died or those who killed them.

"Genocide" is actually a legal term. I have a hard time accepting the imprisonment of human experience inside a legal term that is itself designed to produce a political outcome. The term "genocide" says nothing to me. What we need are real words, real stories, from those who lived through those days. In such stories, there are the killers and the killed, the exiled and the dispersed, the saviors and the saved, the ones who did good and the ones who did ill, the ones who stayed and the ones who returned.

To lock such an enormous history inside a word and a number, to forget the people, to turn that history into something that can be legally agreed upon—that's not right. The moment you start talking about numbers, you create a situation in which not a soul can speak. This can drive a person mad.

What I care about are the people of Turkey. If I thought the word "genocide" would help people of Turkey understand this history once and for all, I would use this word. But we cannot convey this history to Turkish society with a single word. A single word is not enough for us to reach their hearts. We need a whole language.

VARTAN OSKANYAN

Hrant argued that channels of communication could not open without the border between Turkey and Armenia opening first. It was essential that we take advantage of this chance to forge peace and harmony now that people on both sides wished for dialogue. The opening of the border would give both peoples a chance to speak to one other, to eat and drink and sing together. This was what Hrant believed. And so do I.

HRANT

So now how is Turkey going to resolve the Armenian question? There is only one way for Turkey to stop the West from constantly using this against it, and that is to forge a dialogue with Armenians. It must open up three different channels of communication: First, it must open the border between Turkey and Armenia and initiate a dialogue at the level of both society and the state. Second, it must engage the Armenians of Turkey without threat or restriction. Finally, it must win over the diaspora Armenians who are now spread across the world but still burn with longing for their Armenian roots.

ETYEN MAHÇUPYAN

Hrant had a dream: to create independent, unaffiliated groups of activists in both Turkey and Armenia, feeling that these would work together to bring down the fence between the two recalcitrant countries, to forge peace, and to bring the two peoples into unity, thereby healing both. This was the initiative he hoped to inspire and lead.

It was almost as if he believed that this was what he had been put on this earth to do. To open that border, he was prepared to sacrifice all of life's other pleasures if that was what it took. And maybe he was even prepared to defer them for the next time around. Anything, so long as that border opened!

And perhaps why he'd had to go through such suffering to honor the vow he'd made to himself, to open up that border. And perhaps he was not far off from imagining it in those terms.

HRANT

I am a citizen of Turkey. I am an Armenian. I am Anatolian down to my marrow.

Not for a single day have I thought of leaving my country to find my future in that paradise of ready-made freedom that we call the West, to slide like a leech into democracies created through the toil of others.

My sole concern has been to turn my own country into its own paradise of freedom.

When my country wept for the massacre of Alevis in Sivas, I cried, too. When my people fought against conspirators and dark forces, I did, too. I have found my destiny in the struggle to create freedom in my country. As for the rights I now enjoy, or have yet to enjoy, they didn't come free; I paid a price, and I am still paying it.

But now . . .

I am sick and tired of hearing some people—including even those who occasionally find it in themselves to flatter us by calling us "their" Armenians—describe us as the enemies within. I have had it—absolutely had it—with being excluded and dismissed in ways that overlook the fact that I, too, am a normal, ordinary citizen.

I never had the chance to march on April 24 or to erect monuments in commemoration of my forefathers, but I have not left them behind. Nor have I dragged them with me into the present. Instead, I have kept their lives alive in mine. That is what I have done, to the best of my ability. And I have fought without remorse against everyone and everything that has tried to stand in my way.

Of course, I know what happened to my forefathers. Some people call it "massacre" and others "genocide." Some call it "deportation," some "tragedy." My Anatolian ancestors called it "slaughter." I call it the "catastrophe."

And I know that if this catastrophe, this utter destruction, had never happened, our country would be an easier, even an enviable, place to live. That is why I curse those who caused it and those who served as their tools. But when I do so, I am cursing the past. Of course I want the historical facts to be known, but hatred wreaks its own sort of infamy. So let us consign it to history's dark caves. Let us keep it there, I say. I have no wish to make its acquaintance.

It offends me to see my history or my current concerns being mined for political capital in America and Europe. Behind all these caring words, I sense abuse. I reject the sort of shameful arbitration that would strangle my future with my past. I shall not bow to any parliament, or any state, that seeks to arbitrate on my behalf.

The true arbiters are the people and their consciences. What is in my own conscience is no match for the free conscience of a country or a people. And in my conscience, no state has the power to compete with the conscience of the people. My only wish is to speak about our common past with my beloved friends in Turkey freely, and deeply, without so much as a hint of ill will.

I believe, from the bottom of my heart, that one day Turks and Armenians will be able to talk about all this among themselves. Most especially, I look forward to the day when Turkey and Armenia can converse on all matters with ease, allowing me to turn to irrelevant third parties and say, "From now on, you can mind your own business."

The Armenians of the world are marking the ninetieth anniversary of 1915.

Let them do so. It's their right.

The foregoing lines are the thoughts of yours truly.

Part IV

Knowing

27

The Beginning of the End

HRANT

Certain people have decided that "this Hrant Dink" has gone too far and "needs to be put in his place."

And I agree; this claim puts me and my Armenian identity center stage. You may wish to argue that I exaggerate. But this is how it seems to me. The facts about what I have been through leave me with no other explanation. My task now is to share those facts and experiences with you, and then you can decide for yourself.

For now, let's look a little more closely at this business about Hrant Dink going too far. They've been keeping an eye on this Dink fellow for some time now. Since *Agos* first came out in 1996, he has been discussing the problems of the Armenian community and insisting on their rights, while expressing his own views about history, which ran counter to the official state doctrine. And it cannot be said that he has not, on occasion, gone too far.

But the drop that made the glass overflow was the piece about Sabiha Gökçen in the February 6, 2004, issue of *Agos*. In an article, signed by this Dink fellow, the Armenian relatives of Atatürk's adopted daughter Sabiha Gökçen claimed that she was in fact an Armenian orphan, plucked from an orphanage.

KARİN KARAKAŞLI

Hrant took this claim published in *Agos* very seriously, because for him the events of 1915 were not just about the number of dead; he also wanted to trace the stories of the survivors. The surviving Armenians who changed religion were not just taboo in official Turkish history but also in the Armenian world. Hrant thought that the time had come to break this taboo. There were in Anatolia many lost Armenians—survivors of 1915 who had been taken into Muslim families as children or married off to Muslims by their neighbors. He knew this to be the case, but there was a wall of silence obscuring it because to talk about such things was to open up the subject of what happened in 1915. So, by Hrant's reckoning, the Sabiha Gökçen story offered a way to open the subject. Also, this was a bold and eye-catching news story. The weekly magazine *Aktüel* had also been taking a great interest in the claim around that time. But just as we had expected, they didn't print the story. While in *Agos*, it appeared on page 12, under Hrant Dink's byline, and it took up the whole page.

HRANT

She was not just one of Turkey's foremost icons; she was an icon of Turkishness. She was, above all, Atatürk's adopted daughter, and with the power she took from him, she became a model of Turkish womanhood. Her most striking achievement was to become Turkey's first woman Air Force pilot and a national heroine (!) after helping crush the Dersim rebellion. To make a long story short, she set the tone for what a Turkish woman could become.

There have been countless books and documentaries about Sabiha Gökçen, but somehow, none of them got around to mentioning the claim made by the citizen of Armenia, Hripsime Sebilciyan.

Madame Hrispsime worked in Turkey as a cleaner for some time and has now returned to Armenia, but she has something very interesting to tell us: "Sabiha Gökçen is my aunt. We are originally from Antep. We descend from the Sebilciyan family. While my mother and my aunt Hatun were in an orphanage in Cibin, outside Antep, Atatürk came for a visit, spotted my aunt, who was a very cute little girl, pointed his finger at her, and said, 'I want this girl.'

So my aunt became Atatürk's daughter. Her real name was Hatun, but they changed it to Sabiha Gökçen."

To tell the truth, this didn't come as a big surprise to us. This sort of story about Armenian converts is commonplace. There are, in addition, similar oral and written claims to be found in Armenian. The question of converts remains a taboo subject in Turkey, yet to be subjected to serious study. So, for now, we shall confine ourselves to statements and photographs that have so far been limited to the Armenian world, if only to offer a few clues to researchers and scholars.

ERSİN KALKAN

From time to time, Hrant Dink and I would discuss the issue of converts and those who were forcibly converted during the atrocities of 1915. He would tell me what he had heard, and I would repeat to him the stories I'd been told during my travels through Anatolia. One day, Hrant called me and said that he was working on a news story about Sabiha Gökçen. I went over to *Agos* and read the rough draft. It was an extraordinary scoop because it was about someone who had mythic status in the history of the republic. Sabiha Gökçen was not just the first "Turkish" woman pilot, she was also Atatürk's adopted daughter. And for that same reason, this news story was dangerous because it could topple one of the main pillars of official history.

"I want to do this story, too," I said to Hrant. But this meant taking the views of journalists and historians who were in on the secret. Hrant said it would be better for the news to come out first in *Agos*, after which I could put out a piece that filled in the blanks.

This was a subject that historians shied away from, but I was able to get a piece into *Hürriyet*, together with a short interview with Hrant. As we all know, it became headline news. It was presented in a balanced and objective way. Up until this point, there was no problem.

HRANT

Turkey was shaken when this piece appeared in Turkey's top-selling newspaper, *Hürriyet*, on February 21, 2004. It was headline news, soon spreading across the country. For two weeks, a string of columnists offered negative and positive views, while various parties made various statements.

The most important of these was the written statement from the Turkish General Staff. The General Staff came out against this news item, saying that "To open a symbol of this magnitude to discussion, for whatever reason, is a crime against national integrity and social peace." In their view, those publishing this piece were evil-minded and trying to destroy the image of someone who had become a myth and a symbol of Turkish womanhood by stripping her of her Turkish identity.

Who were these impertinent creatures? Who was this Hrant Dink? The time had come to put him in his place!

The General Staff published its statement on February 22. It was a very long statement, which I heard at home on the television news. I didn't feel too comfortable that night. I was sure that something would happen the next day. And, in the end, my past experiences and gut feelings did not let me down.

FETHİYE ÇETİN

When I read the news about Sabiha Gökçen, I thought, "How wonderful!

Hrant is finally putting this issue on the public agenda." I was pleased because my own grandmother was among those who survived by changing their religion, and it was only in the last years of her life that she was able to disclose to me her true identity.

Some time passed. Then, suddenly, *Hürriyet* did a rehash of the *Agos* article, under the headline, "Sabiha Gökçen's 80-Year-Old Secret." The next day, the Turkish General Staff published its famous statement. In summarizing, it said this:

"It is not possible to accept the publication of a story so damaging to national sentiment and values as a work of journalism. At a time when national unity and cooperation needs to be at its strongest, the publication of news targeting national unity and cooperation must, whatever its intent, be viewed as a major assault on a large segment of Turkish society and watched with due concern. Because Turkish society depends on the unity and cooperation it deserves, it falls upon every Turkish citizen and foundation to stand beside the Turkish Armed Forces, to embrace and defend peace, along with Atatürk'sspirit and system of thought, with the common sense worthy of the Turkish people."

When I read these lines, I was not yet Hrant's lawyer, but they caused me to worry for Hrant and *Agos*. Even so, I did not realize how dangerous the situation was. When I look back from today, of course I see this incident as the beginning of the end, but at the time I didn't know it. The General Staff had put out statements like that before, and they had worried us, too, but there was no more to it than that.

HRANT

Didn't I say it? I'd had a sense that something was going to happen. Early in the morning on the day after the General Staff issued its statement, the phone rang. On the line was the Deputy Governor of Istanbul. In a stern voice, he told me to report to the Office of the Governor, bringing with me the documents on which my news story was based. When I asked what the purpose of the invitation would be, I was told that they wanted to talk to me and to see my documentation. I called my most experienced journalist friends and asked them how they read this summons. They suggested that as talks like this were not customary, and as no legal measures had been set into motion, it had probably been initiated with only the documents in my possession in mind.

BASKIN ORAN

When Hrant was called to the Office of the Governor, he asked me what I thought it all meant. It was clear that he had been singled out in the statement issued by the General Staff. It was clear that they had been disturbed by Hrant's story about Sabiha Gökçen in *Agos*. We talked about all this over the phone. We also talked about the possibility of this continuing. But of course we had no idea how far it would go . . .

MASİS KÜRKÇÜGİL

When he told me about the business with the Office of the Governor, I didn't really understand what it meant; everything about it was a bit strange. There is Hrant, publishing *Agos* and using *Agos* to air a whole slew of issues of concern to the Armenian minority, as well as going to all four corners of Anatolia and taking part in conferences, and every time he speaks, they applaud him. Then, he comes back, and the General Staff issues a statement; without naming him, they make it clear it is about him. Then, the next day, he is called to the Office of the Governor and is "warned." And after that, he is again on a television program in which his views are being sought by the leading opinion-makers of Turkey. The truth is, I just couldn't put it all together. If you ask me, Hrant felt pushed about by the tides, too.

HRANT

Thus advised, I gathered up my documents and went off to meet the Deputy Governor. Upon being ushered inside, I saw that there were two people with him, a woman and a man. In the most polite terms, he told me that they were his close acquaintances and asked me if I objected to their being present during our conversation. By the time I had assured him that I had no objection and taken my seat, it was clear to me that this was to be a civilized affair. The Deputy Governor lost no time in getting to the point. "Hrant Bey," he said, "you are an experienced journalist. Should you not take greater care in your reporting? Just look at what a ruckus you've stirred up. We, of course, know who you are, but what does the man in the street know? He could easily conclude that you are publishing this sort of report with another purpose in mind."

After the Deputy Governor had gotten our conversation underway, the other man in the room began to speak, and once he started, he gave no one else the chance to say a thing. He expressed the same sentiments, but more clearly. He advised me to be careful and to avoid entering into subjects that might cause national and social tensions. "We can tell from some of your writing that, however much we take issue with your style, your intentions are not bad, but not everyone can understand this, and you are running the risk of turning public opinion against you." Over and over, he issued his warning. But I confined myself to explaining why I had published this story. First, I am a journalist, and this was a story that any journalist would find interesting. Second, I wanted a chance to discuss the Armenian issue not just in terms of the dead, but also to explore what had happened to the survivors. That said, I was beginning to see this was going to be difficult!

I was just about to leave the room when I realized that they had neither asked to see the documents I'd brought with me nor asked me to surrender them. I was the one to remind them, asking them if they wanted them or not, and then I handed them over.

KARİN KARAKAŞLI

Hrant and I went there together. When we tried to enter that room in the Office of the Governor together, they wouldn't let me in. Some time passed, and then Hrant came out. On our way back to the office, his face was dripping. "They threatened me," he said. "They spoke softly but made their meaning clear." He was very troubled by the fact that the Assistant Governor had said nothing, that the two other people in the room were not properly introduced, and that the third man he assumed to be from the Turkish Intelligence Service spoke for almost an hour.

HRANT

It was easy to read between the lines and understand why they had called me in. I should know my place. I had to be careful , or else it could turn out badly for me!

How true that was! What happened next was definitely not good. The day after I was called to the Office of the Governor, various columnists in various newspapers were plucking one sentence from my series of essays on Armenian identity to suggest that I was running an anti-Turkish campaign.

ERSİN KALKAN

Much as we had expected, there was a lot of noise after the story about Sabiha Gökçen ran in *Hürriyet*. In the beginning, Hrant Dink thought this was a good thing. After all, we believed that there were tens of thousands of Sabiha Gökçens among the survivors of 1915, and here we were, discussing this matter openly for the first time.

ALPER GÖRMÜŞ

The Sabiha Gökçen story in *Hürriyet* was not in the least provocative. The claim was reported objectively. And, in fact, there was, in terms of language and content, not much difference from the piece in *Agos*. But in *Agos*, the story came and went, while the one in *Hürriyet* did not. Suddenly, things grew very tense. This was not simply because *Hürriyet* was a widely read and influential paper. It also came from the newspaper's image. An article that had been framed in one newspaper as a tragic story seemed in *Hürriyet* to contain a hidden insult.

KEMAL GÖKTAŞ

As I wrote in my book investigating the role of the Turkish media in Hrant's murder, the statement issued by the General Staff was seen as a sort of signal flare. The first negative pieces were penned by *Hürriyet* columnists. Then, *Cumhuriyet* followed suit. It was open season, with some writers linking him with "foreign plots" and others finding Armenian insults between the lines. As for the right-wing press, it went even further, charging him of instigating "minority racism." We began to read stories claiming that Sabiha Gökçen was not Armenian but Bosnian.

Even so, the Sabiha Gökçen affair was not enough to turn Hrant Dink into a hate figure in the press. To achieve this, they had to take out of context that famous sentence from his eight-part series on Armenian identity, turning its original meaning on its head. The person who did that was another *Hürriyet* columnist, Emin Çölaşan. Çölaşan had made his name doing character assassinations in the press.

In his series, Hrant Dink had described how the concept of the Turk, and the the Armenian diaspora's fierce hatred of the Turk, had had an adverse effect on Armenian identity; having gone on to argue that it had served as a sort of poison, he had suggested that Armenian identity was now in urgent need of treatment. And so this was the sentence that Çölaşan extracted from the column, using it to say the following: "Freedom of thought is in the rise in our country, and so, too, is freedom of expression. We are racing down the road to Europe! So much so that we can even write what we like about the 'poisonous blood of the Turk!'" That was how the words 'poisonous blood' came to be associated with Hrant's name, whereafter nationalist writers felt no shame in preceding any mention of his name with the word "traitor."

YAVUZ BAYDAR

If you look at the Sabiha Gökçen affair, which began in February 2004, and turned into the media hate campaign against Hrant, you begin to see what this was all about. First, we are talking about the taboos at the heart of Turkish society's dominant narratives of intolerance, and that explains how the media, which is society's ignorant and merciless mirror, would plunge itself overnight into this sort of character assassination. The danger here is clear, on account of the "Armenian taboo." If the "target" was a man like Hrant Dink who was determined to break the taboos, it could quickly escalate.

The interesting thing about all of this was that the signal flare initiating this character assassination came first from the columnists of the mainstream press. During those weeks, and from then on, the personal attacks on Hrant did not stem from debating history or examining the past. In directing hatred and anger uniquely against Hrant Dink, the aim was to frighten a thinking man and, in so doing, to cover up the truth yet again. It was when they failed to achieve their aim that the threat mechanism was put into gear and the stage set for Hrant's undoing.

KEMAL GÖKTAŞ

At this point the newspapers—generally ignored by the left, the democrats, and the liberals but shaping the ideology of lumpen-nationalist youth groups that would come to be used in Hrant's murder—went into overdrive. There were even headlines like "Hrant's Snarl," beneath which he was described as "harboring monkey genes inside a human form" and as a "freak."

The president of the ultranationalist Ülkü Ocakları wrote the following in the *Ortadoğu* newspaper: "If we used the same terms, calling for the Armenians to be drained of their poisonous blood, would this meet the Copenhagen criteria, I wonder? Or are rights such as these accorded only to traitors? . . . It's clear what the game is here: the Zionist-Christian lords will take command of the ruling party, open up a space for the traitors of the AKP , paving the way for all manner of betrayal . . . Let it be known and never forgotten that this cannot continue. May God protect the Turk and raise him high."

If you can recall the demonstration of the Gray Wolves outside *Agos* that day, it begins to become clear how it was another signal flare.

HRANT

Following these articles, on February 26, a group of ultranationalists led by Levent Temiz, head of the Istanbul branch of this youth group, gathered outside the *Agos* building, shouting slogans and making threats.

The police had been given advance notice of the demonstration. *Agos* had taken the necessary precautions inside the office and at the entrance. Every newspaper and television station had been given advance notice and they, too, were outside *Agos*. The group's slogans were very clear: "Love us or leave us." "God damn ASALA." "One night we'll rush in and get you."

In the speech given by the group's leader, Levent Temiz, the target could not have been clearer: "From this moment on, Hrant Dink will serve as the target of all of our anger and hatred, and he will be our target, too." The group did what it had come to do, and then it dispersed. But heaven knows why, on that day and the next, not a single television channel except *Kanal 7* and not a single newspaper except *Özgür Gündem* carried the news. It was clear that the powers that had directed this group of ultranationalists to *Agos* had succeeded in blocking the media from covering it too.

KARİN KARAKAŞLI

That day, the traffic on the avenue came to a complete halt. The ultranationalists were chanting slogans and intimidating everyone. Their leader read out his speech, calling out to Hrant Dink and promising that from then on he would be the target of their anger and hatred. The police force stood behind their blockades, watching the ruckus. The TV stations were there, filming it all. People came from Security Services to say how sorry they were. Then they all went off and left us alone. At the same time, all of the *Agos* phones began to ring. Everyone wanted to know our views. We had prepared a press release, but there was not a single report in the press; the event was not so much as mentioned on a single television program. Evening fell, we closed the newspaper offices, and we went downstairs. Just then, Hrant said to me, "You don't have to walk next to me if you don't want to." It was the first time he had said something like that to me. Maybe he was saying it to protect me, but it upset me terribly.

MAYDA SARİS

When the ultranationalists came and started yelling "Love us or leave us" and "We'll rush in one night and get you," we had a hard time understanding what was going on. After this, plainclothes policemen started paying visits to *Agos*. They claimed to be alerting us to the protests, and with the pretext of protecting us, they would wander up and down the corridors with their walkie-talkies, going in and out of rooms. All of this made Hrant Dink very uneasy, and he told us that we were all free to go home if we wished. "Whoever wants to go home can go." That's what he told us. But, of course, not a single one of us wanted to leave *Agos*.

RAGIP ZARAKOLU

After the demonstration in front of *Agos*, following the Sabiha Gökçen affair and the statement by the General Staff, three of us—Şanar Yurdatapan, the left-wing activist; Abdurrahman Dilipak, a columnist allied with the Islamists; and me—filed a complaint against this ultranationalist group that had caused such a scene with its threatening slogans. But somehow, strangely, the investigation went from being about "unlawful threats" to being about an "unlawful demonstration." Only then did it become clear that these strange groups made up of people of unknown reputation had been organized into a movement. They were the same people who are currently being prosecuted as part of the Ergenekon trial. But it's awfully late, isn't it?

ZEYNEP TANBAY

As Hrant's friends, we did whatever was in our power to stand up against the things done to him in this country. After the ultranationalists did their show of strength in front of *Agos*, we went with Masis Kürkçügil and Aydın Engin to visit Hrant at *Agos*. Ufuk Uras, former leader of the Freedom and Democracy Party, was also in our group. Hrant received us warmly, welcoming us into his room, where we drank tea and talked. That day, he seemed very calm and comfortable. We had such a lovely conversation with him. He was in such high spirits that I left thinking that my worries might be unfounded. Maybe he did this to save us from anxiety.

KARİN KARAKAŞLI

That the show of strength in front of *Agos* received no coverage in the Turkish media was a big shock to us. It was almost more frightening than the demonstration itself. And perhaps this was why the writers like Yıldırım Türker of *Radikal* and Ayşe Önal of *Akşam*, who did stand by us, were so important. "The ultranationalists issued threats to *Agos* and all those who work for it, openly naming its editor, Hrant Dink, as their target," Ayşe Önal wrote. "Hrant is now in danger of being eaten up by crocodiles for his defense of human rights and freedom of expression."

AYŞE ÖNAL

After that piece, they went into a rage, publishing pieces to insult me and set me up as a target. They even went so far as to say things like "Hrant Dink's mistress, Ayşe Önal," or "A. Önal, who shares his bed." These were not things that could get to me or Hrant, but they upset Rakel a great deal.

LEDA MERMER

Then, they came back. This time, they came as the Federation for the Struggle against Unfounded Armenian Claims. Once again, we were inside the newspaper office building. We watched it all from the top floor. They sang the national anthem, as if we were citizens of another country. They left a black wreath in front of the door and left.

After that incident, we spoke about Baron Hrant buying a bulletproof vest. "What's the point? " he said. "They'll just shoot me in the head." It was around this time that he began to pace his office, hour after hour . . .

RAKEL

My husband was very shaken by all of this, of course. First and foremost, he felt very sorry for the people who worked with him. Then, alongside the sorrow, came uneasiness. At home, he tried to pretend nothing was wrong, but those loving eyes of his were glazed, almost. When she found out about the demonstration in front of *Agos*, our daughter Baydzar called from the United States. After he had soothed her, he said, "My little lamb, how it troubles me, knowing that you are there all alone." He didn't want to tell her too much about his troubles, but do you think we couldn't tell, just from the way he was?

DELAL

There's a huge pile of things that my father never talked about, and that includes all of the things he went through. Especially during the last two or three years, he told us nothing, so as not to cause us worry. He shared these things only with our mother.

I was in the States at the time, working on my doctorate. I found out about all this from an email sent to me by a friend. I flew into a panic and called the house. "You're all on your own there; please don't make things worse by worrying about me," my father said. "It's over now. It's come and gone." But when he saw that black wreath they left outside *Agos*, my father was deeply shocked. He told me about this much later. He also told me that the ultranationalist group had demonstrated outside *Agos*, knowing that he was inside to hear their threats. He admitted how troubled he had become when these open threats of theirs were censored in the press.

ARARAT

To tell the truth, from the time *Agos* was founded, we at home had been worried that something might happen to him. Our unease came from knowing how the state viewed Armenians. Over time, we began to relax because Turkey had begun the EU accession process, and there seemed to be not too much of a difference between my father and the other intellectuals of Turkey who were speaking up for democracy. But then came the day when my father became a direct target. A group of about fifty Istanbul-based ultranationalists planted itself in front of *Agos* to remind my father that he was Armenian.

That day, when I got a phone call telling me what happened, I raced home. And that evening, when I spoke to my father, for the first time in his life, he was not able to hide how troubled he was.

HOSROF

My brother came to see us the night of that first show of force outside *Agos*. Or was it the day they left the black wreath? I always mix these two up because they happened in such swift succession. He was lost inside his thoughts. He wouldn't say a word. He just sat there. I remember saying things like, "Don't go anywhere without me." Seeing him like that, I had no idea what to do. That night, I insisted on walking him home. After that, I tried to go with him wherever he went to protect him.

This incident was a clear sign that my brother had been made into a target. This caused me so much anxiety that I was forced to go to a psychologist for help. At my doctor's suggestion, I began to take antidepressants. My brother found out about this, and, from that time on, he shared nothing with me. Once again, he closed himself off and stopped telling me anything.

ZABEL

From the moment Hrant Ahparig walked into the house with my husband that evening, the atmosphere darkened. He walked in and collapsed on the three-seat sofa, and there he stayed. The Hrant I saw that evening was not the strong Hrant Ahparig I knew. This was the first time I'd seen him shaken like this, with his shoulders sagging. You know how they'll say that the light has gone out of someone's eyes? Well, it was like that. He'd become a silent man with a deeply lined face.

We called Rakel at once. She and Sera came right over. Meanwhile, his brother was trying to find out how he could help him. But how helpless he was! He left the house at his brother's side because Hosrof did not want to leave him alone. I watched them leave from the window. Even when he was walking, Hrant Ahparig was a different man. It was almost as if they had killed the living man.

RAKEL

The whole family saw the decline he went into after this incident. I do not know how much he discussed what was happening with his brothers, but my guess is that he didn't tell them much, so as not to worry them. Because he always wanted to protect them.

HRANT

For years now, I have been trying to write about things that are hard to talk about—things like the Armenian issue—with a view to creating new openings. And what a coincidence! Having developed ideas that draw upon the advantages I have enjoyed on account of being both Armenian and a citizen of Turkey, I have succeeded in angering the ultranationalists on both sides! The strangest thing is how similar these two sets of ultranationalists are in what they say, which goes to show how much they have in common.

However, it is essential that we do not leave the building of a new future for the Turkish and Armenian peoples to people like them.

They don't like what they read in *Agos* and they take issue with Hrant Dink's writings because he challenges what they've learned by heart. What one side calls white, the other calls black, and so it goes. If you suggest there might be some gray in between, they are utterly baffled. They forget their lines, and then they get all agitated.

For the first time in my life, I am in danger of being robbed of my human dignity. The first one to try this, during the September 12 regime, was my torturer, who sang folk songs while crushing my fingers under the heel of his shoe. He was having fun with me. He must have heard me singing folk songs in my cell. I used to belt out a pained rendition of "Spring Has Come to My Country's Mountains."

I shall never forget what I went through there. And now I am going through it again, for the second time.

When they label me as an "enemy of Turks," they are subjecting me to nothing other than torture. And the only thing I can do is sing them that song again: "Spring Has Come to My Country's Mountains." And what a lovely song it is when I sing it with the fire of my own beliefs. It is the prisoner's song. A song about loneliness. Especially loneliness.

So, there you have it. These are the tactics they are using to isolate *Agos* and leave us alone and defenseless. What they don't know is that people like us become even stronger when we're isolated. The more they isolate, the more of us there are . . .

28

The Hunt

HRANT

A couple of days later, a group calling itself the Federation for the Struggle Against Unfounded Armenian Claims staged a similar demonstration outside the *Agos* offices. Soon afterward, a lawyer entered the fray—someone named Kemal Kerinçsiz, whose name no one had ever heard before. He brought with him "The Grand Union of Lawyers," the organization, unknown until that day, of which he was the director. Kerinçsiz and his friends went to the Şişli Public Prosecutor's Office and filed a complaint against me. This quickly paved the way for me to be tried under the infamous Article 301, which in and of itself robs Turkey of its dignity.

This was the start of a dangerous process. In fact, I have walked on the edge of danger throughout my life. Either danger loved me or I loved it, and as strange it might sound, I remained extremely innocent.

Now here I was, on the edge of the same cliff once again. There were people after me again. I could sense them. And I knew very well that they were not affiliated with the so-called lawyers of the Kerinçsiz's group. They were not that visible, not that ordinary.

FETHİYE ÇETİN

When we heard about the demonstration staged by the ultranationalists, a group of us lawyers paid a visit to *Agos* to say how sorry we were, but because he wasn't there that day, we weren't able to speak with him.

A few days later, he called me and invited me over to the paper. He greeted me with his usual good cheer, embracing me warmly. Karin was with him. He told me what he had been through, starting with the visit to the Governor's Office. He was very anxious. Most of all, he was worried about the others working at *Agos*. And then, to my surprise, he moved on to his reason for asking me over. A group calling itself the Grand Union of Lawyers, headed by a Kemal Kerinçsiz, had gone to the Şişli Public Prosecutor and made a complaint, submitting a petition calling for a case be opened against him.

This was the first time I had seen Hrant in such a bad way. He even spoke of shutting down *Agos*. He and Karin both gave me power of attorney. This was not something I expected; until that day, Hrant Dink had never retained a lawyer.

HRANT

So long as the Armenians and the Turks are unable to rid themselves of their unhealthy way of looking at one another, it seems unlikely that the Armenians are going to bring their own identity back to health. The real issue is whether or not the Armenians are going to rid that identity of the symbol on which it rests: the enemy, the "Turk." There are two ways in which Armenian identity could set itself free of the Turk: one way would be for Turkey, as a state and as a society, to adopt an empathic approach to the Armenian nation and to display an understanding that makes it clear that they at last share their pain. Even if this approach did not achieve immediate results, in time, it would be possible for Armenian identity to clear itself of the trouble caused by the "Turkish factor." However, it would be difficult to pursue this option at the present time. The second option would be for Armenians themselves to remove from it the imprint of the Turk. This must be the preferred option.

FETHİYE ÇETİN

On November 7, 2003, Hrant launched a long series on Armenian identity. In this series, he explored and analyzed the ways in which Armenian identity had evolved over time in different parts of the world. In these analyses, taking 1915 as their starting point, he was addressing the Armenian diaspora in particular, outlining for them other ways of building a future. But now he was to be prosecuted on account of one sentence taken from that series, and this would lead, in turn, to a string of other prosecutions.

This sentence, which would lead to his being found guilty and branded an enemy of Turkey, came from the seventh installment in the series. Entitled "Getting to Know Armenia," it was, in essence, addressed to the Armenian diaspora, and it advised it to stop seeing the Turk as the enemy because this was doing their identity great harm, urging them instead to devote their creative energies to helping Armenia. This was what made the whole thing so ironic!

HRANT

Having rid Armenian identity of its "Turk," they can enrich it again with something far more vital: the independent state that is Armenia.

If the Armenian world set out to index its future against this tiny country's increase in happiness and prosperity, it would at the same time mark the end to the suffering that has given this identity so much trouble. How to rid Armenian identity of the "Turk?" It's very simple. Stop struggling with it.

As for the best way to find new words with which to forge Armenian identity: help Armenia.

Once the "Turk" has been removed, we shall, in the place of that poisoned blood, see good clean blood running through the arteries that Armenians create with Armenia.

It will be enough just to see that this is the way forward.

FETHİYE ÇETİN

If you look at the series as a whole, you cannot misunderstand what Hrant was trying to say. But what they did was to extract that one sentence: "Once the 'Turk' has been removed, we shall see, in the place of that poisoned blood, good clean blood running through the arteries that Armenians create with Armenia," and used it to lodge a criminal complaint. Hrant and

Karin Karakaşlı, the managing editor (deemed by Turkish law to be responsible for all that *Agos* published) were charged with "deriding and denigrating Turkishness."

Actually, this ran against the Court of Appeals' own interpretation of the law, because a judge is required to base his decision on the entire series and its context. Sadly, a deliberate decision was taken that this trial should serve to libel him, so that he could be set up as a target, and from the very beginning of this prosecution, it was used to serve this purpose.

In effect, it was *Agos*'s Sabiha Gökçen story that triggered this string of prosecutions. But it didn't suit their purpose to prosecute him on those grounds. It was clear that they did not wish for this matter—in other words, the question of what had happened to Armenian orphans—to be magnified or debated. That's why they selected a single sentence from an utterly different piece published long before, using a prejudiced reading of it to begin a hate campaign against him.

HRANT

At the outset, I did not feel overly uneasy about the the Şişli Public Prosecutor's investigation of the charge that I had insulted Turkishness. This was not the first time for me. I was familiar with this sort of prosecution from Urfa. In a speech I'd given in 2002 in Urfa, I'd said that I was not a Turk but an Armenian and a citizen of Turkey, on account of which they had been prosecuting me for "insulting Turkishness." It had been going on for the past three years, and I'd hardly paid attention to the course of this trial. My lawyer friends in Urfa had been handing the hearings on my behalf.

So I went off to the Şişli Prosecutor, feeling pretty indifferent. At the end of the day, I was sure of what I'd written and of my intentions in doing so. When the prosecutor had examined the series as a whole, and not just one sentence that made no sense on its own, he would quickly see that I had no intention of "denigrating Turkishness," and this comedy would end. I was absolutely certain that by the end of the investigation, they would have found no grounds for prosecution. But there's always room for surprise! They decided to open the case.

FETHİYE ÇETİN

The first hearing was in October 2004. Hrant and Karin and I went in together. The complaint had been made by four or five people, but only one of the complainants turned up in court. Hrant made the same statement he had made for the prosecutor earlier. I didn't want Hrant and Karin to come with me to the hearings that followed; I'd decided that I should attend these alone, as their advocate.

KARİN KARAKAŞLI

For a time, the media hate campaign against Hrant stopped. Then it started again. Immediately after that first hearing in October 2004, the ultra-right *Yeniçağ* newspaper attacked Hrant Dink on its front page for a piece he'd written in praise of the EU reforms. When he saw the paper, he said, "Now, this is really going too far."

HRANT

Under a headline in *Yeniçağ*, saying "Take a Look at this Armenian," I was accused of sticking out my tongue at Atatürk, this being an excuse to launch yet another racist attack. To offend these people, you didn't even have to write anyting, actually. If you were Armenian and you put yourself forward as such, this was all the cause they needed. They'd become accustomed to Armenians who never said a thing; it offended them to see people like Hrant displaying their identity with pride.

But there you go . . . Whenever I thought back to what was happening, there was a sour taste in my mouth as I recalled the story about Abdullah the lizard:

The time is 1918, the place a village at the foot of Mount Süphan. It had survived the events with difficulty. The village was crowded with survivors. Everyone had run away from everywhere—these were years when people just clung to one another helplessly. They'd mixed in with the villagers, carrying on with their everyday lives. And so it is with this man, one of God's harmless creatures.

Living in a dark shelter at the edge of a sheep pen, in a gap between two stones in the surrounding wall, no larger than a narrow wound. You know how lizards will crawl right out of gaps like these. So that was how they heard a voice and turned to look at that wound. Well, it was just like that: our fugitive hid, and he survived.

Every once in a while he showed his face, approaching those who still had mercy in their hearts. He would take himself out to the edge of the threshing ground, giving all he sweat he had, and after eating two slices of bread, he would return to his shelter.

It was a time when the land was spitting blood. It took all one's strength just to live a little longer. The new name the villagers had for him was *Abdullah*: "sent by God."

So there he was, somehow surviving in his godforsaken hole. Until the day when he was seen peeing against the wall.

İsmail bends over to fix his shiny eyes on Abdullah's dog's corpse of a cock, and he is shaking with mirth. He skips off, shouting, "Come over here! Come over and look! This one's thing is still unpeeled!"

They say that Abdullah vanished into his shelter as fast as a lizard.

Then they started throwing stones at the shelter. Soon everyone in the village, young and old, is stoning the sheep pen. "Get away from here, you infidel, we know who you are now . . . so get going!" they cry.

After a time, the shouts grow closer, and they turn into footsteps. The gate to the sheep pen opens. The first to enter is İsmail, who has always protected Abdullah in the past. "Where are you, Abdullah? Come out so I can save you. Reach out your hand."

İsmail was about to touch the hand Abdullah had extended when he suddenly shuddered and pulled his own hand back. For what Abdullah had extended was a bloody piece of skin he'd cut off his cock.

İsmail turned around to face the others. "Come on now, boys, let's leave this stranger alone. We're leaving."

They had no worries about Abdullah once he was circumcised. And they never bothered him again.

Now the time is 2004. The *Yeniçağ* newspaper has run a headline saying, "Take a Look at this Armenian." It's clear that some people have gone back to hunting lizards.

And please don't misunderstand me, because I'm certainly not frightened, and certainly not hiding—but I still feel like Abdullah the lizard. Forgive me for saying so, but such is the life of a reptile!

FETHİYE ÇETİN

At the trial's second hearing in December 2004, something happened that I had been expecting: those who had lodged the complaint against Hrant put in an appearance. I could see that they had come to give Hrant a thrashing, and so I was very glad that he hadn't come.

Something happened at that hearing that I've never forgotten. I said, "My client wrote these articles about Armenian identity. There is nothing here about Turks. The piece was about the diaspora Armenians." Whereupon the judge asked, "What Armenians?" When it became clear that the judge had no idea what I meant by diaspora Armenians, I tried to explain what was meant by the term, and I asked that the dossier be sent to be assessed by experts.

HRANT

Yes, they opened a case against me, but I still managed to stay optimistic— so much so that I even took part in a live television program by telephone link, advising the lawyer Kerinçsiz not to get too excited and saying that I was not going to be charged with anything at the end of this trial—and that if I did, I would leave the country. I was sure of my position, and I'd never had the slightest intention of denigrating Turkishness. Anyone who read my essays in full would see this very clearly. Finally, an expert report given to the court by a team of three professors from Istanbul University confirmed this to be the case.

There was no reason for me to worry; the prosecution would falter on so many grounds. But in spite of the expert report, the prosecutor still wanted me punished.

FETHİYE ÇETİN

I shall never forget the hearing at which the prosecutor gave his opinion, and Kerinçsiz stood up and commended him in the name of the Turkish people. After this, the hearing was postponed to a much later date. I presented my defense at that much later hearing and asked for acquittal. But the decision was again deferred. In the meantime, the judiciary went into recess. The judge wasn't able to give a decision at the next hearing, and he once again postponed it. By then, I was beginning to feel seriously anxious. A year had passed since the first hearing.

KARİN KARAKAŞLI

The trial dragged on and on, with the hearings being continually postponed. Meanwhile, something even stranger happened, whereby a new case was opened against *Agos* for publishing the expert report in its favor. But because I had by now been transferred and was no longer the managing editor, it was Arat Dink and Sarkis Seropyan who were prosecuted.

FETHİYE ÇETİN

Actually, according to the law, there was no objection to an expert report being published as news as long as it was not also offering an interpretation. But this time, they opened a case on the grounds that *Agos* had attempted to influence a judicial decision. I had reached the point when I was ready to tear my hair out. The indictment was unlawful—it was a textbook case. This case ended in acquittal, but it involved many, many trips to court.

The decision was finally announced at a hearing in October 2005. Hardly anyone was there beyond a few of the young people who now called themselves the "friends of Hrant." There were, in addition, a few people from *Agos*. That was all. Not really any famous names. Hrant didn't attend this hearing, either. He was waiting for the decision in his office at *Agos*. In the end, the court found Hrant guilty and sentenced him to six months.

KARİN KARAKAŞLI

On the day the decision was announced, we were at *Agos*. Fethiye Çetin called from the courthouse. Hrant had been found guilty, and I was acquitted. Hrant already knew when I walked into the building. He was sitting by himself in his office. His eyes were fixed on his desk. Just then, the phones began to ring. Wiping the tears from his eyes, he answered them all in a shaky voice, saying, "I can't go on with this stain on my forehead. If the Court of Appeals approves this decision, I shall leave this country. How can I face the neighborhood grocer or my neighbour with this label on me?" When he'd hung up all of the phones, he looked at me and said, "This is my death sentence." At that moment, his son and his brothers came into the room. They embraced each other in silence. I left so that they could be alone.

ARARAT

When I went to *Agos* that day, I found my father crying. Even with one prosecution following another, my father had not expected to be found guilty. He could tell that something strange was going on, but he'd still thought himself to be on secure ground. After all, the expert's report was in his favor. That the prosecutor had asked for conviction was normal. That was what prosecutors always asked for. In the end, the judge would make the right decision. That was his genuine opinion. Maybe this was why he was so distraught when he was convicted. It really tore him up. He kept asking, "What am I going to say to people?" and bursting into tears.

ZEYNEP TANBAY

That day a large group of us—we called ourselves the Peace Initiative—rushed over to *Agos* in his support. We were all there at this side, writers and scholars, artists and columnists. He was full of emotion but also very different from the man we knew. Even though he tried to hide it, he was crushed. Speaking to the television cameras that were crowding the office, he said, with tear-filled eyes, "They are accusing me of racism here, but this is a crime I could never commit. All my life, I have opposed racism."

ARARAT

Among the intellectuals who came to *Agos* that day was the famous author Adalet Ağaoğlu. My father was very moved by this show of solidarity, and especially that Adalet Hanım had taken the trouble to come to see him. Then they all went downstairs together, and my father stood in front of the building, speaking to the television cameras. When Adalet Hanım gave him a warm embrace, he couldn't stop himself from crying. I was so proud of my father at that moment. How innocent he was and how pure. *There he is, my father!* I said to myself. *A man stripped bare.*

ADALET AĞAOĞLU

As we stood there in front of the cameras, I couldn't stop myself, and I threw my arms around him. I can remember that day like yesterday, and can you believe it? I can still feel his warmth. Throughout those trials, I had never for a moment doubted in Hrant's innocence, and that day when I saw how the conviction had undone him, I was badly shaken. When we went downstairs, Hrant was right next to me. They were extending their microphones to me as well. And at that moment, something happened, and as I hugged Hrant as tightly as I could, I shrieked, "I'm not letting them take you! They can't take you away from us!" Never in my life have I been the sort of person who shouts or makes a scene. I'm a shy, reserved person. But I don't know what happened. When I heard his voice break, I was torn in two. And then, well, Hrant couldn't hold back his tears, either.

HRANT

On hearing that I had been sentenced to six months, I felt crushed under the painful pressure of all those hopes I'd carried with me from the outset of the trial. I was utterly undone. I had never felt so fragile or so rebellious.

For days, months, I had been telling myself,. "Wait until this decision comes out, wait until I'm acquitted, and then you'll be sorry for all those things." But now the decision had been announced, and all of my hopes were shattered. The truth was, I was in as pitiful a state as anyone can be. The judge had made his decision in the name of the "Turkish people," legally asserting that I had "denigrated Turkishness."

I can take just about anything, but not this. In my view, to humiliate those with whom we live on the basis of an ethnic or religious difference is racist, and there is no excuse for it. It was with this in mind that I spoke with my friends from the media who were downstairs, waiting to find out if I would be leaving the country: "I shall take the case to the Court of Appeals and, if necessary, apply to the European Court of Human Rights. If I am not acquitted at any stage and cannot clear my name by any of these means, then I shall leave my country. Because, in my opinion, anyone convicted of such a crime has no right to continue living with the citizens he has denigrated."

As I uttered these words, I was as emotional as I ever have been. Sincerity is my only weapon.

AMBERİN ZAMAN

The moment I heard about the ruling, I called him, saying, "Let's do a piece for the *Economist* right away. Let's get the word out and drum up some support. I'm coming to do an interview." And he said, "Fine," but in a weary voice. When I got there, he was so upset that he couldn't sit still. "They've found me guilty of racism," he kept saying. "Can you believe it? Racism!" He kept saying the same sentence over and over, wavering between sorrow and anger.

I began the interview with this question: "Why do you think that they opened this case against you?"

Hrant said in reply, "I think they were made to do so. This is the work of the deep state. I think that from the very beginning, it's been the deep state wanting to teach me a lesson. Especially since our report in *Agos* on Sabiha Gökçen. They've already made this clear to me. Things like, "We'll make you pay for this . . ."

The interview kept getting interrupted by phone calls. At every call, he would light up, and his face would fill with emotion. Turks, Kurds, Laz, Armenians, the young and the elderly, men and women, Christians and Muslims, they were all calling him to give him their support. As phone calls came in from all over Turkey, his eyes brimmed with tears. It was clear that these prayers and endearments coming to him at this difficult moment went straight to his heart.

HRANT

I have the reporter from the *Economist* in my office; she's interviewing me about my condemnation. The phones won't stop ringing. I can't let her see my eyes welling up.

I have already been branded a sentimentalist, but I have no other weapon. I might have some brains, but most of me is emotion.

I am neither a cool political analyst nor a politician. Never in my life have I calculated in advance how I should behave. So when I said, "If I am sentenced, I shall leave the country," I meant it from the bottom of my heart.

Tell me, for God's sake, why should I ever need any weapon other than my heart and my sincerity?

RAKEL

Our Armenian elders would come up and say, "We're praying for you; we fear for you." And he would say, "Don't worry, nothing can happen to me, but keep on praying." He used to say that he wasn't a believer, but prayers brought him comfort. Why wouldn't they? Isn't it God's words that give us the strength to go through hard times? And the strong feeling that your friends are on your side.

HRANT

Everyone was in a flurry—and bless them, all week long, they came to visit, offering their support. They picked up the phone and called me. They wrote articles.

The women have gone to be with my wife, to pray with her. They are asking the Lord to protect me. Clearly, they fear for me.

So then, what about me? I cannot say I am not afraid. No, I cannot say that. Not at all. But I'm not about to leave my country. After all, I'm used to living like this. From now on, I'll just live a bit more fearfully. That's all!

YÜCEL SAYMAN

They were not content with convicting Hrant. Exactly one week after the decision was announced, they opened another trial, charging him with "trying to influence the judiciary." I felt so indignant when I heard that. For forty-five years, I'd taught law in universities, and for six years I'd served as president of the Istanbul Bar. But I'd never heard of such a thing.

That article in the Turkish Penal Code was meant to punish the person who made oral or written declarations with the intent of influencing prosecutors, judges, courts, experts, or witnesses. How could that person be the defendant himself? If the defendant himself could not seek to influence the court with his own statements, what else could he do? I called Fethiye Çetin at once and said I wanted to help with Hrant Dink's defense.

FETHİYE ÇETİN

And now, because of the statements Hrant had made to the press about his conviction, they charged him with "trying to influence the judiciary." The lawyer Kerinçsiz and his team ran off to the prosecutor with their template petitions, and the prosecutor drew up the indictments as if he were no more than their secretary. It was abundantly clear that these cases that were being opened up against him, one after the other, were intended to overwhelm Hrant and isolate him. This case, opened in October 2005, would not have its first hearing until May 2006. But there was so much else to live through before that day arrived.

HRANT

The deep forces set out to isolate me in the eyes of the people of Turkey and turn me into a target went so far as to use the statement I made to the press about my conviction as a pretext to open another case against me for trying to influence the judiciary. My statement was published and broadcast everywhere in the media, but only the one in *Agos* drew their attention. So now those in charge of *Agos* and I were tried for influencing the judiciary.

I suppose you could call this dark humor. I am the defendant, and who has more right to influence the judicary than a defendant? But look at what a comedy this has become: now I am being tried for trying to influence a judge.

ORAL ÇALIŞLAR

As Hrant was sent from courtroom to courtroom, it became clear to us that these people were determined. And, in 2006, when we rang in the New Year, there was a great deal of tension. But Hrant was not just sitting there, waiting for the Court of Appeals to rule on his conviction; he was still saying, "I'll do this conference, and you do that one," and running all over the place, giving speeches. It was precisely then that we were invited to a meeting at Antalya's Akdeniz University, where we found ourselves inside a plot that had been prepared for us in advance.

When we entered the conference hall of the campus, we saw the rector of the university, the governor of Antalya, and the commander of the gendarmes sitting in the front row and waiting for us. Among them was the former chief prosecutor of the Court of Appeals, who once had said of Hrant, "This man is taking money from Armenia; he should be tried of treason." The auditorium was full, and the attendants were holding Turkish flags and waving them. And this was where we were to debate freedom of thought!

But in the end, we made it happen. After Hrant took the floor, he gave a moving speech. When the chief prosecutor tried to turn the conference hall into a courtroom during the question-and-answer session, Hrant responded calmly to each of his provocative questions. Hard to believe, but when the meeting ended, the university students in the hall gave Hrant support with their applause.

ERSİN KALKAN

After the conviction was announced, the hate campaign in the press started up again and, with racist and nationalist writers joining in with the mainstream media, it turned into a genuine lynching. Now what you saw in all newspaper reports, especially in my own paper, *Hürriyet,* were turns of phrase like this: "Hrant Dink, who has been convicted of denigrating Turkishness," or "The Armenian journalist Hrant Dink, who has been found guilty of insulting Turkish identity." It went so far that you never saw his name without words like these attached. And rather than condemning Kemal Kerinçsiz and his gang for their attacks, they gave them a great deal of attention, turning them into heroes. It pains me to say so, but a certain group of writers and so-called reporters have a lot to answer for. Their antics helped pave the way for Hrant's demise.

HRANT

Now, they were publishing in the newspapers and on television that I said, "The Turk's blood is poisonous." Each time, I became a little better known as an "enemy of the Turk." In the corridors of courthouses, fascists were assaulting me with their racist curses . . . spreading their insults with banners. And each time, there were a few more threatening e-mails and letters, which had been piling in for months and now numbered in the hundreds.

I kept myself going by telling myself to be patient and wait for the Court of Appeals to make its decision, because when it did, the truth would at last be known, and these people would feel shame for what they had done.

SEZGİN TANRIKULU

Hrant had taken his case to the Court of Appeals, and he was waiting for their answer. In spite of having reached such a critical moment, he did not stop speaking what he knew to be the truth. That was so important for us Kurds, this unflinching courage! In March 2006, we organized a string of seminars at the Diyarbakır Bar entitled "Justice for All," and we invited him, too.

While he was with us in Diyarbakır, he made a very striking political analysis. Speaking as an Armenian and using examples from his own history, he said that we Kurds should not make the same errors. He told us not to seek support from outside powers or engage in nationalism. He spoke of how the "deep state" would be mobilizing the streets to turn Turks against Kurds. With the changing of the world order, he said that the deep state was no longer able to effect dark deeds, such as military coups, and so it had retreated into its own darkness, where it was busy creating a new form of nationalism.

HRANT

Recently there has been an effort to nurture, but above all to manufacture, a new brand of nationalism that can be manipulated at the deepest level.

We are talking about the phenomenon we call the "deep state." It is impossible to define it in concrete, precise, or technical terms. But we all sense it—it's there, even if we can't see it, and every once in a while, it comes to the surface, whereupon nationalism bubbles up. But the new world order lacks the conditions to allow it to surface as it pleases.

So, when the deep state is unable to surface, it pulls society into its own depths instead. And there in those depths it creates a society in its image. This is what I can sense out there. A society sinking deeper and deeper. This is a very dangerous state of affairs . . .

I don't mean dangerous just from the perspective of Turkish nationalists, but also from the perspective of Kurds. For I am saying that it is dangerous for every person living in this country.

The deep state knows this very well: first and foremost, EU accession means the transfer of some of the nation state's sovereignty rights. This is why we are going through such hard times. And this is not the worst yet. We shall endure much harsher times in the days ahead as efforts are made to stop the process altogether. Because the EU accession process is all about about disempowering the deep state. The deep state is more than just a bureaucratic or military body. Above all, it is a mindset. How much we succeed in changing that mindset depends on how much we are able to move toward democracy and away from militarism.

FETHİYE ÇETİN

It was May 2006. We had the first hearing in the trial in which Hrant stood accused of trying to influence the judiciary. Outside the courthouse, it was doomsday. They'd draped a huge Turkish flag over the building. Banners everywhere. The stage was set for a provocation.

I spoke with the police about how I was going to bring Hrant into the building. "Tell him to come in a taxi," they said. "We'll let him in through the garage door." And so that is what we did. Then we went up to the top floor in the elevator. Waiting for us in the corridor was a crowd of agitators. The police had set up a barricade. We were struggling through it, trying to get to the courtroom with all of these agitators spitting at us and hurling curses, waving their fists at the police and threatening them. I couldn't look Hrant in the face. How he kept going through all this, I cannot begin to understand.

It's much the same in the courtroom. While Hrant is struggling to explain himself, they try to shout him down, crying, "enemy of the Turks!" They throw pens, lighters, and loose coins at us. Just then, Arat comes into the courtroom. He is now the managing editor and so is being prosecuted with his father.

ARARAT

When I arrived, the police formed a cordon around me to get me inside. The crowd seemed ready for a lynching. There were ten or fifteen of them on either side, and another thirty behind us—and an endless stream of insults and curses and brandished fists.

In the corridor on the top floor, there were at least a hundred people. Among them when plainclothes police, and you couldn't tell which of them are there to protect you and which of them are there to lynch you. I kept thinking of my father and how he was going to get out of here . . .

The courtroom had been taken over by the agitators. My father was struggling to keep hold of himself. It was all so humiliating. He had suffered such a big injustice already. And now, under all this pressure, he was trying to speak reasonably. They hadn't managed to crush him, but he'd had to crush his own feelings.

These guys were like bad cartoon characters. My father had taught us not to divide people up into good and bad; he told us that every human being had both good and bad in them. But it was only too clear who was bad in that place and who was good. Standing right across from me was the leader of the bad group, Kemal Kerinçsiz. He didn't look like a real person. His yelling and shouting did not sound at all sincere. How clear it was that they were only acting! My father had always laughed at cartoon men like this. But now, he was leaning over to whisper into my ear, "Don't ever laugh. Please, my son. Please." He was worried that their hatred and anger would be focused on me.

FETHİYE ÇETİN

In the end, things got so out of hand that the judge had to postpone the hearing. With difficulty, the police took us into a room, blocking the door so the agitators couldn't get in. We waited there for about an hour. Then they took Hrant and Arat down the elevator and into the garage and out through the back door. What a shame!

At this point I must note something else: a few days before this hearing, the 9th Department of the Court of Appeals approved the six-month prison sentence given to Hrant under Article 301, but on the objection of the chief justice, it had gone to the highest chamber, the Supreme Court of Appeals. While one trial was coming to its nerve-grating end, he was attending a hearing for another trial at which he was assaulted and humiliated.

Anyway, they'd come to the courthouse that day to lynch Hrant. The only other hearing I'd seen like that was that Orhan Pamuk's, which I'd watched on television. I have always wondered why the people who paid so much attention to the others prosecuted under Article 301 paid so little attention to Hrant. Whereas, whether he knew them or not, Hrant always went to their hearings to give them support.

PERİHAN MAĞDEN

I did not go to any of Hrant Dink's hearing. I thought that enough people were going already. I did not stand at his side. But he did stand at mine! One day, he called me and told me he had gone to one of my hearings. When he' seen the same people who'd come to his trial, he'd left, adding that he'd not wanted "to give them an excuse for a provocation." This lovely man was feeling sorry for not being able to remain at my hearing to the end.

VİVET KANETTİ

I didn't go to any of Hrant's hearings, either, but when I went to Orhan Pamuk's hearing in December 2005, I saw Hrant Dink, who had come to give him support, and I witnessed what happened to him.

That day, the corridor on the top floor had been taken over by police and agitators. Suddenly, there was kicking and shoving. Orhan Pamuk's translator, Maureen Freely, who had come from London for the hearing, pushed her way through the crowd with difficulty to come to my side; in the meantime, the shouting in the corridor grew steadily louder, and we heard people yelling, "Get out!" We looked to see where this shouting was aimed, and there was Hrant. He was frozen in shock. When the insults and the curses grew even harsher, he was forced to leave the corridor.

Maureen and I went down to the ground floor. Hrant was still there. "For God's sake, don't go outside," I said.

"What else can I do?" he said. "I'm going out there. Of course I am."

And when he went out, the crowd waiting outside began yelling, cursing, and making threats. What Hrant went through at Orhan Pamuk's hearing was a rehearsal for the provocation he would suffer at his own hearing in May 2006. And what a shame it was that none of us were with him on that day.

FETHİYE ÇETİN

Among these agitators were two unforgettable faces: the first belonged to Kemal Kerinçsiz, the man behind the case for which Hrant was sentenced, and the other was the famous retired general who was a key figure in Turkey's "dark affairs," Veli Küçük. He was there with that group of agitators in the corridor. When they and the ones inside petitioned to be present at the hearing, the judge read out his name. Now both of these men are in prison as defendants in the Ergenekon trial, but it has proved impossible to implicate them in the murder of Hrant Dink.

SARKİS SEROPYAN

After this hearing at which he was attacked, Hrant became obsessed with the name Veli Küçük. I was one of the defendants in this trial, and Arat and I went to one of the later hearings without him. When we were telling him afterwards about Kemal Kerinçsiz being there, he was not at all interested—all he wanted to know was if the other man with him was Veli Küçük.

BELMA AKÇURA

A *Milliyet* reporter told me what sort of things they were shouting at Hrant at that hearing—calling him a vile traitor and saying, "Come over here! There's Turkish blood waiting for you! Come over here where the state can protect you, because who else can?"

When I heard that, I picked up the phone and told Hrant that Kemal Kerinçsiz was becoming steadily more menacing and dangerous. "What they're doing there is not so important," he said, "but you know who really scares me? It's that general. You know, the one who was implicated in Susurluk?"

"Who do you mean?" I said. "Do you mean Veli Küçük?"

"Yes," he said.

"Shall I write about this?" I asked.

"Not now," he said. "Later. There are things I have to tell you about all that."

I understood then that he didn't want to speak on the phone, so I hung up. But my own newspaper didn't pay too much attention to my report titled "Assault on Hrant Dink in the Courthouse," either.

"This should have been in the headlines," I tell them.

To which my colleague at the next table says, "Headlines aren't for who get attacked, they're for people who get killed. Haven't you learned that yet?"

A few hours later, we got news from Ankara that Mustafa Yücel Özbilgin, a member of the Supreme Council of State, has been killed. The assault on Supreme Council of State caused us to forget Hrant.

CENGİZ AKTAR

The funeral of Mustafa Yücel Özbilgin, whose murder during the attack on the Supreme Council of State, immediately attributed to Islamist extremists, turned into a large show of force against them. On the day of the funeral, Hrant and I were attending a seminar organized jointly by the Konrad Adenauer Foundation and the Turkish Union of Journalists. In his speech that day, Hrant had pointed to the possibility of this murder being a provocation, suggesting that the "deep state" might be engineering some "very deep trickery" to impede the EU accession process.

HRANT

With yesterday's attack on the Supreme Council of State and its effect on the national mood, it is only too clear where Turkey is headed. This is not the first time we have seen "political engineering and design." And what we are seeing now are the deep state's "senior engineers" setting the scene for politics in the future and sending the Kurdish issue back into the streets of eastern Turkey. In setting out to exacerbate the Kurdish issue, they are seeking to promote the state of mind I have defined as "rising nationalism." But nationalism alone is not enough. Now, they are also deepening the rift between secularists and anti-secularists.

We can easily say that this sort of "deep engineering" is moving forward to design the politics of the future, which also includes the presidential and general elections. I see this as an effort to create an "alternative government" or a "political order without the AKP."

In the presence of our European friends, I can say this: "In the years to come, Turkey is going to surprise you tremendously. You will be confronted with many other scenarios that will lead you to ask where Turkey is going. But please don't be too surprised; this is Turkey, and Turkey has still not abandoned its way of ruling from the top down. But it's important not to lose hope because there is among its people the deepest desire for change."

AYDIN ENGİN

In June, the media was full of reports about the suspects of the Council of State attack. One of the suspects was even saying, "If we hadn't been caught, we would have gone on to hit the Istanbul Armenians." The *Yeni Şafak* newspaper, which has close links with the leadership of the ruling AKP, even did a report on this. With his customary courage, Hrant rose to the occasion, demanding to know who these Armenians were. This column still serves as an lesson today.

HRANT

"If we hadn't been caught, we would have gone on to hit the Istanbul Armenians." How can we explain how a confession of this nature would be embraced with such indifference?

Our first question is to the *Yeni Şafak* newspaper, which is in the enviable position, thanks to its close ties with the ruling party, to trump the other papers with its access to inside sources. Nevertheless, we must still say this to our friends at *Yeni Şafak*: if you are going to characterize such a statement in your report as a "spine-tingling confession," putting all of the Armenians of Istanbul into a panic, then in the days that follow, you will not run further stories. And neither will you seek statements from the Justice and Interior Ministers to confirm and follow up your report.

Moving on to the other sections of the media—well, what can we say?

Following the Council of State attack, every last outlet in the press and broadcast media churned out all manner of reports, columns, and analyses. There were a thousand news reports, while the columnists did analysis after analysis. Gracious me, can there be anyone who hasn't seen this news? Who was not the least bit interested? Or did someone somewhere decide, huh, no one should be allowed to take an interest in this story, and slap down an injunction?

I ask this because we in the *Agos* family are no strangers to such things. When the ultranationalists held their demonstration in front of our people, saying "One night we'll come and snatch you," an injunction stopped the news from being reported. The entire press corps and countless cameras witnessed that demonstration, but there was nothing about it on television or in the papers.

Is there any difference between the apathy of the press and the apathy of the ruling party, state agents, and state officials? And now I am addressing the justice minister, the interior minister, the governor of Istanbul, and the director of the Security Forces: "Please, I beg you, speak out. Try to bring some clarification to the confessor's statement!"

If the author of the confession had provided a name or an address, things would not be quite so bad. By means of necessary precautions concerning said person or said place, the threat would have been taken under control. However, this confession refers to all of Istanbul's Armenians, and, as such, is as vague as it is wide.

As we know, these men were caught, but they were not the only ones! We invite all those responsible to meet their responsibilities.

At the very least, we shall not stand indifferent, and in the future, whenever we meet with the slightest bother, we shall be sure to badger those who have shown indifference today.

CENGİZ ÇANDAR

The Council of State attack was presented to the public as the work of an extreme Islamist faction, taking its courage from the opportunities created by the AKP government. With this, it was insinuating that the government was creating conditions for a desired religious state, thus the polarization between the secularists and antisecularists was sharpened. Attended as it was by soldiers, members of the judiciary, the main opposition party, and others making catcalls against the prime minister, the victim's funeral turned into a show of force.

And then *Yeni Şafak,* a paper with close ties to the government, reported that one of the attackers had, in his confession, said that if they had not been caught, they had been planning to kill the Armenians. There was not a word about this in any other paper, which is why it failed to create any waves.

But Hrant sees this, and, with his fine political understanding, he writes this piece. In the end, events will come to show that he was right in saying that the Council of State attack was not limited to those who had been caught—it would emerge that figures such as Kemal Kerinçsiz and Veli Küçük were part of the same group. The Council of State assassination would go on to become the backbone of the Ergenekon trial, which in 2007, would charge these men and others with plotting a coup to overturn the government. But what a shame it is that the confession about a plan to kill Armenians also turned out to be well-founded. Only a few months later, Hrant would be killed, in the name of all Armenians.

HRANT

My faith in the "justice system" and in the concept of "law" has been ripped to shreds. How could it not be? These prosecutors and judges went to college, didn't they? Aren't they all graduates of law school? Do they not have the capacity to understand what they read?

As a matter of fact, this country's judiciary is not independent, as a number of state officials and politicians have dared to say. The judiciary does not protect the rights of citizens; it protects the state.

In fact, I was totally sure that even if it was said that the decision was taken in the name of the Turkish people, it was actually taken in the name of the state. That was why my lawyers appealed to the Court of Appeals. Fine, but where was the guarantee that the deep forces setting out to show me my place had no influence there? And since when did all the decisions of the Court of Appeals turn out to be just? Didn't the same Court of Appeals sign the decisions that stripped the minority foundations of their property?

Finally, we appealed, and then what happened?

The attorney general found no crime in my essay, thus confirming the expert report, and he asked for an acquittal; even so, the Court of Appeals found me guilty. The Court of Appeals' attorney general was as sure about my essay as I was, and so he objected the verdict and took the case to the General Council Plenary Session.

But what can I say? Those great forces that were so keen to teach me my place, and that had made their presence felt at every stage of my prosecution in ways unknown to me—yet again, they were standing behind the curtain. In the end, the majority of those voting at the Plenary Session decided that I had "denigrated Turkishness."

FETHİYE ÇETİN

Yes, the final decision came on July 11, 2006, and Hrant's conviction was confirmed. But they didn't stop there. Three days later, they opened yet another case against Hrant, again under Article 301. In a statement he'd made to Reuters, Hrant had said, "Of course 1915 was genocide. By the end, a people that had lived on these lands for four thousand years had vanished entirely." He had gone on to publish it as a news report in *Agos*. It is sadly significant that although the same piece ran in both *Radikal* and *Milliyet*, neither paper was prosecuted.

There was something else surprising about this new case because he had used the word "genocide" as far back as 2005, in an interview with Derya Sazak in *Milliyet*. In that instance, the great Turkish justice system had chosen not to prosecute, but now, for some reason, it decided to do so. The final decision of the Court of Appeals could well be a sign of things to come . . .

AYDIN ENGİN

The Court of Appeals had made its decision known, putting an end to all discussion. And then our wily reporters showed us just how good they were at following up a story by pressing him over and over with the same question:

"Hrant Bey, you said that you'd leave the country if the Court of Appeals confirmed your sentence. So are you going to leave now?" By the time the Court of Appeals announced its decision, the press-led lynch campaign had entered its most extreme phase—especially the racist right-wing press announced the news in a way that openly expressed its hatred against Hrant. They used phrases like, "The Court of Appeals ruled with good reason that Dink's statement was not free expression, but an obscene insult," or "There is no doubt that the expression Dink used was a provocation and an insult against Turkishness." And in so doing, they hung a placard around his neck, labeling him the "enemy of the Turks."

ALPER GÖRMÜŞ

When the Court of Appeals confirmed Hrant's sentence for "insulting Turkishness," I interviewed him for *Aktüel* magazine. This turned out to be the last time we spoke. As I sat in his office at *Agos*, I did not know where to look. As I listened to what he was saying, I felt shame and guilt churning inside me because Hrant was using every bit of energy he had to prove to me why it was impossible for him to insult Turkishness. According to the ruling, Hrant Dink was meant to have insulted the likes of me for being Turks. And now I had this dear man sitting across from me who had struggled all his life against discrimination, saying, "Alper, my brother, how could I ever insult you? How could such a thing ever be? Just look at what these people have dropped me into!" He said this again and again, right up until the moment I left.

HRANT

I was found guilty under Article 301. I was sentenced to six months' imprisonment for "insulting Turkishness," a crime I never committed.

As I continue to be prosecuted under the same article in other cases, I demand an answer to this question: "Almost every other prosecution on charges of insulting Turkishness under Article 301 has resulted in the courts dismissing the cases on technical or judicial grounds and without convictions. Why, then, was Hrant Dink convicted and sentenced to six months?"

If you recall, the vandalism staged during the first hearing of the Orhan Pamuk case disgraced Turkey in the eyes of the world, so much so that the case was dismissed. Pamuk's Article 301 adventure ended with a technical solution. An even lighter solution was found in the Elif Shafak case. Although there was a lot of noise before the case started, it was dismissed at the first hearing, without Elif Shafak having to appear in court. Similarly, other writers and academics who had faced prosecution for the crime of "insulting Turkishness" for writing articles after the Armenian Conference in Istanbul also got away with it, receiving similar slaps on the wrist and nothing more.

Yes, we all need that question answered, and no one more than me.

At the end of the day, I am a citizen of this country, and I insist on equal treatment.In the past, I have, of course, faced discrimination as an Armenian. For instance, when I was doing my military service, after basic training, all of my friends were promoted, but I was not. I was already a man with a family and two children, and normally I wouldn't have cared much. I would have taken comfort in knowing I'd be more comfortable than the others, as I would not be given tough duties or assigned night watches. But the truth is, I was deeply affected by this act of discrimination. I will never ever forget how I hid behind the tin barracks and cried for two hours, alone, while everyone else rejoiced in their promotions.

It goes without saying that it is one thing to miss out on a promotion, and another to be prosecuted, and perhaps acquitted, perhaps convicted, under Article 301.

Just as it should be clear: I am not saying that I shouldn't be convicted if they weren't, or that they should be convicted, too, if I am. But I have to admit that, as someone who has on several occasions faced discrimination as an Armenian, my mind keeps returning to this question: "Does this sentence have anything to do with my being Armenian?"

29

Fluttering Like a Pigeon

HRANT

Until today, I have based my writing on the fundamental principles I hold to be true. While honoring my Armenian identity and history, I have stood shoulder to shoulder with Turks in our struggle for a more democratic country. I went beyond the propaganda on 1915, its concepts, and its themes, to claim, in all its nakedness, the great pain that we have, as human beings, carried with us since then. Because for me, history is not just about disputing laws and documents, it is a question of conscience.

Let us now cede the stage to another intellectual, Krikor Zohrab, deputy of the Ottoman Parliament. Let us look at this idealist lawyer's last letter, dated 1915. "My love, my one and only, for us the last curtain is falling. I have no more strength. If I do not survive, my last advice to my children is this: they should always love and cherish each other, and worship you, and not let their hearts ache too long, and remember me . . ."

ALİ BAYRAMOĞLU

While the rest of us were living our lives cool and calm, Hrant sensed what the rest of us had yet to fully grasp: he'd been chosen as a target. Usually, it is the other way around. Usually, it is the victim who doesn't see the danger and those around him who give the warnings. But Hrant knew what it meant to have one case after another opened against him. This had something to do with his being Armenian. He was experienced enough to know what it meant to be a dissident as a member of a minority. He'd seen certain things as signs. He thought it was a sign that he was called to the governor's office. The ultranationalist demonstrations in front of *Agos*—that was another sign. General Veli Küçük's appearance at one of his trials—that was another . . .

I attended the hearing where Veli Küçük and Kemal Kerinçsiz put in an appearance—though technically, I didn't, because I got as far as the door, and, when I saw the crowd, I turned around.

When you're in the thick of things, you don't understand them. Now, when we look back at the time when Hrant was prosecuted under Article 301 and his sentence was confirmed by the Court of Appeals, is it possible not to see that he was crying out like a man on the way to his execution? But then, we didn't see.

BASKIN ORAN

There were things we couldn't see then. How shall I put it? Prof Ibrahim Kaboğlu and I had prepared a "Minority Report for the Prime Minister's Advisory Board," exposing the current problems of minorities. First, they asked for the report; then, after we had written it, they prosecuted us under Article 301. What I'm saying is that Hrant was not the only one prosecuted under Article 301, but he was the only one whose sentence was confirmed. This was the price of being a controversial Armenian in Turkey. Those who did this may not feel remorse at this moment, but it will bring their children shame.

If you look for those responsible for Hrant's death, you'll find me among them. Because when he said, "If they confirm my sentence, I won't remain in this country; I wouldn't be able to look anyone in the face. I'd leave then and there," I called him and said, "Why should you go? Let them go. Think how many thousands of years earlier than their ancestors your ancestors came here. Time for *them* to leave!" If only I hadn't called him.

HRANT

For me, the most unbearable thing has been the psychological torture I have endured alone.

I see it sometimes in documentaries. The lions are going after a pack of animals, but the pack has left one animal behind. The plan all along is to separate one animal from the pack and then descend on it en masse. I believe that they have isolated me and made me their target in much the same way—and I start torturing myself.

Anxiety is one aspect of this psychological torture. A second is apprehension. A third is caution; a fourth is a deep unease.

I'm just like a pigeon . . .

ORAL ÇALIŞLAR

Though Hrant was greatly loved, he had a solitary side. And I, like all of the others, felt helpless in the face of it. Because I had not paid much attention to the trial process, I did not go to the hearings. One day, Aydın Engin came over and told me about the hearing at which they'd both been attacked. Until then, we'd had no idea. That day was the first time we found out about it. And what did we do after finding that out? What did we do to protect him? I feel so guilty about not having gone to those hearings. It was later that the pain dug into me.

CENGİZ ÇANDAR

Despite our inattention, Hrant never reproached any of us even though we left him to fend for himself during all of those trials.

I didn't go to Hrant's hearings, either. This was partly because I considered Hrant to be "one of us." And this was true for most of us. We forgot he was Armenian.

We had been causing trouble in Turkey for so many years by then—challenging the military, struggling for the Kurds, and fighting against the odds for democratic change—and trials had become so commonplace for us that I didn't see anything particularly dramatic in the Court of Appeals ruling. Orhan Pamuk had been prosecuted under Article 301, as had Elif Şafak. And columnists and academics like Murat Belge, Hasan Cemal, İsmet Berkan, Haluk Şahin, Erol Katırcıoğlu had, too. And after all, I myself was a "marked man," subjected to character assassination after a memorandum based on false statements issued by the Turkish General Staff.

In a country such as ours, those kinds of incidents would be considered ordinary. One minute, we could find ourselves threatened, and the next minute, we were worthy of "friendship and peace" awards. Such things were possible. As a democrat and a man who truly loved his country, Hrant was "one of us." We were fighting for the same cause. But he was Armenian. And we forgot this. We forgot that one of us was Armenian.

HRANT

This happens to all of us.

Sometimes troubles pile up all at once. You feel caught in the crossfire.

First, a friend dies, and then, a loved one falls ill. You're dealt a blow by the state, for political reasons, and you're undone when someone close to you so much as pinches you. You know you have been pushed into a corner. You feel like crying, "Enough!"

Just then, an arm reaches into the dark tunnel where you have taken your woes, pulling you out to see the dawn and whispering into your ear, "Come on now, you must keep trying. You must resist and endure: there's no surrender."

That's how it's been for me these last few weeks. One day, the Court of Appeals hands down a six-month sentence for a crime I didn't commit, and the next day, a few—just a few—people in our community say, "Oh, stop complaining. Your sentence is light, after all."

That's what happens when you're stuck in a tunnel.

Just then, hands reach out, from far or from near. Some you know, some you don't. Some are gathering signatures, sending out statements on your behalf. They share this sentence for the crime you haven't committed, and with the same spirit of resistance, they bring your struggle out into the open. "Come on, now, you must keep trying. You must resist and endure; there's no surrender."

Thank you, friends. It is good that you're here.

TANER AKÇAM

I was then a visiting associate professor of history at the University of Minnesota. After the number of cases opened against Hrant had increased and the attacks grew more serious, we'd started a solidarity campaign. I can't remember exactly where it began. Either Baskın Oran and I started it in Turkey and the Americans joined in, or it was the Workshop for Armenian and Turkish Scholarship, known to us as WATS, that launched the campaign. We collected a great number of signatures, but no one heard about this in Turkey. In addition, intellectuals in Turkey working for democracy did also show solidarity, and they tried hard not to leave Hrant isolated, but he was still very isolated. How could he not be? He was up against a campaign that had targeted him because he was an Armenian. And there was nothing he could do.

MÜGE GÖÇEK

At the University of Michigan at Ann Arbor, we founded an electronic scholars' workshop, bringing together about 600 Armenian, Turkish, and other intellectuals. This group, known as WATS, grew in size, and twice we managed to collect a large number of signatures for petitions in support of Hrant in the years when he was being prosecuted. These petitions, which included names from leading educational institutions, we later sent to the president's office, the prime minister's office, and various other ministries.

Then, one Sunday, Hrant called me on the phone and said he was in Detroit and wanted to come to Ann Arbor to see me. When we met, he told me his main reason for wanting to see me was WATS, and then he said, "Müge, this is a very important thing you're doing. You definitely have to keep this going, OK?" And he got me to promise that I would. I kept the promise I'd made to Hrant, and we set about widening our electronic network even further.

Ufortunately, our work was not enough to challenge the violence and fanatcism in Turkey. We were not able to protect Hrant.

RAGIP ZARAKOLU

It was around then that we rounded up a number of organizations—PEN International, the Publishers Association , and Amnesty International—and went together to *Agos* to show our support. We thought we would be able to protect him through such shows of solidarity; we naively believed that they wouldn't dare do anything to him. Of course, our efforts were insufficient.

It was around now that Hrant mentioned Veli Küçük to me, too. He was extremely troubled by Küçük's meddling in his trial. This was something that preyed on him incessantly. So during Hrant's last months, whenever he was speaking with me, whenever we were together, I felt as if there was a part of him that was absent. His eyes would slide away, and he'd lose himself in his thoughts.

ETYEN MAHCUPYAN

Hrant once told me that he saw Kemal Kerinçsiz as some sort of a street fighter. He was always the one who'd disrupt the hearings by shouting out insults and starting fights. He wasn't someone to be taken seriously.

But the day Veli Küçük turned up in the courthouse was alarming. All he did was to watch, but that was more than enough. It was as if he was keeping Hrant under observation. I remember Hrant saying that he saw him as a real threat.

LEDA MERMER

After the Court of Appeals' final ruling, the mood at *Agos* grew even darker. Baron Hrant became very pensive. And very tense. He began to slam doors. All of his jokes and teasing had stopped; it was as if he couldn't articulate what he wanted. It was at around that time that the hate mail started flowing in continuously. We even had to create a new file called "hate mail." For example, "Love this country or fuck off." Or "When we sound the horn for the attack, Turkey will get too small for you, but a grave will fit you just fine." Or "Fuck off and go live in Armenia. They are going to kill you, son of a bitch, you bastard Armenian spawn!" I sat in front of the computer, so I saw all of these messages the moment they arrived.

In those days, *Agos* was printed by the newspaper *Dünya*. The men working in the printing press were ultranationalists; we knew this. We also knew that they had Armenians in their families because we'd talked about all this while waiting for the newspaper to be printed. But, after the conviction, they became hostile and aggressive. One day, one of them said out of the blue, "So when is your boss leaving?"

"What do you mean?" I asked.

And he said, "He can't last here much longer."

HRANT

It is very clear that those who have been trying to isolate me and wear me down and leave me helpless have achieved their objectives. Already they have managed to convince a sizable group that I am an "enemy of the Turks" with those dirty, false statements they've been feeding to the media. It torments me so very deeply. They keep repeating my sentence, over and over. And every time there is a news bulletin about my trial, they repeat that same sentence in every column they write about it, and each time they do so, I am more deeply marked as an "enemy of the Turks." Unfortunately, I have become a familiar face these days; I can see people turning their heads and saying to each other, "Look at him—isn't he that Armenian?"

MAYDA SARİS

Unless you count his lawyer, Fethiye Çetin, and his family, Hrant was spending most of his time with Etyen Mahcupyan around then. From time to time, there would be a few writers or scholars coming in to show their support, but not that many. He felt very isolated. Especially from the Armenian community, he received no help or support. In situations like this, we Armenians relive the fear of 1915. It's sad to say this, but it is true. And, in addition, his dispute with the Patriarchate had become very serious around then, and they had abandoned him entirely.

At the funeral, everyone walked with us, but where were these people earlier? The crowds pressing into the Patriarchate for the service, the people who couldn't leave him alone at the cemetery, hadn't they waited a bit too long? What a pity!

SARKİS SEROPYAN

During that difficult time when Hrant was branded an "enemy of the Turks," he was also abandoned by our own community. Throughout the time those trials were going on, not a single member of the Armenian community offered him any support, to my knowledge. Hrant was well aware that the Patriarch was behind all this. He felt betrayed. I would even go so far as to say that the gastric illness he suffered around that time could have arisen from these circumstances.

EFRİM BAĞ

My old boss Seropyan is right to say these things. Our community abandoned Hrant. Everyone in the community loved him, but they hid their love out of fear. To tell the truth, we were caught between him and the Patriarchate. As the president of the board of directors of the Meryemana Church, I was just in the middle of it.

My own views were close to Hrant's. He was an honest man who spoke what he believed. And what he said was true. But sometimes he could be a little harsh.

KARİN KARAKAŞLI

Hrant's concern for the protection of the Armenian community was not reciprocated. At just the moment when the state made him a target, he was isolated inside the Armenian community.

The most shocking part of this was the Patriarchate's year-long ban on advertisements in *Agos* in 2006. This embargo lasted until January 19, 2007, when it was lifted to run Hrant Dink's obituaries. Then, the Patriarchate saw fit to criticize *Agos* in the Turkish press—this, too, happened when the trials were at their worst. These criticisms became instant news in the mainstream *Hürriyet*.

So at just the moment when he found himself obliged to explain over and over why he had not "insulted Turkishness," he was going through this other ordeal, and it hurt him deeply as an Armenian.

HRANT

Our struggle outside the Armenian community goes on in the courtrooms and the courthouse corridors. We're forced to defend ourselves. We shall see where this leads us. Our struggle within the community is not much different; again, we are trying to defend ourselves.

When his Holiness, the Patriarch, issued that statement that *Hürriyet* ran on its front page, under the headline, "Dink Insults the Armenian Community," it was deliberate and politically motivated. The remark *"Agos* has failed its role as a community newspaper" shows clearly that the political aim was to isolate and marginalize *Agos.*

Have you noticed how the outsiders and the insiders have come together in this joint statement? Take the word "insult." This is from Kerinçsiz's lexicon. If you say, "I'm not a Turk, I'm an Armenian," then, according to him, you have insulted the Turks. If you say, "I'm not a follower, I am an individual," then, according to his Holiness, the Patriarch, you have insulted the Armenians.

It is just not right for us to take our personal disagreements to the national press. What a shame it is that, having defended ourselves against outsiders like Kemal Kerinçsiz, we are now forced to say the same things to the insiders.

We are not insulting Turkishness or any other identity, nor do we allow others to insult our Armenian identity.

RAKEL

This is what I would have liked: when my husband was branded an "enemy of the Turks," if only the whole community had gone out and organized a demonstration outside *Agos.* Or not even all of us—if 10,000 people, even 1,000, could have come together. If we had made our voices heard, then maybe they would have listened. We have to accept that that the Armenian community was too timid. Timid and frightened. In his last days, during that vulnerable period when he was alone and without defense, the Patriarchate abandoned my husband, too. As part of the community, as his brothers, they should have stayed by his side. But they didn't. As I found out later, those days must have been unbearable for my husband because the death threats were directed not only at him but also at our son.

ARARAT

I knew that after his conviction my father was horribly upset, even indignant, but I had no idea he was worried about me also. In 2006, we had a robbery. It was Easter weekend. Together with my wife and daughter, I spent Good Friday at my parent's place. On Sunday, we got news that our house had been robbed. When we got there, I noticed that he was worried in some new way. "Are you sure?" he asked the police. "This might not really be a robbery." He even asked, "Did they leave a note?" At another point, he said to me, "It's a good thing you stayed with us last night." That day, I could tell from the way my father looked at me that there was a possibility of a threat.

HRANT

My inbox and my hard drive were full of hate mail and threats. How many of these threats were real, how many were fantasies? The truth is that there is no chance I shall ever know.

If it were just me, there wouldn't be a problem. All my life I've put myself on the line, lived on the edge of danger. Let me just say that one of these letters, sent from Bursa, alarmed me because it spoke of immediate danger. And let me add that even though my lawyer turned the letter over to the public prosecutor's office in Şişli, the matter has not been resolved.

SARKİS SEROPYAN

Hrant never shared with me the threats made directly against him. Only once he showed me a letter with threats against his son Ararat and me. The postmark on the upper left corner of the envelope told us that it had been posted in the city of Bursa. "The address is obviously fake, but look, they're even writing down their names and addresses these days," he said. We read the letter together. If it hadn't named his son, he might not have given it so much importance. But that really hit him. "What do they want with my family?" he kept saying . The letter said, "You are going to collect the bodies of your son and Seropyan from outside the gendarmerie on the outskirts of Ankara." The handwriting was terrible, and the paper was poor quality.

At our next editorial meeting, Hrant started asking, "What shall I do, shall I leave? Will you be able to carry on with *Agos*?"

ALİ BAYRAMOĞLU

One day, I got a phone call. I can no longer remember if it was Etyen or Hrant. I was told that Hrant had received another threat letter. They had discussed it among themselves, and then they decided to tell me about it. I got up and went over to *Agos*.

It was a letter from Bursa, signed by an Ahmet Demir. Ahmet Demir is a man whose name is associated with the notorious contra-guerilla, the clandestine paramilitary network organized by vigilantes within the state structure. By which I mean to say that this was not a joke. Hrant was beside himself. Over and over again, he said, "The threats against me don't matter. But what am I to do if it's about my child?"

At this point, I called Hanefi Avcı, who was the head of security in Edirne at that time. When I'd told him what happened, he said, "He should take this letter to the governor's office at once and ask for protection. But I don't think anything much would come from this sort of letter." After this, we spoke for the first time about whether or not he should go abroad.

FERHAT KENTEL

We were at a meeting of the Helsinki Citizens Assembly. After the hall emptied, Hrant called a few of us over and said, "Friends, there's something I want to talk about with you, but I don't know how to say it." And in a shaking voice, he told us about that threat letter he'd been sent from Bursa. Then, he begged us to tell no one else about this letter. And particularly not his family. He wanted to hide his own fear.

HRANT

And then, well, the threats became more concrete. I was left by myself, all alone.

I can't tell my son about this; I can't talk to my family. I have confided only in one or two close friends. And then, when I couldn't stand it any longer, I took one of these

threats and turned it over to the prosecutor, but nothing came of it. This was not an easy time . . .

HOSROF

We spent the summer of 2006 together at Kınalı. We went fishing all the time. On the days my brother didn't go to *Agos*, he'd always call to find out if anything new happened. He'd let them read through whatever messages had come in by e-mail. "Erase these," he'd say.

"More threats?" I'd ask.

"No, there's nothing," he would reply. By now he wasn't telling me anything anymore. We'd just fish together and play cards. We spent the whole summer like that.

RAKEL

I have no idea how much he shared with his brothers. During the last two years, when he came out to the island, he always had Hosrof with him. You could even say that Hosrof became his bodyguard during that last year. Yervant, on the other hand, was at the bookstore, though he certainly shared in our anxieties. As for what they talked about, and how much, I have no idea whatsoever!

One day, we heard a gunshot somewhere near our house. I shall never forget the way Hosrof panicked. He was full of anxiety and fear for his brother. He was always on edge. But so were we all . . .

NECDET KOÇTÜRK

At the end of the summer season we went fishing in Saroz Bay. Then we were looking for a place to play cards. By chance the place we found was just across from the Nationalist People's Party's local headquarters. Hrant got very uneasy, and he even said that we shouldn't sit here. And, can you believe it, it was only then that I became aware of just how tense he'd become. That was when I really got worried. I took him by the arm and said, "While I'm here with you, no one will dare to touch you." He looked at me as if to say, *Are you joking*? I had no idea what he'd been going through.

Just once, he brought up the idea of a bulletproof vest, asking if they really worked, really protected a person. And as a joke, I said, "It wouldn't protect *you*, because they'll shoot you in the head."

Now why on earth would anyone say such a thing? How could anyone? But you see, I said it. I said this to him . . .

ETYEN MAHÇUPYAN

For a short while we both wore bulletproof vests. There was a factory in Manisa; we even had them brought to us from there. But it was hard to get used to them, so we stopped wearing. Hrant didn't want a bodyguard, either.

One day, he talked to me about leaving the country, but he didn't want to go. He wasn't the sort of person who could live abroad. We discussed it throughly. I said to him, "If there isn't a single question mark in your mind, then stay, but if you have the faintest doubt, leave at once."

Hrant kept changing his mind about it. Though he kept telling other people not to worry, that nothing was going to happen, he'd bring up the subject the moment we were alone. At one point, he had more or less decided on leaving. He had a meeting with his family. He brought it up with them. The next day, he called me and told me about the meeting. "We've decided to stay here," he said. "They want to live in the same place as I am."

HRANT

What I experienced was not an easy process, neither for me nor for my family. There were times when I seriously thought about leaving the country, especially at moments when the threats focused on those close to me. On that point, I remained helpless.

I had the willpower to resist this pressure on my own account, but I had no right to subject any of my loved ones to danger. I could be my own hero, so long as my loved ones were left out of it, but I couldn't let myself make a stand that put anyone else in harm's way.

In one of those helpless moments, I gathered up my family, my children. Without alarming them, I wanted to see what we would do if we had to make a decision whether or not to leave. That evening, I found shelter around them and took great comfort from them. They were trusting me. Wherever I was, they would be there for me. If I said, "Let's go," they would come with me. If I said, "Let's stay," they would stay.

RAKEL

One day, we invited Ararat and Karolin to our house. We sat at the table in the kitchen. "Look, children," he began, "it might be necessary for us to leave the country. Because of me, you may have to change your lives." Then he turned to Karolin and continued, "My daughter, it could be hard for you to be far away from your loved ones, from your own family, but I would also have a hard time living anywhere without you." Karolin's answer was so lovely. "Father, wherever you are, I'll come. Don't you worry about me for a minute."

Obviously, he was considering different options. After a while, he said to me, "If necessary, we can find a new way to live; we can leave and the children can go back and forth." With that he brought the conversation toa close. Until the next time . . .

ARARAT

I didn't know there had been a death threat directed against me. My father never told me. It was, I think, at the beginning of the summer of 2006. One evening, he invited me and Karolin over. We were sitting around the kitchen table —Sera, my mother, my father, Karolin, and me. We started talking about the possibility of leaving. If we went to Armenia, we would have the same sort of life, we agreed. In terms of democracy, it's no different than here, we said. Then, we considered going to Brussels, because my sister Baydzar worked and lived there.

Father turned to me and asked my opinion. I said, "You and Mother should go immediately. It doesn't make sense for us to go, too." I had one or two semesters left before finishing college. My little sister Sera wasn't enthusiastic, either. She didn't want to leave her school. "When we finish, we'll join you," I said. We even spoke about what kind of work we could do there. But we did not reach any sort of decision; everything was left up in the air.

Something else happened at the table that night. I kept asking, "What's the sense in me going?", and then my father said something like, "If you only knew." Then, I said, "If they are harrasing you by using my name, it's probably because they want to frighten you." Yes, I said that. Not because I knew anything, but it seemed right to say it at that moment.

In the end, we left it to my father to decide. But we also told my sister Baydzar, who was living in Brussels by that time, to look for a larger house. She did look for a house for us. But my father never said, "It's decided," so nothing came of that, either.

My father was going abroad a great deal to collect the prizes he was being awarded around then. These trips served to calm his nerves for a time. It seemed as if this allowed him to postpone the decision to leave.

DELAL (BAYDZAR)

During those last days, every time he came to Europe, he would try to convince himself: "This is not such a bad place, actually; we could live here, couldn't we?" And then he would wait for me and our mother to give our opinions.

During that last period, when the state was really bearing down on him, there was something; because he was getting one award after another outside the country. He was getting awards abroad, and then he'd go back to Turkey to be found guilty. Once Cemil Çiçek, Minister of Justice, said something strange; something like, "They shouldn't complain too much when they're always off collecting prizes." Comments like this really upset my father, because what he wanted more than anything was to gain the respect of his country. That's why he was very pleased to receive the Ayşe Zarakolu Freedom of Expression Prize in Turkey. Before that he received the Henri Nannen Prize in Germany. And then he went with my mother to Norway to collect another prize. When they stopped off at Brussels on their way back, he said, let's find you a bigger place here, so that we can come and go. This was the first time he mentioned leaving Turkey.

HOSROF

Then one day . . . It is November by now. I am heading home late. I am on the road. I get a phone call from my older brother. He never calls me at such an hour. "Where are you?" he asks. "I'm going home," I said, "or should I come to you instead?" I ask. There is a pause. Then he says no. Later it occurred to me that he'd probably wanted to talk to me that day.

Also in November, something else happened: when my brother and Rakel were out of the country to collect another award, two people turned up at their house. Later, in his statement, the janitor said that they were wearing masks. First, these two men said they were from the police, and when the janitor refused to believe them, they'd made a threat—"Tell him that his days are numbered"—and left. When my brother returned from Europe, the janitor told my brother what had happened. He told the janitor not to worry, and that quieted him down.

I found out about this after they killed my brother. As I said before, he never told me about any of this. He didn't tell Ararat about the death threat against him either. But I didn't get angry with him for any of this. We were in prison together when we were young. He knew my state of mind very well. He knew I would be on his case and say, "You're not a single man living alone. You have a family that depends on you. If something happened to you, what would we do?" He knew that I would put pressure on him to leave. He didn't tell Yervant either, after all. He didn't talk about this with anyone in the family.

YERVANT

If you ask me, my brother didn't bring us to the point of saying, "Time to bow out, we've had enough; it should end here," because he had kept the most important things from us. He'd never told us about the death threat against his son Ararat. You could ask why he hid it from us. Had we known that the children had been pulled into this, we couldn't remain the same. We'd think, OK, this has become something else. He knew that only too well.

During the last months, because of course I didn't know anything about all of this, I was asking, "Dear God, why is he making such noise? Why is he defying everyone like this?" You know, at that point, he began naming a whole list of people, such as the lawyer Kemal Kerinçsiz, General Veli Küçük . . . When he said those names were just the tip of the iceberg, he was implying that who was after him was a great deal more powerful and dangerous scheme. This was his way of saying, "I know who you are."

Later, when I found out about the incident involving the death threat against his son, I figured it all out. That's what he was like; he made himself into more of target. This is not easy to explain, and you could only understand if you knew him well. It was his way of saying, ":Come after me." He was trying to protect his son and his other loved ones.

HRANT

But if we went, where would we go? To Armenia?

But someone like me, who can't tolerate injustice, how long would I be able to endure the injustices there? Wouldn't I get into even more trouble there? Living in European countries just wasn't in me. I am the kind of person who starts squirming even after three days in the West, thinking "Let's get this over with and go back home." How could I bear it if I had to live there?

It was just not in my nature to leave "blazing hells" for "ready-made heavens." We were the kind of people who are willing to turn the hell they live in into a heaven.

To stay in Turkey, to continue to make it our home—it was not just what we truly wanted, it was also a sign of respect for our thousands of friends, known and unknown, who were fighting for democracy in Turkey, who have given us support.

We were going to stay. We were going to resist.

But if we were forced to leave one day, we were going to take the road just as in 1915—just like our ancestors. Without knowing where we were headed. Walking along the same roads as they walked, facing the same ordeals, suffering as they did— we would leave this country with the same wounds. And we would go, not to where our hearts took us, but where our feet took us . . . wherever. I hope we shall never be forced to live through such a departure. To avoid such a departure is already our most precious hope and purpose.

YERVANT

If I go, I'm not going to the airport or anything like that. "If I have to go, I'm going to start from Malatya, my birthplace, and head off in the direction of Der Zor, my ancestors' final destination," that's what he said in his last column. This was his political response to what they had done to him. Or else he would never have taken a stance that would have drawn his children into it. He could never have done this . . .

But, in the end he didn't go, you see. He couldn't. The reason why he couldn't go was very clear: he was thinking how, when we embarked on the road of struggle, there were many others among us. And in one way or another, they're all in trouble. If he left, how could he even bring himself to look them in the eyes? He didn't go because he thought it meant fleeing. He couldn't take that. That's the crux of it.

RAKEL

One day he said, "If I have to go, if I go; I'm going to go the same route as my ancestors."

"My dearest Çutak ," I said, "they went that route because they had to, because they had no other choice. If you decide to go, we have other routes we can choose from."

But he didn't make that decision, you see. He couldn't.

One day, he came home in a very bad mood. I can no longer remember what it was that had upset him, but I can say this much: I had never seen my husband like that before. I thought of my mother-in-law, and a chill went down my spine. When a person is that ill, their expression changes. Their muscles seem to droop. It's not exactly like losing consciousness, but in a way it's similar because the face takes on an absent expression. So that's what I saw in his face that day. I saw my husband in a terrible state. I went and sat quietly next to him. Our dear Sera was at home studying. Once again, we had a conversation about leaving. Our Sera started to cry. She had her school, of course; she didn't want to leave, and with good reason.

In the end, her father said he'd been frightened by the death threats. Sera was still crying, and I was stroking my husband's back. Just then, some lines from the Bible came into my mind like a bolt of lightning. They were: "If God is on our side, then who can hurt us?" I started to speak. "My girl, don't be afraid." And then, in an admonishing tone I said, "Look, Sera, my dear, there's nothing to be gained from fear." And at the same time, I was stroking my husband's back, as if to say, "Try and pull yourself together." And I went on, "There is nothing for us to fear now, because God will help us here."

No one can do a thing to us. We didn't hurt anyone; we didn't do anything wrong. Above all, we must be strong and fearless. If we let our minds disintegrate just once, we won't be any use to anyone, not even to ourselves. We need to remember what we are doing, and we need to stay sane. You will not feel afraid, because Jesus is with you. There's no use crying, it won't help a thing.' I'm saying all of this to my daughter. And all the time, I'm rubbing my husband's back. What I am saying to my daughter, I am also saying to him. What else could I say this to him? How could I tell him to pull himself together? Because I am scared, too. But I knew that when I was afraid, the thing to do was to clamp down on that fear. If two people faltered, the third person had to stay strong. That part fell to me. What is there to say now? If only we'd been more aware. If only we'd forced him to go . . .

HRANT

Now I am taking the case to the European Court of Human Rights. What I know— and this gives me some comfort — is that whatever happens, I shall stay in Turkey until my case is heard.

If the court rules in my favor, then there is no doubt that I would be doubly pleased, for it would mean that I would never have to leave my country. There is no doubt that 2007 will be an even harder year for me. The old cases will continue, and new ones will follow. Who knows what injustices I shall have to face?

RAKEL

When I read his last column, I said to him, "Çutak, dearest, why did you decide to write all of this?"

"Why?" he said. "Didn't you like it?"

"How could I not like what you write," I said. "You write so beautifully, but these are things you know for yourself, so why would you want to provoke them by putting these into words?" "The devil does not like his sins thrown in his face," I continued. "I know what I'm doing" was his answer. "I am going to the European Court of Human Rights, and this will be the statement I make there," he said. I'm going to write more next week. I am a transparent man, he said, I share everything with the public.

It was when he went public that I first learned that threats had been made against his loved ones, too. I knew he'd been getting death threats, but he never told me that Ararat had been threatened, too. Sometimes I think this also played a role in his not leaving. If this was the situation, he couldn't have left and abandoned our son to this. But maybe I am wrong. Maybe if he'd been determined about leaving, Arat would have gone with him. Empty thoughts! It's too late now, what's done is done. We just keep trying to make sense of it . . .

ARARAT

But you know, all these are excuses . . . My father just couldn't bring himself to leave. He looked into his children's eyes, and his grandchildren's. And he just couldn't make that decision. If we'd tried harder, then maybe we could have gotten him to agree, but then he would never have been comfortable anywhere he went. It's an awful state of mind! I've been afflicted with it myself.

As you know, I was also being prosecuted, as the managing director of Agos. After my father was killed, my own family, in order to protect me, played a trick on me and made Rober (Koptaş) the managing director. Then they said, 'You just leave for a while,' and sent me away. Can you imagine: Your father has been killed, your family stays in Turkey and there you are, living an easy life abroad. How could you? You feel awful. I don't think my father made the wrong decision. If it were me, I wouldn't have left either. That's why I don't regret it. We did the right thing.

RAKEL

Now I think that our optimism made us shut our eyes. It gave us a blind spot. "They can't do such a thing," we said. They would never let it, it's just not possible. After all, Turkey is still weighed down by the past that is still not resolved. So just think if they went and killed another Armenian! It could never happen in the twenty-first century, or at least that's what we thought. If we didn't actually utter these words, we were thinking them.

But there you have it: we thought we knew more than God. God was warning us; there were death threats. Fear had entered our hearts. Why are you still wavering? Are you God, that you can know what will come to pass? In this sense, you succumb to guilt. It eats you up inside. But what's done is done. And when all is lost, the Lord shows you how to keep going without caving in.

HRANT

I am just like a pigeon . . .

Like a pigeon, I keep looking left and right, up and down.

My head moves around just as much. My mind, too.

What was the foreign minister saying? What did the justice minister say? "You people are making too much of this Article 301! After all, not a single person has been found guilty or sent to prison yet!" As if the only price you pay is going to prison. Just look at the price . . . Here is the price . . .

Do you know what it means to be locked inside a pigeon's fluttering heart? Do you have any idea? Have you ever watched a pigeon?

While all of this is going on, there is one thing I depend on. Yes, I might feel my heart fluttering like a pigeon's, but I know for sure that people in this country never hurt pigeons. Pigeons live in the midst of cities, surrounded by crowds. And yes, they take flight, but all the same, they are free.

Part V

Dying

30

A Time for Psalms

HRANT

Muslims and Christians, they're all praying for me.
    One is reciting the hadith, the other psalms.
    So what shall I do now?
    Shall I be true to my leftist beliefs and stay far from God?
    Or shall I listen to my common sense and sing the psalms I learned as a child?
    I never had a chance to meet Uncle Abdülkadir.
    He had his daughter-in-law write down his words.
    After asking for my permission to call me his son, he says:
    "Ramadan is here, you know, and I'm praying five times a day, and you are in my every prayer. Don't be sad, my son, I keep begging the Great Lord to look over you and protect you from harm. Put your trust in my prayers"
    But I know Varsenik Hanim; she's my wife's friend. And I know they have gathered together again.They are praying.
    She wants to read me a psalm over the phone. "Please," she says. "At least a stanza." And then she reads these lines from Psalm 46:
    God is our refuge and strength, an ever-present help in trouble.
    Therefore will not we fear, though the earth be removed,
    And though the mountains be carried into the midst of the sea;
    Though its waters roar and be troubled,
    Though the mountains shake with their swelling.
    Let no one see my heart swelling, or the tears in my eyes. Let me find it in myself to recite the rest . . .
    There is a river whose streams shall make glad the city of God,
    The holy place of the tabernacles of the Most High.
    God is within her; she shall not fall;
    God shall help her at the break of day.
    The heathen raged, the kingdoms fall;
    He utters his voice, the earth melts.

HOSROF

We three brothers had no family, and then we made one. Without knowing what a family was, we succeeded in making a family. We all played a part in this, but my brother played the biggest one. He was the one who could see furthest ahead. He look over us and protected us. He was our shepherd. It had been like that since the fisherman's basket. Our feelings for each other, our love; there's never been anything like it. We had problems, and arguments, like all families, but there was one difference. Nothing could separate us. Nothing but death . . .

HRANT

The Lord of hosts is with us; the God of Jacob is our refuge.

Come, behold the works of the Lord, what desolations he hath made in the earth.

He maketh wars to cease unto the end of the earth; he breaketh the bow, and cutteth the spear in sunder; he burneth the chariot in the fire.

Be still, and know that I am God; I will be exalted among the nations, I will be exalted in the earth.

The Lord of hosts is with us; the God of Jacob is our refuge.

YERVANT

From our childhood years, it was my brother who looked over me and kept me safe. He never let it show. He would pretend he wasn't even watching. He was like that all the time, from the time I was three. But on bath days, he was the one who washed me. My brother washed me many times, but I only washed him once: on January 23, 2007.

HRANT

When I was a child, I knew some psalms by heart. And in Armenian, too. I recited the psalms I had memorized and won prizes. But I always thought that when I grew up they would serve me no purpose.

In the end, I grew up, but I couldn't grow wiser, and every time my instincts took me back to those psalms. And now here we are again. Once again, the time has come for psalms.

Oh, brothers! I hope the leftists and atheists among you won't mind if I murmur a few lines from Psalm 23 now. Try and be understanding. Try to understand. I really need you to try.

The Lord is my shepherd; I shall not want.

He maketh me to lie down in green pastures: he leadeth me beside the still waters.

He restoreth my soul: he leadeth me in the paths of righteousness for his name's sake.

Yea, though I walk through the valley of the shadow of death, I will fear no evil: for thou art with me; thy rod and thy staff they comfort me.

Thou preparest a table before me in the presence of mine enemies: thou anointest my head with oil; my cup runneth over.

Surely goodness and mercy shall follow me all the days of my life: and I will dwell in the house of the Lord for ever.

DELAL

In our house, there was always love. My father used to call me Baydzarik. He would carry us on his shoulders. That's how he carried me when I was little. We would ride on his back. When I talk about it now, I can feel his warm head under my hands, and his warm hair . . . right now. It's so hard to speak about it; it brings back the taste and smell of my pain as I speak, but at the same time, my words don't come close to describing it. I'm a stranger to my own words. I can't find a way to heal! Every day, I look for my father. I miss him so much.

HRANT

And I am in the embrace of Psalm 91:
> *He who dwells in the secret place of the Most High*
> *Shall abide under the shadow of the Almighty.*
> *I will say of the Lord, "He is my refuge and my fortress;*
> *My God, in Him I will trust."*
> *Surely He shall deliver you from the snare of the fowler*
> *And from the perilous pestilence.*
> *He shall cover you with His feathers,*
> *And under His wings you shall take refuge;*
> *His truth shall be your shield and buckler.*
> *You shall not be afraid of the terror by night,*
> *Nor of the arrow that flies by day,*
> *Nor of the pestilence that walks in darkness,*
> *Nor of the destruction that lays waste at noonday.*
> *A thousand may fall at your side,*
> *And ten thousand at your right hand;*
> *But it shall not come near you.*
> *Only with your eyes shall you look,*
> *And see the punishment of the wicked.*

ARARAT

If only I could call out to you with all of those clichés. If only I could shout out how proud of you I was, most especially on that day when you couldn't hide your tears from the cameras. As your eyes welled up, I said to myself, *There he is, my father, a man stripped bare.* At your graveside, a hundred thousand people honored you as a martyr. And now I am back there, standing alone, and honoring you as my father. Amen.

HRANT

Because thou hast made the Lord, which is my refuge, and you make the Most High your dwelling,

There shall no evil befall thee, neither shall any plague come near thy dwelling.

For he shall give his angels charge over thee, to keep thee in all thy ways.

They shall bear thee up in their hands, lest thou dash thy foot against a stone.

Thou shalt tread upon the lion and adder: the great lion and the serpent shalt thou trample under feet.

Because he hath set his love upon me, says the Lord, therefore will I deliver him: I will set him on high, because he hath known my name.

He shall call upon me, and I will answer him: I will be with him in trouble; I will deliver him and honor him.

With long life will I satisfy him, and show him my salvation.

RAKEL

It was a week before January 19. "Do you remember", he said, "that love letter I wrote you? Do you know what? No one's ever written his beloved a letter like that."

I brought out the letter. "I saved it," I said. "Come, let's read it again." And then he read it, in a loud voice. Really, it was a poem. He'd written it to me on Valentine's Day.

HRANT

Oh, my love!
Oh, my love, my one and only, my love, my heart!
Please, open my eyes . . .
And remember.
Remember that first time we made love with our eyes, breaking the rhythm of our days, and making our voices tremble.
Ripping the narrow fabric of our lives . . .
And then, those first struggles, not to succumb . . .
Though by now they were writing history, those eyes. Remember.
We were weighed down by our burdens, and they were the heaviest in the world . . .
This is love. Is it ever easy to escape it? Is it easy to make history, to surrender to the mercy of time?
We had to take it on our backs, and carry it into the future. We had to nurture it.
And it did not wane, it grew. It was the seed of that all we became.
In the end, it was our weapon . . . our atom bomb.
No matter how cruel the twists and turns of life, we found a way through.
Our love is with us still. Throughout our history, it has nourished and saved us, just as it always will.
With time, in our every reckoning, and quarrel, and tussle, it was our only shelter. It was the little world from which we carried on our struggle with the big world, it was where we went to defend ourselves, it was our refuge.
Oh, my love, my heart!

You are my star, the peace and calm I've always fought for.

You were the root on my right to be different, my desire for equality, and my love of freedom.

You are not a social right I won over time. You are the founding principle of my life. You are mine. You are me.

You were my secret blessing, the blessing for the price I paid.

Always at my side, and never fading.

My love!

Believe me when I say I have never betrayed you with dishonorable love.

You came at a high price, and I paid it. I shall carry on doing so.

And one day, my love, when my eyes grow heavy,

Call the children to your side.

Open my eyes, one last time.

Show them my pupils of my eyes and say,

"Your father loved me with these."

RAKEL

How beautiful that letter was. My darling's letter. When he read it to me, I couldn't find the words to tell him how much I loved him. I didn't even say how beautifully he'd written it. "You've mixed love up with your political ideas," I said.

"Well, I've never won you over, have I?" he said. "What have you ever written to me? Come on now, let's see it."

"What would I write to you? I gave you my life, after all, and now you want a letter," I said. How could I know that I'd be writing that letter one day . . .

Oh, my love!

It was given to me to be my Çutak's wife. And now here I am, proud and grieving. The children, and my family, and yours, we are all in deep pain. This silent love gives us a little strength. The love we feel is heavy with sorrow. In the Gospel according to John, it says, "Greater love hath no man than this, that a man lay down his life for his friends."

My other half, my love, the father of my children, the head of our family, and your brother—today, dear friends, we mourn him. Today we sing in silence and rise up. Today is the day we begin our journey to the light in the depths.

However old his killer was—seventeen or twenty-seven—and whoever he was, I never forget that once he was a baby. And my brothers, nothing can be done unless we first ask questions of the darkness that turns a baby into a murderer.

My brothers, the love he felt for the rightness of his cause, his love of clarity, his love for his friends. Aall these brought him here. His love, which stood up to fear, was what made him grow. They like to say he was a great man. And so now I ask you, was he born great? No. He was born like you and me. He was not from the sky, but of the earth. In a body that was crumbling just like ours, but with a living soul, it was the work he did, and the way he did it, and the love in his eyes and his heart that made him grow.

A person cannot become great on his own. It is what a person does that makes him great. Yes, he became a great man. Because he had great thoughts, and spoke great words. Today you came here and you all had great thoughts, and you spoke them, too, in silence. You too are great. Don't let today be the end of it. Don't stop at this.

He put his mark on Turkey today. And you have broken the seal. With him, headlines changed, and the way people talked changed, and taboos were broken. For him, there were no taboos. As the expression goes, he wore his heart on his sleeve. He paid a great price for this. Those who pay that price in the future will do so loving the Hrants of the world, and believing in them. We must stop looking down on others with hatred and insults. This will come to pass when we learn to look at those before us as one of our own, and respecting them accordingly.

Oh, brothers, with the help of Jesus, they carried him from his heavenly home. They spread their wings and flew up to the everlasting heaven in the sky. Before his eyes grew weak, before his body aged, before he had lost the pleasure of the things he longed for, they carried up to the heavens.

We'll be joining you there, my love. We shall join you, in that heaven without compare. We must each enter alone, and with love alone. Into that heaven that is higher than the words of humans and angels, and higher than those of the prophet, and greater than the knowledge of all secrets, and greater than the faith that moves mountains, and greater than giving all you own in alms, or surrendering your body to fire. Love and love alone can enter that heaven.

And there we shall live forever, with true love. A love that is never jealous, and never pining for the property of others, and never killing, and never humiliating, a love that holds one's brothers higher than oneself, and puts their interests above yours, a love that harbors no hatred, a love that heals, a love that defends the rights of others. The love of the Messiah. The love that is his blessing.

Who can forget what he did, this love of mine, and what he said? What darkness could make us forget him? Or what fear? Was this a life? Was it oppression? Was he the world's indulgence, this love of mine? Or will death erase his memory? No, no darkness is deep enough to do that.

And so now I too have written you a love letter, my dear. I paid a high price, too. It is thanks to Jesus I was able to write this. My love, let us give credit where credit is due.

You have left your loved ones, your children, and your grandchildren, and from all those others who saw you on your way. You left my embrace. But my love, you did not leave your country.

31

Last Embrace

SERA

After January 19, there was a long time when I had no dreams. When I woke up, all I could remember was a great darkness. Then, finally, one night, I had my first dream. The doorbell rang, and in came my father. We were all shocked. Before we could say a thing, my father began to speak. "That man lying there isn't me," he said. "I'm still alive." To our surprise, he'd come to no harm, he'd just been in hiding. At last, in my dream, my wish came true.

HRANT

This will be the first ceremony of you coming, not to bury me, but to keep me alive.

Stop crying. Listen to your heart. Can't you hear the flutterings of my heart, the heart you thought had deserted you?

Honorable words will be said at my funeral. For that, I am grateful. Yet, I have a few words to tell you, too. they belong to Khalil Gibran.

"Farewell to you and the youth I have spent with you.

It was but yesterday we met in a dream. You have sung to me in my loneliness, and I of your longings have built a tower in the sky.

But now our sleep has fled and our dream with it, and the sun has risen. Noontime is upon us as we rise from our slumber, and now we must part.

If in the twilight of memory we should meet once more, we shall speak again together and you shall sing to me a deeper song. And if our hands should meet in another dream, we shall build another tower in the sky."

We are a community of mourners. Our pain is our greatest asset. You go on placing your death notices. This, here, is the notice stating that I live on.

AUNT SİRANUŞ

Nvart came to me one day. "Sister, I had a dream," she said. "In my dream, I saw Hrant. There were two planks on the sea. Two very long planks. Hrant had propped his feet on them, and he was just lying there, arms spread out to his sides. Then he rose up from the sea and flew off.

"Oh, sister!" I said. "What a lovely dream you had. Hrant will grow up to be a great man. As great as the sea, and he will grow. The world will hear his voice."

"Then what were the planks?" she asked.

"Well," I said, "he propped his troubles under his legs and used them to fly."

And so it was. Even way back when, my sister could see it all. He really has flown off, our Hrant. He spoke to the world, and he made his voice heard.

The End

Epilogue

In Turkey, political assassinations do have a long past. Particularly, since 1980s, due to the Kurdish insurgency, human rights activists and intellectuals challenging state policy and its strictly enforced official history have fallen victim to extrajudicial killings. It is believed that the perpetrators belong to "deep state," a term used to describe a number of clandestine networks closely associated with the Turkish military and state bureaucracy. They were never brought to justice.

By the same token, Hrant's assassination in January 2007 has become a watershed in Turkey's political history. It led to unexpected consequences for those responsible for this heinous crime. The trauma of his murder triggered a strong response from wide segments of the society. The outrage and shame felt for the loss of a distinguished intellectual of Armenian origin was enormous, and Turkey seemed to be on the verge of a profound change.

Hrant's funeral has become an unprecedented gathering of two hundred thousand people, marching and chanting the slogan "We are all Armenians" and "We all are Hrant Dink." In the wake of his tragic death, intellectuals initiated a campaign, which called for an "Apology to the Ottoman Armenians" in an attempt to reconcile with the victims of 1915. More than thirty thousand people signed the petition. The date April 24, the internationally acknowledged day of Armenian Genocide, began to be commemorated in Turkey by the Turks.

Hrant Dink's assassination also led to democratization efforts in Turkey. Legislative changes were introduced to comply with the European Union norms, as the predominantly Muslim country set on the course for integration to the EU. For instance, the notorious article of 301 of the Turkish penal code that had labeled Hrant as "the enemy of the Turks" was amended.

However, the trial of his assassination did not make the necessary breakthrough for a complete overhaul of Turkey. European Court of Human Rights's ruling in 2010, which stated that Turkey failed to protect of its citizen's life and his freedom of speech, was not matched by the Turkish judiciary.

The Hrant Dink assassination trial in Turkey lasted more than five years and led to the conviction of a 17-year-old man as the murderer, while the other 19 suspects who were on trial were acquitted. It did not condemn the real culprits behind the murder. This verdict of the Turkish court created a public outcry and widespread outrage, leading to a profound disappointment with the justice system, curtailing all the prior democratization efforts.

Turkey in 2015 looks to be moving farther from a vibrant and exemplary democratic country. The aftermath of Hrant's assassination did not proceed in a direction that would have been in his desire. The country took an authoritarian turn. Since the publication of the book in 2010, the country has drifted farther and farther away from democracy, and has become a country dangerously polarized, with an uncertain future.

Since Hrant's murder, the very personalities that made up the country's intellectual landscape, have also changed. Allegiances and positions have shifted. Relations, views, and shared values took different turns. Not only is Hrant gone, but also *dramatis personae* in his own life that make appearances in this book are in different places today than they were during his lifetime.

As Hrant Dink has been a larger-than-life figure and become a symbol for human rights issues related to Turkey, his life, and therefore his biography, should also be read and understood as a monograph of Turkey's history during the first decade of twenty-first century.

Tuba Çandar
İstanbul, 2015

Hrant Dink: A Chronology

1954	Hrant Dink is born on September 15th, in Malatya, the eldest of three sons of Sarkis Dink, a tailor from Gürün, Malatya, and Nvart Dink, of Kangal, Sivas.
1960	The Dink family moves to Istanbul due to their father's gambling debts.
1961	While Hrant's father becomes an incurable gambler, his mother succumbs to mental illness. The parents separate, leaving their children homeless. Their grandmother enrolls the boys at the Orphanage of the Gedikpaşa Armenian Protestant Church.
1962–66	Hrant attends İncirdibi Protestant Armenian Primary School. He spends his summers with the children of the Orphanage at the Tuzla Armenian Children's Camp, which he calls "the lost civilization of Atlantis."
1967–69	He receives his secondary education at Bezciyan Junior High School as he and his brothers struggle to make ends meet. At the same time, he starts working as a tutor at the orphanage and the Tuzla summer camp.
1969	Hrant, aged fifteen, falls in love with his future wife, Rakel, an Armenian girl who grew up thinking she was a Kurd. She is the daughter of the chieftain of the Varto tribe, which took the mountains to escape the genocide and survived by hiding their Armenian identity. At the age of nine, she was sent to Istanbul to learn her mother tongue and her religion at the orphanage, where Hrant is working as a tutor.
1969–1971	Hrant is accepted to Surp Haç Tıbrevank Lycee, a prestigious boarding school for Armenian children brought from Anatolia. He comes under the influence of the leftist student movement and is forced to leave after participating in a student protest. He completes his final year at Şişli 19 Mayıs Lisesi.
1970	Hrant begins working as an errand boy for Patriarch Shnorhk Kalustyan at the Armenian Patriarchate.
1971	Hrant is enrolled at Istanbul University, where he studies zoology and becomes a sympathizer of the illegal fraction of the Maoist party.

1972	Fearing the Armenian community might be made to pay for his illegal political activities, he has his name legally changed to Fırat Dink, along with his Armenian friends Armenak and Istepan.
1976	Hrant's long courtship comes to a happy conclusion, when the Armenian Patriarch intervenes to convince Rakel's father to consent to their marriage.
1977	The church wedding takes place on April 23. Hrant struggles to make a living with his wife and two brothers. They take on a variety of jobs: selling watches, printing wallpaper, taking photos, and selling stationery.
1978	Hrant's daughter Baydzar (Delal) is born.
1979	Hrant's son Ararat (Arat) is born. Hrant and his two brothers start a small shop in the Bakırköy district, selling stationery and books.
1980	Hrant and Rakel take over the running of the Tuzla Armenian Summer Camp after its director is arrested in the aftermath of the September 12 military coup.
1981	Hrant and his brother are taken into custody. He spends three months in a military prison, where he is tortured for possible connections to ASALA, an extremist Armenian organization that has claimed responsibility for the assassination of Turkish diplomats.
1985	Hrant's college career, already in its fourteenth year due to the strains of supporting a family, comes to a sudden end when he is called to do his military service. He leaves with a degree from the faculty of sciences.
1986	He does his military service in Denizli. On account of being Armenian, he is dispatched to the "company of suspect soldiers." After a ten-year legal battle, the Tuzla Armenian Children Camp is confiscated by the state and closed down. Hrant's second daughter, Sera, is born.
1987	Returning to Istanbul, Hrant devotes himself to establishing his small bookshop, called Beyaz Adam (meaning White Man).
1988–96	While continuing in the bookstore business with his brothers, he spends the summers in the resort city of Antalya, where he works as a shopkeeper, selling carpets and jewelry.
1994–96	He and his brothers turn their bookstore into a six-story one, one of Istanbul's largest. They gradually expand it into a multi-location business specializing in textbooks.
1993	Hrant is one of the co-founders of Aras Publishing, offering Turkey a "window into Armenian literature."
1996	Hrant is devastated by the suicide of his beloved mother.

1996	Hrant is one of the founders of *Agos*, the only newspaper in Turkey published in Armenian and Turkish. He serves as editor in chief.
1998	Hrant appears on television and speaks out against the minority policies of the Turkish state. He becomes the voice of the oppressed Armenian minority.
	He attends meetings with other public intellectuals across the country, tackling all of Turkey's taboo subjects, from the Kurdish question to the headscarf controversy.
2005	Hrant finally gets his passport, after being denied one for many years. He sets out to engage with the Armenian diaspora and the Republic of Armenia, advocating peace and reconciliation between Turkey and the Armenian world.
2006	After Hrant's publication of the news that Atatürk's adoptive daughter Sabiha Gökçen was an Armenian child taken from an orphanage, the General Staff issues a statement against *Agos*. The next day, Hrant is invited to the deputy governor's office. Ultranationalist organizations spring into action, standing in the street outside his newspaper offices and hurling threats. At the same time, a number of columnists quote from Hrant's essays on Armenian identity, twisting his words to suggest that he is an "enemy of the Turks."
2006–07	Hrant is prosecuted three times for "insulting Turkishness." Following his conviction, the media hate-campaign against him becomes more virulent, death threats against him increase and his son Ararat also becomes a target. Hrant walks towards his death, bearing the label of "enemy of the Turks" like a crucifix. Having exhausted the internal appeal mechanisms, he finally brings his case to the European Court of Human Rights. Two days later, on January 19, 2007, he is assassinated with a shot from behind.

The Voices in the Book

Because the speakers are introduced in the book with their first names, either alone or with their last name, the voices are listed here alphabetically according to their first names.

ADALET AĞAOĞLU   the doyenne of Turkey's novelists; human rights defender who took part in the Armenian Apology Campaign

AGOP KALDILI   Hrant's childhood friend from the Joğvaran orphanage and the Tuzla Amenian Children's Camp; plumber

ALİ BAYRAMOĞLU   scholar, journalist, columnist; Hrant's close friend; one of the organizers of the Armenian Apology Campaign

ALPER GÖRMÜŞ   journalist, columnist; winner of the International Hrant Dink Foundation Prize

AMBERİN ZAMAN   journalist, columnist; Turkish correspondent for the *Economist*

ANNA MAYRİG   the cook at *Agos*

ANNA TURAY   journalist and one of the founders of *Agos*; owner of a public relations firm.

ARARAT (ARAT) DİNK   Hrant Dink's son; architect and writer.

ARİS NALCI   journalist; for a time, the editorial director of *Agos*.

ARMENAK ÇAKIR   Hrant Dink's uncle

ARMENUHİ DIKMEN   one of the children of the Joğvaran orphanage and the Tuzla Armenian Camp; housewife

ARTİN (KEMAL) YASULKAL   Hrant Dink's classmate from Tıbrevank, businessman

ARUS TECER   one of the Joğvaran orphanage and Tuzla Armenian Camp children; tailor

ATİLLA ANAKÖK	one of Hrant Dink's poker friends; antiques dealer
AVEDİS DEMİR	one of Hrant Dink's *Ahparigs* from Tıbrevank High School; physician at the Surp Pirgiç Armenian Hospital
AYDA TANİKYAN	headmistress of Bezciyan Middle School; teacher at the Barsamian School in Nice, Hrant's greatly loved French teacher
AYDIN ENGİN	journalist, playwright, left-wing activist; one of *Agos*'s first Turkish columnists; based at Istanbul Bilgi University's Social Science Institute; one of the organizers of the 2005 Istanbul Armenian conference
AYŞE ÖNAL	journalist, writer, Hrant's closest female friend
BANU GÜVEN	journalist and television programmer
BASKIN ORAN	political scientist based at Ankara University's Social Science Faculty; one of *Agos*'s first Turkish columnists; Hrant's close friend; one of the organizers of the Armenian Apology Campaign
BAYDZAR BOZUK	the Dink family's former neighbor; housewife
BELMA AKÇURA	investigative journalist, writer, ombudsman for *Milliyet*; winner of several journalism prizes for her work on the deep state and intelligence services
BEDRO ANA (YAĞBASAN)	second wife of Siament Ağa (Rakel's father)
CEM ÖZDEMİR	German politician of Turkish descent, joint leader of the Green Party
CENGİZ AKTAR	social scientist; Istanbul Policy Center; columnist; one of the organzers of the Armenian Apology Campaign
CENGİZ ÇANDAR	journalist, writer, columnist and Middle East analyst; for a time advisor to former President Turgut Özal
DELAL (BAYDZAR) DİNK	Hrant Dink's first daughter; chemical engineer; Director of the International Hrant Dink Foundation
DERYA SAZAK	journalist, writer, former managing editor of *Milliyet*.
DİKRAN GÜLMEZGİL	Armenian businessman; Director of the Karagözyan Foundation
DİLEK KURBAN	researcher and writer
DİRAN BAKAR	one of the founders of *Agos*; lawyer

ECE TEMELKURAN	journalist and writer; managing editor of *Birgün*
EFRİM BAĞ	Armenian businessman; one of the directors of the Kumkapı Meryemana Church Foundation
ELİF SHAFAK (ŞAFAK)	world-famous Turkish novelist
ERSİN KALKAN	journalist
ETYEN MAHÇUPYAN	journalist, writer; former managing editor of *Agos*; Hrant's close friend; currently senior advisor to Prime Minister Ahmet Davutoğlu
FATMA MÜGE GÖÇEK	Turkish sociologist at the University of Michigan, Ann Arbor
FERHAT KENTEL	sociologist in the Sociology Faculty of Istanbul City University
FETHİYE ÇETİN	jurist and human rights activist; Hrant Dink's lawyer; a Author of *My Grandmother* and co-editor of *The Grandchildren*
FEYHAN ORAN	Hrant Dink's close family friend
GARABET ORUNÖZ	one of the children from the Joğvaran orpahange and the Tuzla Camp; jeweler in the covered bazaar
GARO PAYLAN	educator, deputy for People's Democratic Party
ĞAZAROS (GAZİ) ÇERKEZYAN	one of Hrant Dink's oldest friends
GERARD LIBARIDIAN	historian and diplomat; advisor to the first Armenian president, Levon Ter-Petrosyan; retired professor, University of Michigan, Ann Arbor
HAGOP MİNASYAN	Catholic Armenian cleric
HALİL BERKTAY	historian, Sabancı University; columnist; one of the scholars who put the Armenian issue back on the Turkish national agenda; one of the organizers of the 2005 Armenian Conference in Istanbul
HARUT ÖZER	businessman; treasurer of *Agos* during its early years
HARUTYUN ŞEŞETYAN	one of the founders of *Agos*; civil engineer
HASAN CEMAL	journalist, columnist, former editor in chief of *Cumhuriyet*, author of *1915: Armenian Genocide*
HAYCAN DİNK	Hrant Dink's nephew; computer engineer
HAYGAN DİNK	wife of Hrant Dink's younger brother Yervant Dink; housewife

HERDEM (ZEKİ)
ÖCAL — one of the children from the Joğvaran orphanage and the Tuzla Armenian Camp

HOSROF (ORHAN)
DİNK — Hrant Dink's brother; bookseller
HÜLYA DEMİR — academic, writer, researcher; Hrant Dink's friend
İPEK ÇALIŞLAR — journalist, biographer
ISABELLE KORTIAN — French Armenian journalist
JEAN KEHEYAN — French Armenian journalist and writer
JOOST LAGENDIJK — Dutch politician, allied with the GreenLeft Party; former member of the Foreign Relations Committee of the European Parliament
KARİN KARAKAŞLI — managing director of *Agos*; poet and short story writer
KAROLİN DİNK — Hrant Dink's daughter-in-law
KEMAL GÖKTAŞ — journalist, writer
LEDA MERMER — in charge of technical services at *Agos*
LEVON
MİKAYELOĞLU — one of the children of the Joğvaran orphanage and the Tuzla Armenian Camp
LORA BAYTAR — cultural and art editor at *Agos*
LUİZ BAKAR — one of the founders of *Agos*; press officer for the Armenian Patriarchate; lawyer
LUSİN DİNK — Hrant Dink's niece; filmmaker
MARAL DİNK — Hrant Dink's niece; journalist
MARİ TOMASYAN
(MARİ MAYRİG) — Hrant Dink's *Mayrig*; mother of Yetvart Tomasyan, one of his closest friends
MARYAM İŞLER — one of the children of the Joğvaran orphanage and the Tuzla Armenian Camp; housewife
MASİS
KÜRKÇÜGİL — Marxist theorist; academic; publisher; politician
MAYDA SARİS — editor of culture and art at *Agos*, publishing coordinator
MELKON
KARAKÖSE — one of the directors of Samatya Surp Kevork Foundation, businessman
MIGIRDİÇ
MARGOSYAN — novelist; former headmaster of Tıbrevank High School
MİKHAİL
YAĞBASAN — Rakel Dink's brother; businessman based in Brussels

MURAT BELGE	literary critic, writer, political activist, columnist; director of Bilgi University's Department of Comparative Literature; one of the organizers of the 2005 Istanbul Armenian Conference
MUSTAFA KARAALİOĞLU	journalist; managing editor of *Star*
MÜGE KOÇTÜRK	Hrant Dink's close family friend; housewife
NECDET KOÇTÜRK	Hrant Dink's close friend, dating back to their time in prison following the September 12 coup; mechanical engineer
NİLÜFER GÖLE	sociologist, writer, academic; Ecole des Hautes Etudes en Sciences Sociales in Paris; recipient of the Legion d'Honneur Award
NURAY MERT	writer, columnist; political scientist; lecturer in the Business Faculty of Istanbul University
OHANNES TECER	one of the children of the Joğvaran orphanage and the Tuzla Armenian Camp; carpenter
OLCAY HALULU	Hrant Dink's army friend
ORAL ÇALIŞLAR	journalist, writer; former managing editor of *Taraf*
ORHAN MİROĞLU	politician of Kurdish descent; writer and columnist
OŞİN (YALÇIN) ÇİLİNGİR	Hrant Dink's close friend; former student leader; civil engineer
PAYLİNE TOMASYAN	Armenian teacher; ArasPpublishing
PERİHAN MAĞDEN	novelist, columnist
PINAR SELEK	feminist; political activist; writer; sociologist at the University of Strasbourg who has been standing trial and facing possible imprisonment for the past fourteen years continuously
RAGIP ZARAKOLU	human rights activist; writer; publisher, owner of Belge Publishing; several cases against him still going through the courts
RAKEL DİNK (YAĞBASAN)	Hrant Dink's wife and life companion
ROBER KOPTAŞ	journalist and managing editor of *Agos*
RONALD SUNY	social scientist and historian at the University of Michigan, Ann Arbor
SAMSON ÖZARARAT	businessman of Armenian descent; one of the facilitators of the Turkish Armenian rapprochement

SARKİS SEROPYAN	the editor of *Agos*'s Armenian section; Hrant's close friend
SELAHATTİN ÜNSAL	the Tuzla Armenian Children's Camp janitor
SERA DİNK	Hrant Dink's daughter; graphic designer
SEZGİN TANRIKULU	jurist of Kurdish descent; politician; one of the directors of the Diyarbakır Human Rights Association
SİLVA ÖZYERLİ	one of the children of the Joğvaran orphanage and the Tuzla Armenian Camp
SİRANUŞ YAŞGÜÇLÜKAL	Hrant's aunt
SÜSLÜ BAKMAZ	the older sister of Armenak (Orhan) Bakır, Hrant's closest friend and comrade in the struggle
ŞAFAK PAVEY	journalist; diplomat; politician; member of Turkish parliament
ŞİNASİ HAZNEDAR	geological engineer; active in civil society
TANER AKÇAM	historian and social scientist at Clark University, Massachsusetts; the first scholar from Turkey to apply the word "genocide" to the Armenain case and help bring the issue of the Armenian genocide into public debate in Turkey
UFUK URAS	politician; the first chairman of the left-leaning Freedom and Solidarity Party
ÜMİT KIVANÇ	journalist, writer; documentary-maker; *Agos*'s first technical director
VAHAKN DADRIAN	sociologist and academic; the senior and major scholar who focused on the scholarly study of the Armenan genocide
VARTAN OSKANYAN	politician; former foreign minister of Armenia
VARTANUŞ ÇAKIR	Hrant Dink's aunt; wife of his eldest uncle Haygaz
VİVET KANETTİ	journalist, columnist; novelist in Turkey
YAVUZ BAYDAR	journalist, columnist
YERVANT (LEVENT) DİNK	Hrant Dink'in younger brother; bookseller
YETVART (TOMO) TOMASYAN	one of Hrant Dink's oldest and closest friends, one of the founding owners of Aras Publishing, which publishes Armenian literature in Turkish and significant works in Armenian

YÜCEL SAYMAN   jurist; academic; former director of the Istanbul Bar Association

ZABEL ÇAKIR   Hrant Dink's aunt; wife of his Uncle Armenak

ZEPÜR DİNK   Hrant Dink's niece; instructor

ZEYNEP ORAL   journalist; writer; columnist

ZEYNEP TANBAY   political activist; dancer

ZİHNİYE CAN   Hrant Dink's university friend

Glossary

1915: One way to refer to the policy of massacres and deportations executed by the Ottoman government beginning in 1915 that later came to be recognized as a genocide.

agha: a Turkish and Kurdish (ağa) feudal honorific given to individuals who are respected and have some influence, such as a land owner or tribe chieftain

Aghtamar: an island in Lake Van in the historical Vaspurakan province of Armenia (now in Turkey). In 915–921, the Church of Holy Cross and the royal palace were built there; in 1113, the Church of Holy Cross became the residence of the Catholicos of Aghtamar.

Agos: the bilingual Turkish/Armenian weekly founded by the Turkish Armenian intellectual and journalist Hrant Dink in 1996 in Istanbul.

ahchig, (aghchig in literary Armenian): girl or daughter

ahparig, (aghparig in literary Armenian): respectful diminutive for aghpar/yeghpayr/apar, brother. Often used for older friends or brothers.

AKP: Justice and Development Party, a social conservative political party that developed from the tradition of Islamism. It has been the ruling party in Turkey since 2002. In the presidential election of 2014, AKP's long-time leader Recep Tayyip Erdoğan was elected president.

Alevi: a heterodox Muslim sect in Anatolia that gives as much importance to Ali (cousin and son-in-law of Prophet Muhammed, and the Fourth Muslim Caliph) as to Prophet Muhammed and integrates Sufism into religious belief and practice. Alevis in Turkey speak a variety of languages, mainly Turkish, Kurmanji-Kurdish, Zazaki, and Arabic, and are estimated to constitute about 15 percent of Turkey's population. Alevis typically do not pray in mosques, and their place of worship and religious ritual, the *cemevi*, is not recognized as a religious institution by the state. This has been a major issue of contestation in recent years.

apar: brother; see ahparig.

Apology Campaign: initiated by Ahmet İnsel, Cengiz Aktar, Baskın Oran, and Ali Bayramoğlu in Turkey in December 2008, the Apology Campaign put forward a text addressed to all Armenians and signed by more than 30,000 people. The text was as follows: "My conscience does not accept the insensitivity showed to and the denial of the Great Catastrophe that the Ottoman Armenians were subjected to in 1915. I reject this injustice and, for my share, I empathize with the feelings and pain of my Armenian brothers and sisters. I apologize to them." The campaign initiated a major debate in the media, particularly in early 2009. See www.ozurdiliyoruz.com.

ASALA: acronym for the Armenian Secret Army for the Liberation of Armenia, a terrorist Armenian organization that engaged in a campaign of bombings of Turkish institutions and assassination of Turkish diplomats, from 1975–1983, in an attempt to initiate an armed struggle against Turkish denialism of the Armenian genocide and for reparations.

Ani: a city in Eastern Anatolia close to the border with Armenia. By the tenth century, Ani became a rich city of prosperous trade, commerce, and culture. The kings of the Armenian Bagratouni dynasty made it their capital.

Article 301: an article in the Penal Code of Turkey that criminalizes any statement that the state finds offensive or views to be an "insult to Turkishness."

Aşık Veysel: a legendary Anatolian minstrel.

baba ganouche: a dish made of roasted/grilled/baked eggplant, sesame seed oil, garlic, and lemon.

Baron: derived from the French, in Armenian it is a designation equivalent to Sir or Master; also used to address a teacher.

Bey: a Turkish and Kurdish (Beg) honorific given to individuals who are respected and have some influence, equivalent to Sir or Mister.

Beyaz Adam:
Catholicossate of Etchmiadzin: the original and historic seat of the Armenian Apostolic church. The leaders of the Catholicossate of Etchmiadzin had the title "Catholicos (Patriarch) of All Armenians." During the Soviet era, Etchmiadzin's role in Armenian life was undermined by communists.

çutak: violin, in Armenian; name given to Hrant Dink by his wife Rakel.

deep state: reference to a clandestine mechanism, believed to consist of elements from military and civilian bureaucracy who consider themselves the true soul of the Turkish Republic, beyond those elected and empowered by the Constitution, and act through extra judicial methods in order to protect the state and the alleged national interest.

Der Zor/Der al-Zor: the largely arid and desolate area in northern Syria designated as the end point for survivors of caravans of deported Armenians during the genocide.

Dznunt: See Surp Dznunt.

Etchmiadzin: see Catholicossate of Etchmiadzin.

Efendi: An honorific for someone who has social achievement, mister.

Elazığ: *harput, hharpert.*

falaka: a beating.

Gaghant Baba: Armenian equivalent of Santa Claus.

Grey Wolves: offically known as Ülkü Ocakları or Ülkücüler, a neo-fascist organization. Formally a youth organization with close links to the Nationalist Movement Party (MHP), it has been described as MKP's militant youth arm. Under Devlet Bahçeli, who assumed the leadership of MHP and Grey Wolves after 1997, the organization has been reformed. Despite this, its members are presumed to have been involved in a number of violent attacks.

Hacı Bektaş Veli/Haji Bektash Veli: an Alevi Muslim mystic, Sayyid, and humanist philosopher from Khorasan, Iran, who lived and taught from 1209–1271 in Anatolia.

hamam: public bath.

harsa: from the Armenian word *hars,* which means "bride" as well as daughter-in-law.

hsgich: supervisor, attendant, tutor.

joğvaran: a meeting or gathering place, used also to designate a place of worship by Protestant Armenians, used here for the Orphanage of the Gedikpasha Protestant Church.

kilim: carpet

Kınalıada: Knale island near Istanbul, a traditional summer resort popular with the city's Armenians.

khent: an Armenian word meaning "mad" or "crazy" but also used for eccentrics or individuals who do not behave by the conventional norms and may have a creative streak or unusual courage.

Kumkapı: An old neighborhood in Istanbul, inhabited mostly by Armenians. The Armenian Patriarchate is located there.

Kurban Bayram: The Festival of the Sacrifice (in Arabic, *Eid al-Adha*), this is a major Muslim religious holiday during which lamb is sacrificed and distributed to neighbors and family to honor the willingness of Prophet İbrahim (Abraham) to sacrifice his son, Ismail.

Kurtuluş: A central Istanbul neighborhood in close proximity to Taksim. Along with Kumkapi and Samatya, it is often regarded as a predominantly Armenian neighborhood.

kuru köfte: fried meatballs.

kutuk: state registry of inhabitants.

kuyrig: an Armenian term, meaning "sister" or "little sister;" a term of endearment to a close female friend or relative

kurush: 1/100th of a lira, an old Turkish monetary unit.

Laz: an ethnic group in the Southeastern region of the Black Sea, mainly Turkey and Georgia. Initially Christian, the Laz converted to Sunni Islam early under Ottoman rule.

Lusavorchagan: a member of the Armenian Apostolic Church, to which most Armenians belong. The term is derived from the name of Krikor/Grigor Lusavorich or Gregory the Illuminator, the founder of the Church in Armenia.

lycee: French word for *lyceum*, a high school.

mantı: Turkish ravioli, served with garlic yoghurt.

March 12, 1971, Coup: The second military intervention in Turkey. Following a memorandum by the general staff minister, Demirel and his cabinet resigned. The military regime ruled through an assembly dominated by conservative parties, with an "above party" government directing behind the scenes. Martial law was declared, youth organizations and trade unions banned; thousands of students, young academics, writers, trade unionists, and political activists were detained and tortured.

Marmara: One of Istanbul's oldest Armenian newspapers.

May 27, 1960, coup: The first military coup d'etat in Turkey, staged by thirty-seven young Turkish military officers outside the staff chief's chain of command against the elected government. The president, prime minister, and several other members of the government were put on trial before a court appointed by the junta. The prime minister, minister of foreign affairs, and minister of finance were executed.

Mehmet Akif Ersoy (1873–1936): a Turkish poet, writer, and academic; a member of the Turkish parliament and the author of the Turkish National Anthem.

menemen: a dish made of eggs, tomatoes, green peppers, and onions.

meydan: a public square; a gathering and meeting place of the town.

millet: a system utilized in the Ottoman Empire to divide the empire into religious communities by placing the right of authority and jurisdiction of each religious group in the hands of their religious leaders. The Armenians, Greeks, and Jews formed separate *millets*.

morakuyr: aunt or close family friend.

muhtar/mukhtar: from the Arabic *mukhtar*, indicating the lowest-level elected/designated administrator in a village or in urban neighborhoods.

Myrig: diminutive of *myr* or "mother,"—"little mother"—or a woman who performs motherly duties.

Nasreddin Hoca: a folk figure embodying popular wisdom who is known throughout the Near East.

oriort: an Armenian term for an unmarried woman; also used to address an unmarried female teacher.

Patriarch Shnorhk Kalustian: Patriarch or head of the Armenian Apostolic Church in Istanbul with jurisdiction over the Apostolic Armenians of Turkey; elected in 1961 and died in 1990. He was instrumental in caring for Anatolian Armenians.

peshmerga: Kurdish guerrilla fighters in Turkey, regular army of Iraki Kurdistan.

rakı: the Turkish word for a traditional anisette drink, also known as *arak* or *uzo* in the Mediterranean region.

Ramazan/Ramadan: The Islamic month of fasting, during which Sunni Muslims do not eat or drink anything between dawn and dusk. The meal that breaks the fast is called *iftar.*

Ruhi Su (1912–1985): a Turkish opera singer, folk singer, and saz virtuoso of Armenian origin.

Mevlana/Rumi (1207–1273): Persian Sufi mystic, poet, theologian. Born in Khorasan (in modern-day Afghanistan), he lived most his life under the Seljug Sultanate of Rum (the Anatolian peninsula that had belonged to the Byzantine or Eastern Roman Empire and known as the geographical area of Rum) and died and was buried in Konya (in today's Turkey). Following his death, his followers founded the Mevlevi Order, also known as the Order of the Whirling Dervishes, famous for its Sufi dance known as the *sama* ceremony. His major work is *Masnavi.*

saz: traditional Armenian stringed instrument.

September 6–7 riots: On September 6, 1955, on the basis of a false report that Mustafa Kemal Atatürk's birthplace in Thessaloniki had been bombed, organized mobs attacked mainly Greek, but also Armenian, Jewish, and other non-Muslim homes and businesses in Istanbul. At least ten people were killed and many were injured; more than 4,000 homes, 1,000 businesses, 73 churches, a synogogue, and 26 non-Muslim schools were attacked and plundered. The attacks resulted in the emigration of tens of thousands of Greeks to Greece.

September 12, 1980, coup: A military coup d'etat in Turkey—the third since 1960—led by General Kenan Evren, it deposed the government led by Suleyman Demirel and established a harsh military dictatorship that lasted for three years.

Şişli: A central neighborhood in İstanbul known for its cosmopolitan population.

Srpazan: Form of address to a bishop, equivalent to "Your Eminence."

Susurluk: A small town and a district of Balıkesir Province in northwestern Turkey. It was the site of a scandal involving the close relationship between the Turkish government, the armed forces, and organized crime following a car crash on November 3, 1996.

Surp Dznunt: Holy Christmas.

Surp Hach Tbrevank: Holy Cross Seminary.

Surp Zadig: Easter.

Shnorhk: see Patriarch Kalustian.

Taksim/Taksim Meydanı: Istanbul's main square.

tashnag: "piano," in Armenian.

Tashnags: Also known as Dashnaks or Dashnagtsutiun (Armenian Revolutionary Federation). Refers to members of or to an Armenian political party established in 1890 and dedicated to the freedom of Ottoman Armenians; often used as a generic term for Armenian revolutionaries of the Ottoman period. The party is still active in the diaspora and Armenia, dedicated to the recognition of the genocide and reparations from Turkey.

Tıbrevank: a seminary for the preparation of clergymen; a prestigious boarding school in Üsküdar district of Istanbul, founded in 1953 for Anatolian Armenian boys and later transformed into a secular high school.

tombala: lottery game traditionally played on New Year's Eve.

tulumba tatlısı: dougha deep-fried pastry that is soaked in syrup.

Three Horan Church: Church of Three Altars in Beyoğlu district of İstanbul. *Horan* is derived from the Armenian word for altar, *khoran*.

Ülkücüler: see Grey Wolves.

Vartabed: Priest in the Armenian Apostelic Church

wealth tax: levied in Turkey in 1942; a one-time tax on Turkish citizens to prepare the country for war. In practice, Jewish, Greek, Armenian, and Levantine citizens suffered disproportionately from the tax. Those who could not pay their tax dues were sent to labor camps in Aşkale, Erzurum, in eastern Turkey.

Yezdi/Yezidi/Ezidi: predominantly Kurdish-speaking religious group, whose religious practice is based on a unique combination of Zoroastrian and Muslim Sufi belief. Yezidis in Turkey are strongly discriminated against by all other groups (including Sunni Kurds). According to Yezidi belief, if someone draws a circle around a person, that person cannot move unless the circle is erased by others.

Yılmaz Güney (1937–1984): Turkish film director, screenwriter, actor, and novelist of Zaza and Kurdish origin. He won the Palme d'Or for the film *Yol* at Cannes Film Festival in 1982. His works were devoted to the plight of working-class people in Turkey. At a gathering in 1982, Guney referred to the events beginning in 1915 in the Ottoman Empire as genocide.

Yunus Emre (1270–1320): Turkish poet and Sufi mystic. He is, with Ahmet Yesevi and Sultan Walad, one of the first known poets to have composed works in the spoken Turkish.

Zaza/Zazaki: a cultural-ethnic community speaking Zazaki, which is regarded as an independent language by some and as a dialect of Kurdish by others.

zhoghvaran/zhoghovaran: See joğvaran.